TRADING TRIADS

Unlocking the Secrets of Market Structure and Trading in any Market

Felipe Tudela

WILEY
A John Wiley and Sons, Ltd., Publication

This edition first published 2010.

Registered office
John Wiley & Sons Ltd, The Atrium, Southern Gate, Chichester, West Sussex, PO19 8SQ, United Kingdom

For details of our global editorial offices, for customer services and for information about how to apply for permission to reuse the copyright material in this book please see our website at www.wiley.com.

Library of Congress Cataloging-in-Publication Data

Tudela, Felipe.
Trading triads : unlocking the secrets of market structure and trading in any market / Felipe Tudela.
p. cm.
Includes bibliographical references and index.
ISBN 978-0-470-74843-5
1. Investment analysis. 2. Stocks–Charts, diagrams, etc. I. Title.
HG4529.T84 2010
332.63′2042–dc22

2010013115

A catalogue record for this book is available from the British Library

ISBN 978-0-470-74843-5

Typeset in 10/12pt Times by Aptara Inc., New Delhi, India
Printed and bound in Great Britain by TJ International Ltd, Padstow, Cornwall

Contents

Acknowledgements

I want to thank first the three persons, today my friends, who provided the support that enabled me to create and develop the Triads market model. These three friends are Olivier de Ducla, Patrick Sauty and Joël Villecroze.

I conceived the Triads back in 1997 when Olivier de Ducla, who was President of AFATE, and Patrick Sauty, who later became Vice President, invited me to lecture and give seminars on Triads.

Joël Villecroze, CEO of Trium, Equity and Derivatives understood the value of Triads and created a website for them, as well as other applications for third parties.

I deeply appreciate the support of Thierry Bechu, former President of AFATE, teacher at Dauphine and fund manager for SGAM (Société Générale Asset Management) who found my Triads model to be 'simple and consistent' and dedicated a section of his book, *L'Analyse Technique. Pratiques et Méthodes,* to it.

I would like to thank all of the authors whose thoughts and ideas inspired and led me to the creation of Trading Triads and, in particular, W.D. Gann, Jesse Livermore, William Dunnigan, Frank Tubbs, George Bayer, Richard D. Wyckoff, Tom DeMark and John Crane.

Thanks also to my friends Don Mack and Albert Labos for their insightful trading knowledge and support.

I want to thank in particular, my wife, Annie, whose love, help and support have made this book possible.

Also a word of thanks to Aimée Dibbens, Alec Dubber, Karen Weller, Lori Boulton, Pat Bateson, Rachael Wilkie and all of the people at John Wiley & Sons, Ltd. without whom there would be no book today.

I would also like to thank the Equis Metastock Reuters Thomson technical support team and formula team for their readiness to help and their excellent service.

Thanks also go to George Robinson who gave attentive and focused care to the edit and Jose Antonio Pancorvo who took the time to read the book and make suggestions for its improvement.

Lastly, I thank all of my other friends and students whose names do not appear here, but who helped me along the way.

Acknowledgements

Introduction: The Road to a New Level of Mastery

THE AGELESS SCIENCE OF TRADING

The objective in writing this book was to provide a tool that will enable you to read the markets better. The information in this book will permit you to analyze and trade with or without indicators. The book blends the old with the new in a unique approach. This approach will give you a perspective of markets that will help you to gain a better understanding of the different points of view of technical analysis and market structure analysis.

We do not discard any method. Instead, we try to enhance your knowledge of market reality with a more profound view of how markets operate and how trading methods relate to them. It is important to state that what we are giving you is a method to read and to trade the market. Our method is a model that enables you to describe market actions accurately. Is the market trending or consolidating? Is the market rising or falling? These questions may seem evident from a distance, but are not as obvious as they first appear. Not everyone is able to 'see' what the market is doing without a certain degree of practice.

Most persons are uneasy about their ability to forecast markets. However, they give little importance to assessing correctly what is going on now – in the present. We think that it is much more important to describe accurately what a market is doing now. For the trader or analyst who is able to do that, forecasting will take care of itself and there will be no need to forecast.

All that you must do is attempt to understand what the market has been doing up to the present. This is all that the market asks of you. You must not let yourself be distracted from that task.

Our method is a tool for achieving this. Use it to learn the lessons that the market is waiting to teach you.

WHY MOST TRADERS FAIL

There are many reasons why traders fail. Most traders aren't winners. Trading is a difficult endeavor in which it is easy to lose money. Many would-be traders try many trading methods and, after having tried almost everything, end up with losses. In many cases, losses bring the trader down emotionally. He or she then abandons trading forever. You can avoid this. There is no reason to become a permanent loser in the market.

Why, then, do these failures occur – this continual loss of money by these would-be traders? Here are some of the reasons:

1. Lack of knowledge and lack of practice. The would-be traders approach the market without understanding what markets are and what being a trader means. They think that a newsletter, an advisory service, or a trading method is all that they need in order to become wealthy. This is not so.
2. They don't know how to define the main market phases. They think that a market is going up when, in fact, it's going down, or vice versa. Even if the would-be traders are able to correctly identify a trend or phase, they go against the flow. They sell when the market is going up or buy when the market is going down, in the hope of making a small gain on the reaction. (A reaction or correction takes place when a market gets to a certain level and then returns to an equilibrium point. Assume, for example, that the market goes from 30 to 40 in an uptrend and then returns to 35. You wait for the reaction from 40 to 35 before buying.) When the would-be traders incorrectly identify a trend or phase, they misplace their stops. The trader's stops are almost always touched and they end up losing.
3. Even if a would-be trader knows how to read the market correctly and place his stops correctly, he often 'overtrades' as he is not aware of the risk. He has no trading discipline and ultimately ruins himself. This has been the fate of many great traders and market wizards.

All of these mistakes can be avoided, although it is not always easy to do so. How? Simple! By acquiring an understanding of the science of markets. Let me explain the foundation of all success in the market.

THE KEY TO SUCCESS IN THE MARKET

An understanding of the science of trading is the key to success in the market. It is a science that is an accumulation of centuries-old wisdom. It is a science that has not needed to wait for modern mathematical indicators – or for complex software programs – to be profitable.

The science of trading is an old science that is self-sufficient, although it is able to benefit from the newest tools in mathematics and the best software available. It enables an expert trader to know what the market is doing by simply examining a chart. Mathematical indicators can tell us nothing, except what already exists in the market.

The objective in writing this book is to teach you how to read market structure. You will need only charted bars.* What we have done is create a simple tool that, with only a set of simple elements, will enable you to read the market as the old traders used to do. We give you a new tool to use in conjunction with the oldest of methods – charted bar reading and swing trading. In other words, you will learn to identify and read the oscillations of the market.

Old traders, such as George Douglass Taylor, who was a trader in 1950, knew how to read market fluctuations. He had such familiarity with, and intimate knowledge of, the grain market that he earned his living in it.[1] Taylor was a true swing trader. A swing trader does not forecast. Instead, he follows the natural flow of market fluctuations. He understands that the market has its own language, which he must learn.

The way to do this is by acquiring such a knowledge of fluctuations that you develop a sixth sense of the market. Then, you will be able to identify turning points and take advantage of them. However, there are many ways to read charted bars and each trader has his own approach. The question for you is how to measure the natural movement of the market objectively.

Here I offer a new answer. It does not depart from the old trading methods. Instead, it confirms their well-based foundations and wisdom.

What I have created is a model of natural market movement that enables you to measure market fluctuations without imposing your own subjectivity on it. This model uses only three elements – the pivot, the triad, and the swing. They will be discussed in the next chapter.

This ternary model not only provides a way to measure market fluctuations and their patterns objectively, but also enables you to discover the 'market's inner strategy.' Every market has its own hidden strategy that tells you how to trade it. The triad model will enable you to discover such a strategy and use it to your advantage.

The triad formulas in Metastock are available in Appendix I.

* We use the more accurate term 'charted bar' in this book, instead of the term 'bar chart' that is found in most trading books. 'Bar chart' denotes a chart that contains more than one price bar, whereas 'charted bars' refer to the individual bars on one particular Chart. 'Bar charts' means more than one chart, each of which contains a series of price bars.

1
The Oscillatory Nature of Markets: Their Component Elements

MARKET SCIENCE, THE SCIENCE OF OSCILLATIONS

What is an oscillation? An oscillation is a vibration. A market has a rate of vibration. Prices are not fixed, but exist in a flow, a stream that appears as quotes or charted bar on a screen.

The underlying market structure is made from these oscillations or vibrations. What we are trying to do is to understand them. They are the origin and cause of market structure. All patterns derive from oscillations.

This is why you must learn about the oscillatory nature of markets. A market's oscillations or vibrations will exhibit a rhythm. This rhythm has an inner harmony. Changes in the inner harmony provide clues about market behavior.

These oscillations take place in time and space. Their rhythm not only configures the different market patterns and structures, but also the market's cycles and time forms. Discovering the vibratory rate of a market gives you the key to trading it efficiently. Each market is a law unto itself, and this appears as the specific personality of that market. Commodities have personalities of their own. For example, metals do not vibrate like grains. Stocks differ from financial futures.

Let us take a grain futures chart, such as a chart for soybeans, and compare it to a stock chart, such as that of MMM (that is, Minnesota Mining and Manufacturing Company). Their individual personalities will become immediately evident on first examination – intuitively – even before we know why. A more careful examination enables us to define the characteristics that make them different. For instance, the soybeans chart is cyclical in form with huge bull markets at intervals in time. The MMM chart resembles a continually ascending, noncyclical flow.

Why are they different? It is because their vibratory rates differ. They oscillate to different rhythms and in different ways.

This is why it is so important for you to become acquainted with their underlying natures and to try to understand them. You need to identify the specific vibratory rate of each market – its key number. By knowing this, you can unlock the market's personality and trade in harmony with it.

This is not new. A trader and writer, R. D. Wyckoff, always had this vibratory rate in mind. He called it the personality of a market. This is why he advised others to trade only a few stocks, so that they would be able to understand the stocks' subtlest behavior.

In his book on tape reading, Wyckoff provided a way to penetrate and understand each stock's personality.[2] To Wyckoff, some stocks are leaders and others are followers. Some stocks behave in certain ways and others behave in other ways. What Wyckoff calls the personality of a stock has its origin in its vibratory rate.

Every stock and market vibrates in a unique way. This is the real key. Here is the secret of the markets. If we had to reduce all market structure and technical analysis to one thing, it would be the vibratory rate from which all fluctuations and movements arise. It is each movement's specific vibration that gives it its specificity.

Now, where do these vibratory rates or oscillatory rates originate? In answering this, we arrive at a confluence of technical analysis, market structure analysis, and fundamental analysis. We find ourselves confronted by the market's deepest core.

Why are oscillations the underlying foundation of a market? The answer is that oscillations comprise a primary law concealed behind a market. The rate of vibration expresses the true personality of a market in a single element – its fundamental conditions, technical conditions, and structure. They all stem from it.

When we talk of fundamentals, we are referring only to a perspective from which to evaluate a market. Technical aspects comprise another perspective and market structure comprises still another. What makes them one is the vibratory rate.

All these perspectives emerge from a unique, invisible rate of vibration. This is the essential and profound personality of a market.

We will not delve into the differences between technical and fundamental analysis and market structure here. We will approach this subject in a later chapter. We simply want to emphasize the importance of a market's vibratory nature.

It is important for you to be able to define and describe the oscillatory nature of a market as the foundation of its market structure. Market structure is the price/time structure that forms the basis of technical analysis. This time/price structure is a flow that vibrates at its own rhythm. We need to understand this market structure and its vibratory rate as they make themselves apparent in the time/price flow of a market.

We can say that volume is also part of such a structure and that we cannot set it apart from the flow of price and time. This is why, for any given price at any given point of time, we have a definite and unique volume.

When dealing with futures, we can also add open interest.

In this book, we will only deal with the time/price elements that define market structure and cause its vibration rate to be evident by the sequence of its oscillations. This sequence will have a definite pattern. The oscillatory rate that appears in market structure must be precisely identified for any market, whether for stocks, stock sectors, commodities, financial futures, or indexes, etc. There is no market or anything that flows that is not subject to a given oscillation.

From an understanding of this law will come our understanding of markets and how to trade them. The vibratory rate will be our clue to understanding the language of the market. An inner law will emerge from behind every market. In the end, as Wyckoff suggested, you must be acquainted with the personality of each market that you will deal with. This will give you a definite advantage in your analysis and trading.

Now, let us turn to the fundamental market structure that arises from this vibration core.

The Fundamental Structure of the Market

The market has its time/price flow underlying its market structure. What our triad model does is describe this structure simply and objectively. By objectively, we mean without human intervention or arbitrary conditions.

By human intervention, the subjective element, we mean such things as counting waves or counting charted bars. For instance, Elliott wave devotees must count waves. They have arbitrarily fixed the number of waves at five. However, it doesn't work. Also, where does a wave begin and end? You can have as many different answers as there are Elliott wave followers throughout the world. This is not what we want. We need something that is single, unique, and valid for all observers.

We do not mean by this that the Elliott wave theory is useless. There are some traders who succeed with it. However, it is somewhat of an art form that isn't based on any generally agreed way to define market structure. Traders who use the Elliott wave, a theory that provides interesting market insights, would in this sense benefit from trading it in conjunction with the triad market structure model. This would give their trades an objective frame of reference that would allow them to avoid many false signals coming from incorrect wave counts.

Then, we have, for instance, bar counts. Gann, for instance, has swing charts that are based on two-bar chart counts or three-bar chart counts. This does work. Once you decide that you are on a three-bar chart count, everyone who uses this number will come up with the same answer.[3] In this sense, Gann swings are objective, do work, and are very useful. Gann swings are a type of swing that is attributed to W. D. Gann, who was a trader during the first half of the twentieth century and born in the previous century.

However, this method still requires counting. In our method, there is no counting – of anything at all. The market, itself, decides its swings in a natural and completely objective way. The advantage of this procedure is that it enables you to obtain an objective market description that is valid for all observers of the market who use the same descriptive method.

This market model, which the triad makes possible, is so simple that anyone can understand it. It can be used in conjunction with other methods. In the right circumstances, this market model is very convenient and can enhance your trading and analysis.

Our model gives us a general background and a common market language whereby all methods can find a common ground. This enhances the positive features of those methods. You can trade, basing actions only on the market structure described by our model. You can also use our model with mathematical indicators. You can use bar counts or any market approach, system, or method. For instance, you can trade Gann swings, or indicators, such as stochastics or moving average convergences/divergences (MACDs). A moving average becomes an efficient tool when used in conjunction with triads.

In summary, every trading method is significantly enhanced when used with triads. Before explaining triads, let's continue with our explanation of the fundamental market structure. Markets oscillate. The time/price flow of a market is far from uniform. It is not a line, but rather an oscillating curve. From this oscillatory curve, a market structure will arise. The oscillations within this market structure are called swings. The swings go up and down in an indefinite sequence.

The primal market cycle is composed of these indefinite upward and downward swings. Markets go up and down in a cyclical fashion. All free markets are cyclical in their structures – up, down, up, down. ... Cycles exist and do work. We can be sure that an upward market will be followed by a downward market and vice versa. This was true yesterday. It is true today and it will be true as long as free markets exist.

These cycles can vary in length, from micro-oscillations to multiyear bull or bear markets. Also, they resemble Chinese boxes. An oscillation can contain many other oscillations or be contained within many other oscillations. They are fractal in their nature. A swing or market fluctuation is an oscillation. A market oscillation can be composed of other market fluctuations.

What is necessary to understand is that all cycles are oscillations and that all oscillations are cycles. Market swings are market cycles, irrespective of their amplitudes or lengths. Market structure, as defined by these oscillations, was correctly understood by Charles Dow, the father of modern technical and fundamental analysis.

Charles Dow was far ahead of his time. Surprisingly, very little has changed since he made his major discoveries. What Einstein is to modern science, Charles Dow is to modern finance and market analysis. An understanding of his market theory is a must for any serious student of the market. Let us briefly explore his main ideas concerning the structure of the market and his method to read the market's mind.

For Charles Dow, market oscillations held the key to understanding the market. He developed a theory of markets that enabled the investor and analyst to understand their structure. The principles that Charles Dow discovered are universal and have passed the test of time. He developed a robust model. His theory was not developed systematically, but is found in the collection of articles that he wrote for the *Wall Street Journal*, and was later studied and developed by Hamilton and Rhea.

Now, let us examine Dow's idea of market structure. For Dow, markets can be reduced to three kinds of movements:

1. The main trend or market direction
2. The secondary reaction
3. The daily fluctuations.

These three movements have the following traits: first, each is an oscillation or, in market jargon, a swing; second, the smaller movements are contained within the larger ones. The daily fluctuations are contained in the secondary reaction and in the main trend.

Each of these three movements has a time span – years for the main trend, months for the secondary reaction, and less than one day for daily fluctuations. Each of these three movements or swings has a time/price ratio. These are the three kinds of waves on which the market is constructed. These three types of waves and how they are assembled provide the fundamental market structure. Let us examine each of these three waves.

The primary trend has a duration of several years. It is the market's long-term tendency. There is no method to define its precise duration. However, the past provides some clues. This primary trend separates into a primary bull market and a primary bear market, each of which has three phases.

The primary bull market's three phases are:

- First, a return to confidence. Hope returns to the investing public. The economic landscape is seen again in a positive light. This coincides with the beginning of a rise in prices.
- Second, a reflection of the public's hope for higher stock prices. The stock market, as a whole, rises and people again trust the market.
- The third and final phases, speculation and inflation, return. Stocks become overpriced. It is the beginning of the end.

A moment comes when the market reverses itself and the primary bear market takes the place of the previous primary bull market.

The primary bear market also has three phases. They are the reverse of the phases of the previous bull market. The primary bear market's phases are:

- First, a loss of confidence in the market. The investing public does not trust the economy, the future looks bleak, and shareholders abandon hope.
- Second, as a result of this gloomy outlook, shareholders sell their stocks and companies see their earnings decline noticeably.

- Third, as a result of the selling, panic follows. Now, massive selling occurs. The public sells, regardless of the value of the stocks. The stocks drop sharply in price and the economic landscape is perceived negatively. This phase marks the end of the primary bear market.

Each of these two main waves or market swings includes a powerful reaction that Charles Dow called the 'secondary reaction.'

In the secondary reaction, the market retraces between 33 and 66 % of its primary movement. This retracing takes the form of a wave or swing in a direction opposite to the main trend. It is very often mistaken for a change in the main trend. Confusing and mistaking the secondary reaction for a change in the main trend is an error because the market, when the retracing ends, will resume its original main direction. The duration of this secondary reaction can range from many weeks to many months.

The third kind of wave or swing is the daily fluctuation. These swings are less than a day in length and are oscillations that Dow considered to be meaningless 'wavelets.' Each main market movement, with its secondary reactions, will encompass a total of five or six waves. This is not a dogma for Charles Dow, nor was it for W. D. Gann, for whom the market had between three and six or seven waves.

Charles Dow has given us a simple model that defines market structure with a minimal number of elements. This gave rise to his index, the Dow–Jones Index of Industrials and Transport. He used a sample of companies to represent and mirror the entire market. The behavior of this sample will be described with his three-waved market structure.

For Charles Dow, his index was a tool with which to observe market reality. With the Dow–Jones Index, he was able to discover the true tendencies of the market. It was a systematic index that enabled him to 'isolate the daily fluctuations from the waves and the waves from the current.'

Charles Dow looked at market structure as being multilayered. To him, markets had different levels. With Charles Dow, we have a phenomenological approach to markets. This means that the perception of an event or phenomena is observer-dependent.

For instance, a market can be moving downward in the very short term, but at the same time going up in the medium term and long term. This depends on your position as observer. For a day trader, a market can be going down, while for a long-term investor or medium-term trader, it could be going up. This means that a market, in itself, is neither going up nor going down nor anywhere. Such qualifications as 'up' or 'down' are categories or attributes imposed by our minds as a function of our space/time positions as observers.

A principle emerges from this. It is that the observation of a market event or economic event is defined by the space/time scale of the observer. A market or an economic indicator can have an ascending vector in one time scale and a descending vector in another time scale.

This notion of scale is fundamental for the trader or investor. Often market participants are at a loss in relation to the time/price scale. By this, I mean that many people confuse time scale with price. For example, they may watch the news in the morning and hear that the Dow has dropped by 1 %. Therefore, they think that the market in general is going down. They do not realize that the market can be going up steadily and that it is normal to have downward and upward fluctuations as it moves up in price. Thus, they confuse a one-day reaction with the general tendency of the market. This is because the market can be going up relative to a given time window and down relative to another time window. In the daily chart and weekly charts, a market can be rising, while in the intraday 30-minute chart, it can be falling. To judge whether a market is going up or down, we must first define a time frame in relation to which the market is moving. For example, how often have we heard someone say in the middle of a bear market that the Dow is rising and that he has bought stock, although the rise was only a daily fluctuation and not a reversal of the main trend?

The market index that Charles Dow used as a model of the entire market was actually two indexes, an industrial index and a transport index. They worked together. His indexes enabled him to verify his market theory and to anticipate market behavior.

Charles Dow's theory of market behavior is based on three movements, which, as we have already explained, define fundamental market structure and three postulates.[4] Let us examine his three postulates:

- First: the postulate of nonmanipulation. For Charles Dow, the primary or main movement of markets cannot be manipulated. Only daily fluctuations and short-term movements can be manipulated. This postulate is useful not only for long-term investors, but also for short-term traders who must beware of market manipulation that so often traps day traders.
- Second: the postulate of anticipation. The market anticipates the future. All markets contain, within their prices, a synthesis of the factors that form their behavior. The price is the result of the knowledge, hopes, and fears of the market participants.
- Third: the postulate of noninfallibility. The Dow theory is fallible. Forecasts may be wrong from time to time. In order to succeed, one needs a study in depth of market conditions. It is necessary to correlate economics, politics, technological events, and sociological factors, etc. This is only possible within a historical perspective that enables the investor to anticipate the main economic tendencies. The Index is the tool to accomplish this.

William Hamilton, Dow's disciple, used to call the index the market 'barometer.' This barometer must be used in conjunction with as complete a study as possible of the market and the factors that compose it.

The three postulates that we have explained imply that the Index is among the best of tools to use to anticipate the undercurrents of economic events. This is due to the fact that the Index integrates in its composite price all factors that determine market behavior. This integration includes all factors, whether known or unknown, in an objective way that cannot be manipulated.

Using the Index and market structure, Charles Dow was able to determine the direction of the market, using the principle of *convergence divergence.* In fact, he is also the creator of a method that we find applied now to other indicators. The two indexes, the industrial index and the transport index, must converge or diverge in relation to each other

We have convergence when the movement of one index confirms the other. If the industrials and the transport index are both rising in their primary movement, and then both reverse downward, we have a confirmation of the reversal – indicating a change in the main trend. In Dow theory, the behavior of one index alone is not sufficient. Both indexes are required to confirm a market reversal.

Divergence is the opposite of convergence. In this case, both indexes move in opposite directions. When one has reversed, the other continues in its previous trend. The meaning of a divergence is negative. If one index reverses and the other does not, it means that a change in the main trend may not happen, although it could happen. It is a signal of uncertainty.

An investor who had acted on the signals provided by Dow theory would have earned around 14 % per year on average. This would have been earned for only acting on the signals of confirmation of both the industrial and the transport indexes.

The results above would have been even better if, instead of buying the whole index, the signals were used to buy low-priced stocks with strong fundamentals. Fundamentals are also a tenet of Dow theory. Charles Dow is also the father of fundamental analysis. In fact, he combined the best of both – the technical and the fundamental – and he even delved into the psychology of investing.

Now, let us explore some of his ideas in the fundamental realm. For Charles Dow, fundamental analysis ruled over technical analysis. In the long run, prices will reflect values. Value controls price. Divergences are due to perceptual gaps, but sooner or later they will come together.

The real purpose of technical analysis is to anticipate price changes in order to be able to buy high-value, underpriced stocks when there is a divergence due to a gap in perception. This means that, when the public perceives all stocks as valueless, due to their state of fear or panic, combined with ignorance, some experts recognize the gap between price and value, enabling them to buy cheaply stocks that offer great value. This gap between price and value originates in a gap in perception by the general public. When panic has pushed valuable stocks down to rock bottom prices, we can buy them at the right time, thanks to the signals that the indexes give.

The converse occurs when the markets are exuberant and frantic speculation has created overpriced stocks. Then, as soon as the indexes signal a reversal, we can sell the overpriced stocks to repurchase them later at the right price – when prices are at, or below, par value.

We see that, for Charles Dow, technical analysis and fundamental analysis are like two sides of the same coin. Both are needed – one to describe market behavior and time our investment decisions and the other to make us aware of the real value of our investments.[5] Therefore, the investor must be able to anticipate two things – changes in price using technical analysis and changes in underlying value using fundamental analysis.

The investor must be a thorough student of the market. He must know all factors, both fundamental and technical. Dow tells us that 'the main purpose of study is to define, first, the value of the company whose stocks the investor has, and then the right time to buy.' These two conditions define in a nutshell Charles Dow's investment theory. Right value and right time make for a good investment.

Then Dow tells us about the right conditions for an investor. Here he dwells on the psychology of investing. An investor needs patience. Dow tells us that 'the biggest profits come from the greatest patience.' Also, he emphasizes that the investor must 'sit over his investment for months or years' to realize its full profit potential. Further, it is important that the investor does not become a victim of the nervousness that surrounds markets. He must be alone, isolated from market action, in order to remain serene. He must not let himself be provoked into doing something impulsively that would defeat his goal.

It is because of this that Dow tells us that the optimal conditions for investing are those of an investor who lives outside the city. This investor won't fall prey to fear or be disturbed 'by rumors and sudden price fluctuations.' Dow tells us that the biggest advantage of an out-of-town investor, the advantage that prevents him from becoming a victim of fear, is that he is unable 'to see the market.'

This kind of investor buys, according to Dow, on the basis of 'demonstrated conviction.' This is not blind faith, but a true knowledge that the price is below the real value and that prices will sooner or later reflect the real value. The investor is a man of knowledge. He knows value and can look beyond appearances. Even if prices drop for a while after he has bought, he knows that they must come back eventually to their real values.

In Charles Dow, we find a complete approach to markets. He includes all factors and uses them in a simple and efficient way. His approach to market structure, defining it as an integration of waves or oscillations, is the key to our model of market behavior. However, we must also say that market structure by itself is not everything. Market structure is a tool to help you understand the real world of trading. As long as you do not forget this, you will be able to use market structure to your advantage.

Let us return now to fundamental market structure and consider time. Time's behavior is important. Time also oscillates. Time oscillations are indivisible from price oscillations; that is, time oscillations and price oscillations are so interrelated that, when price is considered, time should also be considered and vice versa. Every price fluctuation takes place in time. Changes in price always imply changes in time. Time changes show definite patterns.

Every fluctuation or swing is cyclical. Upswings are always followed by downswings. There is a constant cycle. However, these fluctuations are not random. They follow patterns. Most swings will be contained within a price/time range. At a given level of volatility, upswings and downswings will have similar lengths and times. This is true not only of small fluctuations, but also of large price swings that take years to develop. Bull markets and bear markets are often similar in length.

This cyclical behavior in time is natural since it follows the cyclical behavior of price. A study of these long-term patterns will prove to you the existence of market cycles that belong to definite time lengths.

These time cycles, swings or waves, can be static or dynamic. A static cycle has the same recurring time length, while a dynamic cycle changes its length according to an inner law. An example of a static cycle is a ten-year cycle, while an example of a dynamic cycle is a Fibonacci time cycle.

Cycle clusters occur when many cycles of different lengths begin or end around the same date. When these dates arrive, significant events occur in markets. A significant event, for example, might be the end of a bull or bear market.

The past will repeat itself in the future, which will then become the present. All past events will be repeated at some time in the future. Bull markets and bear markets, recessions, and expansions will occur again and again.

In all these repetitive cycles, there is an element to consider. We must never ask the past to repeat itself exactly in the future. Here comes the rule of analogy. Events that repeat in cycles are analogical, not identical.

When we compare two similar events, we must look for their differences and not simply their identities. For example, if we know that a bear market might be just around the corner and that it might be similar to another bear market in the past, we must ask how it will differ this time. We must be able to pinpoint the difference in the similarity. This will put us ahead and we will avoid becoming rigid. Nothing repeats itself twice in the same way. Never.

Time, therefore, is an important element in market structure. Measuring time periods and identifying the difference in their similarities is as important as measuring price waves. The market is an interrelated whole, as Charles Dow explained. Nothing must be excluded. It is important at all times to keep an open mind and to not fall captive to market dogmas that could blind us to market reality.

Now, let us return to market structure.

THE KEY ELEMENTS OF MARKET BEHAVIOR

A Simple Model to Describe Market Behavior

Our goal is to describe market behavior in a simple and easily understandable way. Our descriptive model needs no arbitrary wave counting or bar counting system. You, the user, will have nothing to add or take away. The results will always be the same. We will have a kind of background or universal market description language. When you use it, it will clarify what the market is doing at that given moment. It will also make past behavior self-evident.

This model will also enable you to trade the markets objectively, eliminating a great deal of guesswork. You will be able to do this because what is invisible with many trading methods becomes visible with our method. This is why our method or model of describing markets can be used in either of two main ways to trade.

The first approach to trading is to use the method as a standalone system. Learn the language of the market. You will then know what the market asks of you and be able to trade it. This first approach should be used at the beginning. It's a good starting point.

Once you have practised with the first method, you can use the second approach. It is using the triad method in conjunction with other trading methods. Triads enhance every trading system. They will check the signals of any system against market reality. This will enable the analyst to confront his own analysis or system with the market background that, due to triads, will become visible and reveal its true meaning.

Think of our method as a safety net that is there to protect you. This does not mean that our method is infallible. It is not infallible and is not meant to be. Its only purpose is to describe market behavior accurately at a given moment. Forecasting is not needed if you have an accurate description of the present. Your only goal is to describe markets in the here and now!

Perhaps I should elaborate. Let us begin with market structure.

The Market: Its Ternary Structure

The market has a ternary structure. By this I mean that it has a structure born of oscillations. Oscillations are the primary elements of market behavior.

What we want to know is how markets oscillate and how oscillations combine and change direction in a perpetual stream of market flow. For this purpose, we have created a simple mathematical model that has the ability to describe market structure. This model is built on three elements:

1. The pivot
2. The swing
3. The triad.

The structure that is defined by these three elements is what we call the 'fundamental market structure.' This structure is at the base of every market movement and every market pattern. It explains every market behavior from the standpoint of price and time.

Price and time help you to understand market conditions. For example, they help you to identify market strength at any given moment. This will help you to know, for example, whether a reversal is a true reversal or only a reaction within the same movement.

The fundamental market structure will also help you to identify the length of a movement. You will have clues to tell you whether a movement is near its beginning, near its middle, or near its end. It will be most useful in helping you to place stops where the chances of the market hitting them are minimal, if you make your trade in the correct direction.

With the pivot, swing and triad, you will also understand the inner logic behind all patterns. You will understand the common thread behind figures, such as double bottoms or tops, head and shoulders, triangle patterns, etc. Above all, the relative importance of each market price as positioned in space and time will be made evident. What before was a simple sequence of highs and lows will become a qualified series of points – and their relative meaning will stand out. The market will acquire a new dimension of profundity that it did not have before.

Therefore, these three elements in their simplicity are essential. We will now examine them.

We will begin with the first element, the pivot.

The Pivot

The pivot is the origin of every market movement. It is the foundation point (Figure 1.1). The pivot is at the beginning and the end of every market swing, movement, or wave (Figure 1.2), and is a turning point or reversal point. The market changes its direction at a pivot.

The pivot is an energy point, the elementary market particle. It acts like a magnetic center or pole from which a movement originates – or at which a movement ends

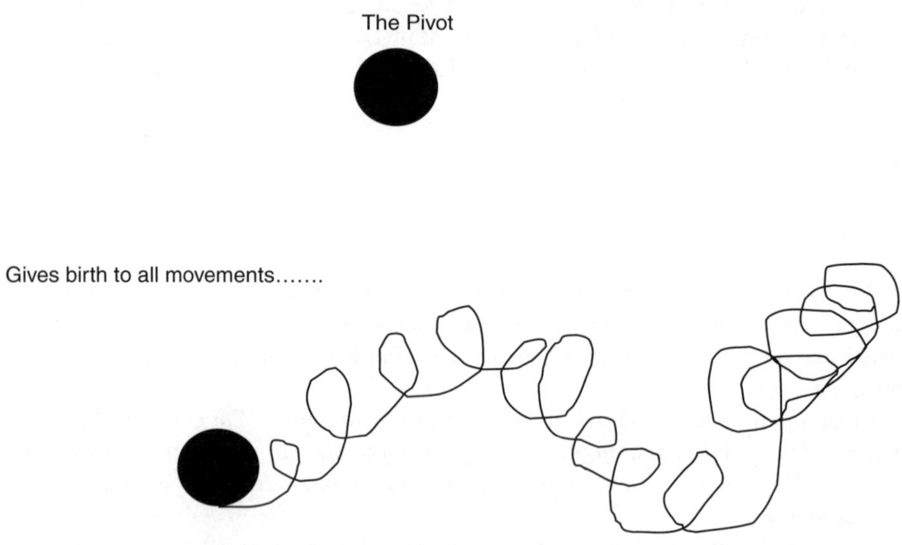

Figure 1.1 The pivot.

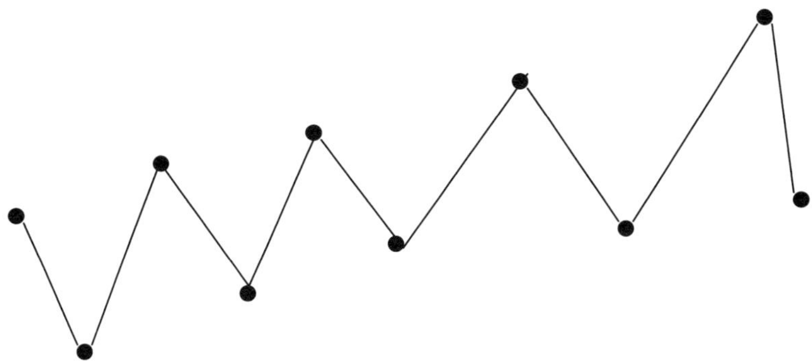

Figure 1.2 Swings.

and another movement begins. In this sense, pivots are creative. They are always the origins of new movements.

Also, not all pivots are the same. Their relative positions make them more or less important. It is from pivots that triads and swings are born.

Understanding the relative importance of pivots is essential to an understanding of market behavior. For instance, the simple position of a single pivot may mean that the market has definitely reversed. A multiyear bull market can be completely reversed at a single pivot. Even though there may be other pivots around the reversal, there will be one key pivot that will signal that a reversal has truly taken effect. The former is simply one possible case among many others. This is to say that pivots are energy points charged with meaning, and that each pivot must be analyzed on its merits alone, according to its position within the entire market structure.

Imagine a ball that bounces. To bounce requires energy. This energy must come from somewhere, but the ball will absorb it and react to it. Now, if you throw the ball to the floor, what will happen? Your ball will be stopped by the floor and then bounce. It will rebound and rise up until, for an instant, it will stop. Then it will fall, initiating a new movement in the opposite direction. For its new movement, the ball has acquired energy of different polarity. There are two points, clearly defined, where our ball stopped before reversing direction. At both points, its energy reversed direction. The energy for each of these turning points was not the same.

The example of our ball and its turning points is akin to pivots, turning points in the market, and energy centers that are not homogeneous. Like the bouncing ball, market pivots vary in strength according to their overall positions. These pivots are the origins of market movements. These market movements are called oscillations, fluctuations, swings, or waves. They are worth examining in some detail.

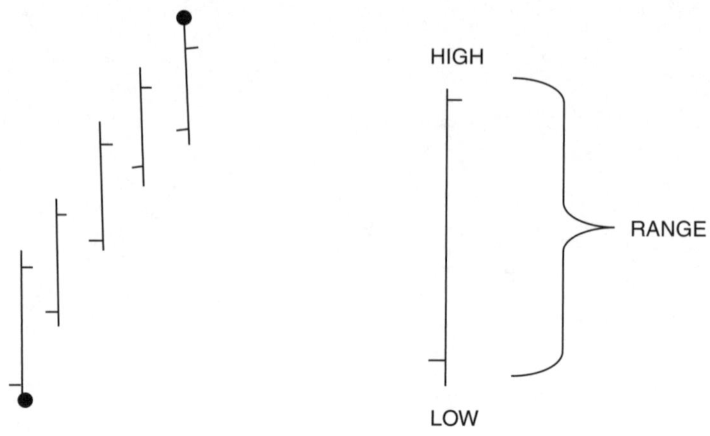

Figure 1.3 The swings are divided into time/price units, i.e. charted bars.

The Swing

The swing is a market oscillation. It is born in a pivot. All swings are contained between two pivots – an origin pivot and an end pivot. The end pivot of a swing is the beginning pivot of a new swing in the opposite direction.

Every swing results from the movement of a pivot. A market line is created by such a motion. This line is expressed in time price units. Time price units can be represented as a series of ticks or a series of charted bars (Figure 1.3). Markets are cyclical and the swings alternate constantly. The alternation of swings is the primary market cycle. All other cycles come from this initial cycle. We find the law of action and reaction operating here (Figure 1.4). The law of action and reaction is behind the alternating motions of swings and indicates that there are two contrary forces acting in the market. As soon as one swing ends and a new one begins, one of the forces ceases, giving way to an opposite force. Both forces and their interaction are the energy that feeds the market. The market behaves like an electrical motor, the revolutions of which are the result of two poles alternating – a positive pole and a negative pole.

The law of action and reaction gives us three kinds of swings. The first kind of swing is the horizontal swing, the second is the upward swing, and the third is the downward swing.

A horizontal swing indicates that market forces are at equilibrium. This is a neutral point. Prices stay the same along a time line. Buyers and sellers have an equal impact on the market. This horizontal line or swing seldom occurs in free markets. It occurs when price controls prevent prices from expressing their true nature. When a horizontal swing does occur in free markets, it occurs in rather illiquid markets

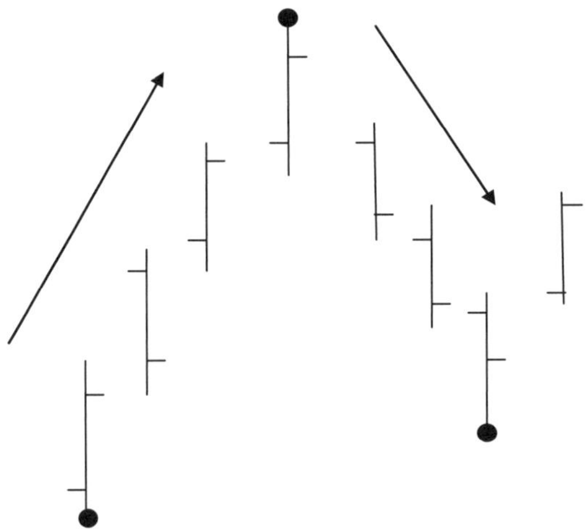

Figure 1.4 The swings follow the law of alternation. This is why markets oscillate. The pivots link swings together and are their beginnings and ends.

or intraday markets for very brief periods where buyers and sellers are momentarily indecisive.

Upward and downward swings are the most common swings. They occur in free markets where prices can oscillate. The swings alternate between up and down, even in sideways markets. An upward swing denotes an imbalance between buyers and sellers in which buying strength exceeds selling strength. There is a net buying flow. A downward swing denotes an imbalance between buyers and sellers in which selling strength exceeds buying strength. There is a net selling flow.

The horizontal swing has neither speed nor acceleration. It is static. That is why it appears geometrically as a horizontal line. Upward and downward swings have both speed and acceleration. That is, they have a uniform or a variable rate of change that can increase or decrease. This is shown by the angle of the swing. The greater the angle of a swing, the greater is its speed.

Speed differs from rate of change. If the rate of change is uniform and equal for each time period, we will have a certain angle. The steepness of the angle will be a function of its speed. If the rate of change accelerates, we will have multiple angles that develop as a fan. To accelerate, a price must change its angle. It must become steeper. Therefore, swing angles define the rate of speed and rate of change.

A swing can contain other swings within itself. This is due to the fractal nature of markets. Each of these inner swings has, in turn, its own speed and rate of change. A trend line shows this. A trend line helps us to make visible a swing that is composed of other swings. The same is true of a charted bar. If we look at what takes place inside a daily charted bar, which itself is a swing, we will discover many fluctuations.

There is something to remember about trend lines. Their function is not to trade the markets, but to measure the direction, angle, speed, and acceleration of a market movement or swing. Trend lines are lines that you draw on charts, so that you can examine them. By examining them, you have a better idea of the market trend and its direction, angle of elevation, speed and acceleration. Of course, this does not exclude the use of trend lines as trading tools.

Now, let us examine triads, the reversal structure that joins swings together.

The Triad

We will begin with a definition of a triad. A triad is a series of charted bars, not necessarily consecutive, that satisfy the following conditions:

- The high of the middle charted bar is higher than the highs of the adjacent lateral charted bars (given any three charted bars) and the low of the middle charted bar is higher than the lows of the adjacent lateral charted bars. In this case, we have a descending triad. The high of the middle charted bar is lower than the highs of the adjacent lateral charted bars (given any three charted bars) and the low of the middle charted bar is lower than the lows of the adjacent lateral charted bars. In this case, we have an ascending triad (Figure 1.5).

These two kinds of triads, the ascending triad and the descending triad, are found at the beginning and end of every swing or market oscillation.

Here we are dealing with simple triads that can be either ascending or descending. This triad can be found in any time frame, whether daily, weekly, monthly, hourly, etc. The triad has a fractal nature and will be found in every time/price market level.

The triad is also a miniature mirror of the entire market cycle. In an ascending triad, the left side is descending and the right side is ascending. We have a downswing

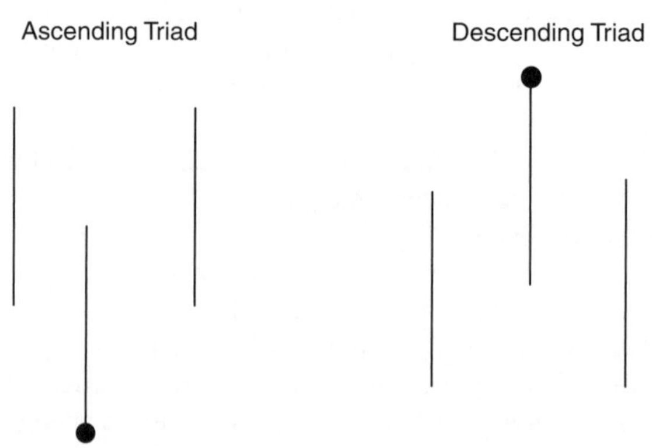

Figure 1.5 Triads can be ascending or descending.

and an upswing. This is true, irrespective of the close of the triad charted bar. From the high of the left side charted bar to the low of the middle charted bar, we have a downswing. From the low of the middle charted bar to the high of the next adjoining charted bar, we have an upswing. In the descending triad, we have the reverse. First, we have an upswing followed by a downswing. In both the ascending triad and the descending triad, we find a primal market cycle where upswings alternate with downswings and vice versa.

Thus, in the triad, we find a miniature model of the market and its primal cycle. This is why triads always work as turning points, because the triad contains a miniature market reversal in itself. The high of the descending triad is the ending pivot of an upward swing and the beginning pivot of a downward swing. In the case of the ascending triad, the lowest low is the end of a descending movement and the starting point of an ascending movement.

This means that the triad is the smallest geometric structure to contain two opposite swings linked by a common pivot. The triad is the smallest turning point and the basic building block of the fundamental market structure.

Let us now examine the types of triads.

Types of triads

The two main types of triads are the ascending triad and the descending triad that we have already defined. These two kinds of triads can be simple or complex. The ascending and descending triads that we have defined are cases of simple triads. A simple triad is one that has only three charted bars.

This leaves us with the complex triad. A complex triad is one that comprises more than three charted bars (Figure 1.6 and also see Chart 1 in Appendix II).

The additional charted bars are inner charted bars between the middle charted bar and the first charted bar of the triad, and between the middle charted bar and the last charted bar of the triad. For example, between the middle charted bar of an ascending triad and the left charted bar of the triad, we can have one or more charted bars that have a lower high than the middle charted bar and a higher low than the middle charted bar. The same can apply to the interval between the middle and right charted bars of the ascending triad.

Our example shows that triads, whether ascending or descending, can have intermediary inner charted bars. These intermediary charted bars are contained within the only three charted bars that are sufficient and necessary to define a triad, as explained earlier when defining the simple ascending and descending triads.

In conclusion, the triad structure is the minimal structure of charted bars required for a change in market direction. It is the minimal, turning-point structure.

Here we must explain the difference between the triad and the ringed charted bar. The ringed charted bar identifies only a high charted bar in relation to its adjacent highs or a lower low in relation to its adjacent lows. This differs from the triad that requires a lower low and a lower high or a higher high and a higher low, which enables

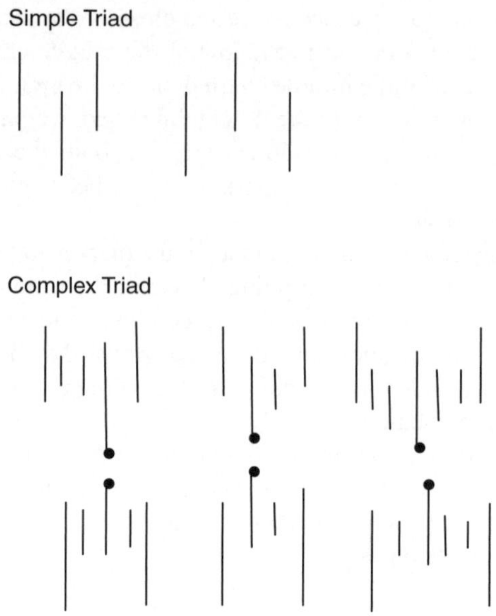

Figure 1.6 Triads can be simple or complex.

us to have a complete market movement or a swing first in one direction and then in the other.

Another difference is that the ringed charted bars are not meant to be a turning point structure that will signify the end of one movement and the beginning of another movement in the opposite direction. Every swing of any length is always contained between two opposite triads. A swing is the market oscillation that is contained between an ascending triad and a descending triad, the lowest low of the first and the highest high of the last being the starting and ending pivots of the entire movement.

Also, a ringed charted bar does not indicate market direction as does a triad. It lacks the necessary third and last charted bar with a higher high than the middle charted bar for an ascending triad or a lower low than the middle charted bar for a descending triad. This higher high or lower low confirms that a turning point and a full movement have occurred.

The ringed charted bar also fails to indicate market strength because that is not its function. The triad defines strength by the fact that at least the last charted bar of an ascending triad has a higher high than its middle bar or, alternatively, the last bar of a descending triad has a lower low than its middle bar.

This is not to minimize the function of ringed bars. They represent a tried and true approach that has worked for traders since times immemorial. All we are saying is that they are not triads and that they don't have the meaning or functions of triads.

Let us now examine the function of a triad.

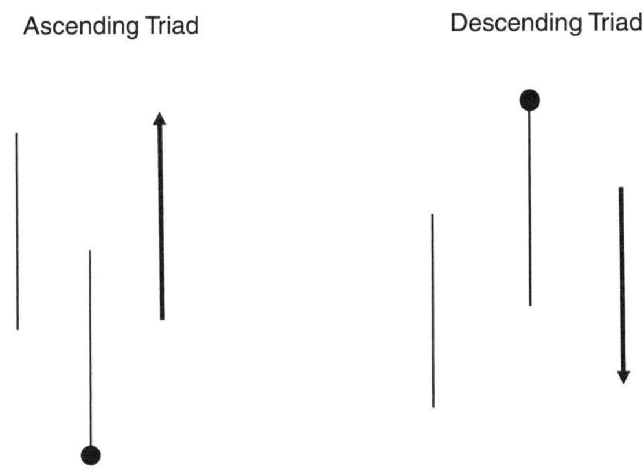

Figure 1.7 The triad has direction and thrust.

Functions of Triads

A triad has three main functions:

1. First, it validates pivots and swings. A pivot is the high or the low of the middle charted bar of a triad and is validated only when the third charted bar of the triad is complete.
2. Second, it has a directional function. It contains a vector that indicates a new market direction. The triad has thrust.[6] The last charted bar of the triad is a breakout of the high pivot of the central charted bar in the case of an ascending triad or a breakout of the low pivot of the central charted bar in the case of a descending triad (Figure 1.7). This breakout is a thrust in the new direction where the market is headed. Thrust gives the triad its full power and enables the trader to enter the market at low risk high energy points.
3. Finally, the triad measures the strength of the market by the range and the closing position of the third and last charted bar of the triad.

Let us go over each of these three functions in greater detail. With regard to the validation of pivots and swings, until a triad is complete, it is impossible to know if we have a triad at all or if a new market pivot has been defined. The triad is not a market forecast. It needs to be complete. The function of a triad is to describe the market now – at the present moment. The complete triad is both in the past and the present.

In summary, the triad is a geometric structure that is like a hinge that links a market fluctuation to the next market fluctuation in the opposite direction. The triad also defines market pivots. A market pivot is the geometrical dot that links swings or fluctuations together. This dot, which corresponds to a real price in the market, is only known when a triad is complete.

The triad itself has the following structure: it has a middle charted bar that has a lower low and a lower high than its contiguous left side and right side charted bars – or it has a higher low and a higher high than its contiguous left side and right side charted bars. In the first case, we have an ascending triad and, in the second case, we have a descending triad.

Triads can be simple or complex. The simple triad has only three charted bars. The complex triad can have more.

Whatever happens at the exact moment when a triad becomes complete (assuming that we are there to observe it), happens in the present. This present, which begins upon completion of the triad, instantly becomes the past as the future begins to unfold – a future that is unknown to us.

It is at this point that the directional function of the triad, its second function, comes into play. Upon completion, the third and last charted bar of the triad signals a new direction in the market. This new direction is an accomplished fact in the last charted bar of the triad. Within the triad, the market has changed direction.

The triad does not forecast a new direction, but signals an accomplished fact. The market will not reverse after the triad because it has already done so within it. It is at the completion of the triad that the present gives rise to the future.

This future may or may not continue the new direction that the triad is signaling to us. We assume that the new direction will continue, not as a forecast but only as a possible scenario reinforced by the fact that the market already has a direction. For us, this new direction is market reality. To suppose that it will change or stop is to assume something that does not belong to market reality. All we do is continue to follow the new existing direction. Therefore, what we do is simply follow the new direction of the complete triad into its future.

Next is the third function of the triad, which enables us to assess the strength of the market. This strength will be directly linked to the continuation of the new direction into the future that the triad signaled. If the new direction is strong, this strength will carry into the future. The clues with which you can assess this strength are the closing point of the last triad charted bar and its range. For example, if the last charted bar of an ascending charted bar closes over the high of the middle charted bar and has a great range, the new force vector is strong. This means that the new ascending swing is strong.

Thus, triads enable us to define pivots and swings, to signal market direction, and to signal market strength. Having said this about triads, let us resume our discussion of the fundamental market structure.

THE FUNDAMENTAL MARKET STRUCTURE

This is the market's ternary structure. We have defined the fundamental market structure as being composed of three elements – the pivot, the swing, and the triad

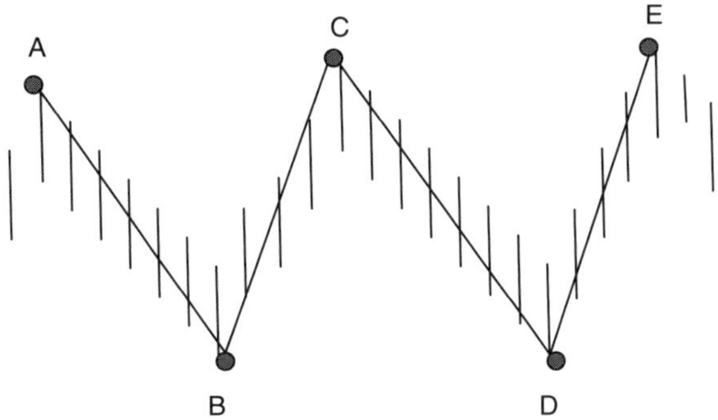

Figure 1.8 Pivots, swings and triads.

(Figure 1.8). The pivot is the origin of swings. A swing is limited by a pivot at each of its ends. The triad is the hinge that links two swings. It is a complete turning point.

This ternary structure will enable us to understand the language of the market. We will be able to look at charts in a new way (Figure 1.9). By identifying a chart's swings, pivots, and triads, whether ascending or descending or simple or complex, the market will begin to reveal its secrets spontaneously.

As an exercise, try to identify the ternary structure in charts. This ternary structure is responsible for the alternating motions of swings. These alternating swings follow rules. Patterns develop. These patterns will appear by themselves once we are able to observe the links between swings and their pivots and triads.

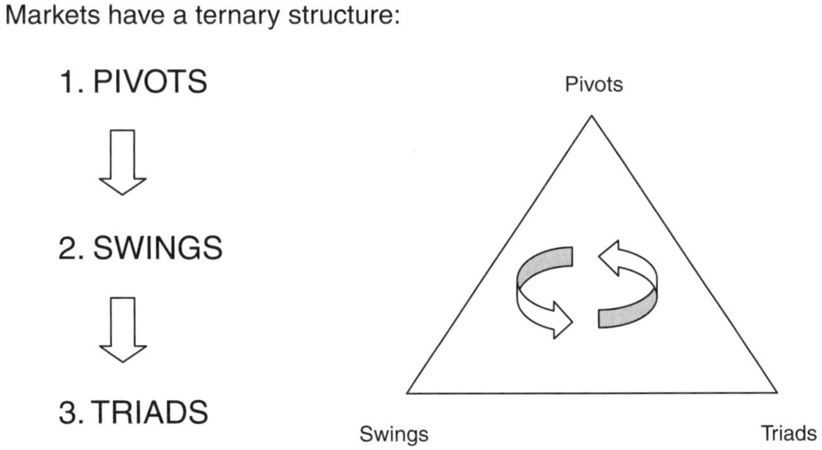

Figure 1.9 The fundamental market structure.

This ternary structure is circular. Each element of the ternary structure feeds on the others. The pivot, the origin or first element, engenders the swing or first market movement. When this first market movement reverses and becomes a swing in an opposite direction, the triad is born. In conclusion, a first pivot engenders the swing, which engenders the triad, in turn.

From this first development of fundamental market structure, an indefinite market movement proceeds. The market is born. From this point onwards, pivots will engender swings and triads, swings will engender pivots and triads, and triads will engender pivots and swings. This initial circular motion becomes a spiral motion of circles that evolve into an ever evolving future.

This ternary market structure enables us to read the market without having to engage in forecasting. This is because it enables us to do something much simpler – to describe the market accurately.

Nevertheless, to describe the market is a challenging task. It is not easy to describe accurately what the market is doing now. Few people have this ability, even among professionals. Attempting to forecast the market is often the result of inaccurately describing it. If we describe a market correctly, not only will we be far ahead of most traders but we will have all that we need to trade that market.

We believe that there is no need to forecast. All we need is to be in the market now. The fundamental market structure is the tool that enables us to accomplish this. This market tool enables us to describe oscillations. It enables the market to define its own oscillations without imposing an arbitrary distance for the oscillations from the outside.

This is possible due to the existence of the triad. A triad appears not because we define it, but because the market does. Let me explain. As we have seen, we have a starting point for every market movement – the pivot. The pivot is the origin of price change and so we have a swing. Now, this swing is a mystery to us. We do not know when or where it will end. When will it end? It will end when a new pivot appears – a pivot that marks the end of the swing. For a new pivot to appear, a condition must be satisfied. We need a triad.

Once this triad appears, the swing ends in its final pivot. This final pivot does not exist until the triad is complete. The triad can be either simple or complex. Who will decide when the triad will appear to end a swing? The market will.

Also, who will decide if the ending triad will be simple or complex? The market will. This means that, by observing the pivots that are engendered by the triads, we will learn the length of a swing and its duration objectively. The market itself will tell us the price changes and time changes of its oscillations.

This makes it much simpler to observe the market than trying to fit the market movements into a predefined and arbitrary number of waves – or counting charted bars. Again, we should mention that we are not against bar counting. It is a very useful technique that is fully compatible with our market tool. We actually encourage bar counting methods in their appropriate context. Bar counting is useful in specific trading setups. Our triad method can also use bar counting, but within the background of fundamental market structure.

Wave counts are a different story. Wave counts do work if they are used as Charles Dow and Gann used them, not rigidly and dogmatically. It is true that waves occur in bull markets and bear markets and that we need to be aware of them.

The problem comes when we believe in advance that the market should have a unique and fixed number of waves. This approach does not work, especially for trading. Thus, we are back to our triads. The triad is the element that enables the market to define its own oscillations. It enables us to define with precision the length and duration of each swing. This applies to every time frame.

From Dow's wavelets to long-term market waves, from the smallest swing to large movements, the fundamental market structure lets the market explain its own story objectively and the same for every observer. The fundamental market structure enables us to discover the natural and objective movements of the markets.

Measuring oscillations is a key aspect of fundamental market structure. The market structure enables us to measure oscillations in price and time. Measuring swings is made possible for the same reasons that enable us to describe oscillations. Each swing can be divided into time/price units called charted bars. This division can be done in different time frames.

For each swing within a given time frame, we will find a definite change in price and in time. What is important is that we can measure these changes and that measuring them will enable us to recognize repetitive changes. These repetitive changes, which we can call price patterns and time patterns, will give us clues to the usual behavior of a market. Its personality will appear.

For instance, we will observe that, if a swing exceeds its usual length by a given number, a reversal could be near – or if a pivot is exceeded by a given number of points, the movement will continue. By measuring time, we will be able to make similar observations. For instance, we will discover certain ratios between time and price. We will observe that certain swings have price changes that correspond to given time changes. For example, we could have eight-point swings that carry on for sixteen days.

Many other relationships will appear. The reason why these price and time measurements appear is that the fundamental market structure, as described by triads, enables the market to define its own length and its own duration of the swings it creates. Once again, it is the triad that, by defining the beginning and end of swings and the appearance or absence of pivots, will determine the length of each swing in price and duration in time (see Chart 1 in Appendix II).

These price lengths and durations are natural. They belong to the market's inner structure. A triad's only merit is in making this structure visible simply and easily.

Now, let us learn how triads help to explain the primal market cycle, the swing. The primal market cycle is the swing because it is the unit of each market movement. There is no smaller market movement than a swing. Swings can vary in length and duration, but the market moves in swings.

Market movement is nothing more than the alternations of its swings. Swings link themselves in an indefinite market chain. Ascending swings are followed by descending swings in an unending dance. This alternation of swings is cyclical.

It repeats itself. An ascending swing is followed by a descending swing and vice versa.

The link between swings, which constitute the cyclical nature of markets at its primal level, is once more made possible by the triad. The triad not only makes possible the existence and appearance of the pivot that ends the preceding swing but also creates the new swing that appears as the opposite of the preceding swing. This would be impossible without the triad.

In conclusion, the triad creates the primal cycle from which all market cycles are born. However, there is more. In the case of the cycle, the triad itself is also a cycle. The triad is cyclical.

You will remember that a triad has three main elements that may or may not be consecutive. These elements define a miniature upswing, its turning point pivot, and a miniature downswing – a complete market cycle. In an ascending triad, the market goes down in order to turn around and go back up. In a descending triad, the opposite occurs. The market goes up in order to turn around and come back down. In both kinds of triads, ascending and descending, whether simple or complex, we find a miniature, full market cycle.

Triads have helped us to explain why cycles must occur. They must occur because of a mathematical law. This law operates where there is change in the form of fluctuations. The price and time fluctuations in the market engender triads.

A triad is a specific kind of number pattern that expresses itself geometrically in a price chart or arithmetically in a quotation screen or spreadsheet (see Charts 2 and 3 in Appendix II). Both ways express the same reality, namely a microcycle that contains the market structure in miniature and that creates the points that link the market fluctuations or swings. This is the real power of triads. Triads go to the core of the market itself.

Let us explore now why triads are also the foundation of market phases. Market phases originate in swings. A market phase is a specific behavior of swings. Not all swings behave in the same way or are positioned in the same way. As in a Lego game, swings can be assembled in various ways. By being assembled in different ways, their sequences can assume different forms. These forms will depend on how swings of different lengths and duration are put together.

In all of these phases, we have main pivot points and secondary pivot points. These are the turning points that come into existence as soon as a triad ends an oscillation to begin another. Again, the triad, as the hinge that connects swings, has the role of linking swings of different orders of magnitude in size and duration. These different orders of magnitude define the importance of the pivots.

Triads arrange themselves according to market behavior to create market phases. These phases will be easily visible, as will be their pivots and the relative importance of the pivots. The arrangement of the triads follows a sequential order as they arrange themselves as a 'series' of triads. For instance, if we want to analyze the behavior of the market according to Dow theory or to identify the main trend and the secondary reaction, all we must do is highlight the triads in a chart with an adequate time window. In a weekly or monthly chart, the highlighted triad will make the main wave and subwaves of the primary trend and its pivots visible automatically, as well as the main wave and subwaves of the secondary reaction and its pivots. Triads make any market behavior self-evident and easily recognizable by the observer. They make the most important events visible.

The pivots and waves obtained in this way are caused by the market's natural movement as revealed by triads. We are not making any kind of adjustment from outside. No optimization of parameters is possible in any way at all.

Triads give us an objective and truthful way in which to analyze the market and arrive at the same conclusions concerning general market structure. In other words, this means that any two persons who observe the same chart will agree on the number and position of the pivots – and the number and position of the waves or swings in it. All of this is simply the result of letting the triads do their own work.

After the market structure with its waves and pivots assembled in phases has become visible, it is up to the trader or analyst to assess correctly the final meaning of it all, because the meaning depends on his specific strategies and goals.

Now let us see how triads influence the specific patterns that the market creates. Triads are not only behind market phases, but also behind market patterns. A triangle, a double bottom, a pennant, a channel, or any pattern that we can think of, has its origin in triads and the pivots and swings that originate from them.

As with phases that give us the bigger picture, patterns are specific formations that occur within that bigger picture. Those patterns are precise ways in which swings assemble themselves, which give rise to the forms we know – the triangle, the triple bottom, the head and shoulders, and the top, etc. In fact, we have no patterns at all. Instead, we have assemblies of swings that tell us that the market is changing its behavior. This meaning is not found in the pattern itself, but in the way the market is behaving. It is revealed to us by the new way of assembling the market's swings.

The market is revealed to us as consisting of several layers. Each level shows us a different reality. This way of describing things is called a phenomenological analysis, where phenomenological comes from the word phenomenon. A phenomenon simply means any event or thing that we perceive with our senses. A flower in a vase is a phenomenon.

The usefulness of this approach is that it forces us to describe things as they appear to us. It is like obtaining a pleasant drawing or a photograph of something. If we are able to recognize the subject of the drawing or photograph, we are already way ahead of the competition. When this approach is applied to the market, it enables us to make a drawing or photograph of it, analogically speaking, that enables us to recognize objectively what is going on.

When we recognize a triangle in a chart, this is taking place at a level at which we can see the triangular image. If we go a layer deeper, we will find market fluctuations assembled in a particular way by triads and pivots. Think of a chart on which prices create a triangular pattern known as a 'triangle' in technical analysis. We recognize this pattern as a 'triangle,' but if we shift our viewpoint and look at it as a series of fluctuations, we will have a contracting series of fluctuations that create the illusion of a triangular form.

Now, although we have many market patterns, we have an even greater number of small particular market setups that traders use in their daily activities. However, we must remember that all of these patterns and setups are combinations of swings that are linked by pivots that originate in triads. A pivot is only known when a triad is completed, but the pivot occurs in time before the triad. So, in a way, pivots originate in triads and triads originate in pivots. A pivot is defined at a completion of a triad.

What is the use of all of this? What is the advantage of knowing that phases and patterns and market setups dissolve at a given level of observation into an assembly of fluctuations linked by pivots that originate in triads? The advantage is that once we know this, all phases, patterns, and cycles are reduced to a few simple laws that explain market behavior. Phases and patterns will become only particular cases of a general law. When this happens, the behavior of phases, patterns, and cycles that seemed somewhat arbitrary to us before will become self-evident and meaningful. Once again, we see the power of triads.

Before we leave this chapter, we should understand what a 'market setup' is. In fact, the usual term is 'trading setup.' This means that the market has, at a given moment, a particular condition (or conditions) that enables the trader to buy it or sell it. However, a trading setup is also a market setup, since the market positions itself in a given pattern or figure. For example, buying the breakout of a consolidation would be a setup. The trader would wait for the market to consolidate to move horizontally and, as soon as the market breaks out of the horizontal range (consolidation), he would buy it if the breakout is on the upside or sell it if the breakout is on the downside.

2
How to Measure Oscillations

THE PRIMORDIAL MARKET CYCLE

Measuring the Primal Cycle: The Swing

We have seen that all market fluctuations are cyclical. The market is a never-ending alternation of its primal cycle. This primal market cycle consists of swings in alternating directions, with one swing following the other endlessly, and is what enables us to trade or to invest in the market. We will take positions at given prices and times within this primal market cycle.

We can, for instance, enter an upward-moving market reaction. In that case, we will wait for a descending swing to complete itself. As we know, the market has a primal cycle law. We can be sure that the market will retrace itself at a particular moment. If markets were not cyclical, we would not wait for it to retrace itself.

The same can be said of any other setup, such as buying a double bottom or the breakout of a triangle. We know, because of the cyclical law, that any market position will evolve into its opposite. We can call this cyclical law of the market 'the law of the same and the different.' Markets go from the same to the different. Every movement from the same to the same can only be done by a previous movement from the same to the different. According to this law, every movement from the different to the different must pass first from the different to the same.

Within this cyclical law, our first task in order to understand the personality and behavior of the market is to measure its cyclical elements. This means measuring its swings. It is imperative that we measure all market swings. The measuring must be done for all possible time frames. Measuring every time frame will reveal a great deal of common behavior. The personality of the market will emerge.

Very few traders measure market swings. In fact, most people approach markets by trying to recognize chart patterns or market setups. Failing this, they will attempt to see if a moving average crossover has occurred – or if an indicator is giving its signal.

This is not the way to understand or trade markets. The way to a real understanding will only come by becoming familiar with the market's fluctuations. This familiarity will come only when you are able to measure the fluctuations correctly.

Now, let us discuss how to measure market fluctuations.

How to Measure Market Oscillations

To measure the market means to measure each and every one of its swings under every possible time frame and under every possible angle. We must acquire the 'measuring habit.' This means that we must keep on measuring the market until it becomes second nature to us.

This requires discipline. We must measure the market in a consistent fashion. We must do it daily, weekly, or monthly, depending on our investing or trading time frame. If we are short-term traders, it might be convenient to measure the market swings daily. If we are intermediate-term traders, we could measure the market swings weekly, although if we are long-term traders or investors, we might do this monthly.

You should assign yourself a time at which you will regularly study the market's fluctuations. The more of it that you do, the more practice you will have gained. Acquiring the discipline required for the measuring habit will furnish you with the discipline and attitude necessary to trade the markets successfully. The habit of measuring market swings is far more important than the actual action of measuring. Always measure. Measuring only once will give you a feel and a practical understanding of the need to measure. However, it is only by making this measuring activity a habit that you will be able to receive its full value. Think of the measuring habit as a form of investment capital for life that has far greater ongoing value than liquidation value.

Money from the markets is the result of a trader's market knowledge. This knowledge converts to money, when correctly used. However, the real value is not in the money. The real value is in your market knowledge. It is market knowledge for which you will be paid. How you are paid for your knowledge is secondary. First must come the knowledge.

For example, if you are an analyst, your market knowledge will convert itself to money for the value of your analysis. If you are a financial writer or lecturer, the public will pay for your market knowledge as others wish to learn what you know. If you are a trader, your market knowledge will transform itself into trading money. The same holds true if you are an investor.

The market has many ways of paying you. Money is not the only form of payment. The pleasure of knowing about the markets is a reward in itself. True success comes only to those who do something from a sense of vocation or calling.

At the beginning of this market knowledge should be the measuring habit. This habit will provide you with unique knowledge of the market. Therefore, to know how to measure the market, begin by developing the measuring habit. The more you measure, the more you will learn. The more time that you spend measuring and studying the market, the more you will know about it.

This knowledge comes in many ways. The first is measuring the swings or fluctuations themselves. By measuring them, you will be able, with practice, to classify the different kinds of swing sizes and swing durations. Also, you will begin to develop a sense of sequencing and alternation. You will begin to make educated guesses about what swings usually follow others within specific market phases or periods.

Classifying swings can only be a result of constant practice because the differences among swings can be subtle. Also, their sequencing can be difficult to grasp at first. With sufficient practice, you will not only learn the kinds and sequence of swings but also you will detect clusters of market events. For instance, you may conclude that the end of a pattern will coincide with the end of a swing of a given size and duration and with the end of another intermediate swing, and also with the end of a smaller swing that, at the same time, ends any retracing of the former swings.

A clustered event like this gives us a clue that an important market change may occur. Clusters of events, such as the end of swings of different lengths around the same place at the same approximate time, occur not only within a given time frame but also in different time frames. The superimposition of different time frames, such as a monthly chart, a weekly chart, and a daily chart, will enable us to perceive such clusters and add to our overall knowledge of markets.

All of the foregoing should come naturally to you as a consequence of developing the measuring habit. The measuring habit will change forever the way you look at markets.

Measuring the Market is Creating Its Reality

The unique something that you will discover is that, by measuring the market, you create market reality in a fully objective way. What will take place is a paradox. You will create market reality.

At the same time, this market reality will be fully objective. Any number of observers can confirm its reality in the same way. This reality occurs because, as an observer, you are actively creating it.

Our perception is selective. It is the result of an act of choice. This choice is made consciously or unconsciously. We choose what to perceive. This choice gives us the building blocks with which we form our perception of the world.

This choice operates through attention. Have you noticed that some people are very attentive to certain things that you give little or no attention to? They are building their world in the same way in which you are building yours. You also are attentive to certain things that others around you don't notice. You are constantly building your world. And your world is not exactly the same as someone else's world!

Why does attention select different things for different people? Here is where your belief system comes into play. Your belief system conditions your choices and guides your attention like a beam, as you search for what you are seeking. Your belief system is subjective. It is within you. However, attention projects your belief system outward until it finds and selects what it is looking for. Once it has found what it was looking for, it becomes fully objective. It is really there and, because it is a real thing, its validity is the same for all observers.

Market perception is the intersection of two coordinates – your inner and subjective belief system and the market's outer objective reality. When they meet, the market is born. This is truer in market analysis and trading or investing than anywhere else. Your belief system will define what you see objectively. The degree of objectivity will depend on the strength of your belief system. This requires further explanation. If your belief system is based on sound judgment and reasoning, it will not only condition the way you perceive reality but also the way it functions. Reality is reasonable and so are the markets.

The laws of market logic and market thought are pale reflections of the real thought about markets in the outside world and in your inner, invisible world. One thing is your conception or perception of reason, and quite another is reason itself. This concept will be extremely important later when it is taken into account in our market studies.

The thing to remember now is that your belief system as a trader will direct your attention until your mind finds what it is looking for in the outer world. However, your mind can find things that belong to a sound trading belief system or to an unsound belief system. A sound trading belief system will guide your attention to building an outer trading reality that works. If you explain it to someone, he should find exactly the same things in the markets that you find – if your belief system is sound. For example, if you present someone with a weekly chart and ask him to measure all swings created by triads, the results will always be the same, no matter who does the measuring.

Once the same concepts of the belief system are shared by two observers, their realities are identical. This is the test of objectivity. If the belief system is not sound or grounded in reason, it will not be possible for two observers to share the same results. For example, let two observers count waves according to the Elliott theory. Their results will differ. There is a lack of consistency.

A sound market model will enable your attention to create market reality and to share it with others on a fully objective basis. Of most importance is that, by measuring the market, you not only are creating its reality but also are making it yours.

Measuring the Market Makes it Yours: The True Way to Own the Market

The act of measuring the market will cause you to perceive market reality in a unique and, at the same time, objective way. If your belief system is correct, all of the measurements of fluctuations that you make will be real and also your own. What happens is that your perception, guided by your attention and your market beliefs, is selective. Because your trading system is grounded on reason, it is objective. It is real for you and, because you are the one who does the measuring, it is subjective at the same time. It is only yours.

This is true until you decide to share your findings with others. As long as you decide not to share them, you will have a fully objective and real market perception. However, at the same time, and as far as you know, it will be yours only.

It is possible that someone else may have measured the same swings in the same way. However, it is also possible that this is not the case. Because the market is so large, it is unlikely that everyone will measure the same swings in exactly the same way. Some market students will give more significance to some swings or to some movements, phases, or patterns than to others.

These choices will depend on the specific trading strategy or analytical perspective of each person. However, all choices will be objective and real in their meaning. This means that measuring market fluctuations using triads will enable you to create, as a trader, a unique approach to the markets that will remain your secret, unless you decide to share it.

Think about it! There are a multiplicity of markets and, in each market, a multiplicity of phases and a variety of patterns. To this, we must add the multiplicity of time frames in which markets can be analyzed, as well as their combinations. Within this universe, even the soundest trading beliefs based on market reality, and what really works, will not give the same results in the same way for all traders. The market is too large and traders will not select exactly the same area to study.

In this sense, the market is also yours. This is due to the fact that, because you are a unique individual, your market perspective will also be unique, according to the different elements that determine your choice.

Some traders will measure fluctuations in order to trade them directly. Other traders will analyze the structure that the market presents within a given period and time frame and deal with the market according to the structure that is defined by triads. Still another trader could use channels, or moving averages and other indicators or systems, in conjunction with market structure to trade the markets. Therefore, the number of possible approaches to studying and trading the markets is great. However, in all cases, it is important to have a sound knowledge of market structure and to measure the market fluctuations constantly.

If actively measuring the fluctuations was a trader's only method, he would have all that he needed to trade well. Simply measuring, if you do nothing else, will put you far ahead in the trading game. I can assure you that very few people take the time to measure market fluctuations actively. Triads make this task simple and easy because they define each and every market swing in an objective and visible way.

Now, it is time to learn the measuring technique that we will apply to market oscillations.

MEASURING THE MARKET

The Two Key Market Measures: Price and Time

Market fluctuations or swings are measured in price and time. We measure every upward swing and its consecutive downward swing. As we have seen, swing fluctuations and their alternations form the primal market cycle.

The swings that are measured will fall within a range, although this range can vary. We will recognize that the swings of a given measured size will be repeated at given intervals. Also, we will notice entire sequences occurring within a range. For example, a series of swings will occur within a range of three points. This means that, from pivot low to pivot high, the distance will be three points. After such a series, the new swing will be larger and display a greater range of volatility.

It is important to measure the individual swings in price and time, as well as to measure the series of swing that occur within a range. We must also measure in price and time the major swings that contain minor swings within them.

Many swings will repeat within their range the same time/price ratios. This means that their size (measured in number of points) will be related to their duration in charted bars. Both measures must always be taken together since they are closely related. We must always measure the time and price for each and every individual swing, as well as for each and every subswing.

As we have said before, many patterns and clusters will emerge from these measured swings. We will notice swings of a given time and size that return many times so that we can almost anticipate their return (see Chart 3 in Appendix II). Also, multiple swings of different time/price ratios will end at approximately the same time. These swing clusters give us important information with regard to impending market turnarounds.

The same can be said of the series of swings that occur within a range of given price/time ratios. The same series can reappear later. It is important to measure the entire series, and sets of series, in price and time. The same must be said for major swings and their subswings since they tend to repeat. In these cases, we must not only measure each major swing individually but also count the number of swings that occur within each.

This will give us an idea of the number of waves that make up major swings. We will recognize that they tend to repeat, roughly speaking, under certain market conditions. We must also count the number of swings themselves that occur within a phase, a pattern, or a significant period of time.

Once we have measured the swings and the number of swings in price and time, we must record this information. This will enable us to discover hidden relationships within them. It will also enable us to use the information.

Now that we know what to measure, let us learn how to measure price.

Measuring by Points

Price is measured first by the number of points. We measure each swing from its pivot origin to its ending pivot. This gives us the change in price from a pivot low to its pivot high for an ascending swing and from a pivot high to its pivot low for a descending swing. We measure the number of points for each individual swing, as well as for any composite swing that consists of a series of swings.

Table 2.1 Measuring the composite swing by points

Swing	Price	Points
AB	15–20	5
BC	20–18	−2
CD	18–35	17
DE	35–25	−10
EF	25–45	20
AF	15–45	30

Here are some examples. Let us suppose that we have an upward swing that starts at a pivot of 35 and ends at a pivot of 38. The swing measures 3 points from a pivot low to a pivot high. It follows a downward swing from 38 to 34 from the pivot high to the pivot low, measuring 4 points.

In our previous example, we measured two consecutive swings. The first had a value of three points and the second had a value of −4 points. As in the above example, we assign a positive value to the number that we obtain by measuring an ascending swing and a negative value to the number that we obtain for a descending swing. In the case of an ascending composite swing, we could have, for example, a swing pivot low of 15 and a swing pivot high of 45. The value would be 30 points. Within this swing, we could have five minor swings: a swing of 15 to 20, a swing of 20 to 18, a swing of 18 to 35, a swing of 35 to 25, and a final swing of 25 to 45.

These minor swings within our composite swing measure 5 points, −2 points, 17 points, −10 points, and finally 20 points, respectively. The composite swing has a value of 30 points. Let us tabulate this (see Table 2.1).

Measuring in points is our first way of measuring swings. This method of measuring alone will increase our understanding of market fluctuations and sharpen our analytical and trading skills. However, measuring fluctuations by the number of points is only the first step. We still have to learn other ways of measuring the same fluctuations. Let us look at a second way.

Measuring by Percentage

The second way of measuring swings is by percentage. We measure the percent increase from a pivot low to a pivot high for ascending swings and the percent decrease from a pivot high to a pivot low for descending swings (Figure 2.1). As with measuring by the number of points, recurring percentage patterns will emerge. We will discover that swings tend to cluster around a given percentage change of fluctuation. This will help us to recognize and anticipate their behavior.

Measuring by percentage keeps the high-priced and low-priced swings in proportion. The change for high-priced issues is greater in points, but not in percentage. This means that a 5-point ascending swing for a stock valued at 10 points is a 50 %

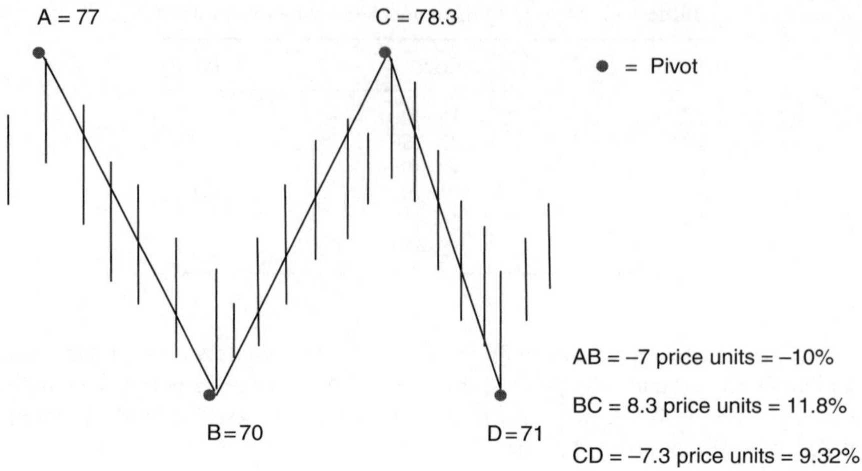

Figure 2.1 The amplitude of a swing is measured in price units or in price percentages.

increase, whereas the same 5 points for a stock valued at 50 points is a 10 % increase. The percentage measure provides a more consistent way of valuing swings, since it uses a common ground in valuing changes, irrespective of their point changes.

Let us take our previous example for points, but use it for percentage changes this time. In the case of an ascending composite swing, we could have a swing pivot low of 15 and a swing pivot high of 45. The value of the change would be 200 %. Within this swing, we could have five minor swings: a swing of 15 to 20, a swing of 20 to 18, a swing of 18 to 35, a swing of 35 to 25, and a final swing of 25 to 45.

These minor swings within our composite swing would be percentage changes from pivot low to pivot high and vice versa, of 33, −10, 94, −28, and 80 %, respectively. The composite swing would be a 200 % change from its pivot low to its pivot high. Now, we will tabulate them (see Table 2.2).

Learning to measure the swings as percentage changes from their origin pivots to their end pivots will enable us to discover the recurring percent changes in market

Table 2.2 Measuring the composite swing by percentage

Swing	Price	Points (%)
AB	15–20	33
BC	20–18	−10
CD	18–35	94
DE	35–25	−28
EF	25–45	80
AF	15–45	200

fluctuations. Now that we have measured the price changes in price points and percentage points, we will turn our attention to the measurement of time.

Learn How to Measure Time

By measuring time, we mean measuring the duration or time length of a swing. Swings vary in time length. Some swings last less than a day, whereas others last for a few days, a few weeks, months, or even many years. For the sake of simplicity, we can classify swings as intraday, short term, intermediate term, long term, and very long term. A swing is intraday if it lasts less than a day, short term if it lasts a few days, intermediate term if it lasts a few weeks, long term if it lasts months, and very long term if it lasts a year or more.

This classification is necessary. It gives us perspective and teaches us what to expect of the markets. Time is essential in analyzing and trading because everything will happen and have validity only for a given time frame and time window.

This needs elaboration. If we are not conscious of our time frames, a short-term trade can become an intermediate-term trade or even a long-term trade. Once we have it clear in our minds what to expect from short term, intermediate term, long term, or very long term, things become easier. This is due to various reasons. One reason is that the longer the time frame is, the more robust is the market behavior. If, after a significant fall in the market, I buy in after a one-week rise to hold for a year, my decision could be catastrophic. The market could very well continue its drop after a few weeks or months. I would have an against-the-trend investment.

In the case above, I would have been mixing time lengths. A one-week rise is a short-term period and is inconsistent with my holding goal of one year. If I had purchased only after a nine-month or a one-year rise, my action would be more reasonable for an objective of holding for a long-term period. A multiyear bear market may very well have ended, if the market rises again for a year after its last bottom.

Now, take another example. Suppose that, within a long-term bull market, I buy an intermediate-term correction of a few weeks after it has turned around for a few days, with the idea of holding it a few more days or even weeks. This would be a reasonable goal. My time frames are then in synchronization – in harmony. Because the strength of the trend is also a function of time, we must always know beforehand our time frame and the market's different time frames.

We will find that time lengths of swings recur as frequently as do price changes. It is here where measuring the duration of fluctuations is so important. Remember Charles Dow. He was fully aware of the importance of the relative time lengths of the main market swings.

Measuring time is essential. It will give us many advantages, such as knowing the relative duration of a given market movement, and help us to know how much longer a trend will continue before it ends. The knowledge of when a trend will begin, what its duration will be, and when it will end will only come to you if you make a habit of measuring time swings. Measuring the time of each fluctuation gives the secret of market timing in its purest way. Market timing begins with the act of measuring market oscillations. We can almost say that it doesn't matter how you measure time, as long as you manage to do it for every swing.

Recurrences and clusters of time ranges and time beginnings and endings will appear everywhere. Your attention to this will help you to do the job, like a powerful reflector that illuminates many time relationships within swings.

In this manner, a new market landscape will appear before your eyes. All you need to do is to measure the duration of fluctuations. You measure the duration from pivot low to pivot high for ascending swings and from pivot high to pivot low for descending swings.

Now, let us take a look at the many ways of measuring time swings.

Measuring in Charted Bars

The first way of measuring a time swing is by counting the number of charted bars that it contains from its pivot origin to its ending pivot. For ascending swings, we count the number of charted bars contained between the pivot low and the pivot high. For descending swings, we count the number of charted bars contained between the pivot high and the pivot low (Figure 2.2).

In doing this, we are defining a swing only in terms of time. A charted bar is a price/time unit, but is mainly a time unit that contains a price unit. In other words, the time element is more important than the price element, although each needs the other.

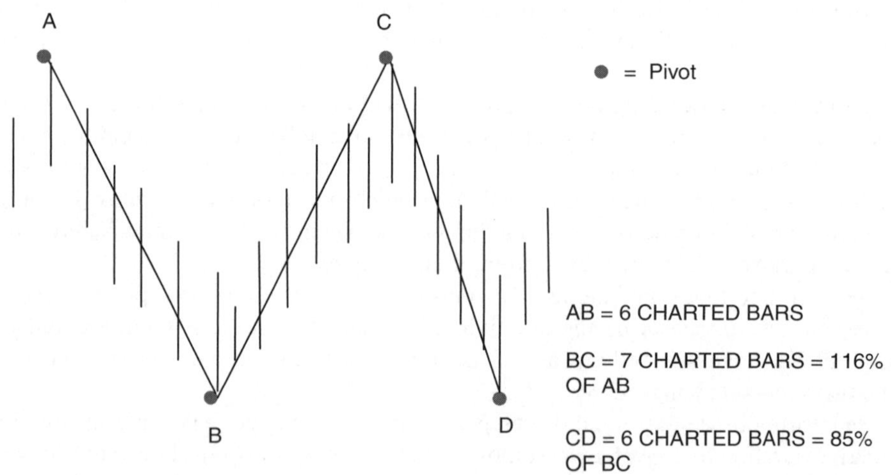

Figure 2.2 Measuring the length of a swing in charted bars.

Time limits price! Therefore, each bar is a time unit within a swing and a swing is a set of such time units. These units, as we find them in charts, are usually intraday, daily, weekly, monthly, or yearly.

By counting the bars, we measure the duration of the swing in actual trading days or trading time units. We must count every time swing – every fluctuation – by the number of its charted bars. Then we must tabulate all time swings and classify them by their duration in this manner.

As with price swings, we will find simple time swings and composite time swings. The simple time swing is either ascending or descending. The composite time swing also is either ascending or descending, but contains within itself a series of ascending and descending swings. It is important to measure the charted bars of the composite swing as a whole, as well as to measure the charted bars of the subcomposite and, finally, of the individual swings. This natural way of measuring time will give us all the time spans that we need in order to understand the durations of the different market fluctuations or waves.

Certain time spans will recur. Time cycles will reveal themselves. As always, the same cyclical law that underlies price will be present in time. We will find upward time swings followed by downward time swings.

In measuring time, we must not limit ourselves to one time window. We should also measure the same time period in different time windows, such as those in monthly, weekly and daily charts. The succession of different time windows enables us to discover certain ratios, such as that which exists between the length of uptrends and downtrends.

As you proceed, you will discover certain truisms. For instance, one of them is that uptrends last longer than downtrends. It is only by actively measuring that the truth of time will appear. By doing so, you will dispel many myths about time and markets.

Take a chart. Choose a time window – a daily, weekly, or monthly chart – and count the charted bars of the different swings created by their respective triads. Repeat this exercise constantly. You can be sure that you will learn a few things about markets.

Now, let us concentrate on another method to measure time.

Measuring in Calendar Days

Time should also be measured in calendar days. This includes trading days plus weekends and holidays. The measurement of swings in calendar days should be done from the origin pivot to the end pivot for each fluctuation (Figure 2.3). All swings, composite and simple, should be measured by this technique. For this, we take the date of the origin pivot and the date of the end pivot and calculate the number of days in between.

We should apply calendar measure to all time windows. This means that we should measure the number of weeks for weekly charts, the number of months for monthly charts, and the number of years for yearly charts. These measures of calendar time

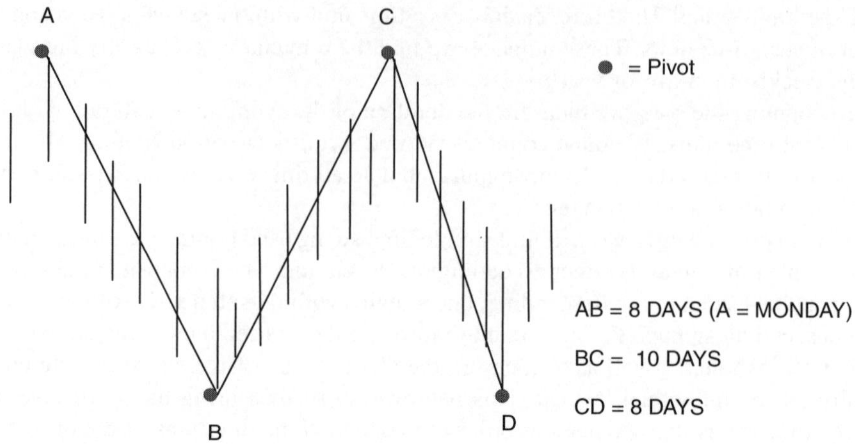

Figure 2.3 Measuring the length of a swing in calendar time.

will give us the main durations or time lengths of long-term swings, intermediate-term swings, and short-term swings.

We will notice calendar time patterns emerging. Some average times for long-term, intermediate-term, and short-term movements will appear. The key days of the year for some market events will also appear. For example, May is a month in which market instability begins and upward swings momentarily reverse. October is a month for major market reversals. Some holidays or key days are also known for specific market behaviors. All these dates will be included within the different calendar market swings. This is why we should also note the beginning date and ending date of each movement when measuring calendar time.

The beginning date for the pivot is the date on which the move originates. The end date for the pivot is the date on which the swing ends. By defining not only the number of calendar days of each swing but also their beginning and ending dates, certain dates will appear again and again. You will notice that reversals and significant turning points appear on approximately the same dates.

This will enable you to trade time. You will be able to describe market behavior within a time length quite accurately.

The movements measured in calendar days of differing lengths will sometimes form clusters. These clusters are indicative of a potential turning point or change in market behavior. The dates around which these clusters form become magnetic points in time. These magnetic points in time will continue to exercise their force on or around the same dates in the future. We are not forecasting here, because many forces act upon markets and they do change. We are only observing scenarios, the causes of which are definite points in time.

These time points may or may not appear again, but we are aware of the possibility. This differs from a forecaster's frame of mind. In our case, we simply take into account a real possibility and take action only after the market itself has confirmed the validity of such a time magnet by definite market action. Not only will time swings that differ in calendar days cluster around the same date but also certain calendar dates, even in the absence of a cluster, will be key dates for reversals or turning points.

By our calendar measurements of swings and identification of their beginning and ending dates, we should be able to locate those reversal dates accurately. You should tabulate all of your findings from your study of time in the markets. You should take the last five or ten years and tabulate the different calendar durations of swings, as well as their starting and ending dates. Also, you could tabulate the beginning and ending dates for each season, whether spring, summer, autumn, or winter. The reason to do this is that each season has its major financial events, such as tax filing time, which will be reflected in markets. To this you should add the presidential cycle. Is it an election year or first presidential term year, etc.? Your tabulation should include this for the beginning and ending dates of swings.

All your measurements of calendar time should be made for the different time frames across which new clusters will appear.

Now, let us consider measuring time in the markets from still another perspective.

Measuring Time in Percentage Value

As we did for price swings, we should also use percentages when measuring time swings. The measurement in percentages should be done as follows.

We should measure the percentage of time for every swing in relation to the year. The year is considered to be a complete time revolution of 100 %. Each swing has a calendar duration that can be expressed as a percentage of the entire year. For instance, a swing that has a 90-calendar day duration is a 25 % swing in relation to a year of 365 days. A 10-day swing is a 3 % swing in relation to the year. This percentage measure of the duration of swings should be applied to upward swings, as well as to downward swings, and then tabulated.

Reducing all time swings to a common denominator in percentage terms has an advantage. It gives us a sense of the duration of the main ranges of movements in relation to the year. We will know how much of the year is taken by each swing. This fractional perspective is invisible when you measure only in days, whether trading days or calendar days.

Knowing each movement's share of the entire year will make its relative significance more evident. For example, if an upswing lasts 270 calendar days and its following downswing lasts 90 calendar days, and another upswing lasts 30 days and its following downswing lasts 10 days, and a third upswing lasts 27 days and its following downswing lasts 8 days, we can measure these relative to the length of the year. The first swing measures 74 % and its following downswing measures 25 %.

The second downswing measures 8 % and its following downswing measures 3 %. The last swing measures 7 % and its following downswing measures 2 %.

Once again, by tabulating our information, we will find clusters of percentage times relative to the year. This will give us a sense of the average length of a swing relative to the length of the year for many long-term, intermediate-term, and short-term swings.

Now, we will apply statistics to our different ways of measuring time.

Statistical Measures of Price and Time

It is useful to apply statistics to our measured swings. The first step is to tabulate our information. We must tabulate our measures of swings in price points, in price percentages, in trading days, and in calendar time. Once we have done this, we obtain the measures of central tendency (i.e., averages) for our data. For each sample, we want to know the mean, the mode, the median, the maxima, and the minima.

These measures will give us valuable information about the market swings and overall market behavior. With these measures of central tendency, in addition to the sets of measured swings, we will be able to decipher the oscillatory key to the market that we are studying.[7] Each market has its own oscillatory key. This consists of a number that expresses its vibration rate. This vibration rate will make itself known in many ways. However, we will end up with a unique number in every case.

For swings, this unique number is the oscillatory key. This key will show itself as a retracement ratio that recurs and repeats again and again, or in a swing length that reappears frequently, or in a given number of waves within a trend.

Once our number has been identified, we will have a powerful trading tool. We can use this tool in many ways – to buy or sell retracements or breakouts or support and resistance, or to enter an existing trend. The average (i.e., arithmetic mean) will give us the average of all swings, upward and downward, in price and time. It will enable us to know the average length of swings in points and in percentage. We will know the size of the average upward swing and the average downward swing within a given time frame. Also, we will be able to know the average duration of upward and downward swings in trading days and calendar days. The average size of swings help you to enter and exit positions with lower risk, as well as to calculate the possible duration of those swings in order to enter and exit them at the right time.

The arithmetic mean is not always the best measure to use when evaluating a market movement. The median is another measure of central tendency. It is the size of the swing that is in the middle of the sample. In other words, if you arrange all sample values in ascending or descending order of size, the median will be the value that is located in the middle. It will be the fifth value in a sample of 9 values, the tenth value in a sample of 19 values, or the fiftieth value in a sample of 99 values. The median is a swing size that usually differs from the mean swing. The median will be calculated in points and in percentage and applied to price and time as an average.

The mode is the swing size in price or time that appears most frequently within the sample. It is useful for evaluating the frequency of swings of a given length.

The maxima is the greatest swing in the sample. The minima is the smallest swing in the sample.

These measures can be determined for all swings. They also can be determined separately for upward swings and downward swings. Occasionally, a set of values contains one or two extreme values that distort the arithmetic mean. In cases like this, the median or mode may provide a more accurate measure of the average of the sample. These measures will be helpful in many ways, some of which will be unexpected. For instance, the mode can help you to take a position with knowledge that a swing of a particular length will be repeated.

If you identify the frequency of swings of a given length within a time period, you can also measure the time length between their appearances, having an idea of other time lengths that could appear between – or following – a given swing. If a given swing is repeated a number of times during a given period (e.g., assume that a swing of 10 points occurs four times in three months), you can measure the time that has elapsed between each of these swings. You can also note swings of other sizes that occur between any pair of 10-point swings during that three-month period.

Many applications that can only be imagined as a result of direct observation and practice will appear when using such statistical measures as those described above.

Another measure that must be used is the standard deviation. It is imperative to know the standard deviation for your swings, upward and downward, in price or time. The reason why such a measure is so valuable is that it gives us the frequency of occurrence of swings of a given price or time length and also provides a unique way to calculate automatically the probability of appearance of each of your swings.

The normal distribution curve is a magic curve. It is also a probability curve and therefore we need to evaluate the probability that a given swing of a given length in time or price will make its appearance. The main idea to remember is that two standard deviations include 95 % of the probability of occurrence of any given event. This means that swings that are within two standard deviations of the arithmetic mean have the highest probability of occurring. In other words, most swings take place within two standard deviations of the mean. The other swings have only a 5 % probability of occurring.

The usefulness of this is evident if we think about it. There are many ways to use the standard deviation. It is possible, for instance, to enter corrections that are beyond two standard deviations.

It is not our purpose to go into trading tactics or strategy here. That subject will be covered in a later chapter. Here we simply want to emphasize the need to tabulate swings using all of these measures. Also, within the normal distribution curve, these statistical measures can be applied to subsets of our main swings. A subset is a set of upward swings or a set of downward swings. However, we can also create new subsets, such as one for all of the swings within a given volatility range or a given market phase. What we must remember above all – and practice – is to measure the market constantly. We must make a commitment to acquire the habit of measuring.

Now, let us explore how time and price interrelate.

The Time/Price Factor

Time and price go together, as is evident when measuring swing lengths. Each swing measured in terms of price change also implies a measurement of time change. The units that express this are time/price units, such as charted bars or Japanese candlesticks. Such a unit is an indivisible whole. Each price change happens within a time frame, whether it is a day, week, month, or another period.

The link between time and price is of such importance that it cannot be ignored. Because of this link, market change and market behavior are fully understood. To understand this link is to understand that time is more important than price.[8] Time is what rules market behavior and, once we understand why, market action becomes more transparent to us.

The first law relating to time and price is that every price change implies a time change. Price cannot change, except in time. Time rules price in the sense that price must change at its natural rhythm.

This requires an explanation. The evolution of price is not arbitrary. Behind price we have fundamentals that rule it. As Charles Dow said, 'Price always will in the end rejoin value.' However, this value is unknown. Even the best fundamental analysis can only hypothesize about it. What is real – as a perceived fact – is the evolution of prices in time. This evolution that we perceive is guided by fundamentals that we do not perceive, as well as many other factors that we ignore. Although it has its natural time, this evolution often involves excesses that deviate from, and must return to, their natural timeline.

We can compare the evolution of price in time to the growth of a plant. The plant has a given time for its full growth, which is contained as a program in the seed. However, external conditions may cause the actual growth to stray from the initial plan. A tree is able to grow more under certain conditions and less under others. For example, if a seed is planted in a shady location, the resulting tree may delay its growth until the gardener transplants it to a sunny spot. Then, nature will correct its course, according to the initial plan.

The same is true of prices. Their evolution in time is not regular. It oscillates. In its swings, the price searches for its own balance. This hidden balance is ruled by time – the natural time that the stock price needs to achieve its full growth. Sometimes the price of a stock will exceed its real value. Sometimes it will lag. It will always oscillate. In addition, the price will always seek to act within the time allotted to its real value.

This link between price and time implies that we must measure price and time not only separately, but also together. We must also measure the rate of change of each swing. By rate of change, we mean by how many points a swing changes per unit of time between its origin pivot and its ending pivot. Knowing what the price change per time unit is will enable us to know the speed and acceleration of price in time. It will also permit us to know whether price is exceeding, or lagging behind, its own natural rhythm.

When initially measuring the time/price ratio, we need to measure it in all swings. The measurements will enable us to know where a price will be if a swing continues to evolve at the same speed. For instance, if a swing increases by half a point per day and is an upside swing within a larger uptrending swing, and if such swings within that kind of uptrend have an average duration of 6 days, we can anticipate a 3-point increase from that swing's initial pivot to its ending pivot. Of course, we are assuming that the swings will continue to behave as expected.

We always have conditional scenarios. Our market judgment involves only the present. We judge the future as a set of mutually exclusive conditions that we are aware of, so that we can take appropriate action when any of the scenarios becomes market reality.

We can know the actual market rate of change for a given swing. Its future is within a specific set of possible scenarios. We must never act upon these scenarios, but only upon definite market action that confirms market behavior in a given way. For example, we initiate a trade on an upswing after a significant retracement. We expect that such a kind of swing could have a length of eight days at an increase of half a point per day, according to our previous measurements. We enter the trade when the swing has advanced one full point. Then we trade the possible scenario of an additional three points advance, based on our time/price ratio for that swing.

We are not forecasting the market here. Nobody can know and 'forecast' what the market will do. All we are doing is trading a given possible scenario because it is probable. However, probability is not fact.

We have seen the importance of the time/price ratio of swings. Now, we will examine a new concept – the meaningful or master swing.

THE MEANINGFUL SWING

Defining the Meaningful Swing or Master Swing

The concept of meaningful swing is elusive. The meaningful swing is a swing within a trend or a consolidation that may not coincide with any measure of central tendency. It is an individual swing that retraces an amount in order to make it meaningful. Some swings within a trend are greater than others. For instance, within a trend we will find retracement swings that are larger than the average swing. Some of these swings are too large and will not repeat again within the same trend.

Other retracement swings within the trend are large enough to enable you to take a position with low risk, but not so large that there will be no chance of them repeating within the same trend. These kinds of swings are what we call significant swings or master swings. For a given market movement, these swings will contain the oscillatory key for that movement. Each market will have a number of significant swings that will tend to repeat under the right circumstances.

Those swings enable us to analyze and trade a given market. It is possible for us to know how many of these swings will appear on average for any given movement. This gives us a measure that enables us to know whether a movement is at its beginning or its end. It also gives us a low risk point for trades. The reason for these swings to be significant is that they are unique to the market that we are studying. Each stock will have its significant swings. Each commodity also has its significant swings.

You must choose your significant swing after observing your charts. There is no hard and fast rule to define the swing. Here is why. Perhaps you choose as a significant swing a retracement of 10 points within a trend made up of a series of swings. You have observed that the 10-point swing repeats itself and occurs twice in similar swings. However, another analyst or trader could choose as a significant swing a 7-point retracement that repeats itself more often, say three or four times. Both choices are correct. Both numbers are reflections of the oscillatory key for that market. Each of the two swings has a number that is unique for its kind within that chosen market.

Identifying the Master Swing

To identify your master swing, you must know that:

1. The master swing stands out from the majority of swings in a simple visual inspection of a chart or a spreadsheet.
2. The master swing will not necessarily coincide with any central tendency measure of swings.
3. The master swing repeats itself.
4. The master swing is fully objective. It exists as defined by triads without any tweaking by the observer.
5. The master swing is subjective. You choose a meaningful swing from among the swings out there that everyone can see.
6. The master swing is an expression of the oscillatory key of a specific market.

These are the main conditions to identify the master swing in any market. The important thing in addition to the conditions above is that the master swing must be meaningful to you (see Chart 2 in Appendix II). This means that it must be consistent with your market analysis, study goals, and trading objectives.

Every market should be studied to find the master swings that it contains. Depending on the different phases and levels of the market, many meaningful swings can be found. If you are in a low-volatility period within a consolidation after a market low, you can find the meaningful swing for that level of market volatility. Similarly, a highly volatile market where swings are larger will have a meaningful or master swing.

A given range of swings within a market also has its meaningful swings. For instance, if you choose the small swings, instead of the medium or the large swings, within a movement, you will find some swings that are more meaningful than others among the small swings. The same applies to the medium or large swings. The choice of a meaningful swing depends on what you are going to do with it.

The meaningful swings bring us to the quest for meaning in the markets. Every aspect of a market, whether trend, retracement, pattern, or consolidation, has a meaning. So it is with swings. Each swing and category of swing has its own meaning for you to discover. This is why it is also important to study the meaning of the different swings. As an example, let us look at small swings within a consolidation. These small swings are telling us of very low volatility. If these small swings build themselves into a consolidation, they could be telling us that an explosive move could be waiting around the corner. This example only serves to say that the meaning of swings must not be disregarded, whatever their size.

We will come back to this, but let us first learn how to measure a master swing.

Measuring the Master Swing

Now we know what a master swing or meaningful swing is. Our next step is to measure such a swing.

Within a time period we have a series of swings that we have already measured in price and time. We have also established their price/time ratios. We have then tabulated this information on a spreadsheet. This information in chart form and spreadsheet form gives us a clear picture of swings and their behavior. It is here that our search for the meaningful swing begins. We observe in our chart and spreadsheet that some swings are outstanding and immediately attract our attention. It is from among these swings that we will choose our meaningful swing.

The choice will be made according to the conditions that we have already specified above. Once we have chosen our candidates for significant swings, we compare their sizes and measure the number of times that they repeat within the same movement. We select not only those meaningful swings that repeat within the same movement, but also those that occur only once within a movement. In many cases, those swings will coincide with the maxima. (Remember our discussion of central tendency measures?)

From our selection of swings that repeat within the same movement, we select the one that is in accordance with our goals and keep a record of its measurement in time and price, as well as its price/time ratio. With our selection of nonrepetitive swings within the same movements of master swings, we check for repetition of the same master swing, not within the same movement but within another movement of the same kind. If the candidate repeats itself in other movements, we select it also as a meaningful or master swing. Once again, we keep a record of its measurement in time and price, as well as its time/price ratio.

For both kind of master swings, the one that repeats within the same movement and the one that repeats only in a different market movement, we carefully note the number of repetitions and the date on which each of these swings occurred. Then we proceed to tabulate all of this data to have it ready for use.

We should add that, among the master swings that do not repeat within the same market movement, we have big movements, such as the secular bull and bear markets. (Secular bull or bear markets are those that last for a very long time – perhaps years or even centuries; see Chart 3 in Appendix II) Within these big movements, we might even find some that have existed only once and are waiting to make a comeback in the future.

This kind of master swing brings us to the subject of signatures.

The Master Swing as a Signature

A signature is a very powerful market tool. The origin of signatures is very, very old. It was used extensively by wise men of past ages. Signatures are significant events that announce impending change. In the middle ages, the term used to designate signatures was 'signatura rerum,' the signature of things.

Signatures were frequently used in medicine. Doctors, such as Paracelsus, used them and even based their theories upon them. A classical signature was the kind found in a plant that had the shape of a heart. It was believed that, due to its shape, the plant was beneficial for that organ. In many instances, this was true.

With regards to events, signatures were the different signs that announced changes, such as storms, earthquakes, eclipses, plagues, wars, appearances of comets, etc. The interesting thing about this 'signatura rerum' convention is that, if correctly understood, it works. In fact, it works very well. The logic behind it is failproof. If this seems strange, it will seem evident and logical after you understand the principle.

Let me elaborate. The principle behind the concept of 'signatura rerum' is one of significant change. A significant change is one that suddenly alters the balance of things. This is true regardless of what is being discussed.

You can use signatures to anticipate weather changes, economic changes, and political changes, or even to forecast the outcome of a football match. Of course, the concept applies to markets and, consciously or unconsciously, many market students have applied it. For example, the 11 September destruction of the Twin Towers was a 'signatura rerum.' It announced a radical change in the balance of the world and, indeed, our world changed forever. The same can be said of Pearl Harbor or the assassination of the Archduke Ferdinand I, the event that gave rise to World War I.

Any event that significantly alters the usual course of events is a 'signatura rerum' and we must heed its signal. This kind of event may seem inconsequential to many, but the event becomes a signature of things to come to those who can see the significant change in the balance of things.

For instance, when Paul Volcker, chairman of the Fed, was called in by President Carter to solve the inflation problem in the United States, the hard and unexpected measures that Volcker took were a 'signatura rerum.' It announced the beginning of the Reagan Era.[9] Also, when on 28 May 1987, a West German student, Mathias Rust, flew from the Helsinki-Malmi airport in Finland to penetrate the iron curtain and land his Cessna aircraft in Moscow's Red Square, he became a freedom folk hero. It was an insignificant and inconsequential event for many. However, it became a signature of the fall of communism for those who had the eyes to see.

Big changes in history, politics, economics, and the markets are heralded by events that radically change the balance of things, even though they may seem inconsequential at first. In the markets, we find such signatures in swings. Signatures are tools used by many market students, such as W. D. Gann. Although he does not use the term 'signature,' Gann told us that 'when a time period on a decline exceeds the time period of a previous decline, it indicates a change in trend' (W. D. Gann, *45 Years in Wall Street*, p. 11).[3] Therefore, when a swing appears that exceeds the normal oscillations in a trend and we have a signature that announces a change in the nature of the market, it could be a reversal or the beginning of a consolidation.

If most swings in a trend are within a given range, but suddenly one swing greatly exceeds the normal range of the other swings, it indicates a rupture of balance within the trend. If we imagine a trend as being a diagonal line rising upward, prices will not follow the line exactly, but will oscillate around it. Sometimes, they will be above this imaginary line and sometimes below. The fluctuations from above the line to below and vice versa will remain within a range. They are in a state of relative equilibrium or balance. Now, if a down movement within this trend greatly exceeds the average range of swings suddenly, the normal equilibrium or balance is lost, meaning that a change is coming soon.

In this sense, a master swing can repeat itself a few times. However, a change of phase will occur sooner rather than later. We must observe market events that break the normal rhythm of market fluctuations and disrupt its normal behavior. When, for instance, we have a market correction that is very significantly greater than preceding ones, we must be aware that a change in trend could be near.

When a bull market is about to end, we have such a signal. The unusual bull market correction mentioned above is a signature. A bear market may soon begin. This was the case of the bear market that began in October 2007. Before it occurred, we had corrections that were signature events announcing the end of the bull market (see Charts 3 and 4 in Appendix II). Therefore, always be attentive to market movements that are signature events. Also, identify such past signature swings and tabulate them. They will teach you about a market's specific personality.

Using the Master Swing to Act on Markets

Now, we will discuss the use of the master swing. The master swing helps us to understand where we are within a trend. Master swings do not occur just anywhere. The master swing usually occurs after the beginning of a phase, then around the middle, and finally around the end. By becoming familiar with these kinds of swings, you can obtain an idea of how much longer a given swing may still have to go.

The master swing also gives you a low-risk entry point for trades, usually short term, but also long term. For instance, after a strong reaction, you could buy the market on an uptrend or short it within a downtrend. Having measured the master swings, you know what to expect when one arrives and a trading opportunity presents itself.

The master swing is also helpful as a signature. When a unique swing occurs that disrupts the habitual balance of a movement, it becomes a signature that announces an impending market change. The normal balance of a movement is the usual range of fluctuations around its equilibrium or balance point. A signature increases that range significantly above average. With this knowledge in hand, you should double your attention in order to avoid being caught unaware of a change in market condition.

If you are a long-term investor and this kind of signature swing occurs within a secular bull market, it would be possible to begin improving your positions, reducing your commitment in the markets. As a trader, it would be possible to take this signature swing as a signal of a reversal that will enable you to take short positions on stocks as soon as the market gives definite proof of the reversal and perhaps the beginning of a bear market.

In all cases, you must always wait for definite action by the markets. You must never act on the basis of a forecast or attempt to forecast. Your action must be a consequence of market action and not taken in anticipation of market action. This relates directly to signature swings and master swings. You must never act based on them alone. You must always wait for a clear indication from the market that the moment is ripe for a change in market condition.

The moment is ripe when the market condition has already changed. For instance, if a master swing repeats itself, do not take a position within the swing itself in anticipation of a reversal. Instead, wait for a clear indication that the reversal has occurred and then take your position and go along with the market. Your intention should always be to have a clear description of the market's present behavior. If you achieve this, everything else will take care of itself.

Now, we will learn how to recognize the different market phases and their underlying origins and causes.

3
Market Phases: Learning to Recognize Them Is Your First Step Towards Success

THE ORIGIN AND NATURE OF MARKET PHASES

Mind Rules Market Behavior

Market behavior is always human behavior. In a free market, this behavior is conditioned by the multitude of free choices of all market operators. These choices can be varied and even opposing.

This is seen clearly in the fact that there is a seller for each buyer. The positions here are opposite. This often means that one party is right and the other is wrong, although not in all cases. For instance, a short-term trader can liquidate a position that a long-term investor is buying for a long-term profit that he hopes to achieve. Their time frames differ and their actions also differ, although their ultimate goals are similar – to make a profit in the market. Everything in the market balances in the end and market fluctuations are only the movements of minds seeking an elusive point of balance between price and value.

In these movements, the operators often reach a point of equilibrium where there is a balance between buyers and sellers, until suddenly the balance is broken and either the sellers or buyers take control of the market. These fluctuations are the result of the operators' combined mind movements that oscillate between fear and greed. However, these two poles of the mind – fear and greed – are not sufficient to explain the behavior of markets or the mind fluctuations of their operators.

Many traders and investors are not excessively greedy or fearful. They have a rational fear of losing by overstaying the market when their science of markets tells them that they shouldn't. Therefore, they sell. They are not greedy, although they desire a legitimate gain as the result of their knowledge and study. These operators are truly the real market insiders. They know the markets in depth and act accordingly. Their actions are seen in the market when they are quietly buying before the public becomes aware of what is happening. Their actions also take place when they quietly sell before the public suspects that a reversal is at hand.

The different ways of thinking about the market, as well as the different degrees of market knowledge, have their specific behaviors. These behaviors are behind the market's behavior. There is no phase in the market that cannot be explained by a specific mind frame of the market operators. If each market has its own personality, it is because the majority of the operators in that market have their specific frames of mind. Nothing happens in a market that has not happened first in the minds of the market operators.

Market Phases and Patterns Reveal the Mind of the Market

The study of the different market phases must take this into account. Each market phase must be read as a specific mind frame of the market. Each market phase is the outward expression of the mind of the market.

The same can be said of all market patterns. Every pattern has a definite meaning in the mind of the market. Each pattern is telling us what the majority of the operators who are active in the market are thinking about its present and future conditions.

In this sense, market phases and market patterns, as seen in charts or read in spreadsheets or quote machines, are only the images of an invisible dimension, the mind dimension that is reflected in the oscillating movements of market swings, as well as in the phases they become and the patterns they create. As an analogy, we can think of a hypercube that has four dimensions, whereas our visible three-dimensional world of objects is only the imprint of this invisible fourth dimension, which is the real cause of all things that appear in our world and their movements.

Our study of the market, its swings, its phases, and its patterns, is really the study of the swings of the mind, the phases of the mind, and the mind patterns of the market operators at their different levels. In this sense, market behavior is people behavior. People's behavior is caused by their free will in a free market. Their free will does not exist in a void. It is the free will to choose and the act of choosing implies limits or options.

All freedom is subject to conditions, and exists as freedom because of its conditions. Those conditions are simply the necessity to choose from among opposites. In market language, this gives us two choices – to buy or to sell. Those two key free choices will decide all market action. We could also count within this market action what results from a third choice – the choice to not act and, instead, to postpone for a time any buying or selling.

This gives us three kinds of market operators – the buyers, the sellers, and those who stay out of the market until their time comes. All three will pass through these three stages. At times they will be in a waiting stance, and then they will become buyers or sellers. Traders who wait for a moving average crossover might be on the sidelines, while fundamental investors could be buying and short sellers could be selling on a given market pattern.

This also tells us that every market perspective is important from the viewpoint of the market itself. This is because the market participants are all part of the market and their thoughts will play a role in the end result – market behavior. The technical analysts and traders, the fundamental investors, the tip followers, and the new followers within the general public all play their parts in this scenario called the market. This is why we must understand their minds and ways of thinking, as well as the weight of each in the overall market behavior.

The Fundamental Market Structure as an Image of Market Behavior

We will now study the mirror that reflects the mind of the market as a series of oscillations, phases, and patterns. We will study the fundamental market structure and the way by which it mirrors market behavior. In doing this, we will try at the same time to read the mind of the market. We will explain the thought that is behind each of the market phases, as defined by this fundamental market structure.

We must remember that this fundamental market structure is defined in each of its movements by the triads, which define pivots and market direction, since each triad is a small replica of the market itself. The fundamental market structure defines market behavior because it adapts geometrically to the actions of the market participants. As we have said, this action will be reflected in the lengths of swings and how they assemble themselves to create the various market figures and patterns. It is by reading these market shapes and patterns that the intention of the market participants or of certain groups of participants will become apparent.

These triads, the minimal expressions of the market, are the hinges that link the pivots that hold the swings. By linking together swings of varying lengths, the triads give rise to shapes and patterns. These are the same shapes and patterns that enable us to read the mind of the market.

The triads help to describe in a simple fashion the fundamental structure that enables us to read the mind of the market, as well as the mind of its specific participants. In this description by triads' pivots and swings of the fundamental market structure as the reflection of the minds of market participants, something unique happens. The image or imprint becomes autonomous and acquires meaning by itself.

At this point, we have the birth of market structure analysis. Although the minds of the market participants are behind each phase or pattern that develops within market structure and we can read the thinking behind the market in the geometry of the market, it is possible for us to work directly with the structure. This means that we can use market geometry to analyze and act in the market, without taking into account any further the thinking of the market participants who gave rise to such structure.

Market geometry, through the fundamental market structure, becomes a language in itself. It becomes a code that enables us to work directly with market structure by manipulating the geometrical ratios within that structure into an operative language that tells us directly about market behavior. For example, when we buy a swing retracement or sell short the breakout of a support, we do not need to refer to the minds of the market participants who gave rise to that specific swing or that breakout that enabled us to take market action.

The mind of the market is already contained in the geometrical language of the market that speaks through the fundamental market structure. This was pointed out by Charles Dow when he said that market prices contained the result of all the actions and intentions of the different market participants. This geometry of the market, its fundamental market structure, ultimately expresses itself through its swings or oscillations.

Oscillations are the Market's Ultimate Foundation

In the end, oscillations are the market's ultimate foundation. The different ways in which oscillations assemble themselves and then behave give rise to all market-specific geometrical structures and their laws. These oscillatory laws are perceived by us through geometrical structures that relate to each other in specific ways. We can momentarily forget that the market oscillations are the mind oscillations of its participants. All we need is the oscillatory language itself. Simply by knowing this oscillatory language, it is possible for us to understand and participate in market actions. This oscillatory language is the market's secret language that is waiting to be discovered and used by us.

We must now learn oscillatory language in order to read the markets. This is an easy thing to say, but a difficult thing to do. As in learning any language, it may seem simple at first since the concepts are easily understood. However, as any language student knows, it is only by constant practice that a language is really learned. A dictionary is of no use if its words are not learned. We must acquire and practice with a vocabulary that is large enough for our use.

With market language, it is the same. We must constantly practice and apply the oscillatory language of the market until it becomes second nature to us. How to acquire this vocabulary has already been explained. It is by measuring swings, the market ultimate's foundation, that we will learn to communicate with the market. Within this is also the learning of different market phases and market patterns, all of which are made up of oscillations.

This oscillatory language is what will reveal the nature and personality of each market to us. Each market that we study or act upon will have a definite and unique personality that communicates with us through its oscillatory language. Each market will show its oscillatory rhythm and harmony to us as it teaches us all of its subtleties and hidden relationships.

Take a few charts, one for a stock, another for an agricultural future, such as soybeans, and another for a metal, such as gold or platinum. Now compare them. You will see that they are different. Their personalities will immediately become visible to you.

This specific personality for each market, which for the moment you are only feeling, comes from the pattern of its oscillations. Soybeans do not oscillate like gold. Gold does not oscillate like pork bellies. Each market has its own oscillatory language.

You must go beyond this feeling that you have gained by comparing charts. You must convert your first impression into real knowledge by study and by practice – by learning the fundamental market structure and using it to study and to act. This knowledge can only be obtained first hand by direct acquaintance with each specific market. This comes only by study and practice. These are the real keys to market success.

Oscillations: The Birth of Time and Space in the Market

In our previous exercise in which we compared charts for different markets, we had a distinct feeling that each chart differed in the overall behavior of the market that it represented. It was as if each market had its own distinctive personality. Under closer scrutiny, we conclude that this difference among charts is produced by how these markets oscillate. We discover that each market's specific way of oscillating gives it its own distinctive personality. Or, rather, it could be the inverse. It may be that, because the personality of each market is unique, it oscillates in its own particular way. The fact is that oscillations are how a market expresses its own being. It is through the language of oscillations that we discover each individual market's particular ways of acting.

This brings us back to one of our main concepts, the pivot. We will remember that market structure's first element, as defined by triads, is the pivot. Although we need a triad for each consecutive pivot in order to define it, the first pivot of the first swing is born from a void, an empty space. This primordial pivot was the first price ever for any market. Once this first price point appeared in space, it began to oscillate, giving birth to market action that evolved in everything else – swings, triads, other pivots, phases, patterns, etc.

Let us think of this first pivot as a point that suddenly exists in a previously empty space. This point then begins to move slowly. It describes in its movement a curve that is more of a spiral than anything else. By its movement, a market space is generated. A point has no dimensions. Only when it begins to move do the dimensions of the space appear. It is the same here. The birth of the market space begins when the first pivot begins its first movement.

However, this first movement of the first price pivot takes time. It does not happen in an instant, as does the first pivot. The evolution of the pivot creating market space and its different forms, such as swings, phases, and patterns, takes time. Each market needs its own time to grow and evolve. This time is not only clock time. It is real time that depends on the peculiar nature of the market involved. Some markets evolve more quickly into phases or patterns than others. Other markets grow slowly. Some markets are volatile, whereas others are not. All depends on how they evolve in their own space according to their natural time. In turn, this depends on their natures and personalities.

Now, we are back to oscillations. It is by oscillating that a first pivot creates space and time, market space and market time. The way in which a pivot oscillates will differ according to each market. Different markets never oscillate in the same way. Each market has its own way of oscillating, according to its inner and hidden personality.

Here we come to the core of oscillations. The way in which each market oscillates is its personality. This way of oscillating comes from a deeper level – the seeds of oscillations – that is contained in its pivots. This deeper level is the fundamental nature of the market. It is not the visible, fundamental nature, like that shown in financial statements, but the invisible nature, the hidden essence that gives rise to what a company really is or what a commodity market really is.

Everything else that we can see is only the expression of this invisible core. This takes us back to Charles Dow who said that price evolution reflected everything about a market, the known and the unknown. However, this unknown is much more relevant than the known. It is the unknown that is the cause of the known. In other words, the true being of a market, whether it is a stock, a commodity, or anything else, will always be unknown. It will never be otherwise, nor can it be.[10]

Here we are at last at the core behind pivots and oscillations. Behind them we have the invisible being that we can call the soul of a market, its inner invisible law that brings together all else – all market elements. All that we can see and know about a market, fundamentals or technical aspects, depends on an oscillatory rate or vibration rate that enables this invisible law that rules each specific market to make it appear as it is and behave as it does.

In conclusion, oscillations create the space and time in which a market, and all that belong to it, becomes visible to us. Its oscillations in price and time evolve into phases and patterns in accordance with the fundamental market structure.

Now, we will examine the main phases into which market oscillations evolve within the frame of our fundamental market structure.

THE WHEEL OF TIME

The Three Market Phases

We have seen that, according to fundamental market structure, a pivot evolves in a swing or market oscillation. This initial swing or market oscillation ends in a second pivot that was created by a triad. From that point onwards, new pivots, swings, and triads are brought into existence indefinitely. Then, it is their turn to evolve into phases that form in space and time. These phases can have distinctive patterns.

Market geometry is born. What are the phases into which the pivots, swings, and triads evolve and create a new layer or level within the fundamental market structure by this act? These phases are essentially three in number:

- The trending phase
- The consolidation phase
- The turning point phase.

Every event within market behavior will belong to one and only one of these three phases (see Chart 5 in Appendix II). Each of these three phases can have within it many patterns. In fact all patterns can be deduced from these three initial phases.

This is why, when studying a market, the key question is: 'In what phase is the market that is being analyzed?' Once the market's phase has been identified, the next question is: 'Where are we now within the existing market phase?' Finally, we can ask: 'How long does this market phase still have to go until it ends?'

The answer to these three questions will enable us to know our position exactly in a given market in time and space. We will then know what the market is doing and how long it may continue to do it. We will know the phase, its price range, its present time length, its probable price, and its future time length. From here, we can go an extra step and define what the next step or phase in the market's evolution will be. Also, it will be possible to make an educated guess about the possible scenarios into which the next phase may evolve.

When analyzing the scenarios into which the following phase may evolve, we are in the domain not of probability, but of possibility, since these scenarios have their own inner logic, which is independent of what will or will not happen in the future. We will study this later as it belongs to the inner logic of market phases.

For now, let us simply discuss each of the three market phases. We will begin with the trending phase.

The Trending Phase

Each phase of the market is created by a unique way of assembling pivots, swings, and triads. In this sense, the fundamental market structure defines each market phase exactly. This is the case with the trending phase. In this phase, the market is either ascending or descending. It is never moving horizontally.

This market phase has its origin in the first swing born from a first pivot. This first swing can be ascending or descending. If it is ascending, that is, if its price changes increase – or if it is descending, that is, its price is decreasing – it is in a trending phase. This is a trending phase within a unique swing. However, this unique swing evolves into other swings. This swing ends with a triad that develops into another swing. This triad contains an ascending or a descending trend.

The first charted bar of the triad that ends an ascending swing is ascending. The third charted bar that completes the triad and initiates a possible new opposite swing is

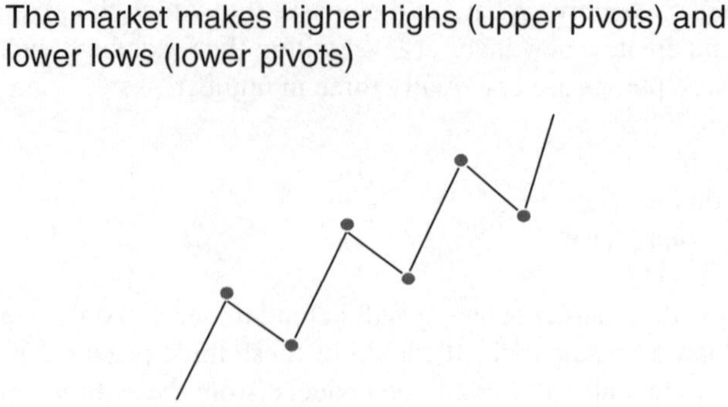

Figure 3.1 Trending market: uptrend.

descending. Therefore, each triad contains a miniature one-bar chart ascending phase and a miniature one-bar chart descending phase. It is from here that all trending phases originate and evolve.

Now, let us see how the trending phase builds from this initial pivot and triad into the market trends that consist of a series of swings that are the trends that interest us from the viewpoint of analyst, investor, or trader. Trends that consist of a series of swings are sets of swings that can be ascending or descending. They are defined as follows.

The market is in its ascending trending phase when:

- The swings within an ascending trend are ascending. The series of their pivot lows and pivot highs are ascending.
- The counter trending swings within the trending phase have their pivot ends above the pivot lows of their origin trending swings. Otherwise there is a consolidation.
- In summary, the market makes higher highs because of the ascending end pivots and higher lows because of the ascending origin pivots (Figure 3.1).

The market is in its descending trending phase when:

- The swings within a descending trend are descending. The series of their pivot highs and of their pivot lows are descending.
- The counter trending swings within the trending phase have their pivot ends below the pivot highs of their origin trending swings. Otherwise there is a consolidation.
- In summary, the market makes lower lows because of the descending end pivots and lower highs because of the descending origin pivots (Figure 3.2).

To continue, a market is in a trending phase when it is making either higher highs and higher lows or lower highs and lower lows. In the first case, we have an ascending market. In the second case, we have a descending market.

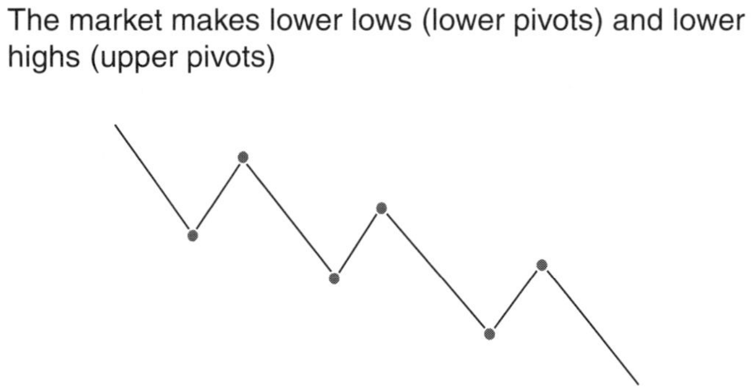

Figure 3.2 Trending market: downtrend.

Each swing within the trading phase is linked to its contrary swing by a pivot that, in turn, is defined by a triad. Thus, in a trending phase, we have a trending series of triads. The fundamental market structure ternary elements assemble themselves into trending phases.

Now, we will examine the consolidation phase.

The Consolidation Phase

Each phase of the market is constructed by a unique way of assembling pivots, swings, and triads. In this sense, the fundamental market structure defines exactly each market phase. As it was for trending phases, this is the case for the consolidation phase.

In this phase, the market is not ascending or descending. It is moving horizontally. This market phase has its origin after the first swing born from a first pivot. This first swing can be ascending, descending, or horizontal. If it ascends, that is, if its price changes increase, it is in a trending phase. Also, if it descends, that is, if its price is decreasing, it is in a trending phase. However, if the pivot moves horizontally, that is, if the price moves in time while not increasing or decreasing, we have a primary consolidation.

A primary consolidation is a nontrending phase within a unique swing. This unique swing evolves into other swings. Thus, consolidations are rarely formed from a unique pivot moving statically in time and generating a horizontal line. In markets, consolidations are usually the result of a series of ascending and descending swings that, as a whole, do not trend. This means that they neither rise nor fall.

The first charted bar of the triad that ends an ascending swing is ascending and the third charted bar that completes the triad and initiates the possible new opposite swing is descending. At the high or low of the central charted bar of an ascending or a descending triad, we find a pivot. This pivot is the dividing point between its ascending movement and its descending movement, or vice versa in the case of a descending triad. It is a static point. In this static point that divides a triad, the previous movement, upward or downward, stops. This cessation of movement for an instant before a change in direction is a consolidation.

Thus each triad contains a miniature image of market consolidations, as the pivot where a movement ends before another movement takes place. It is from here that all consolidations originate and evolve. Consolidations are waiting moments before a market starts to move again.

Now, let us see how the consolidating phase builds from this initial pivot and triad into the market ranges made up of a series of horizontally alternating swings. Consolidations that consist of a series of swings are sets of swings that will be alternatively ascending or descending. They are defined as follows.

The market is in a consolidating phase when:

- The swings within a consolidation are successively ascending and descending. An upward swing is followed by a downward swing. A downward swing is followed by an upward swing. The series of their pivot lows and their pivot highs are horizontal.
- The series of the pivot lows and the pivot highs of the successive alternating and contrary swings are within the same horizontal range. The pivot highs of the alternating swings are at the same horizontal level. Their pivot lows are at the same horizontal level.
- The contrary or alternating swings can have exactly the same length and, if not, they are always contained within the same horizontal range that is created by the swing of greatest length.

In summary, the market creates similar swing highs and similar swing lows within the same horizontal range (Figure 3.3).

Each swing within the consolidating phase is linked to its contrary swing by a pivot that, in turn, is defined by a triad. In a consolidating phase, we have a nontrending series of triads that are contained within a horizontal range. The fundamental market structure ternary elements also assemble themselves into nontrending, but consolidating, phases.

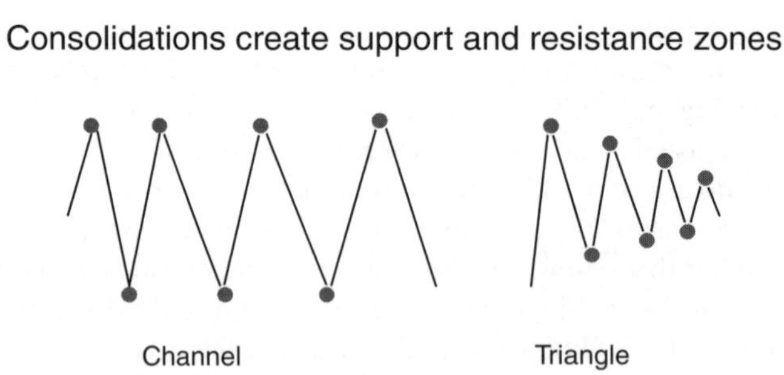

Figure 3.3 Consolidation: horizontal range.

A single pivot can move in only three possible directions – up, down, or horizontally. The consolidating phase has its origin in the horizontal movement possibility.

Now, we will examine the turning point phase.

The Turning Point Phase

Each phase of the market is constructed in a unique way of assembling pivots, swings, and triads. In this sense, the fundamental market structure defines each market phase exactly. This was the case for the trending phases and is also the case for the turning point phase. In this phase, the market is not ascending, descending, or moving horizontally. In a sense it contains the three movements within itself. In this way, this turning point market phase differs from the two others.

Relative to the first or original pivot, the turning point is the transitional step from the dimensionless pivot to the first direction that it will take, whether upward, downward, or horizontally. In the case of the first pivot, this transitional step is contained within itself. This is because a pivot has the property of not moving upward, downward, or horizontally. In fact, every pivot of every triad is also a turning point. It contains a transitional moment within itself.

By extension, every triad is a turning point. This is because a triad is the hinge between two swings of contrary direction. From this property of all pivots and, by extension, all triads do all turning points come:

- The turning point phase within a series of market swings can be defined as follows. A turning point always contains the end of a trend and the beginning of the contrary trend. A turning point is a moment of equilibrium that also contains an extreme consolidation, the last one before a market reversal.
- In a turning point, the market reverses from low to high or from high to low.

In summary, a turning point is the last stage before a market reversal. In it we find the end of the previous movement, its final consolidation and the beginning of the next movement.

The triad exemplifies this. In a triad we find the end of a movement in its first charted bar, the consolidating instant and turning point of its pivot, and the inception of the new contrary movement in its last charted bar. This is why the triad pivot is the turning point of the triad itself, since that pivot contains all three phases at the same time. It is also the reason why the triad as a whole is a turning point relative to the contrary swings that it links together.

Now, we will discuss the two kinds of turning points – the reversal from low to high and the reversal from high to low.

The Reversal from Low to High

These are the conditions that define a reversal from low to high of trends that consist of a series of swings:

- The market is at the end of a descending trend and is not making any further lower low pivots and lower high pivots (see Chart 6 in Appendix II).
- The market begins to break on the upside of the high pivots of the preceding trend. These pivots are resistance points that are broken on the upside (see Chart 7 in Appendix II).
- The market makes at least one higher bottom than the lowest bottom of the preceding downtrend.
- The market stops making lower lows and lower highs and begins to make lows around the same level and highs around the same level. It consolidates and stabilizes for the last time (Figures 3.4 and 3.5).

These are the conditions that define a reversal from high to low for trends that consist of a series of swings:

- The market is at the end of an ascending trend and is not making any further higher low pivots and higher high pivots (see Chart 8 in Appendix II).
- The market begins to break on the downside the low pivots of the preceding ascending trend. These pivots are support points that are broken on the downside (see Chart 9 in Appendix II).

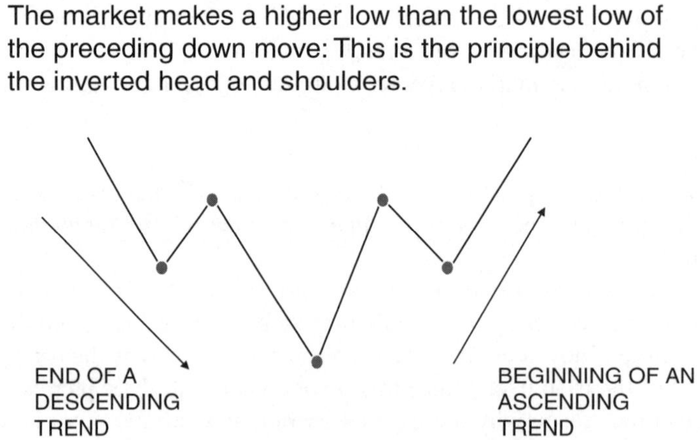

Figure 3.4 Upward turning point.

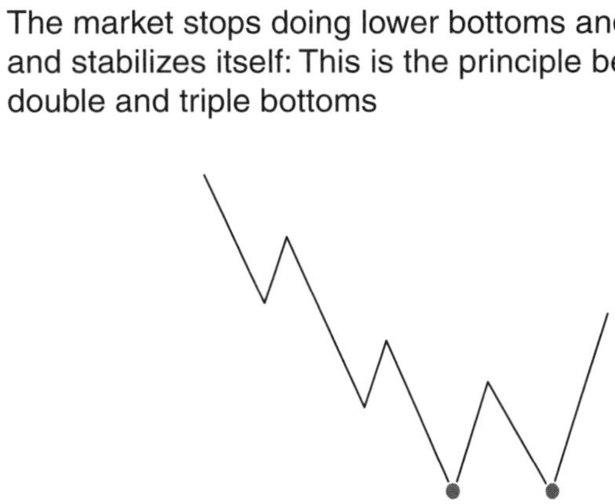

Figure 3.5 Upward turning point.

- The market makes at least one lower high than the highest high of the preceding uptrend.
- The market stops making higher highs and higher lows and begins to make highs around the same level and lows around the same level. It consolidates and stabilizes for the last time (Figures 3.6 and 3.7).

These are the conditions that define a turning point. However, its validation needs an additional condition. Here is the explanation.

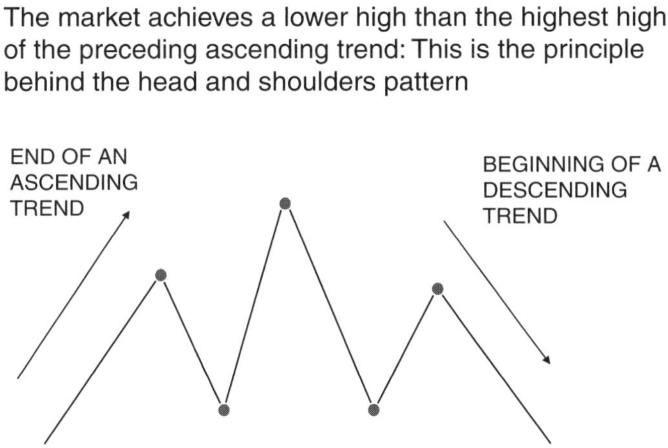

Figure 3.6 Downward turning point.

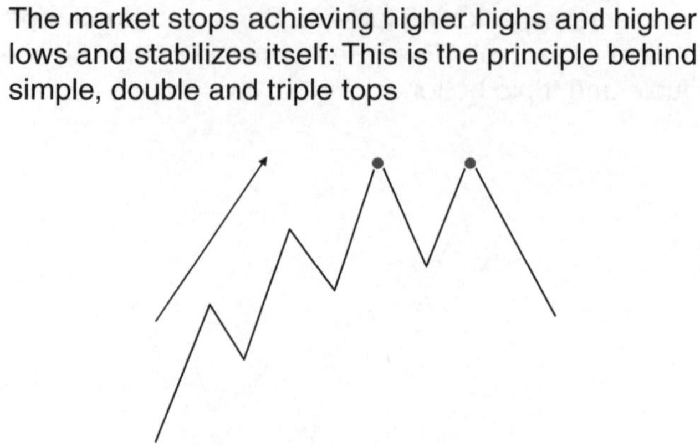

Figure 3.7 Downward turning point.

Validation of a Turning Point

Every turning point can also be a continuation pattern. There is a reason for this. The reason is that reversal patterns and continuation patterns are both included within a consolidation phase. This is why, for example, a triple top within an ascending trend could very well happen to be a continuation pattern, instead of a reversal pattern.

For a turning point, a reversal, to be effective, an additional condition is required. There must be a significant change in the balance of power between market participants. This change must follow the equilibrium period at the turning point apex. If this occurs, it is imperative that we recognize this change in the balance of power between market participants and operators. We need to be able to identify the market signals that announce such a change within the market's fundamental structure.

Here, once again, the fundamental market structure and its ternary composition of pivots, swings, and triads come to our aid. Through this structure, the market itself will tell us of such changes in the balance of power.

This will be the subject of the next chapter. For now, let us remain with the market phases since we still have not finished with them.

The Inner Logic of Phases: The Perpetual Sequence of Phases and the Mind Behind Them

We have defined the three market phases – the trending phase, the consolidation phase, and the turning point phase. We have explained their origins from a primal pivot and also their working within a complex market that consists of a series of swings of varying configurations.

These three market phases have an inner logic. This logic is in their sequential nature. They form a natural market sequence that goes on and on indefinitely. The trending phase develops into a consolidation phase and this consolidation phase develops either into the continuation of the previous trending phase or into a turning point that anticipates a reversal.

This sequence of trending phase, consolidation phase, and turning point phase constitutes the sequential logic of the market. The three phases form a cycle that can occur in the following sequences:

Trend, Consolidation, Turning point

or

Consolidation, Trend, Turning point.

These sequences repeat indefinitely. The repetition enables us to know which phase of a market cycle will be next. For example, if we have a trending phase, we can be sure that the next phase will be a consolidation phase. Also, we know that such a consolidation could give rise to a continuation of the trend or to a turning point phase where a reversal will take place. If, instead of a trending phase, we have a consolidation phase, we will know that the next phase will be either a trending phase or a turning point phase at which the consolidation becomes the beginning of a reversal.

This sequence must be mastered before you can read the market. Being able to recognize each phase is what will enable you to know what the market is doing at the present moment. This ability to recognize phases will enable you to choose the strategy that is best suited to the phase that the market is in. These phases have a sequence that has an inner logic, but this inner logic responds to a mind behind the market participants who are present in each of these phases.

In the trending phase, we have buyers who are more powerful than the sellers. Market participants want to buy. They want to buy because they expect that prices will rise and they will be able to sell at a profit. Profit is the motivation for their buying and the reason is their expectation that prices will continue to rise.

In the consolidation phase, there is doubt and uncertainty. Buyers are confronted by a lot more selling. This selling is sufficient to stop the trend, but still not enough to reverse it. The sellers believe that they have a profit to take. The belief of the buyers is that the market will continue its previous trend or that they can trade the consolidation range. This is why they stay in their positions. A consolidation is a market that is uncertain of its next action, but where the majority of participants have positive expectations that the trend will continue.

The turning point phase is a phase in which market participants experience doubt and fear. They doubt that the market will continue to rise and they fear losing their profits. They therefore become sellers. Buyers become a powerless minority. After a period of doubt and uncertainty, the market finally reverses and the bears take the lead.

This sequence of phases – trending, consolidating, and turning point – takes place in time. A market needs time for its different phases to evolve. Let us look at this.

The Spiral of Time

The market phases repeat themselves indefinitely. They never stop. Consolidations follow trends. In turn, consolidations are followed by reversals that, once again, begin new trends followed by consolidations and reversals. This gives us the impression of a never-ending circular movement. However, this is not to be. To be circular in nature, the phases must repeat themselves in exactly the same way every time.

This is certainly not the case. A market is a living organism and time is the evolution or movement of its own inner nature. Time results from the nonsimultaneous deployment of the market's own nature. This implies that first one thing appears and then the next one, etc. A market adapts itself continually to new events and circumstances. It is part of a living history that seeks its own meaning.

In this sense, time is not a blind quantity. Time is the time of the market and, in the way that a man is born and then grows and passes through many stages in his growth until he declines and dies, the same happens to markets. They have their own invisible law that rules their destiny.

Thus, market phases are never circular, since they never repeat. Instead, they are spiral, with each sequence differing from the preceding one and having different patterns, different durations, or different lengths. Their similarity is only an appearance behind which is concealed the difference that gives their true identity. Identifying the differences between two similar phases is what uncovers that which is unique about the most recent phase.

This spiral of time involves two laws:

1. The past will always repeat in the future and the future is nothing more than an image of the past. This is the law of circularity. This is the law that makes two events similar that are distant in time.
2. The past will never repeat itself in exactly the same way in the future. This is the law of the spiral. It is almost a circle, but not completely. It is a spiral that evolves into the future.

These two laws make up the spiral of time. They enable us to be always on the lookout for a repetition of the past. The past will always return due to the circularity of time. However, at the same time, we must be aware of the differences between similar circular events that we observe and their past equivalents. The spiral of time is there at work and what at first seems to be a circle is, in fact, a spiral. This ability to see the difference in similar cycles is necessary to succeed in the markets. It enables us to use past events as references without rigidity. Here is where the fundamental market structure comes again to our help.

Understanding how the market evolves into its different cyclical phases, the fundamental market structure enables us to see their formations, similarities, and differences, and to judge every event not only by its past behavior but also by what the market tells us today.The way that trends, consolidations, and turning points behave within the spiral of time is a direct consequence of the fact that time moves in a spiral way, not in a circular way. This is why these phases always evolve into different patterns and never repeat themselves in exactly the same way.

Let us look at these patterns that evolve within the spiral of time.

THE INNER STRUCTURE OF ALL PATTERNS

The Fundamental Market Structure is Behind All Phases and All Patterns

The perpetual sequence of phases will repeat indefinitely with variations that are contained within a possible number of patterns. Patterns are the different ways in which phases develop. Within these evolving market phases that are trends, consolidations, and turning points, we have ways in which swings assemble themselves in a self-evolving construction, thanks to their pivots and triads.

These phases never repeat themselves in the same way. They change within a number of possibilities, which we call patterns. These possibilities have inner logic.

Patterns are types of phases. A simple pivot vibrates for the first time. Its vibration evolves into a series of swings that, because of its vibration rate, evolve into many phases that, in turn, conform to different patterns. In the end, it is the market's vibration rate that constructs all of the market's phases and forms. This way in which the market creates itself has the fundamental market structure behind it.

In analyzing patterns, you can see that the behavior of the phases develops another layer of structure – the patterns. Behind them always are the builder, the oscillating pivot, and the rules established by the fundamental market structure. The market is a whole with many superimposing levels, each with its specific function and meaning.

It is for us to discover and understand not only how the market is built from its first principles but also how it transforms itself into its many levels. It is also important for us to understand and define each level by itself and in relation to the entire market structure.

Geology offers us an analogy. In that discipline, we must understand not only each layer of the earth's crust but also how each layer relates to the one below it in order to ultimately make sense of the whole as nature created it.

So it is for us with markets. We will try to understand each of its layers, as well as how each relates to the layers below. This will enable us to make sense of the fundamental market structure as a whole, as well as to understand its first principles. What we must now try to understand are the patterns that evolved from the phases and are contained within them.

Now, we will examine how the three market phases give rise to all of the patterns that we know about.

All Patterns Can Be Deduced from the Three Market Phases

The three market phases are:

- The trending phase. The market makes higher highs and higher lows in the ascending trend and lower highs and lower lows in the descending trend.
- The consolidation phase. The market makes swing highs around the same level and swing lows around the same level, staying within a horizontal range.
- The turning point phase. This contains the end of a trend, its consolidating point, and the beginning of the next phase.

These three phases give rise to the following market patterns.

Patterns Generated by Trends

If, when it makes swings, its highs when linked and lows when linked make two parallel lines, the trending phase gives rise to an ascending or descending rectangle or an ascending and descending channel. When the two previous lines within a trend converge, instead of remaining parallel, we have a pennant.

The different ways in which swings transform themselves into trends generate the different patterns within trends. As long as these conditions are fulfilled, any pattern that forms within a trend is a trending pattern.

Patterns Generated by Consolidations

The consolidation phase also evolves into many such patterns. As examples, we have horizontal channels and triangles.

A horizontal channel is a consolidation range in which all swing highs are at the same level and all swing lows are at the same level. This is the typical horizontal channel.

When the swing highs and the swing lows tend to converge as the consecutive swing lengths diminish, a triangle is formed. Many trends change into temporary triangular consolidations that usually are resting periods before the trend resumes its course.

As long as the conditions that define a consolidation hold, any pattern formed within these conditions is a consolidation pattern.

Patterns Generated by Turning Points

These patterns satisfy the conditions of all turning points, namely having the end of a movement and the beginning of the next. Among such patterns we find multiple bottoms, including simple, double, and triple bottoms, and all multiple tops. We also find the head and shoulders type of pattern as a type of turning point.

In simple tops, an ascending trend stops reaching consecutive higher highs and higher lows and reverses itself immediately into a downtrend.

In simple bottoms, a descending trend stops achieving consecutive lower highs and lower lows and reverses itself immediately into an uptrend.

In head and shoulder patterns we have the same structure of the simple top, including within the formation the previous lower high of the ascending trend and the next lower high of the new descending trend.

In the inverted head and shoulders patterns, we have the same structure of the simple bottom, including, within the formation, the previous higher bottom of the descending trend and the next higher bottom of the new ascending trend.

In multiple bottoms, the market stops achieving lower lows and lower highs and stabilizes, creating a support zone. This is a consolidating period before reversing in the opposite direction and initiating a new uptrend.

In multiple tops, the market stops achieving higher lows and higher highs and stabilizes, creating a resistance zone. This is a period of consolidation before reversing and initiating a new downtrend.

We have seen examples of patterns that show how they all develop from one or more of the main three market phases. Therefore, what we call patterns are actually types of market phases.

How Every Pattern is a Phase

Every pattern is a phase of some kind. The reason for the patterns as natural formations of the phases within the fundamental market structure is found at a descriptive geometrical level in the market structure itself and its pivots, swings, and triads. All patterns are oscillating contractions, oscillating expansions, neutral oscillations, or combinations of the foregoing. For example, a triangle is an oscillating contraction, an inverted triangle an oscillating expansion, a channel a neutral oscillation, and a head and shoulders a combination of an expansion and a contraction.

On another level, those three phases' multiple types, which we call patterns, that can expand, contract, or do both are evidence of another dimension, a third dimension beyond the space and time of market prices and volumes. This is the dimension of fundamentals and all other invisible factors that form a specific market and its behavior. Within this dimension is the mind of market participants and their expectations.[11]

In the same way as we saw that each of the three market phases responded to a certain frame of mind of the market participants, specific patterns give added precision within each phase to the general frame of mind of its participants. It is at this mind level that we see again the consistency of the relationship between phases and patterns as an outgrowth of each specific phase. All that a pattern contained within a phase does on this mind level is reinforce the idea and meaning behind the phase.

Let us explore this concept. We will take a look at a triangle, a type of consolidation phase. In the consolidation phase, the market participants are uncertain. The market itself is taking a rest and deciding on its next movement. We have also said that, in a consolidation, there is still a positive expectation that the market will resume its trend. If this is not the case, we would have a turning point and not just a consolidation.

In the case of our triangle as a type of consolidation phase, we have the frame of mind of the consolidation itself. This is uncertainty with a positive expectation, plus the reinforcement of this positive expectation in the triangular form of this phase. The triangle is a consolidation of diminishing swings where volatility declines drastically because there is an expectation that the market may explode upward at any moment. This, of course, is only an expectation. In their expectations, market operators become very attentive and careful, and buying and selling diminishes until the market gives a clue to its new behavior.

In summary, every pattern is a phase and every pattern reinforces the behavior of its phase positively or negatively.

How Every Pattern Contains a Time/Price Factor

Patterns as types of phases also contain a time/price factor, as does every market movement. This time/price factor must be accounted for. All market patterns have a range of prices and a length of time. All market patterns tend to repeat in the future. In this sense, all market patterns are cyclical.

This is why we must measure the market patterns in terms of their price ranges and time lengths. This will give us clues to how long we should expect a pattern will take to complete itself before a significant market change occurs.

Market patterns are important and you should know their types. You should tabulate the main market patterns and their time/price ratios. Also, within this study, you should include the number of times that a pattern is resolved by a continuation or a reversal.[12] Many patterns that are thought to be reversal patterns are, in fact, continuation patterns. Many patterns that seem to belong to turning point phases do not become such until there is a proven market reversal. This is why turning points must contain both movements – the ending movement and the new movement that is beginning.

An example of what we could call a turning point trap is a triple top, or a head and shoulders top. Often when these appear, the market does not turn around, but resumes its trend.

It is useful to tabulate all these movements for the market that one trades or invests in. If we learn them, our market vocabulary will expand and we will become more attuned to market reality.

How many would-be bottoms or tops have failed to become turning points and what were their time/price ratios, their price ranges, and time lengths? These failed bottoms or tops are a type of consolidation phase before a resumption of the previous move. A failed triple bottom is a consolidation before a downward breakout that continues the previous downtrend. A failed triple top is a consolidation before an upward breakout.

This is why we need definite confirmation of market action before assessing the nature of a move. A bottom is not a bottom until an upward reversal has occurred. A top is not a top until a downward reversal has occurred. This is why, after a careful study of a market's phases and patterns, we should always wait for definite market action before becoming involved in a market.

Having studied phases and their patterns (i.e., types), we must examine the conditions that cause them to change to others within the indefinite cycles of market movement.

Now, let us consider market strength.

4
Market Strength: The Conditions for a Change of Phase

THE FUNDAMENTAL MARKET STRUCTURE: THE KEY TO MARKET STRENGTH

Why Strength Matters

Market structure with its pivots, swings, and triads and the phases and patterns that they develop into are like a fine work of engineering – intricate machinery that is ready to work smoothly and regularly. However, in order to work, a machine needs fuel. It needs an external energy source with which to power its revolving cycles. The fuel is the strength that comes in the form of buying power and selling power.

These are the two poles that move market machinery – the positive pole or selling power and the negative pole or buying power. Buying power is negative because it occurs when a void must be filled. This void is created by low prices or expectations of low prices that move the market upward from its negative low point to its positive high point. The positive pole is what generates selling power. Selling occurs when prices are positive. They are full; they are not cheap. It is at this moment that selling and sellers appear on the scene.

During this selling period, prices go from high to low, from positive to negative. For example, they go from a bull market secular high to a bear market secular bottom. With these two poles alternating, the market goes from more buying than selling to the opposite – more selling than buying. This is a cycle of power that alternates continuously, making the market machinery turn over and over.

This external power that comes into the market and the different phases in the balance of power between buyers and sellers are what enables a reversal to be a true reversal and a trend to be a true trend. How great a force enters the market will determine how much staying power the new market phase will have. If a bear market reverses itself, sufficient energy is required not only to stop the bear market but also to change the balance of power drastically. Only new, fresh power can stop a trend, reverse it, and then enable it to continue

Only a new force injected into the market can enable a trend to continue. If the force disappears or changes direction, the trend will end before it is really born. This is how many market movements lure us into believing that they will become trends when they do not. Therefore, we need to be able to distinguish true market movements from false ones at their inception. This can be done only by identifying the force that is behind each movement.

How this is done is not easy. Therefore, we will once more ask the fundamental market structure and its pivots, swings, and triads to come to our rescue.

How the Fundamental Market Structure Tells Us about New Strength Coming into the Market: The Three Laws of Power

We will now ask the fundamental market structure for a clue or warning of any new force about to enter the market and alter the balance of power between buyers and sellers. Let us see if market geometry has something to tell us about these changes in force within the market.

As you know, markets originate from simple pivots that oscillate, creating swings. These swings come into existence when a triad appears. This triad containing the seed of the contrary swing reverses the market. This is how every swing in one direction engenders a swing in the opposite direction. The apex of these swing changes is always a pivot. This pivot is the turning point where the balance of force changes.

For a contrary swing to occur, we need the arrival of an opposite force that can meet two conditions:

1. Be able to exercise a force equal and opposite to the existing one.
2. Be able to exercise a force greater and opposite to the existing one.

If these two conditions are met, we have a reversal. If only the first condition is met, we have a consolidation. This is what differentiates turning points and a consolidation phase from a perspective of force.

These two conditions explain that, for every swing in one direction, there is an alternate swing in the opposite direction. This is why we have swings, even within composite trends. In a simple swing and its alternate swing, we have two opposing trends, even if short lived, which are linked by a pivot. The triad is what ends a simple swing, and the triad already contains the contrary swing in its minimal reversal expression.

The pivot that exists as soon as the triad appears contains the two conditions mentioned above in the exercise of a new force. Thus, every triad contains a force that is greater than, and opposite to, what exists. Therefore, within each triad, we have the minimal condition necessary for a reversal. Its third charted bar is the reversal. Its appearance is due to the second condition for the exercise of a force.

Now, where is the first condition met? The first condition is met in the pivot within the triad. The pivot is the point of equilibrium where two opposing forces nullify each other. In the pivot, we have the end of the previous force by the appearance of a new force. Thus, in the pivot of the triad, the old force is met by the new one. Our first condition is met, namely to be able to exercise a force equal and opposite to the existing one. However, it is only in the third charted bar of the triad that the second condition is met so that a reversal occurs.

A triad reversal of a swing into its contrary swing is not enough to explain the force coming into complex trends, those that we actually will be dealing with in the markets. A contrary swing can be as short as its triad reversal itself. However, in many or most cases, the shift in the balance of force within the triad is enough to make the contrary swing go further than the reversal of its initial triad.

We want to be able to know when a force has entered that is able to reverse complex trends, namely trends that are made from a series of swings linked by their pivots – trends that evolve into patterns of every kind of correction. To be able to identify that kind of new force, we must first identify it in the simple swing. We are interested in knowing what makes a simple contrary swing go beyond its minimal triad reversal.

This is where a third condition for the exercise of force in the market enters the picture. This third condition is:

3. Being able to exercise a force that will continue its function if nothing opposes it.

This third condition explains why some swings go beyond their triad reversal. The reason is that they encounter no opposing force in front of them. The swing continues uninterrupted until an opposing force stops it and reverses it.

Within a complex trend, these two opposing forces create the oscillating swings that create the trend. The direction of the trend will indicate from where and with what intensity the force is moving. What we want to know is when this complex trend will stop and reverse. We understand how a reversal applies to simple swings. Now, we want to know how composite swings that evolve into trends are reversed.

The Power of Pivots

To understand how trends that are constructed of composite swings reverse, let us take a look at how simple swings reverse beyond their initial triad. If we can detect a sign that will enable us to confirm that a new swing that has just completed its reversal can go beyond the triad that gave birth to it, we are on the right path. Let us try to find such a sign that will help us anticipate a continuation of a swing.

The first thing to do is to examine a number of triads, ascending and descending, in as many charts as possible. Here we find something interesting. Most triads in their reversal go beyond their reversal charted bar. This extension of the reversal beyond the triad in the majority of cases tells us that the force that caused the reversal is strong enough not only to stop the current movement but also to reverse it beyond the initial charted bar triad. This means that a reversal has enough force in it to develop a triad into a larger swing. This gives our first sign of a force strong enough to continue a triad into a swing. This sign is the triad itself.

If we want more precision, the breakout of the triad's pivot is, in itself, the proof that a force that exceeds the previous one has entered the market. Without a breakout of this pivot, we would never have a triad to begin with, much less a reversal.

Thus, here we have our general rule: the breakout of a pivot is the sign of a force that is capable of stopping a previous movement and reversing it. It follows from this that our attention must focus on the pivots.

Let us extend this concept to complex swings, such as trends, upward or downward, which are composed of a multitude of swings. In the case of these complex swings, how will we be able to know that a change in the balance of forces has taken place?

If we begin to look for a change in the pivot at the end of the trend, we will not find it. The reason is simple. A trend is composed of contrary swings that alternate. The pivots always imply a reversal within the trend. This does not mean a reversal of the trend. The final pivot of a trend has the same quality as any other pivot within the trend in order to be the origin of a contrary swing. However, we need more than this for a true reversal.

A reversal of a trend occurs when a new trend occurs in the opposite direction. This new trend will be as complex as the preceding trend. It will be formed by contrary swings linked by their pivots and born from their triads. Thus, our reversal sign must be something different than the final pivot of a trend, upward or downward.

This reversal signal will be a pivot, but not the final pivot. Why? Because the final pivot is the pivot of a simple swing, not a complex one. The only reversal signal for a complex swing must be the breakout of a pivot within the old trend, linking two swings. In the case of an upward trend, the last pivot low will be such a point.

If the market reverses an uptrend, the first signal will be when the low pivot of the uptrend before the reversal took place is broken. This signals us that a new force has been able to stop the previous trend and reverse it (Figure 4.1 and also see Chart 9 in Appendix II). If the reversal is the reversal of a downtrend, the signal that there is a force to continue such a reversal into a new trend is the breakout of the last pivot high of the preceding downtrend (Figure 4.2 and also see Chart 7 in Appendix II). In both cases, we find our initial rule, the breakout of a pivot. However, instead of being simple triad pivots alone, they are the pivot highs that link the last two swings within a movement.

Now, this is only a minimum. If the new complex swing or trend breaks the two last pivots of the preceding movement, the new force receives further confirmation. If the breakout is the breakout of a pivot of an important corrective wave within the last trend that is being reversed, the signal is even stronger.

Let us suppose that the two high pivots of a descending trend are broken to the downside. This is a strong signal. If the pivot high belongs to an upward correction that itself is made of many swings, the signal is even stronger. Let us now suppose

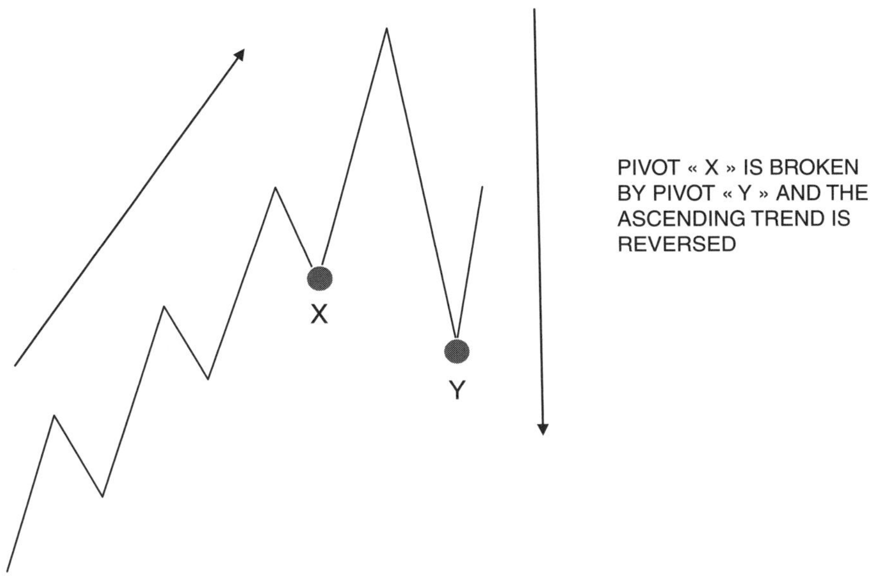

Figure 4.1 Sign of a new force that has the power to stop a trend and reverse it: reversal from an uptrend to a downtrend.

that the two low pivots of an ascending trend are broken to the upside. This is a strong signal. If the pivot low belongs to a downward correction that itself is made of many swings, the signal is even stronger. Such is the power of pivots.

The Power of Tops and Bottoms

This power of pivots as a signal of a new force that can reverse a trend appears in the breakout of pivots of the preceding trend as the market reverses. This new force will also manifest itself within the new trend that is taking shape. We have said that a new trend must be, of necessity, a complex trend if it is to reverse a previous complex trend. This new trend, in its inception, must be complex to exist. If the new trend shows minimal complexity, it is evidence that a new force has been able not only to reverse the previous trend but also to give rise to a new one.

Here we apply the same principle that we found in the triad, but on a larger scale. The triad itself is proof of the reversal of a simple swing at its minimal degree. For complex swings made up of swings, the same applies.

Let us define this minimal complexity needed for a reversal as a new trend in inception. Here we need a reversal swing from the extreme pivot of the old trend being reversed, as well as a contrary swing that creates a new top for a descending swing or a new bottom for a descending one. This new top or bottom to be validated needs its contrary swing, which breaks the previous pivot of the new trend. This means that, in an uptrend reversal, we will have a lower high and two lower lows

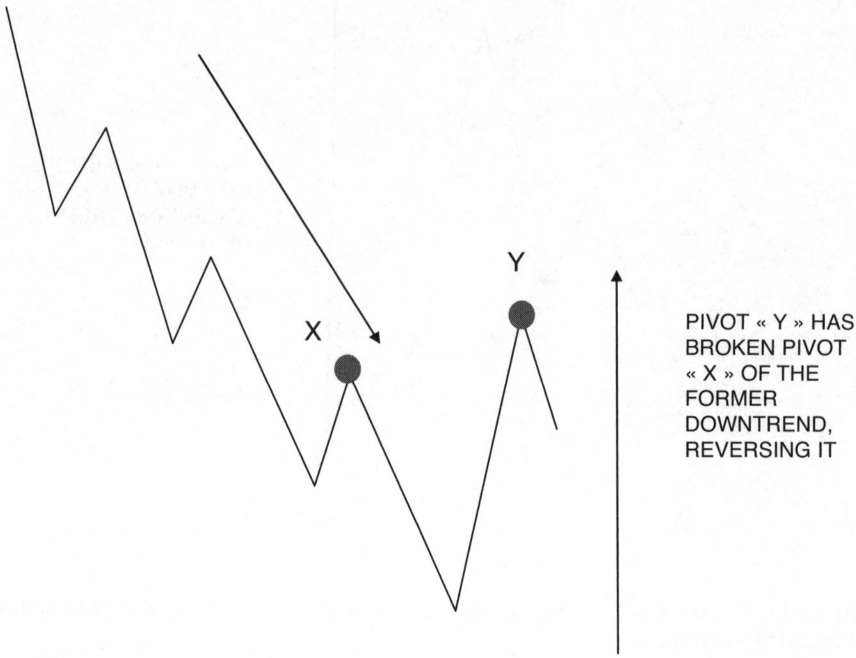

Figure 4.2 Sign of a new force that has the power to stop a trend and reverse it: reversal from a downtrend to an uptrend.

(Figure 4.3). In a downtrend reversal, we will have a higher low and two higher highs (Figure 4.4).

In both cases – the upward reversal that initiates a new downtrend and the downward reversal that initiates a new uptrend – we have pivot breakouts within the same trend, as well as higher highs for the new uptrend and lower lows for the new downtrend. It is the pivot position and number, and the pivot breakout within the same trend, that tell us that a new force is driving the new trend. We know that a chance exists for the newly born trend to develop into a mature trend.

We have two ways of learning that a trend has ended in a reversal that is giving rise to a new trend and that a new force has entered the market that is not only capable of stopping the old trend but also of reversing it and maybe continuing it. These two ways are:

1. The breakout of pivots, or important resistance or support from the previous movement, and
2. The formation of higher consecutive highs and higher consecutive lows in the case of a new uptrend, or lower consecutive highs and lower consecutive lows in the case of a new downtrend, both within the new trend.

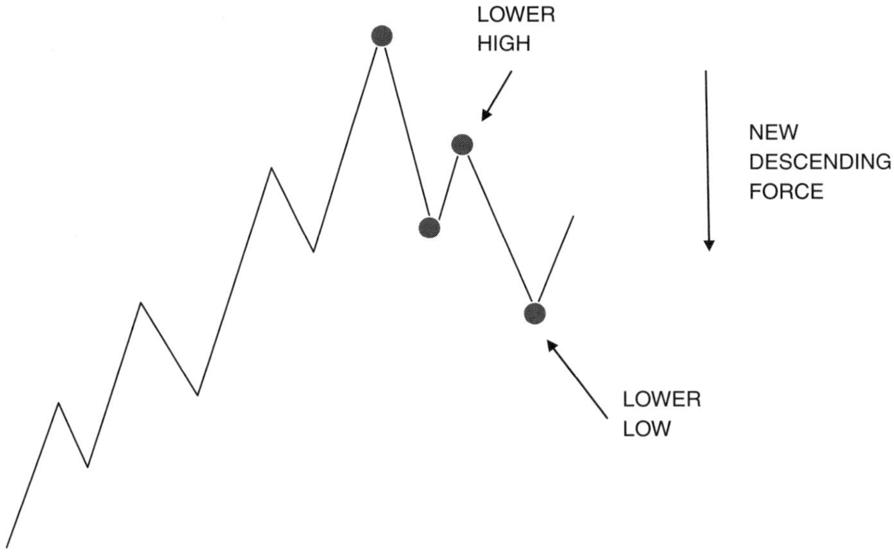

Figure 4.3 Sign of a new force that has the power to stop a trend and reverse it: reversal from an uptrend to a downtrend.

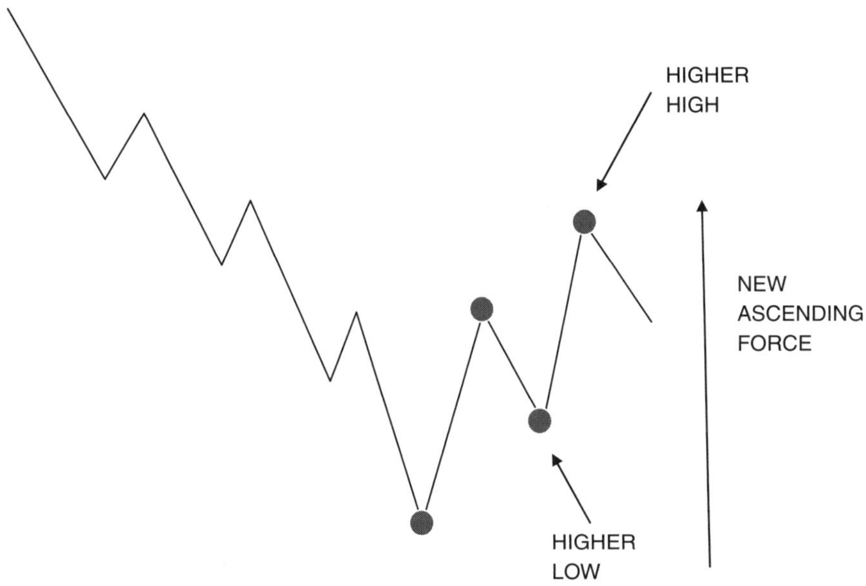

Figure 4.4 Sign of a new force that has the power to stop a trend and reverse it: reversal from a downtrend to an uptrend.

These two ways, by which the market can signal us that a new force has appeared that is capable of reversing a trend and developing into a new one, have greater strength when they are both present (see Chart 7 in Appendix II). This means not only that the new trend has broken important pivots or levels of the old trend but also that it has formed new pivots or levels within the new trend.

The fundamental market structure with its pivots, swings, and triads has once again given us a clue to identify a change in the balance of forces within the market. We have limited ourselves here to the breakout of price pivots and price levels of a previous move or the creation of new price pivots and price levels within the new movement.

There is still one element missing for our strength approach to be complete. It is the time factor. Let us see what the fundamental market structure has to tell us about time and its link to market strength.

Market Strength and the Time Factor

Time and market strength are intimately linked. Market strength can be compared to a magnet that bends time. Significant changes in the balance of forces within the market deeply affect time. Time oscillations can become larger or shorter when confronted by changes in force that arrive suddenly and enter the market. The shifts in force translate into changes in time. This gives us another tool with which to identify underlying changes in market strength.

Time becomes a signature that tells us that the balance is changing and that a reversal is around the corner. This ability to change the pattern of time is as meaningful as a change in the pattern of price, a pivot breakout, or trending pivots to indicate the presence of new strength in the market.[13]

Before explaining how time changes denote shifts in the balance of power in the market, let us discuss the idea of time patterns. Time patterns are as real and valid as price patterns. Time patterns are of many kinds. Examples include changes in the time length of swings and their time pivots and specific lengths of time that measure market behavior or key dates.

Time pivots are the extremities of time lengths. If a movement has a length of ten days, the first moment of day one is the beginning time pivot and the last moment of day ten is the ending pivot for that time swing. If the length of the next movement exceeds that, it has broken the former time pivot. If it does not, the time pivot is still intact.

Another kind of time pattern is the simple time length. Here we simply measure different time lengths since a movement began. This fixed time length signifies another kind of time pivot. A movement can reverse after 18 days or reverse after 45 days or reverse after 90 days, etc. Here we have fixed lengths where reversals or market changes often occur. They can also be measured in weeks, months, and years. The 5-year cycle, the 10-year cycle, and the 20-year cycle are examples of this kind of movement.

These movements create clusters. If we have different market movements where different time lengths or swings coincide, we have a cluster that could spell significant change. Such time patterns can also be dynamic. Here we have time lengths that change their span according to a ratio, such as the Fibonacci ratio. Key dates are another time pattern. Key dates are time pivots where reversals occur.

We are interested here in only one kind of pattern. It is the pattern that will tell us that a new force is entering the market and altering its balance and that a reversal is coming soon.

I should explain this. Price swings can be measured in time lengths. The time length is the number of trading time units. The number of trading time units is the number of charted bars of the swing. We can also measure the number of calendar time periods between swing pivots. These time periods, whether trading or calendar, tend to always remain within a range. They are cyclical. The limits of the range repeat themselves indefinitely. When the range varies significantly, we are faced with a possible reversal.

In a downward trend, the main direction of the force is down. Therefore, the strongest swings are the downward swings. They have the greatest number of charted bars. Time shows an inclination towards a downward movement. In an upward trend, the opposite happens. The swings that last the longest and which have most charted bars are the upward swings. Time favors an upward movement.

The time factor then favors the direction of the movement. When this time factor changes its balance and reverses, it shows a change of market direction. This change in the time factor can only occur with the arrival of a new force.

We now have an element that will enable us to judge if a new trend is in its buildup phase. This element must be present if a change of trend is to occur. It will enable us to distinguish between real reverses and fake ones.

We have seen that, in upward trends, upward movements within the trend tend to last longer in trading time and calendar time than downward movements. We have also seen that the opposite happens in downward trends. In downward trends, the downward swings tend to last longer than the upward swings. It is when that ratio changes significantly that a new trend begins to form.

For example, if, in an upward movement, the upward swings on average have five charted bars and last seven calendar days and the downward swings on average have three charted bars and last three calendar days, but this ratio changes, the trend will change sooner or later. If, during the uptrend of our example, a downward swing appears that, instead of having three charted bars and lasting three days, lasts six charted bars and seven calendar days, the time factor has changed from three to six. This announces that a reversal is near, even if the market still continues for a while, as it will, with its uptrend (Figure 4.5 and also see Chart 10 in Appendix II).

Let us reverse this for a downtrend. If its downswings lasts five charted bars and seven days and its upswings last only four days, but within the trend at a given moment the uptrend changes from four days to eight days, the time factor has doubled and a reversal is forming. Even if the market in our last example continues its downtrend

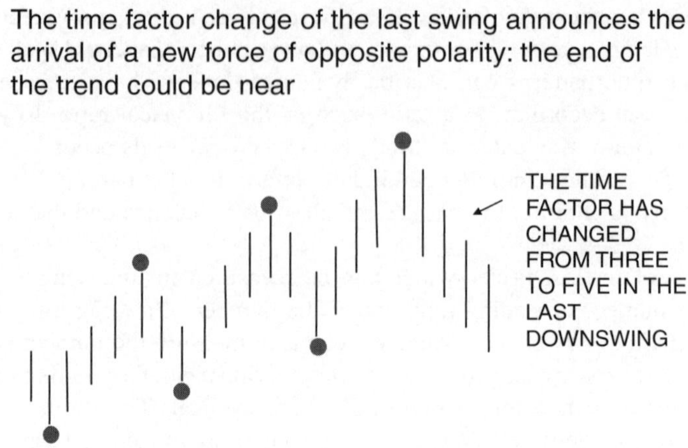

Figure 4.5 Time factor in an ascending trend.

for a while, the correction that lasted longer than the others is an indication that the reversal is near. This signal should always be heeded. It is powerful (Figure 4.6 and also see Chart 11 in Appendix II).

Once again, the fundamental market structure with its pivots, swings, and triads gives us a way to describe and identify easily the appearance of a new force in the market. With this knowledge, we will be able to determine when a new trend has begun in earnest. It will help us to avoid confusing reactions within a trend with a real change of trend.

In our market analysis, we must use as tools (a) the time factor and (b) the breakout of important pivots and the creation of new pivotal levels within the new trend that is in its birth stage. Having seen how the time factor works to produce a reversal, let us explore the energy factor.

THE ENERGY FACTOR

The Law of Action and Reaction

Energy is what moves markets. Buying and selling are ways in which this energy flows. This flow of energy is behind market oscillations. Each market is a vehicle through which energy circulates. This vehicle will give shape to the flow of energy that will oscillate in a given way. A market is a kind of oscillator that creates oscillations with the energy that it receives. In turn, these oscillations create the market movements, phases, and patterns.

The energy vehicle of a market is always the same. It can move around, but it can never be destroyed. The energy will build to the point where an opposite

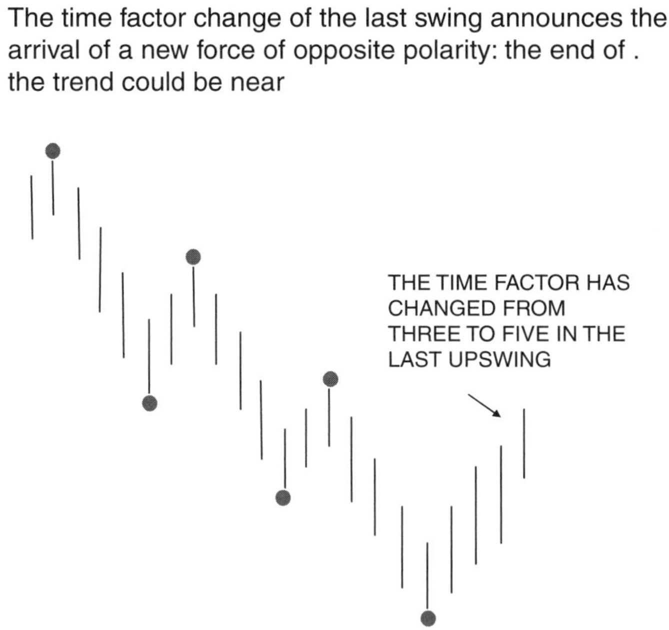

Figure 4.6 Time factor in a descending trend.

movement will come into existence. This pendulum-like movement of energy is what an oscillation is all about. It is the law of action and reaction. This law will manifest itself in time and price. For example, a secular bull market will build its energy to the point where it reverses with the same force that it had when it came to be, but in an opposite direction. We then will have a bear market for many years.

The same happens with time movements within a trend. If they last long in one direction, they will reverse and last in proportion to their initial direction. The time and speed may change, but the energy spent will still be the same. For instance, a bear market often lasts a third as long as its corresponding bull market. However, it compensates for its shorter time with speed and volatility. In summary, the energy behind the market is the same.

This energy factor tells us that the market will always cycle between opposites to maintain its state of initial equilibrium. What seems like disequilibrium and movement is only a new way of keeping balance. There is always a balance and, as soon as a movement is complete, the opposite movement begins. This is why bull markets do not last forever and never will. Bear markets, however steep, will always end with a new bull market.

When prices are high, all of the energy will be spent selling. When prices are low, the same energy will be spent buying. The cycle will always repeat. Markets are permanently circulating. When we know this, we learn to wait for the right time. We know that every market will sooner or later come back in one way or another. We know that, no matter how gloomy the outlook may be, the energy of the market is there, waiting to appear.

Also, we know that only energy remains the same. Everything else will change. Therefore, we will wait for the moment when the market acts in a particular way that confirms that its energy is creating movement and direction. In this sense, every market phase or pattern has more or less energy – more or less potential. We have said that this energy may be in use or may be on the sidelines waiting to come in.

This concept differs from the one of force. Force is energy that is already in the market, driving a movement actively. Energy itself is always there and ready to move the market when its moment comes. It is present and existing, even if not active.

To recognize energy's existence is to recognize how it is behaving at each stage. Let us see how energy acts within a consolidation.

The Zero Point or Neutral Point: The Energy Behind a Consolidation

Consolidations are examples of the energy behind movements. In a consolidation, the market's energy is waiting and self-contained. It is neutralized and, at the same time, building up huge, secret reserves of explosive power.

Ted Warren, a trader and author, developed the strategy of buying consolidations. This is not the best strategy for us. It is better to wait for a breakout of the consolidation. However, he made a point. He demonstrates that consolidations contain huge potential energy. They are market energy accumulators. This energy accumulates progressively. The longer the accumulation period, the more powerful is the movement that follows (see Chart 12 in Appendix II).

During the consolidation phase, market energy builds up due to the zero point of markets, where the market participants' opposing forces neutralize each other. An equilibrium where nothing happens is reached between buying and selling. This equilibrium of opposing forces builds up a constant market interest where equal selling and buying exists. The longer this equilibrium exists, the more difficult it will be to break.

This difficulty creates the energy accumulation. This accumulation is potential that develops, but is purely virtual. In other words, a huge amount of energy would be necessary to break a long-term consolidation. This energy would never arrive. However, if the consolidation ends, a huge amount of energy will be needed or the consolidation will not break. A long-term consolidation is a market habit that conditions the minds of the majority of its participants.

To break this psychological habit, as well as to break the fundamental and technical conditions to get out of the consolidation, requires lots of energy. This energy is already there, as potential that is ready to break loose if market conditions should change. This is what makes long-term consolidations interesting – not to buy or sell, but to watch until the time is ripe. A consolidation could be compared to a dam that contains thousands of tons of water. That is its potential energy. If the dam broke, the avalanche of water and its force would be devastating. This is due to the potential energy that is waiting. The same is true for consolidations.

The potential energy contained in the consolidation is the reason why it should not be traded for big profits. Potential energy is not actual force. The two are opposites. Within a consolidation, everything is like petrified rock. The buyer or seller of a consolidation becomes immobilized and neutralized. He loses time and movement. This is why consolidations should be avoided for the market action of trading or investment.

For the same reason that potential energy and actual force are opposites, consolidations become great watching-only opportunities. We should watch consolidations because of their potential energy, which could change into actual market force one day. Consolidation phases are needed as resting periods before the real action begins.

Using a metaphor, we could say that the market sleeps during a consolidation and during its sleep it recovers its lost energy. The longer its sleeping period, the greater its recovery and the stronger its awakening. Another analogy is one involving the sea. A consolidation is like a calm sea just before a storm strikes. Both examples, consolidation as a sleeping period and consolidation as a calm sea, tell us of the enormous amount of energy that is concealed behind apparent market stability.

Now with this energy perspective, let us look at trends.

The Energy Explosion Behind a New Trend

If consolidations accumulate energy, trends use it. In a trend, all of the potential energy accumulated during the consolidation phase is used to create a force that enters the market. This force is different from the energy potential. When force enters the market, the potential stays as a reserve, declining gradually. This diminution of energy occurs as more and more force is used to move the market. This force uses up the potential energy. When the force is exhausted, the energy changes polarity and is used up by a contrary force (see Chart 13 in Appendix II).

As a movement uses up energy that transforms it to force, energy of the opposite polarity begins to accumulate. Energy always remains the same. It only changes polarity. Polarities change, but the energy behind remains. It is always potential.

Energy is like the shadow of actual market action and its force. Energy is always potential until it becomes actual. Once energy is actualized as force, new potential develops to equilibrate its active pole.

Thus, markets oscillate not only in price and time, but also between a potential pole and an actual pole. As the actual pole develops, a potential pole of the opposite polarity begins to develop. For example, a trend near its end has converted energy into force. As this energy is converted into directional force, this same energy transforms itself into energy of the opposite polarity. If we had to add both energy polarities, they would amount to the entirety of the market potential at that point in time and space. This entirety can be expressed as 100 %. This is how it happens.

Let us examine any directional trend. Let us say that a directional trend is exactly halfway – at its midpoint. We would have 50 % of the potential energy needed to fuel the market direction that has consumed itself as force. This force is an actual force that is pushing the market its way. It is the real action of market participants. This force, if halfway, has still another half to go. There is another 50 % of the energy left that will be converted to actual force in the immediate future.

Now, the 50 % of energy that has already been spent as a force of a given polarity has converted itself into 50 % energy or potential for a movement of the opposite directional polarity. As soon as the trend reaches its end, it has converted 100 % of its potential energy into actual force. At this point, this potential energy has been converted fully to its opposite polarity and is ready to fuel a movement in a different, if not opposite, direction.

Let us examine the polarities of upward and downward reversals. We will begin with an upward reversal.

The Negative Pole: The Energy Behind an Upward Reversal

For an upward reversal to take place, there must be movement from less to more. Prices are low and attractive for buyers. There is a profit potential that expresses itself as how high prices can go. This profit potential acts like a magnet that attracts buying action. The market begins to rise and an uptrend begins.

This movement from less to more, from a market low to a market high, can be equated to a move from negative to positive. The low prices are at the negative pole of the market. This will attract buying power. This new buying power will move until its positive end, when prices will be overvalued. Then, we have the opposite of a void and the market must discharge itself and empty itself again. Here we have a reversal.

At the beginning of the uptrend and its buying power, we have a great deal of potential energy that will transform itself into buying power. This energy fuels a buying force, in the same measure as it does when it converts itself into selling potential energy. As the upward trend advances from negative to positive, this selling potential energy grows until we have 100 % selling potential energy and 0 % buying energy. This is when we reach the positive pole and the trend reverses.

If a consolidation occurs within the uptrend before the market reverses, what is left of the buying energy, which is very small, is compensated by selling energy, until the buying energy is exhausted. The act of consolidating is a signal that selling force has increased to the point where the rise is flattened into a horizontal movement. In this particular case, the consolidation is due to an increase in the selling force coming into the market, while the buying force remains the same or declines.

A consolidation within an upward movement is a sign of incoming additional selling force, with the angle of the market phase tending to 0°. In a consolidation, a market is not going up or down. It is horizontal. It moves along a 0° line. Thus, when a force comes into a market that it trending at a given angle, and bends it, the angle goes to 0° as soon as the market stops rising and flattens for a while. Angles in the market not only tell us about the speed and acceleration of a movement but also tell us about market potential and market force.

When an angle, as in a consolidation, tends toward zero degrees, initiating a horizontal line, the forces are in equilibrium and the opposite potential energy pole is beginning to convert itself to actual force. In the case of our uptrend, the consolidation is telling us that the accumulated selling potential energy for a reversal is beginning to change into a new, actual selling force, although not enough to reverse the trend.

Now, we will examine the downward reversal.

The Positive Pole: The Energy Behind a Downward Reversal

For a downward reversal to occur, the movement must be from more to less. Prices are high and attractive for sellers. There is profit potential that expresses itself as how low prices can go. This profit potential acts like a magnet that causes selling action. The market begins to drop and a downtrend begins.

The high prices are at the positive pole of the market. This will drive selling power. This new selling power will move to its negative end, when prices will be undervalued. At the beginning of the downtrend and its selling power, we have a great deal of potential energy that will transform itself to selling power. As this energy fuels a selling force, it converts itself into buying potential energy. As the downward trend advances from positive to negative, the buying potential energy grows until we have 100 % buying potential energy and 0 % selling energy. This is when we reach the negative pole and the trend reverses.

If a consolidation happens within the downtrend before the market reverses, what is left of the selling energy is compensated by a buying energy, until the selling energy exhausts itself. The act of consolidating is a signal that the buying force has increased to the point where the downward movement flattens into a horizontal movement. Thus, in this particular case, the consolidation is due to an increase in the buying force relative to the selling force, while the selling force stays the same or diminishes.

Within a downward movement, a consolidation is a sign of incoming additional buying force or, at least, a diminishing of selling force relative to the buying force, the angle tending to 0°. In the end, these forces always balance themselves at a deeper level. What seems to be a trending phase, a consolidation phase, or a turning point phase are only conversions of potential energy from one polarity to the other.

Market potential is always there, although it can be hidden. There can be obstacles blocking its action. Nevertheless, it is always there as a virtual force, which can be unleashed when market conditions justify it. This is the real energy that is always in balance. It transforms buyers to sellers and sellers to buyers, trends to consolidations and consolidations to trends or turning points. Appearances change, but the goal behind is the same.

The profit potential is what makes buyers buy and sellers sell. It is also what converts the former to the latter, the actual buyers becoming the future sellers and the actual sellers becoming the future buyers.

In summary, the energy or potential for a reversal is accumulated during a movement in a given direction, the energy polarity changing progressively until this change is complete and the energy potential changes to the new force that will actively fuel the market in its new direction.

We must ask now what the relationship is between this bipolar market energy and the time factor, which we explained previously.

THE TIME FACTOR

Energy Manifests in Time

Market energy is, as we have stated, potential waiting for the right conditions that will enable it to be used. This implies a particular relationship between energy and time.

Energy itself is outside of time in the sense that it is only potential. It is energy for something that could happen, but is not actually happening. We can think of it as unused fuel. Fuel has energy potential that will only be unleashed by an explosion. Before this happens, we have fuel in space and time, but not potential. The potential is a direction that fuel could acquire given certain conditions.

Think of oil. For centuries, it was valueless. It was only when it was needed as a fuel to drive vehicles and machines in the modern era that oil became a first priority commodity. The potential was always there, but it was not in a specific time period. Oil's potential was there even before oil existed. It was contained in the oil formula. If some day oil existed on earth, it would exist with all its possibilities.

The same happens with market energy. It is there, but only as a possibility waiting for the right conditions to use it for something – in this case the development of a market phase. For that market phase to arrive, the right conditions are required. Among those conditions is the previous market phase, which will serve as an accumulator for this energy. At that precise moment, the energy will appear in time. Its appearance will manifest itself as a specific polarity or potential pole. As we have seen, an uptrend will make real its cumulative opposite potential – that which will make possible the reversal – during its development in time and space.

Time, in this sense, will be the container of energy. Time, as far as the market is concerned, is the development of the market itself within its own space until the cycle has been completed. This means that markets will be there as long as there are humans who need to trade things among themselves. Trade will continue as long as exchanges are needed for life. Profit in terms of money is only a symbol of real profit, the real use of something for one's life and existence.

Thus, time is the time that the market needs to develop its necessary swings, phases, and patterns, according to the expectations and goals of the market participants in their trading activities. Time is therefore a specific stage of the market's cyclical evolution. Time is not a void and abstract quantity, but implies a quality. Thus, time will contain market energy. The longer a market stage takes relative to other market stages, the more energy will be accumulated. This is why time gives us a clue to the pure potential of a market.

Let us look at a practical example. Suppose that we have an upward trend, a bull market, which lasts six months. This means that during these six months, the potential energy for a reversal has been growing steadily day by day. From this, we know that, if the market reverses once this potential is at its highest, the reversal will be in proportion to the time spent by the market rising upward.

Now, we will look at a longer time frame, ten years this time. This longer time frame will accumulate a greater potential for reversal simply because energy manifests itself in time. As the market develops, creating a greater likelihood for a reversal with every passing day, energy accumulates.

It is the time length of the phase itself that will reverse in the future that is telling us about the accumulated potential that will fuel the reversal. The greater the time length of a phase, the stronger will be its reversal (see Chart 13 in Appendix II).

Now, we will explore the oscillatory nature of this time energy.

Variation in Time Oscillations Anticipate Changes in Market Strength and Coming Reversals

Time oscillates. We have the time swings of trends and consolidations. The time is the time of something. It is the time of an uptrend or the time of a downtrend or the time of a consolidation or turning point.

Moments in time express potentials. Those potentials were waiting for their time to come. They came into time within a given market phase that created the potential energy to be there. This means that each time oscillation accumulates the energy of its own reversal. The length of time, as we have stated, gives us a clue to the strength and length of the reversal. Long time swings mean long and strong reversals (see Chart 13 in Appendix II). Here again is an example of the law of action and reaction.

Identifying the energy potential of the different market phases can be applied to the balance of force produced by changes in the time factor equation. We have seen how this happens. If, within a movement, one of the oscillating swings changes in its time length significantly, this becomes a signature of a nearby trend change. This signature has another meaning, in addition to indicating a change in the balance of power indicated by the change in the length of one of the oscillations within a movement.

This time change becomes the signature, but also contains an indication that the market potential that had accumulated during the phase where the signature occurs is approaching its apex. However, there is more. The signature tells us of the potential for a reversal accumulated during the entire movement in advance. We can see this in changes in the balance of power in secular bull movements.

For example, the change in the balance of forces within the bull market that ended on 11 October 2007 with the S&P at a high of 1576 was an example of this. The strong signature told us that great potential for a reversal had accumulated during the bull market before it ended. From a market energy point of view, the corrective signature that started on 16 July 2007, with the S&P 500 attaining a high of 1556 and ending on 16 August of the same year with the S&P 500 reaching a low of 1371 and correcting 185 points was a meaningful event. It not only anticipated a change in trend and the end of the bull market, but also told us that the energy accumulated during the bull market was important (see Charts 3 and 4 in Appendix II). In addition, it told us that accumulated energy was going to be used by the market for its reversal. This gave a scenario of a possible strong reversal.

Without forecasting, but by simply looking at the present market movement at that time, we gained useful information. The first information was that a signature altering the balance of force had occurred. The other information was that potential energy that could be used for a reversal had already been accumulated. If a reversal was to take place, it would be huge. No forecasting was needed or prophets or market gurus. A reversal was only a possible scenario, but it was all that we needed.

Now, we will return to our triads and pivots in relation to market energy. Since, along with swings, they are the building blocks of our fundamental market structure, we must approach them from a perspective of potential energy.

Price Triads Are a Mirror of Time Triads

Triads exist in time and price. A time change is an indication of a price change. As we have seen, all reversals are signed by previous time events. These time events should also be mirrored in triads.

In a triad we have three charted bars. They all belong to the past and indicate a possible present and future. Within this past, we find a reversal event within the triad that creates a pivot.

All pivots are created by reversal events. The pivot exists after the reversal has taken place, but the pivot is before the reversal. Its position is only known by us in the future, the third charted bar of the triad. The price point that is potentially a pivot already exists. If, at that precise point, the market does not turn around, but continues to move in the same direction, the price point does not stop existing. However, it will not become a pivot. This is why a pivot is known only after the reversal has occurred. The triad is such a reversal. This gives us another way of denoting time with a triad. The first triad charted bar is the past. The middle charted bar, where the pivot occurs, is the present and the third charted bar, where this pivot becomes known, is the future.

The triad from this perspective encompasses the three time windows of past, present, and future. The present is only revealed in the future. When it is now, it is already past. When the third charted bar is complete, only then is the pivot known.

In a triad, the future, its third charted bar, is a reversal of the past. From the perspective of a pivot, its future is the next charted bar in time that defines it. Its past is its previous charted bar.

The time triad is defined as market past, market present, and market future, where time is qualified in a concrete way. Something happens in time and the three time phases must each correspond to specific phases within the market development. The past then is a phase, time 1, signified by a definite event. The present is always a time pivot. It is the moment when change occurs. It is time 2. The future is the new event resulting from this turning point instant. It is time 3.

The price triad is a specific case of the time triad. If the past is an upward swing, the present is the pivot, the precise moment where the polarity of the movement changes. The future is the new movement, the downward swing.

If the past of a triad contains a downward swing, its future will necessarily contain an upward swing. The reason for this is that the past and the future have inverted polarities. Time cycles from past to future, its turning point being the present.

The price triad mirrors this time triad, which is more general because it applies not only to price and markets but also to many other kinds of phenomena. Each time change implies a reality change and thus a change in polarity. This means that the past reflecting itself in the future will pass through the present and, in doing so, will change its polarity.

Let us look at a market example of this. The first example is the triad. If the past is an upward charted bar, the future will be a downward charted bar. The door through which the change occurs is an instant, the present. We call it the pivot, due to the fact that polarities change.

Let us now assume a more general event. A bull market in the past will be followed by a bear market in the future, changing in a present where the market turns around. What happens if two market events are exactly the same? Well they cannot be. At most, they will be similar. The future event can be similar to the past event. For similarity to happen, a change of polarity is needed. The past is not equal to the future. The 'is not' signifies a change of polarity that creates the similarity.

This teaches us never to expect that things will repeat exactly in the same way as in the past. A difference must be acknowledged and difference is always a change of polarity of a certain kind. Therefore, when we think about time in the markets, we must not think of it as only empty clock time, but as real time, which moves because of the market's inner clock, which has its own rhythm and harmony and beats in keeping with its own nature.

MARKET TIME AS DIFFERENT FROM CLOCK TIME

We have seen that market time is not clock time. It is not empty time, but factual time. Each unit of market time corresponds to a concrete event. We can explore further this concept of market time as being concrete and different from clock time.

Let us get back to our definition of time in general. Time is the measure of movement. This definition comes from Aristotle. It suits us well in our efforts to define market time. We measure a movement by comparing it to another movement.

The time of a first movement is given by the number of times a second movement fits within the first. For example, if writing a chapter of this book took two complete rotations of the Earth, the time taken to write it was two days. What we call time is the result of comparing the movement of something relative to another movement of something else that we use as a reference.

Time is sequential. To be in time is to be first and then second, etc. – first one thing and then the other. Time then is not simultaneity, but movement. It can only exist relative to things that move and can be related by those to others. We measure the year by a complete movement of the earth around the Sun.

Each day of the year is a complete rotation of the Earth around its own axis. If we divide this rotation from sunrise to sunrise into 24 parts, we have our 24-hour day. If we create a machine that rotates 360° from sunrise to sunrise and divide its dial into 24 parts, we have created clock time. By a further division of each 24th into 60 equal parts, we have the minutes, which, when divided by 60, give the seconds.

In summary, movements within movements enable us to measure time.

Now, in the same way that planet Earth time is measured by motion relative to the Sun and divisions of these motions, the market can be measured by the movements that take place within it. This inner market time is different from measuring time in only trading days or calendar days. If this inner market time is to be defined, we should say that each market movement is a time. Time in the market is, therefore, the sequence of its individual movements. This sequence creates an *after* and a *before*, and a transition within both that could be equated to the present. The *before* plays the role of the future and the *after* portrays the past. This sequence differs from time outside the market.

What are the units of this market time? Every movement is a unit and there is a hierarchy of movements. The tick is the equivalent of the second. Thus, a tick develops into a charted bar and the charted bar can be equated with the minute.

However, these time units do not stop at the charted bar. The charted bar develops into the swing. The swing can be equated to the hour. Then, the swing develops into the phase, either a trend or a consolidation or turning point. We have arrived at the market day.

We also have our market inner year. Once the market has gone through the entire cycle of its phases, the market year is complete. The market, we had said, repeats the same phases indefinitely.

Now, you may say, these units are heterogeneous beyond the tick. Two charted bars will not have the same number of ticks, two swings will not have the same number of charted bars, and two market phases will not have the same number of swings. The same can be said of our market year. Two complete cycles that contain the sequence of market phases will not be equal.

However, here we must answer that market inner time is not an arbitrary, externally-imposed, homogeneous time. We are facing a qualitative time here that is elastic – a time that sometimes will go faster and sometimes slower, but that in the end will balance. An analogy of this phenomenon would be subjective time versus clock time.

Clock time is the same for all of us, but one hour is longer if I'm in a waiting room and bored than if I'm immersed in doing something that I like.

It is similar with market time. Movements can have unequal numbers of units, but they represent one market movement, i.e., one unit of time in its corresponding degree. If the market moves three charted bars, it is a three times movement. If the market moves three swings, it has moved three times a swing and if it has moved a whole phase, it has moved one time a phase. If it cycles once through all three phases in different combinations, it has completed one full circle of market time.

Now we will explore how this inner market time, which is essentially elastic, works for us.

How to Use the Market's Inner Time

Market time is elastic. One time or market movement can have a different length than another similar movement. These units can be measured. These measures can also be compared. These comparisons give us measures that will repeat cyclically. For instance, separate the swings. We will measure their time units, their charted bars. We then will have the inner time for each swing. Some swings will have more charted bars and some will have fewer. Their elasticity means that some swings lose time and others gain time.

A swing that advances too quickly in price, at too a steep angle, and with fewer than average charted bars or time units will fall back again quickly and be short lived. It cannot be trusted to attain a price target by itself. It loses its illusory gains quickly. A swing that advances slowly, with a greater number of bar time units than average, will probably be on target more often, without giving up what it had won in the price advance. Also, a series of large swings will tend to be balanced by a series of short swings. When market time expands in one of its time units, it will contract in the next ones. We can have series of expansion and contraction.

However, markets always tend to find a balance in their total time units. In practice, this means that a series of small moves will beget larger moves and vice versa. An example of this is that low-volatility swings at the beginning of a movement will end with high-volatility swings at the end of the movement.

This brings us to large movements, such as trends composed of many swings. Here in the market's *inner time*, the units of trends are the swings. A trend measures its number of time swings. This enables us to measure the inner time of a trend by counting the number of swings it contains. This is not price, trading day time, or calendar time. It is the market's own inner time within its own created units.

Once again, the principle of elasticity comes into play. Some trends will have large price movements in a short inner time with a smaller number of swings. These trends will be balanced by trends with large price movements with a greater number of inner price movements. Again, if time unbalances price, sharp corrections will follow.

The usefulness of this inner time, relative to trends, is that we generally can learn how many swings a trend has. In observing many such inner times of trends, clusters will appear. We will get to know the duration of trends by the number of their swings. This enables us to project the probable length of the trend that we will study or that we are planning to trade. We will observe that certain key inner time unit numbers tend to repeat. Then, the market will deliver its vibratory rate secret.

It is the same with consolidations. By counting their swings, we get an inner time measure that will tend to repeat and give us a tool to make projections. During a consolidation a market makes time. It waits. Time does not go forward, but repeats itself statically. To go forward means to go forward in price. This does not mean a price rise. It means a rise if you are long or a decline if you are short.

In an upward trend, a market gains time. As the price rises, profits can be made in a shorter time. In a downward trend, the market loses time. Multiyear gains can be lost in a few months when markets retreat.

There is also a time relative to the trader. In an uptrend, the trader gains time. It advances if you are long or decreases if you are short. Also, in a downtrend, a trader loses time. It advances if you are short or decreases if you are long.

Thus, in a market it is possible to make time, to gain time, and to lose time. This is why it pays to be conscious of the market's inner time and its inner cycles. Lack of this awareness can have disastrous consequences, whereas being aware of the market's inner time and its inner cycles can enhance your market results.

If, for example, you take a long-term trend at the right moment and exit it at the right moment, you will have gained time. This means that you will have profits that would have taken longer to achieve with a buy and hold strategy. If you make 20 % per year by trend trading, when the indexes make 9 % per year, you will have gained time. If compounded, the time gained is huge.

If you are in a bear market and do not sell in time, losing 50 % of your equity, we know that, to recover your losses, you will need to make 100 % on your equity. However, that is nothing compared to the time that you will need. The recovery could take more than double the time it took to make your initial equity. The time loss in this case could be more significant than the price loss.

Learn to think not only in terms of price, but also in terms of time. This attitude could save you a great deal of time plus profits.

We have now explored the fundamental market structure and the different perspectives from which it can be studied. Now, let us turn to the trading part of our book. You will learn how to trade using the fundamental market structure.

5
Basic Principles and Strategies for Trading Success

USING THE FUNDAMENTAL MARKET STRUCTURE TO TRADE THE MARKETS

A Trading Strategy that Works with Core Market Principles

The trading method that you will learn here is based on the fundamental market structure and its core elements. This method is, in itself, a kind of method of methods. It will enable you to use a multitude of trading approaches using only one basis.

You will be able to select from different trading systems based on different market strategies or perspectives. You will be able to trade the market alone without indicators, based only on the fundamental market structure. You can trade chartist patterns, using them in conjunction with the fundamental market structure. You can also trade, using moving averages or channels or bands or different kinds of mathematical indicators, such as stochastics or MACD, and in conjunction with the fundamental market structure.

This fundamental market structure gives you a finite number of elements that will be the tools of your trade. These elements, your market tools, are:

- Pivots
- Swings: simple and composite
- Triads: simple and complex
- Phases: trends, consolidations, turning points
- Patterns: tops, bottoms, triangles, channels, etc.
- Time and price cycles.

These tools will help you to define your trading strategy and tactics, your entry and exit points, your stops, and your risk control and money management systems. These tools are simple and precise. Precision trading and precision investment are natural consequences of the tools themselves. Simplicity here brings precision. Each tool can be identified without confusion by anyone.

Anyone can recognize a pivot or a swing or a triad. Anyone can recognize a phase or a pattern. They can be visually identified in a chart or in a spreadsheet. They can be expressed in chart format or spreadsheet format. They are geometrical or arithmetical. Once identified, they can be easily used. They do not need to be optimized, nor is it possible to optimize them. You recognize the tool, its actual position within market time and space, and use it, if the market tells you to.

Each tool has its precise trading function. Once you understand the function, you will be ready to use it.

Precision and simplicity are essential parts of our approach. Not having anything to optimize gives us a framework that forces us to trade well within it. Also, we must concentrate our trading on only one system with the fewest possible parameters.

Complex systems are theoretically possible. However, they are not humanly workable or practical. If simplicity can replace complexity, we should stay with simplicity. Simplicity brings precision. It is very difficult, if not impossible, to be precise with complex systems.

The fundamental market structure and its tools have additional trading features.

A Trading Strategy that Applies to All Markets

One consequence of a trading method that works with core market principles is its generality. It will work because of its own inner laws. It can do nothing, except follow its own rules. In other words, it will work in every market. This is due to the fact that every market follows, and is built on, the fundamental market structure. This structure offers us the same tools, irrespective of the market, since a market must conform to the rules of this structure.

Therefore, we can trade every market using the same tools and the same basic methods. We can trade stocks and stock indexes and different stock sectors. We can trade futures, commodities, or financial or agricultural stocks or stock indexes. We can trade any kind of free market imaginable.

There will be only one basic trading strategy: use the different tools that the market structure offers. Use pivots, swings, triads, market phases, market patterns, and time and price cycles and patterns. Each of these tools, as we will see later, has a very specific way to be used for trading. No guesswork is involved. Instead, there is a set of definite and precise rules to follow. These rules will always remain the same. No optimization or tweaking is needed.

A pivot will be used for trading in a number of specific ways. A triad also will be used in a specific number of ways. The same can be said for the rest of the other tools. This makes trading simple. It makes it simple and easier, but this does not mean that little work is required. Effort is needed to achieve simplicity and to use it effectively.

When something appears to be easy, it is only the visible part that we are seeing. Concealed behind it is hard work.

Although we can trade the market with exactly the same tools and in exactly the same way, these simple and relatively few tools present many combinations. This gives us the opportunity to choose. Our choices are quite numerous. They can depend on the market, as well as on the trader's personality, style, and specialization. This enables the trader to develop a multitude of systems within the same market strategy.

A trader can specialize in a given market and narrow it down to the smallest details of the personality of that market. He will recognize specific recurring behaviors that will give place to definite trading setups. Another trader may specialize in trading short-term swings, while another will trade a specific pattern within a swing, but always using the same general strategy – the fundamental market structure and one or more of its tools.

A Trading Strategy That Applies to All Time Periods

This general strategy applies to every kind of market and also to all time frames and time periods. The same strategy, in exactly the same way and using exactly the same tools, can be used to trade one-minute charted bars hourly charted bars, or any other intraday time frame. In other words, this strategy can be used for day trading.

This strategy can also be used without changes to trade end-of-day charts. The trader can use it for very short-term trades or medium-term trades within an end-of-day time frame. The same can be said of the weekly, monthly, and yearly time frames. All of them can be traded using the fundamental market structure and its tools. In each of these time frames, different ways of trading are possible.

With this general strategy of trading triads, many substrategies can be built within any time frame. A yearly time frame, or a monthly, weekly, daily, or an intraday time frame, can be traded with the same secondary strategy for the same market. This simplifies the task of trading different time frames. However, it is convenient for the trader to specialize in only one time frame, learning to recognize in it the personality of a given market and its subtleties. This specialization will simplify study and practice.

This general strategy is applicable not only to all time frames but also to every time period. The reason for this is that the fundamental market structure is the same and its laws always remain the same, regardless of time. Where there is a market, this structure will be present and functioning. This structure asks only that one condition be satisfied – that a market exists.

This enables you to know that you could have traded triads in the far past, that you can trade them in the present, and that you can trade them in the future. It would have been possible to trade triads in ancient Egypt, ancient Greece and Rome, seventeenth century Europe, or any other century. This way of trading is possible wherever markets are free.

We could have traded the stock market or other market in the same way in the 1920s or in any other year of the last century or this century. This is possible because the same causes have the same consequences. In this case, the fundamental market structure has been the cause of the market's behavior. This causes any market to act in the same way, whatever its era or time period. Consequently, a strategy based on the fundamental market structure is beyond any specific time and encompasses all periods.

The generality of this method goes beyond itself. Let us see how.

A TRADING STRATEGY THAT IS NOT EXCLUSIVE OF OTHER TRADING METHODS

This method is not only compatible with every time frame and time period but also with almost every trading or investing method known, whether technical or fundamental. Any method will be enhanced in conjunction with the trading triad methodology.

The triad methodology will give added precision when trading chartist patterns or mathematical indicators, such as moving averages, stochastics, MACD, etc. It will give the trader precise entry and exit signals. In addition, it will inform the trader who is ready to accept a signal within his own system whether the signal, such as a moving average crossover, is true or false.

In this last example, the trader will know if the crossover goes with the market's real direction or if it is only a reaction that is contrary to the direction of the market and should be avoided. The trader will also know that the crossover, in this case, is a false signal. Here is the sequence of pivots and swings that will tell the trader about the validity of his signal. If high and low pivots are ascending with their corresponding swings and are in the right position, he can act on the signal. If this is not the case, he is facing a false signal and must step aside. In summary, the fundamental market structure will enable him to recognize false signals in order to avoid taking action on them and to recognize true signals that he can act on.

This method's ability to recognize true signals and to avoid false signals is the reason why it is compatible with, and can be used in conjunction with, almost every other trading method or perspective. This ability to distinguish true from false signals comes from the fact that the method reintroduces qualitative critical points that the averages and other methods have eliminated to obtain their smoothing results.

Once again, the market and its structure become visible. It highlights in unique fashion its main components against the signals of the trading methods, used so that the former become transparent to the trader and appear as they truly are. This enables the trader or investor to trade all technical methods and setups that have as background the visible market structure that will validate or invalidate what he is about to do. This is true not only of methods that rely on technical analysis but also for methods that are rooted in fundamental analysis.

With fundamental analysis, you know when the price is right, based on its value as determined by such financial parameters as earnings growth, etc. However, a market may not be acting in accordance with fundamental values. This happens very often and an underpriced stock can remain underpriced for years and never reach a price that corresponds to its real value.

It is here that technical analysis and fundamental market structure come in. They will tell us if the market behavior is right to buy a fundamentally sound company. This structure and its method will give us the right timing. In addition, the fundamental market structure and the trading method that is the outcome of that structure will enable us to recognize if market conditions, as revealed by the fundamental structure of the market, endorse buying a fundamentally sound stock or selling short a fundamentally overpriced stock. In each case, whether you are using technical analysis, fundamental analysis, or both at the same time, the fundamental market structure will enhance your trading and investing decisions.

Trading triads, the trading method that will enable you to do this, is simple. Its simplicity is based on its strength.

A Trading Strategy That Does Not Depend on Complex Mathematics

The triad trading method is based on simple concepts and simple tools. The arithmetic and geometry behind them are profound, but easy to understand. The triad itself is a simple reversal structure that enables it to define pivots. The pivots defined by triads define the extremities of swings. The swings will alternate at different angles, which will determine whether we face a consolidation or a trend.

Points, lines, parallels, and angles are the geometric figures that define our tools. With them, we can build the market structure. We will also have growth, rate of change, linear and nonlinear, exponential and nonexponential, logarithmic and arithmetic elements. All of our geometrical elements can be expressed arithmetically with numbers. Pivots are specific price figures, angles are definite price increases or decreases, and lines are angles that follow specific growth patterns.

A spreadsheet will show our mathematical tools as numbers. A chart will express them as geometric forms – a point, a line, an angle. These, in turn, will form series of points, lines, or angles.

We have also vectors. They show us the direction of our lines. We have price vectors and time vectors.

All of these tools, numerical and geometrical, are easy mathematical elements that visually attract our sense of market reality. The market structure emerges as if by magic from the simple combination of these elements.

A deep intuitive sense of numbers and forms makes us sense the precision and truth of the information that we receive. This market truth becomes self-evident as soon as these points organize themselves in ordered series of pivots and the lines in ordered series of swings. These simple series combine in more structured phases and patterns and the market reveals its hidden structure and meaning.

Mathematics does not need to be complex to be useful. The opposite frequently occurs. Simplicity outsmarts complexity. We find many examples of this in the world of trading and investing.

This is the case with normal distribution curves. An average that is a measure of the central tendency within the curve will often obscure the facts, instead of telling things as they are. An example of this is a moving average. A moving average does not correspond to real prices, but to average prices – to prices that may not even exist. Also, it homogenizes prices, withdrawing essential information from them. Confronted by prices that do not exist and information that is withheld from us, our vision of the market becomes distorted. A market is made up of real prices, not averages. Averages are fiction.

Within a market, we do not have homogeneity, but diversity and structure. Not all prices are created equal. Some price points are more important than others. This will depend on their particular positions within market space at a given time. The visual inspection of such a structure will be hundreds of times more useful to us than an average. This is not to denigrate averages or other mathematical indicators, but to indicate their deficiency, which arises from their complexity. Averages do have a place as tools, but only when integrated into market reality and its simple elements.

As to indicators, we can say the same. The best of them are the simplest. One of the simplest types of indicator is the moving average. A simple moving average can become a very efficient tool when it adds market structure as background. In the markets, as well as in trading and investing, it seems that the best tools and strategies tend to be those that are the simplest. Simplicity always beats complexity.

This is why we will base our trading strategy wherever possible on the simplest of tools and on the simplest of strategies. The simpler your approach, the easier it will be to understand and to manage. Outstanding results in the market always come from simplicity. This is true of technical analysis as well as fundamental analysis. The best traders use only one system. This is true also of the best investors.

In technical analysis we have, as an example, the famous Turtles. They traded a simple Donchian system and became the best at doing so. In fundamental analysis, we have Warren Buffett, who invested on the basis of a simple earnings growth idea. All the rest flowed from it. So be simple, think simple, and trade simple.

Now, we will explore a key distinction that is essential in learning how to trade the difference between patterns and principles effectively.

THE DIFFERENCE BETWEEN PATTERNS AND PRINCIPLES

What is a Market Principle?

A market principle is a law that applies to every market and is at the core of market reality. A market principle is invisible. It cannot be seen. What we observe are simply the outward effects of market principles. An example of a fundamental market principle is the law of action and reaction. We know that every action has a reaction. This is also true in the markets. The opportunity to trade depends on it.

Here is another aspect of principles. They are necessary. The possibility to analyze or trade the markets depends on them. Without principles, no markets would exist and no traders or investors would be able to operate.

Returning to our principle of action and reaction, let us consider the consequences for markets. One consequence is that we would not have swings. In order to have swings, we need alternation and whoever says alternation is saying action and reaction. Without action and reaction, we could not buy low and sell high or vice versa. Without action and reaction, we would have no turning points or bull markets and bear markets. A turning point is the passage from action to reaction. A bear market is a reaction to a bull market and a bull market is a reaction to a bear market. Action and reaction.

This principle of action and reaction is probably the most powerful and useful market principle that we can have. It is a principle that deserves to be fully understood and constantly studied. It can be applied in a multitude of ways and in many circumstances. Many trading methods have been built upon this principle and many future methods will be built upon it. It is essential to focus on the principle of action and reaction to succeed in the markets.

Another powerful market principle is the principle of alternation. The market alternates between opposite poles that are like magnetic attractors. It is a principle of polarity. Market energy oscillates between two poles. This principle manifests itself, for example, in the polarities of low and high, volatile and nonvolatile, large and small, etc.

This principle of alternation or polarity tells us the way in which market energy is flowing. If market prices are at their lowest extremes, they will go higher. If the market has extremely low volatility, it will move towards greater volatility. The same will happen in the opposite direction, from higher prices to lower prices and from higher volatility to lower volatility.

Having explained what market principles are, let us discuss what a pattern is.

What is a Pattern?

A pattern is a specific figure market structure that occurs within a phase. For instance, a triangle is a pattern. Triangles can develop within trends and consolidations.

A triangle is a shape that can be found in many chart configurations. Triangles can be of many kinds. We find small triangles within trends that indicate an explosive move is near. We find ascending and descending triangles, and large and small triangles. Similarly, we have pennants and flags. They also can be ascending and descending, each with a specific meaning. A bottom is another kind of pattern, which can be simple, double, triple, or multiple. A specific kind of behavior is attributed to each.

All of these patterns have visibility in common. They have shapes that can be observed. Their shapes give clues to the behavior of market participants. For instance, a triple bottom tells us that a strong buying support zone is developing. This hints that market prices are already low enough for market participants to develop buying interest. It also gives us a clue to the value of such prices. The prices could be undervalued.

The same can be said of tops – simple, double, triple, or multiple – but in the opposite sense. They tell us that a selling resistance zone is developing and that prices are overvalued or that market participants perceive them as being overvalued.

Channels, for example, exist when prices are in a range. A range can have different angles. Ranges can be horizontal, ascending, or descending. Prices will go from one boundary of the channel to the other. In channels, prices will alternate between extremes. This tells us that prices are contained within limits. Market participants are ready to buy and sell, but only within a given limited range. Prices slowly seek their balance as they flow from boundary to boundary.

Flags have something in common with channels. A flag is a channel that develops as a consolidation phase emerging from a trend. If the flag is descending, the market supposedly should break up. If, on the contrary, the flag is ascending, the market could break out on the downside. Flags are really consolidations that can have a trending component within them. They are a kind of consolidating reaction.

This reactive component is what makes flags incline downward in uptrends and upward in downtrends. It is also the reason why they break in the direction opposite to their inclination. Flags are an indication that market participants consider that prices are momentarily too high and should go a bit lower, although not much. This is why the price perception of market participants is held within a range. This means that they are ready to sell if the price rises beyond a certain number of points, but ready to buy if the price falls by more than a certain number of points, although not by so many. This is why prices are bounded within a range.

We have many other patterns like those that we have mentioned. It is sufficient to say that they are shapes that designate a type of market behavior.

Now, we will explore the difference between patterns and principles.

Why Market Patterns Are Not the Same as Market Principles

It is essential that you understand the difference between market principles and market patterns. Patterns are the outward side of principles. Behind every pattern, a principle is at work. We must always be on the lookout for the active principle behind the pattern.

Although principles shape patterns, they go far beyond them. We will find them acting behind market structures in ways that are not always defined as shapes when they appear. For example, the vibrational rate of market swings will be expressed by a number, rather than by a shape. This vibration rate is a principle. It will configure the oscillatory rhythm of a market.

The same can be said of the principle of action and reaction. It will not be embodied in a specific shape. Its nature is sequential. A strong bull market should engender a bear market of commensurate force.

The principle of alternation or polarity is the same. It does not necessarily embody itself within a shape. It indicates a pendular movement between two poles. An example is the alternating movements of swings. Swings oscillate between opposite directions. A swing goes in one direction and is followed by another swing in the opposite direction. They alternate indefinitely and in doing so manifest the principle of law of alternation. High volatility is followed by low volatility and vice versa. This is another example of the principle of alternation.

Another principle is the law of balance. When prices are balanced, we have consolidation phases. The consolidation phase will have a visible pattern, such as a channel or a series of tops or bottoms. This visible side is not the principle, nor is the market structure, which, in this case, is the consolidation phase, which gives it birth. The operative principle behind the channel, and even behind the consolidation phase that is embodied in it, will be the law of balance.

Another market principle is the law of imbalance. In its invisibility, it is the active cause of many market events. In the same way that the law of balance creates a static kind of market event, such as a consolidation, the principle of unbalance creates market movement. A trend is the phase that expresses this law.

The law of balance tends to eliminate all movement, the market then becoming static. In contrast, the principle of unbalance creates movement, since it attempts to fill a void. The movement lasts until the void is filled. This is why, when the market consolidates, one can say that it is in a horizontal range and is momentarily in balance. It becomes a static market since it is not actively moving, as when it is an upward or downward trend. In consolidations the market goes nowhere, with the same prices repeating along its horizontal range. Such a market is in balance for a while, until a trend starts.

Market movement would be unthinkable without a state of active disequilibrium, which pushes or pulls the market in a given direction. A dynamic unbalance is what moves the market forward.

In these examples, we have shown the difference between patterns and principles. We have explained how principles are the laws that operate behind market phases and market patterns. Phases and patterns are embodiments of market principles that go far beyond them.

Let us now discuss how to use these market laws and the patterns that they control.

How to Use Market Patterns and Market Principles to Create Sound Trading Methods

When market principles are known, market phases are understood. When market phases are understood, market patterns become meaningful. Then, markets can be traded. Why? The reason is simple. Market principles are universal. As they are universal, they always work. Their truth is fact beyond statistics and tests. A market principle or market law is always true.

Market laws embody the more general law of cause and effect. The real cause behind the market structure behavior and even behind the market participants' behavior are the market laws. The market laws are the cause. The market structure with its phases and patterns is the effect. This is an example of the law of causality.

Real causes belong to a level different from the level of their effects. The market principles that are invisible and immaterial, made of mind stuff, are the real cause of visible market phenomena. In addition, by learning to manipulate the market's laws, we learn to manipulate market events. This is a shortcut. Instead of trading market structure or phases or patterns, we will directly trade market principles.

The advantage is their core reality. They are always true. When the market gives a visible sign that an invisible law is acting behind, we go with the law. We can never go wrong. It is easier. This does not mean that we must not test. We must always test. However, knowing the principle that is behind market action enables us to know why the market will act in a given way.

Sometimes the market does not act as we expect. A principle can be overcome by a stronger one – or its effect can be less than we thought. However, this is seldom the case. In all instances, the principle will be there, even if its intensity disables our trading scenario. More often than not, the market will follow the principle and our trades will generally be successful. It cannot be otherwise if we follow market principles. This is why you must learn to see principles and learn to trade principles.

Most traders are too concerned with market appearances, phases, patterns, and setups and do not develop the habit of looking first and always at the principles behind all market phases, forms, and events. Make a habit of recognizing market laws – always. Then you can trade.

An Example of the Advantage of Working with Principles

To make our point about the importance of market laws or principles as tools to trade the markets, let us look at some practical examples of trading with them. For our first example, we will forget all that we know about technical analysis and fundamental analysis. Let us assume that all you know about markets is the principle of action and reaction. You only know one market law, the law of action and reaction, and you have decided to trade with it.

This is what might happen:

- At first you are not even thinking about a given trade. You know that, in a particular sector, mining, there is eager buying and inflation of stock prices. You have witnessed huge falls in the past after such overly enthusiastic buying.
- Suddenly, there is a market collapse and the mining sector stocks come crashing down. Many lose 70 % or more of their value.

- Time goes on. A few months pass and the market does not recover. You remember that when this happened in the past the market in the mining sector experienced a huge rise after a period that ranged from one year to a few years.
- Therefore, you arm yourself with courage and buy the five biggest stocks in the mining sector and decide to hold them until the huge rise comes again.
- After one and a half years, there is an enormous rise in the mining sector stocks. You sell and pocket your profit.

Why you did this? We assume that you are not a professional trader. You simply were aware of the mining sector, perhaps had friends who worked in it, and live in a mining environment. Near your home town is a well-known mine. You did this because you knew that big market collapses in the mining sector are followed by enormous short-lived rises. In summary, you had a feeling for the law of action and reaction and acted on it. In your past experience, when the mining market sector had a significant drop, it always recovered sooner or later with a proportional, significant rise. Action and reaction.

Here you are not trading with knowledge of technical and fundamental analysis. You knew nothing about triads and the fundamental market structure. Also, let us assume that you are financially illiterate and knew nothing about the company's finances. You simply had the good sense to buy the five companies that had the greatest equity among the group. You did this to diversify. The five big ones cannot all go wrong at the same time. Also, you invested a small amount of your savings – no more than 30 %. You succeeded because of your ingrained sense of the law of action and reaction due to past experience. This same law also helped you to control your risk and manage your money. You knew that you could win big, but you also knew people who had lost big.

Once more, big wins – big losses – action and reaction. Therefore, you diversified and invested a small amount. You did all of this, using a single market law.

This example is not given with the intention of giving you a way to trade. It is intended only to give you a practical example of the workings of the law of action and reaction. Although I know of people who actually trade in this way, it is not the way you should trade. To trade using this law, you also should have knowledge of the fundamental market structure and risk control and money management techniques.

The random trader in our example used good risk control and money management skills. He diversified among five companies, the strongest ones, and used only a percentage of his equity to invest intuitively. Although his intuition was correct, study and planning are needed in real trading to succeed. It is the only way in which you will be able to trade successfully.

The lesson here is about the practical power of principles. It is possible in fact to trade only the law of action and reaction. The results are powerful. They come from the invisible core of market action.

Now we are ready for our trading strategy.

BASIC TRADING STRATEGY

Engineering the Trading Strategy

Now we will learn how to trade using the fundamental market structure. The first thing we must know is that knowledge of market behavior is hardly enough to be able to trade, let alone trade well. Trading is a complete activity that includes, as one of its elements, market knowledge. The other elements of sound trading are money management, risk control, a trading plan, a trading system or method, and awareness of the psychological side of trading.

All of these elements are so interrelated that it is not possible to take them apart and succeed. Money management, for instance, will be affected by our market structure knowledge and both, together, will condition trading results. Therefore, our first rule for engineering a sound trading strategy is to take into account all elements and integrate them into a single whole. Never, ever, trade before doing this. Learn to integrate everything before you trade. You will be years ahead of the competition.

Here is the list of things that we need before we will be ready to trade:

- A set of trading principles.
- A model of the fundamental market structure.
- A set of trading rules: entries, exits, setups.
- A set of risk control tools: price stops, time stops, money management stops, market structure stops. You may choose one or many.
- A set of money management tools: position sizing, diversification, asset allocation, margin of safety, trading system ratios.
- A set of trading systems: market structure-based, indicator-based, volatility-based, etc.
- A set of psychological tools: confidence builders, emotional control method.
- A plan that combines all of the above.

These elements are indispensable. It is not possible to abandon any of them. All of them must be integrated. Each will exercise its influence upon the others. The interrelationships must be considered.

To engineer a trading strategy, it is essential to know how each element within a specific trading plan interrelates with the others. For example, stop placement will differ according to the trading system. If a system is based on market structure, its stops will not be placed in the same way or locations as the ones for a system that is based on mathematical indicators. The same can be said of our entry strategy. It will differ according to the market model behind the system. A market structure model, such as ours, will differ greatly from a fully indicator-based model.

The same applies to money management. Market structure will define position sizing differently from a system that is based only on indicators.

The trader's psychology can also be affected by the kind of model that he uses. It is one thing to have a market structure-based model in which market action becomes visible and quite another thing to trade a system that is based on a faith in statistics.

The lesson here is that all elements interrelate and that we need them all, the entire list, before we begin to trade. Now that we have our list, let us review it.

Foundational Principles of the Trading Method

The first building stones of our trading method are its trading principles. We have already explained what they are and how they work. Now we will itemize the principles that we will use as our main trading tools.

These principles can be used alone to trade the markets. Also, many trading systems can be constructed on them. However, the right way to use them is in combination with market structure elements and money management and risk control tools.

We will now list our first trading tools, the trading principles or market laws:

- The law of vibration
- The law of action and reaction
- The law of alternation
- The law of balance
- The law of dynamic unbalance
- The law of inertia.

These are our market laws. Here is how to use them.

The Law of Vibration

Each market has its own vibrational key, its rate of vibration. Market swings will vibrate in accordance with this law. This vibration will be known by certain numbers that repeat. For example, if a descending swing has a length that repeats regularly (e.g., it has happened twice per month for many months), the length has a number. This number gives you the vibration rate.

This number has given you a key vibration. Thus, you decide to trade it. As soon as a downswing appears that arrives at that number, you will buy it. As soon as the market turns around and the correction has nearly ended, you will sell it.

Let us say that a correction swing that repeats according to a vibrational key number corrects nine points. You have your vibrational number, nine. As soon as you see a swing correcting around this value, you will buy it. As soon as the correction has neared its end, you will sell it.

This is only an example and is not intended for actual trading. In order to trade it, all of the other elements of a sound trading plan are required. This is for illustrative purposes only. It shows that the law of vibration can be traded.

The Law of Action and Reaction

An example of how to trade this law was given previously. If a strong market correction occurs, another strong movement in the opposite direction should end the correction. Strong actions breed strong reactions.

You can trade strong market movements, taking the opposite side once the strong market movement has already occurred, knowing that the markets will react as strongly in the opposite direction. This is how to use the law of action and reaction.

In our example, you buy a market correction that, by its strength, has never or rarely occurred during the last few years. An equally strong contrary move should end the correction.

We must repeat that you should not attempt to trade this law without the other trading elements being present.

The Law of Alternation

This is the law of alternating sequences. For example, a consolidation follows a trend, then a turning point follows the consolidation, then a reverse trend follows the turning point, then a consolidation, then a turning point, and then another trend again in the initial direction. A practical application of this principle of alternation might be to buy a consolidation at a market low knowing that it will be followed by a trend. This is what Ted Warren did and he made a fortune doing it. He bought long consolidations.[14]

Again, we must warn you that this is only an example. There are better ways to trade the same law, as, for instance, waiting for the consolidation to break in accordance with all the market structure rules.

The Law of Balance

Markets move in search of a balance point. Sometimes, markets turn around that balance point and are bound within a horizontal range, not doing anything otherwise. This is what we call a consolidation.

If the range of contrary fluctuations around this balancing horizontal line is large enough, it will be possible to trade the boundaries created by the balancing point that acts as the magnet that holds the horizontal pendular movements within the range. We then buy the support boundary of the consolidation channel and sell the resistance. Another trading strategy is to simply use those moments to avoid the market and stay on the sidelines. This last strategy is often the best one.

Once again, this is only intended as an example of how to use the law of balance in our trading action.

The Law of Dynamic Nonbalance

Here, movement occurs as a rupture of equilibrium. A new balance must be sought. The market moves to its new equilibrium point. This is how trends are born. Price and perceived value break out of their former balance.

A new balance point between value and price is created and the market rushes to fill it: a trend. With the balance point having been reached, the disequilibrium ceases to exist, until it also is broken and a new movement begins.

Breakouts are ruptures of the balance point. From that starting point, a movement proceeds until it finds its new equilibrium or balance. This new movement has direction. It is nonrandom. It has a dynamic nonbalance. We can think of it as a controlled forward fall.

It is a homeodynamic movement, which differs from a homeostatic one. During its fall, when balance has been lost, it follows a path that has a moving center of balance. The nonbalance is dynamic and within the boundaries that guide it. Equilibrium is not fully lost. It guides the movement.

Trends, upward and downward, are examples of this. To trade them, as soon as equilibrium is broken and balance is lost, we jump on to the trend and follow it.

Once again, this way of trading a controlled loss of balance must be done in accordance with all of the other market structure rules and trading rules.

The Law of Inertia

This law tells us that a market movement or phase will continue until a force stops and alters the phase. A consolidation will carry on until something causes it to break. A trend will continue unless something stops it.

According to this law, we can expect a market movement to continue until something stops it. This is the principle behind jumping on to a trend and expecting it to continue. It will continue because of the principle of inertia.

If the law of dynamic nonbalance is necessary to start the movement, the law of inertia is what makes the movement continue until the end. We buy a trend because the balance has been broken and we expect that the new balance point will not be reached immediately. This gives us a chance to profit from the trend.

Thus, we have our set of general market laws or principles upon which we will build our trading. We will use them to trade in accordance with the fundamental market structure. We will now explain our trading method based on triads and all of the foregoing.

Where to Initiate a Trade According to Triads

A trade is based on our market laws or principles. These principles will act in every market phase. This means that we will act in a specific market phase as soon as a sound market law tells us to do so. Any trade will be initiated in a trend, a consolidation, or a turning point. In each of these cases, we will work in conjunction with a market principle and with the rules of the fundamental market structure.

We trade these three phases as follows.

Trading Trends

When there is a trend, we will take the trend based on the different market laws. The law of vibration asks us to know the lengths of different trends. This study will give us a vibratory key that will tell us the possible price length and time length of the type of trend that we are about to trade. We must measure all former trends to find the magnitude that interests us. Also, we should study the conditions of its development.

The law of action and reaction asks us to study the significant trends and to classify them by significance. Do not expect a secular bull market to begin from a simple market correction of a few points. In practical terms, this means that we must take a trend after an opposite direction trend that we expect will be commensurate in strength and duration with the new trend. For instance, if we want to enter a secular bull market, we will have a better chance if we buy after a secular bear market. This is the law of action and reaction. We must expect the reaction to be equivalent to the action.

The law of alternation asks us to expect upswings and downswings during a trend. In this case, we will buy a corrective swing – if we buy a trend – in order to minimize our risk. Alternatively, we may buy a swing in the direction of the trend, in which case we must make provision for a correction.

The law of balance tells us not to enter a trend trade by buying a consolidation. Many people buy multiyear consolidations thinking that the market is bound to go up. It seldom does. Do not trade against principles.

The law of dynamic nonbalance tells us the opposite of the law of balance. Enter a trend only when a balance has broken. A trend is essentially a state of dynamic nonbalance. Do not go against it. Use balance breakout to get in. For instance, if a consolidation breaks into a trend, then get on board.

The law of inertia asks us to take a trend if it is bound to continue. You will know this by applying the law of vibration to tell you the range that a trend should have as a reaction to its contrary previous trend. Essentially, the law of inertia asks you to avoid obstacles. Inertia is nullified by obstacles. As long as there are no obstacles on the horizon, a trend should continue. These obstacles are old resistance or old support.

Expect a trend to slow as it approaches old strong support or resistance. This is where reactions do occur.

Trading Consolidations

The law of vibration tells you that you should measure consolidations. They can be classified by their lengths. A few good length numbers should be found. Then the law of alternation tells you that consolidations are followed by trends.

Because profitable trading requires a movement strong enough to be profitable, here is where the law of action and reaction comes in. Long consolidations give birth to long trends. Thus, you should favor long consolidations as Ted Warren did.

The law of balance tells you to wait while the consolidation continues. The law of dynamic nonbalance tells you to enter the market only when the balance of the consolidation is broken and an unstable state takes over the market. This is the breakout point, which tells you that a long trend could be forming.

The law of inertia tells you that a consolidation will last until it breaks out. More importantly, it tells you not to enter during the consolidation since the latter could last for a very long time, until something breaks its state of equilibrium.

In summary, all of the laws tell you to wait until a consolidation breaks before trending and that consolidations, especially if long, are good waiting signals for you to look for an entry opportunity. A waiting signal is market behavior, which tells you that a trading opportunity will present itself at any moment. Therefore, you must be alert and wait attentively until it arrives. For example, if the market has been in a horizontal range for a while, a breakout of the range could happen at any moment. You must now wait for that breakout to occur in order to be able to buy it.

Trading Turning Points

Turning points are traded like consolidations. All of the market laws apply in almost the same way. Turning points have numbers that you can find, applying the law of vibration. How long they last and how many tops or bottoms they have are the issues for which such figures can be found. This enables you to choose the most suitable turning point function of your trading system.

The law of action and reaction tells you that strong and long trends tend to have strong and long turning points. Remember that a turning point is a consolidation at the end of a movement. The difference is that it presents itself as having a top or bottom.

The law of alternation tells you that, after a trend, either a consolidation or a turning point will materialize.

The law of balance tells you that, at turning points, the market is momentarily in a state of balance or indecision. This is why you must not trade turning points at their beginning or their middle, but only at the end.

This is the difference between a turning point and a simple consolidation. The turning point includes the reversal. You do not trade a breakout of a turning point, but the reversal that has already begun within it.

This is where the law of dynamic nonbalance comes in. When the turning point has actually turned and the market is actually pointed in the direction opposite from where it came from is when you take the trade. You do not trade a breakout, but a reversal.

Having studied the main market and trading laws or principles, and how they apply to trade each market phase, let us now become specific and explain exactly where to enter or exit the market.

The Precise Buying and Selling Point

The fundamental market structure and its three constitutive elements – the pivot, the triad, and the swing – give a precise and unique buying point and a precise and unique selling point. Entries and exits are always executed within a triad.

When you sell or when you buy, you should sell or buy a triad. The reason is that the triad defines the pivot that ends every swing. Without a triad, no swing can be defined between two pivots. Every swing is contained between two triads. The triad is the turning point of the swing. The swing can be simple or complex. It can be a small or very large movement. It does not matter. You will always find two triads, one at the beginning and one at the end.

Because the triad is the natural turning point of the market, initiating your trade at the closing bar of a triad gives you the minimal reversal amount for a new movement to begin in a new direction. The new movement has already begun at that last closing bar. This new movement that begins at the close of a triad is the seed of the movement that will follow. Taking the movement at this point not only maximizes your chances of going with the new market direction but also minimizes your risk.

Minimal risk comes from the fact that the turning point is at its beginning. So the distance between your entry and the low or high of the market at that point is the distance between the close of the triad and the center bar of the same triad. If you place a stop when trading a triad, you would place it at the pivot of the central bar of the triad. This gives you minimal trading risk and a natural stop placement location.

When trading triads, your entry point could, of course, be at the opening of the next bar after the close of the triad. Also, the stop could be at a previous pivot point, instead of the one on the triad on which you initiated the trade. However, the above are only variations and adjustments that will follow with practice. The entry point is the close of the triad and the stop is generally at the extreme pivot of the triad.

The important thing that must be emphasized is that your buying and selling points are given by the market itself, since the triad is its main turning point element. This is why the third bar of a triad generally has a higher probability of continuing with the new market direction than the opposite.

The same entry rule applies to simple and complex triads. You always buy the final bar of the triad at its close. You buy the final bar of ascending triads at their close and you sell short the final bar of a descending triad at its close.

Now, take a chart. Identify 25 triads. Count the number of times that each triad follows its new direction. Do this before continuing to read. As a further exercise, apply all the general market principles to the triad behavior that you have observed in your sample.

The Results to Expect

If you have done the previous exercise, you already have confirmed how triads work and you may even have discovered some interesting things. You have experienced the advantage of having a precise and unique entry and exit rule that does not need to be optimized. A triad is a triad and there is nothing that you can do to change it, even if you want to.

Also note that the entry and exit points are unchangeable. A triad is not a triad until the close of its final bar. Thus, to use a triad as an entry or exit, you can do nothing but enter at the closing bar or wait for that closing bar if, for practical reasons, you choose to enter at the opening of the next bar. Not only can you not optimize triads, but there is nothing that you can do to change your entry or exit point. This also cannot be optimized.

A consequence of this is that you are obliged to find a triad whatever trading system or approach you use within the fundamental market structure method of trading triads. This is a constraint that the nature of the market forces on you. It is a constraint only if you want to begin a trade at the minimal reversal point and minimal risk point as defined by the market structure. However, what may seem to be a constraint is, in fact, liberating.

When you find your triad, you will have found an adequate spot to begin a trade – a location that is based on a market structure that will always be the same and that defines reversals and engenders pivots. This is the nearest that you can get to selling a low and buying a high. By constraining you, triads have enabled you to think about other things within your system without having to worry any more about the precise entry or exit point, regardless of the state of the market.

Your entry with a triad will always be at the end of a previous movement and at the beginning of the following movement. Also, your entry will always be after the market has minimally reversed. To add to this, your entry will always be near a pivot. Being near a pivot is being at a relatively significant turning point, as near as possible to the beginning of the new movement and as near as possible to a point where a stop can be placed and a trade can be exited with minimal risk, if wrong.

This brings us to the subject of failed triads. As you have already observed, if you have done the previous exercise, after the close of the final bar of a triad, it happens that occasionally the market reverses at the next bar and does not continue in the direction signaled by the triad. In this case, it is not the triad that has failed, but our trade. The market reversed, because a triad includes the reversal. What happened is that the reversal did not follow through.

This happens and will always happen. It is unavoidable. However, the market usually will do what the triad signaled. This is an edge in trading. Most triads, in their simplicity, do work. Like everything else, you must learn to use them. Then, practice will make you better.

The triad method is a toolbox with a few simple tools that are generated by the market itself. They can be used in a staggering number of ways. Your imagination is the only limit. Let us continue learning how to use them.

6
The Key Buying and Selling Patterns

WAITING PATTERNS

Preparing the Ground: The Triad Trading System

To trade the first step you must know in advance what to trade, and also have a plan with all of its elements ready – a system to trade, money management, risk control, and psychological rules. However, before the plan is organized, you need a trading system that works. The system can be discretionary or automatic. It can use only the market structure or can rely only on indicators or can be a combination of the two.

Our method is based only on trading the fundamental market structure or trading indicators on the fundamental market structure rules, phases, and patterns. In both cases, the fundamental market structure is the primary trading tool. It is important to know this before looking for market opportunities to trade. Let us have a look at both perspectives, the discretionary and the automatic.

A discretionary approach to trading is not systematic. It consists of identifying what you think is a market opportunity based on your market knowledge – and making the trade. Nothing prevents you from having this knowledge and using it successfully. This can only be achieved by testing. You must be sure that a setup generally works with the odds on your side. This implies that you have a system. Therefore, the successful discretionary trader is really not discretionary.

From the outside, the discretionary successful trader seems to be discretionary. In fact, he knows that given setups do work, has tested them, and uses different ones at different times. So he does have a system, or rather many systems, but all are automatic. Let us go further and define what automatic means in a trading system. Automatic means taking all signals. In a discretionary system, you take only the signals that you want. This is why some traders override their systems' signals at times.

In automatic trading systems, you do not choose your signals. This means that you do not choose when to buy or sell since it is the system that chooses for you. In discretionary trading, the trader selects his trades according to his own criteria, knowledge, intuition, etc. This means that there is conflict between automatic and discretionary that is ultimately a conflict between being able to choose and not being able to choose. What often happens in practice is that traders override the signals of their own automatic systems. Overriding a system that is meant to be automatic usually brings catastrophic results, although not in all cases. This is a different approach in which the meaning of automatic and discretionary are justified, but in relation to a given specific system that you override when it is obvious that the signal is wrong for you.

Overriding a system usually is not the thing to do, unless your market knowledge of general conditions tells you to do so. This is seldom the case. You are much better off trading a system automatically and relying on your risk control rules to protect you.

What you need to do is to study a trading setup with an entry and exit that will put the odds in your favor, and then always trade this setup in exactly the same way. When the conditions are present, you will not need to override your system. This is possible due to the fundamental market structure and the simplicity of the tools used to trade triads. This is why the triads trading system is automatic, not because it takes all of the signals, but because it takes all of the signals that are confirmed by the fundamental market structure.

This implies that the system is always observing the market as it is now and avoiding false signals within the limits of the possible. The system is discretionary when it is built up, because the trader chooses what to trade, but at the same time it is automatic in its execution. Once the conditions of the system have been defined by the fundamental market structure and the trader has tested them to verify that the odds are in his favor, he will automatically trade the same setup whenever it appears.

Let us now examine the different possible setups indicated by the fundamental market structure.

Choosing the Phase for the Trading Setup

The triads system can be built upon three kinds of setups that are suggested by the market itself – trends, consolidations, and turning points. Each of them has its own approach and uses one or more market principles in combination with the fundamental market structure trading rules.

Therefore, as a first step, you must choose the kind of setup that your trading system will use. You can trade trends. You can trade consolidations and you can trade turning points.

Trading trends means jumping in while a trend is ongoing. This type of trading consists of entering the trend at a reaction swing after the market resumes the trend.

Trading consolidations means to either trade the upper resistance and lower support levels of the consolidation or trade the breakout of the consolidation, which then becomes part of trading a trend.

Trading turning points is trading reversals, usually around tops and bottoms, minor and major – for instance, trading the reversal of a swing for a minor one and trading the reversal of a bull or bear market for a major one. For this, it is necessary to observe the behavior of the different phases and choose the one that you want to trade:

- Trends. Identify the trends that have taken place during one year, and their lengths in time and price. Then, identify the trends that have lasted less than one year and more than one year. This will give you an idea of the length in time and price of the main swings. Study them in the daily, weekly, and monthly charts. Begin with the monthly charts and work backward. Also, study the time intervals between significant trends and identify the consolidations that take place within the trend.
  - Consolidations. Identify the consolidations that last less than a year and also more than a year.
  - Turning points. Examine all the simple tops, double tops, and triple tops occurring during the year under study. Give attention to their price range and how long they last before the reversal occurs.
  - Exercise. Take a monthly chart and identify eight trends that have lasted less than three months, less than six months, less than one year, and more than one year. Also, study them in the weekly and daily charts. Do the same with consolidations and turning points. Write down your observations.

Once you have studied the three market phases, you must choose one of them to prepare your trading system. Choose to trade short-term, medium-term, or long-term trends, turning points or consolidations:

- Exercise. Based on the preceding exercise, choose the type of trend that you want to trade. Study its price range from beginning to end and its duration. Choose a trend that lasts less than a year.

Wait Until Ready

Having defined what you are going to trade, you must then wait for the phase you intend to trade. This requires learning to wait and never acting before it is time. This waiting period can be long or short. If you are trading short-term trends, you will have a few during a year, and the waiting period will not be long. However, a secular bull or bear market can take quite a while. Even their turning points take time to develop.

It is easy to trade anything at any moment just because you want action. This is always a losing proposition. Your trading setup must be fully identified and tested before you trade it. This excludes trading anything in between. Many apparently good opportunities will pass while you define your trading strategy, tactics, and setup. You must let them pass. It is part of your training.

In summary, it is imperative that you do no trading while you are building your trading system, its strategy, and tactics. You must take your time to study the market and refine your system.

Refining your system will begin with a rough estimate of the behavior of the market phase that you have decided to trade. Once you have this estimate, a refining period must follow and more extensive testing must be done. All of this takes time. You must abandon forever the idea that your system, even with the most simple of setups, will be ready immediately for you to trade. Arriving at a robust trading proposition will take you at least a couple of months, if not much longer. As in any business, there must be preparation and testing time.

Later, in another chapter, we will come back to the subject of building a trading system and, more importantly, a trading plan. This is not our concern at the moment. We are simply at the trading tools definition and use step.

The reason why we have proceeded with this subject is to warn you about rashly trading the tools that we are presenting in this chapter. First, you must fully understand the tools that you use and only then must you build them into something useful.

Before we continue, I want to warn you about an especially dangerous market phase.

The Tunnel of Death

This occurs within the consolidation phase. Consolidation phases can be the death of a trader. When you buy a consolidation before it ends, you are losing time and money that could be used in better ways. Also, consolidation periods are highly indecisive and the time involved in staying in them does not justify the risk of staying. It is better to stay out of consolidations.

The long horizontal range consolidations are dangerous. For the trader, it is like entering a tunnel in which everything is in a state of suspended animation. Nothing happens. Although it helps that nothing is there, the risk increases with time. This is why long-range consolidations are the 'tunnels of death.' Nothing happens while they last and it is like being dead. Avoid them.

Equally deadly are the short consolidations, such as those that appear within a trend before it resumes. They also must be avoided. They are equally lethal.

This is why consolidations, large or small, within trends or turning points, should only be traded at their breakout point, once the market comes to life again. Not only will you avoid unnecessary risk and time in the market, but also your profitable trades will increase. Breakouts are the real way to trade consolidations. In a breakout, we wait for the consolidation to end and for the market to initiate a new movement. Here, you must be aware of false breakouts.

False breakouts occur very frequently. Most inexperienced traders buy or sell a breakout of a consolidation to see their trade fail and the market fall again within the consolidation range. The way to avoid false consolidation breakouts is by using the fundamental market structure. As you will see later in this chapter, the fundamental market structure will enable you to buy or sell a consolidation breakout with a high probability that the new movement has begun in earnest.

The principle behind a true breakout is that the new market movement has really begun, using the accumulated energy of the consolidation period. The balance has been broken and a trend is developing. To apply this principle means to buy a consolidation breakout only when the trend, to which the consolidation has given rise by breaking its balance, has already begun. This means buying later rather than sooner. Do not buy the breakout as soon as it occurs. Instead, give it time to develop.

It is the fundamental market structure that will tell you when to buy this kind of breakout, as you will soon see within this chapter.

It is There, but Still Not Ripe

Buying consolidation breakouts too soon brings us to another subject before we deal with buying and selling setups. This subject concerns buying a market phase or pattern before its time. Here you must distinguish between false signals and getting in too early. Many supposedly false signals are nothing but getting in too early by taking a signal that is not one at all.

A true signal is validated by the fundamental market structure. When a consolidation breakout is bought according to the triad method, what seems to be a breakout is excluded and will not be traded. Some of these trades taken on a true signal will fail, but this is because the best of market setups do fail from time to time. In this case of a failure, you have a false signal. With the triad method, you will have false signals, but to a lesser degree.

The lesson here is that you must always wait for confirmation of the triad before taking any trade or signal. This jumping into the market too soon happens not only with consolidations but also with trends and turning points. The getting-in-too-soon syndrome crops up here for the same reasons as before. It happens because you have not waited for definite confirmation by the market. This is why people jump into trends too soon, buy or sell at turning points too soon, and buy or sell patterns before the time is ready.

This is why you must always wait for definite market confirmation before entering a trade. It is better to get in later than too early. Get in later when the market has given robust indication of its new behavior. This new behavior of the market is not its future behavior. There is no need to forecast the future. All you need to know is that the market phase that you need is already there and working.

One reason to use the fundamental market structure when trading is to have definite confirmation from the market itself that the new movement has begun. It prevents you from entering the market too soon. The idea of entering the market too soon is the same as that which lurks behind, trying to sell tops and buy bottoms. Waiting for the top to sell or the bottom to buy is a losing proposition in all cases. Instead of waiting for a top or bottom, the thing to do when trading trends, for example, is to get a chunk of the action. You do not need to enter exactly at the beginning of the movement and exit exactly at the end to have a reasonable profit.

Triads and the fundamental market structure are your best protection against entering the market too soon. Triads enable you to enter the market at the right moment for any kind of phase or pattern that you decide to trade. This will enable you to trade with the odds in your favor and with the minimum possible number of false signals.

Vehicle Selection

When trading triads and the fundamental market structure, it is important to take into account vehicle selection. Vehicle selection is one of our most important choices. This selection is more important than precise timing. Choosing the right stock, which is in the correct market phase, is a key decision. This key decision has more importance than the exact entry or exit point when buying or selling that chosen stock.[15]

When trading stocks, it is important to identify the leading and more active stocks of the best performing sectors. Also choose among them the ones that trend better and with better profit ratios than other stocks. The same applies when selecting from a wider range of vehicles, such as stocks, commodities, currencies, bonds, etc.

In addition to vehicle selection, when trading triads and market structure we must consider the market's general conditions.

General Conditions and Economics

This is the open secret of successful trading and investing. Above all else, general conditions rule the markets. Before entering a trade, you must wait for the right general conditions of the market to be in place.

This is why a master trader, such as Jesse Livermore, gave such importance to general conditions. This is also why W. D. Gann, one of the greatest market theoreticians of all time, tells us to first assess the general behavior of the market, that is, its general conditions.[16] This is the most overlooked aspect of the market. Very few people look at general conditions and realize the truth about the market. Perhaps almost no one does this because of the inherent simplicity of this truth. General conditions are in plain view, in front of us and asking to be looked at.

The best way to know general conditions is to look at your charts and to have the right economic perspective. Looking at your charts will tell you more about what is going on in the markets than anything else.

Have a look at the indexes, the S&P 500, the Dow Jones Industrial, and the NASDAQ. If you trade stocks, do not go against them. Have a look at the stock sectors to assess their behavior. Keep an eye on interest rates and on commodities, especially the price of oil and gold.

The above will give you an idea of general conditions within the markets and the economy. Always give priority to what your charts tell you rather than to what the theoretical economists tell you about the economy. While the charts always tell the truth about what is happening, economists at most can hypothesize about the causes of a given market behavior. There is no hard and fast rule for the market behavior, and economists are wrong more often than not. The reason for this is that economics rests on decisions by human beings that are free. Free human action is the ultimate economic truth. This is why economic analysis should be fitted to real market behavior – to the truth that your charts are telling you – rather than the opposite. Economic theory and reading markets badly are the causes of erroneous and ineffective forecasts. Above all you should be a chartist economist. In this way, you will be adapting theory to reality and not the other way around. Charts are powerful!

A word is due about economics. The more you know about economics, the better prepared you will be to assess general conditions by looking at your charts and the more you will benefit from your trading. However, as in trading, you need the right approach. This is why our economic school of thought does matter as it can help our market success. For instance, a Marxist approach would cause us to become losers in the markets. The same can be said for a Keynesian approach. If your approach is from the Austrian school, you could make a fortune.[17]

In my book, *The Secret Code of Japanese Candlesticks,* I have further developed the subject of general conditions and the economy as the foundation for successful trading and investing. In trading triads, the practical way of using general conditions is never to trade against what general conditions are telling you. For example, you should go long on stocks only when the stock indexes are rising and have given a definite indication of a recovery and uptrend. Similarly, you should not go short unless the stock indexes have given a definite indication that a bear market is ongoing.

Taking into consideration the behavior of indexes, as well as the behavior of the other sectors of market and economic activity, is the most powerful factor for success in trading or investing. Let us repeat the idea: the general conditions rule!

Now, it is time to examine the entry and exit points of the triad method.

BUYING PATTERNS

The Buying Entry Point

The entry point is always the close of the final charted bar of a triad. In an ascending trend, you buy the last bar of the triad at the close. You can also buy the next bar after this last one at the open. There is no other buying point. In all cases, it is the same. You buy the close of the last bar of the triad. The triad can be simple or complex. You buy whichever of the two comes first (Figure 6.1).

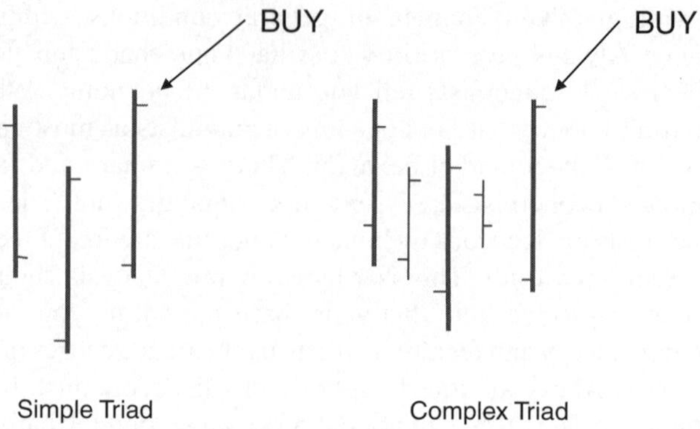

Figure 6.1 The triad as a buying entry point.

With this buying point at the third bar of a triad, you can trade any variety of market phases and patterns. Triads give you a unique buying point for all kinds of trades. This simplifies the task of choosing an entry. In addition, it forces you to find the entry point without optimizing. To trade any market phase, you must identify this unique buying point. This unique buying point always exists and is always the same. It cannot be otherwise.

The reason that this is a natural buying point is that it belongs to the fundamental market structure itself. All that the triad method does is formulate something that is already there – that already exists in the market. The reason that it exists in the market as a natural entry point is because triads define pivots that are the natural turning points of swings. A turning point pivot that ends a swing does not exist until the triad that gives it existence is complete.

It is only when a triad is complete that a swing is complete and ends at its final turning point pivot. This means that the triad implies that the market has already fully reversed by defining the final pivot of a now previous swing and the beginning pivot of the new swing.

This triad completion is at its third bar, more specifically at the close of the third bar. Before the close of the third bar, the swing has not ended in its pivot and the reversal is not yet real. At the close of the third triad bar, three things happen:

- The previous swing is defined.
- A new pivot marks the end of the previous swing and the birth of the new contrary swing.
- The reversal is complete at that precise instant. Not before. Not after.

This makes the close of the third bar of the triad the only natural first entry point after a reversal pivot. Any other entry place would be too early or too late. The close of the third bar of the triad is the natural and perfect entry point. This natural entry point is created by the market itself. It is implied in its own behavior and structure. This is why you must always buy at the close of the third charted bar of an ascending triad.

Now that you have your buying point, you need to know the buying setups. These are the conditions to buy at the lowest risk and with the odds in our favor. There are four main buying setups. Let us examine each.

The Upside Reversal

An upside reversal takes place when a market makes a bottom and then reverses itself and begins an upward movement that can develop into an upward trend. For an upside reversal to occur and have the possibility of developing into an upward trend, you need at least a new higher low pivot above the bottom one and a high pivot above the preceding high pivot. This means that, after the bottom pivot of the previous down movement, the market turns around and creates a higher low and two consecutive higher highs. These are the conditions for a trend reversal. Ideally, the new higher low pivot will not overlap the bar of the bottom pivot.

As soon as these conditions are satisfied, you will buy at the close of the third charted bar of the next ascending triad (Figure 6.2 and also see Chart 14 in Appendix II). When this ascending triad, which is your buying point, is complete and you buy, a new low pivot appears. The newly generated upward movement then has two higher lows and two higher highs, forming a parallelogram. From time to time a double bottom may be formed instead of the second higher low. The number of swings in this new upward movement is four. Your buying point comes after a reaction from

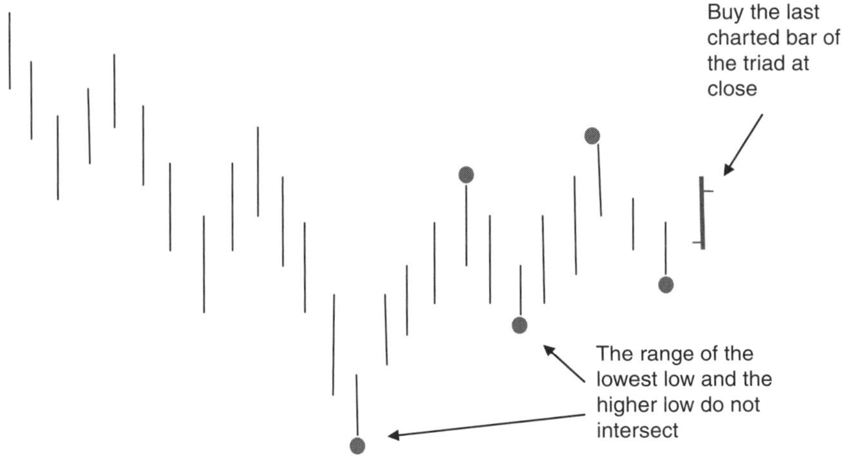

Figure 6.2 The upside reversal setup: buying two higher highs and a higher low.

the second higher high and after the market turns around, bringing about a second higher low with the completion of the third charted bar of a triad.

Here you see the triads in the act of building pivots and swings. The fundamental market structure demonstrates its inner mechanics. What the triads have achieved here is to define a minimum complex swing or, in other words, a trend. A simple swing is not really a trend. In fact, trends are composed of fluctuations. Each fluctuation is a simple swing. Their combination forms a trend that lasts as long as the market continues to make higher consecutive highs and higher consecutive lows, in the case of an uptrend. The minimal trend composed of multiple swings will require a low pivot that is higher than the pivot low of the preceding movement and a high pivot that is higher than the preceding pivot of the new upward movement. Your entry point comes after an additional higher low pivot confirms that the upward trend is already in existence and validated. You enter when the trend already exists, as a minimum.

As mentioned before, these pivots, high and low, are built by the triads that are the market's nanoengineers. They build the swings and pivots, using them to create a variety of phases and patterns. You wait until the triads have finished building a minitrend before entering an upward turning point. That is your entry point. You do not enter too early on a simple upswing or too late when the swing is already overdeveloped. Your entry point is exactly where the up movement has finally become a trend.

Whether or not your new trend will be short lived, you do not know. However, at least you know that you are in a trend and that you have bought at the moment of its birth. Of course, this is only a buying setup that enables you to buy a new trend. We must caution you not to buy all of these setups. Remember the market laws, such as the law of action and reaction, the law of alternation, and the law of nonbalance. These laws will define the quality and strength of the buying setup. This is why you must define the type of previous downswing that will engender an uptrend – its price length and time frame. All of this has an effect on the new swing to be born.

Therefore, before using this buying setup, study the swings and their times and price lengths. Then choose an average time and price length of swing and test it. Always study the market before acting on it and prove to yourself that a principle or rule really works. This will save you time and money.

Now comes your second buying setup.

The Breakout of a Downtrend Pivot

Here you buy the breakout of a high pivot of the previous downtrend. You buy it after the market has turned around and the new upward movement has broken the previous high pivot of the downward trend. Your buying point here is again an ascending triad after a corrective movement following the breakout of the pivot high that creates a higher low pivot from the absolute bottom for that movement.

You buy the close of the third charted bar of the triad that has created the new higher low (Figure 6.3 and also see Chart 15 in Appendix II). Again, you have two

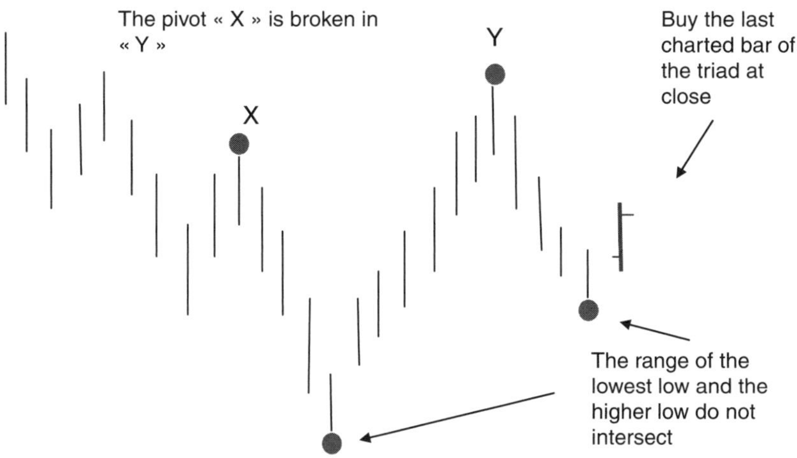

Figure 6.3 The upside reversal setup: buying the breakout of a downtrend pivot.

higher highs and one higher low. The difference with the former setup is that one high pivot belongs to the old down movement and the other high pivot to the new up movement.

The principle at work here to justify your buying is that the breakout of a former pivot, which is a strong resistance point, means that a new force has entered the market. This new force was able not only to stop the downtrend but also to reverse it. The presence of this force is indicated by its ability to break the high pivot of the previous trend. This means that this new force is much stronger than that of the old and dying previous uptrend that it was able to turn around.

It is possible to give added strength to this setup by combining it with the former setup and waiting for an additional higher high within the same new movement, taking the absolute bottom of the new up movement as the point of departure. This added condition enables you to avoid the risk of having a corrective complex swing after the breakout. In this case, if you buy the first triad after the correction, the market could still move a bit further down before it resumes the new trend.

This happens more often than not for the same reason that the high pivot is broken. What has been broken is strong resistance and, as a consequence, a strong reaction is due, although not strong enough to nullify the previous trend. The high probability of such a correction is deduced from the law of action and reaction. A force that is great enough to reverse a trend by breaking one of its high pivots and resistance points is due to test its breakout with an equal force. This is what engenders the complex correction made of many descending swings, instead of only one.

This is why it is convenient perhaps not to buy the first corrective triad after the breakout of such a high pivot, but to wait for the new uptrend to reassert itself by making an additional higher high and its corresponding consecutive higher low. This higher low then is your entry point at the close of the third charted bar of the triad that gave birth to this higher low pivot.

Again, do not buy outright, and without study, any breakout of the high pivot of the former trend. Not all pivots are the same and some pivots are stronger than others in downtrends. Some pivots correspond to the high of a consolidation during a down movement or to a high pivot after a complex upward correction that is made of a multiplicity of swings and with a wide price and time range.

This last kind of high pivot is much more significant than the high pivot of a simple swing during a downtrend. This is why the magnitudes of high pivots must be classified and studied. This study will enable you to choose the pivots most likely to see a breakout and a sustained change in trend.

In this setup, you also had a miniature complex uptrend in the beginning, but with a slight anticipation where an additional bottom is exchanged by greater market strength or force coming into play, which broke the pivot to the upside. Again, studying the market and identifying the best conditions for this setup to work is a must. For this, take a number of samples of this setup within different time windows – daily, weekly, and monthly – and test them. Begin with the monthly charts and proceed from there to the weekly and daily charts. Experiment with different lengths and durations of downtrends and breaking of their last significant high pivots. Once you have done this, you can identify a time and price length and its time window, and test a trading scenario based on this setup.

While you study this setup, never stop thinking about the first market laws or principles, such as the principle of action and reaction, the principle of alternation, and the principle of inertia, etc. Remember that, although you may think that you are trading a given setup, you are really trading principles and laws.

In this breakout of the pivot setup, the more significant the pivot is, the more meaningful will be its breakout. Action and reaction are proportional. Significant breakouts mean significant movements. Think about it. Prove it to yourself. Always test and experiment.

Now, let us define your third buying setup – the simple, double, or triple bottom.

The Simple, Double, or Triple Bottom

This is one of your most important buying setups. You will buy simple, double, or triple bottoms as soon as a triad appears when the formation ends. As usual, you will buy the third bar of the triad at its close, since this is your general buying setup for all cases.[18] The buying of each kind of bottom has its different approach. Let us begin with a simple, or single, bottom.

The single bottom is a bottom that is isolated within a trend. Any bottom can be considered as singular, but this is not the case here. A single bottom for us is one that has no company. No other bottoms can be found at the same support level.

The single bottom that you will buy is the bottom that is within an uptrend. An uptrend is made up of alternating rising and descending swings that form consecutively higher highs at their ending pivots and higher lows at their origin pivots. These higher lows within a trend are the single bottoms that you will usually trade. In your first setup, the upside reversal, you are buying a single bottom. It is also the case in your second setup, the breakout of a pivot. In the case of the second setup, you wait after the high pivot breakout for a correction and a triad that is the turning point of the correction by creating a new pivot that constitutes the single bottom that you are buying.

Single bottoms enable you to enter a trend at any moment during its ongoing movement. You always buy at the close of the third bar of the triad that builds the bottom (see Chart 16 in Appendix II). These single bottoms are created by the presence of a market force. For prices to rise and a trend to exist, you need a force that has not been used to its fullest. The law of nonbalance and the law of inertia are present here.

The law of nonbalance is driving the market to seek its new point of equilibrium. This point of equilibrium is an opposing force of a contrary nature. As long as such a force does not appear, the trend is bound to continue due to the principle of inertia. These nonbalance and inertia principles are behind the higher single bottoms. As there is no equilibrium yet, even momentary, bottoms cannot be at the same level, but are at different and ascending levels. Also, because there is no opposing force to create a balance point, the trend must continue. Thus, its reactions create higher and higher consecutive bottoms.

These single bottoms are among the foundations of trend trading, according to the fundamental market structure. Your triads, driven by nonbalance and inertia, create higher and higher pivots, giving low-risk buying points within a trend.

There is an exception to this kind of single bottom. It is one that appears in very volatile markets at an isolated level and not exactly within a trend. This is the case for some markets, such as pork bellies, where sometimes a single bottom that is not within a trend is seen. In this case, the bottom is the end of a bear market that ends at a higher level than the previous bottom. These isolated single bottoms are not as strong as the upward swing bottoms within a rising trend.

A double bottom is a much more reliable bottom than a single bottom. Double bottoms can occur within trends or in isolation. Double bottoms within trends occur when the trend rests for a while and consolidates before resuming its ascending course. A double bottom within a trend provides a good way to enter an ongoing trend with minimum risk. It is very important here to have measured other trends and calculated a target from the double bottom consolidation area.

Buying the double bottom should not take place when the market creates the new bottom, but when it resumes its course after having created the bottom. Here you wait for a triad to be complete in order to have a bottom pivot created by the triad. You then buy the upward triad that creates the bottom at the close of its third charted bar or at the open next day (Figure 6.4 and also see Chart 17 in Appendix II).

The second way to buy a double bottom is to wait for a consolidation to be broken. In that case, you buy the first triad that is over and does not overlap the consolidation

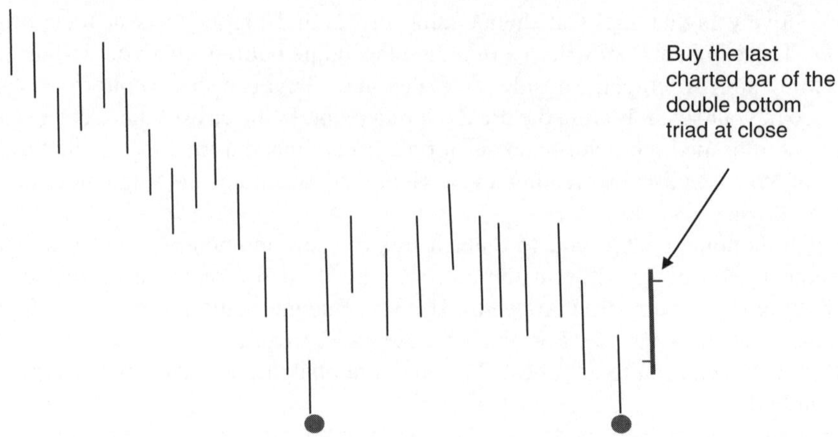

Figure 6.4 Buying bottoms with triads: double, triple, ...

range. You buy at the third triad bar, its end bar at its close (see Chart 18 in Appendix II). This second way is the safest.

The strongest bottoms are triple bottoms. They are the safest and entail the least risk.[19] They are bought in exactly the same way as double bottoms. You buy the triple bottom at the close of the third bar that brings it to completion (see Chart 19 in Appendix II).

The second way of buying a triple bottom is to buy the first triad that is above, and separate from, the consolidation range that includes the three bottoms. You always buy at the close of the third bar of the triad or at the open of the next bar.

Double and triple bottoms either occur in isolation or within a trend. They are a safe way to enter a rising trend or to enter a new trend.

Another safe way of buying single, double, and triple bottoms, and one of the best, is by combining all previous setups. This gives the greatest confirmation possible that the new trend is on the move. In this case, you will buy the new single, double, or triple bottom as soon as the market has made an upward reversal setup, or a pivot breakout setup, or both. This creates a very strong buying point (see Chart 20 in Appendix II). The reason for this is that the fundamental market structure with its engineers, the triads, creates a cluster structure that defines the new upward trend as fully born and complete.

A double or triple bottom shows strong buying support. The upward reversal setup implies that a new force has been able to create a new trend. The high pivot breakout gives still stronger evidence of the new force.

These three elements cluster together to build a robust structure that validates the new trend in a unique fashion. Now we will discuss how resistance that has become support, our fourth buying setup, should be traded.

Resistance That Has Become Support

Another setup, a classical setup, is the buying of support and resistance. There are two main ways to buy resistance that has become support. The first is to buy old tops that become new bottoms within the same trend. The second consists of buying old tops that become new bottoms, but that are not within the same trend. Let us examine each.

The first way of buying resistance that becomes support is to wait within an uptrend for a high pivot to be made that is higher than a previous one. As soon as this new high pivot is there, a correction follows that will usually end near the previous high pivot. Within this trend, a new higher low pivot that creates a single bottom will occur. This single bottom and its defining pivot occur because the market stops its downward correction around the last high that had been the old resistance.

This old resistance, now support, will stop any corrective downward reaction within an upward trend. It becomes a safe place to buy and to enter a new ongoing trend. As usual, you buy at the close of the third bar of the triad that creates the new higher low pivot, which is testing the old resistance before the trend resumes (Figure 6.5 and also see Chart 21 in Appendix II). Testing the old resistance means that the market wants to know if all selling will be absorbed at the level of the old resistance, now new support. If so, the trend will continue its rising course.

You never know in advance what the new trend will do and if the test of the old resistance, which now is the new support, will succeed. This is why you buy at the close of the triad or at the open of the next bar. The reason for this is that once the triad is in place, the test of new support around the previous high top has succeeded, at least in a minimal way. You must remember that you do not want to anticipate, but want to be in movements that have already begun. The triad ensures that you will be.

The second way of buying old resistance that is now new support is buying around old tops that become the new bottoms and are not within the same trend. If you

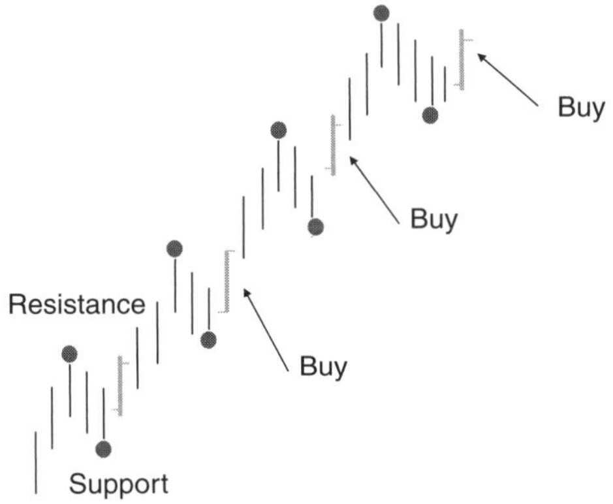

Figure 6.5 Buying within a trend old resistance that has become a new support.

examine a chart, you will see how many old tops that sometimes were created years ago, become the new bottoms where the market tends to stop The way of buying them is the same, but with a caveat. They are not the safest way of buying old resistance that becomes new support. If you simply buy the first triad that appears after the market corrects to such an old bottom, everything could go wrong.

The problem is that there are many levels of old bottoms and not all are of the same supporting strength. Therefore, although it is true that the market will always find support around an old resistance top, the difficult part is to know around which top. For example, in a bear market, the market could break many former historical bottoms before finding its equilibrium around some of its former old tops. This is why, when buying this kind of old resistance, we need to refine our technique.

Again, the previous setups come to our rescue. Triads and the market structure that they build again suggest what to do. To trade these old historical tops, which are months or years apart, and that are now support that will contain a market that falls, you will combine once more many setups that integrate themselves naturally. You will wait until the market chooses its old top and makes it a new support and will ask the market to give you proof that the old top will become its new support. To do this, you can combine some or all of the previous setups.

As soon as the market ends its fall around an old top, and this can be above or below it, a single, double, or triple bottom will form. You wait for one or more of them to form. Then you buy them. If it is a single bottom, you wait for the upside reversal and the high pivot breakout setups to occur and then, as usual, you buy the triad that ends the corrective movement, creating a higher bottom pivot. You buy at the close of the upward triad or at the next bar (see Chart 16 in Appendix II). In the case of buying after a double or a triple bottom formation around the old top, now new support, you follow the setup that we explained previously about trading such bottoms (see Charts 17 and 19 in Appendix II).

Here is a word about your buying setups. All setups combine in a unique mechanism. Each fills and fits perfectly a specific void within the market structure. This is because they are based on a market logic that is based on pivots, swings, and triads. This enables you to have confirming, and not conflicting, parameters as trading setups. This is because your setups are market structures in themselves. This is why they fill, fit, and fully integrate within themselves.

This makes your trading necessarily more secure and complete. The upward reversal fits perfectly with the previous high pivot breakout, and the bottoms and old tops that become support are component parts of an upward reversal movement that is breaking high pivots as it goes along and makes support. Therefore, all of these elements, as they integrate and confirm their inner logic, give your trades added validity and robustness. In fact, it is not us who are the traders, but the market that is trading for us. All that triads and the fundamental market structure do is teach us how to follow the will of the market and go along with its flow.

We have studied our buying patterns where, for all our buying setups, the unique buying point is at the close of an ascending triad or at the next bar after it. Now, we will define the main selling setups used by the triad method. These selling patterns are the reverse of our buying patterns. Let us examine them.

SELLING PATTERNS

The Entry Point

The entry point is always the close of the final charted bar that defines a triad. In a descending trend, you sell the last bar of the descending triad at the close. You can also sell the next bar after this last one at the open. There is no other selling point. In all cases, it is the same. You sell the close of the last bar of the descending triad. The descending triad can be simple or complex. You sell whichever comes first (Figure 6.6).

With this selling point at the third bar of a descending triad, you can trade any variety of market phases and patterns. Triads give you a unique selling point for all kind of trades. This simplifies the task of choosing a sell or short sell entry point. In addition, it forces you to find the entry point without optimizing. To trade any market phase, you must identify this unique selling point. It is always the same and always exists. It cannot be otherwise.

The reason why this is a natural selling point is that it is defined by the fundamental market structure itself. All that the triad method does is formulate something that is already there, that already exists in the market. The reason that it exists in the market as its natural entry point is that triads define pivots that are the natural turning points of swings. A turning point pivot that ends a swing does not exist until the triad that gives it existence is complete.

It is only when a triad is complete that a swing is complete and ends at its final turning point pivot. This means that the triad implies that the market has already fully

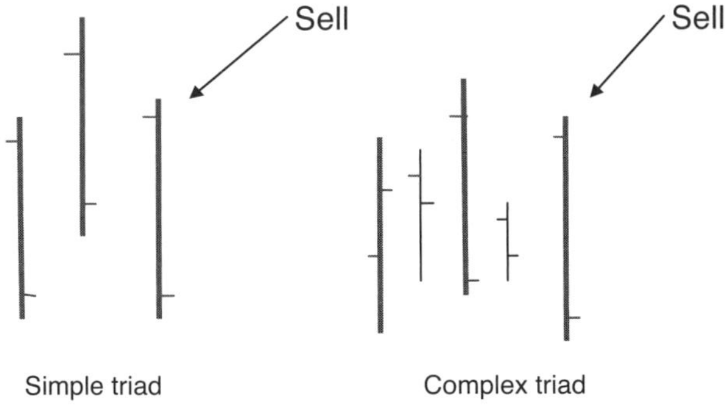

Figure 6.6 The triad as a short selling entry point.

reversed by defining the final pivot of a now previous swing and the beginning pivot of the new swing.

This triad completion is at its third bar, more specifically at the close of the third bar. Before the close of the third bar, the swing has not ended in its pivot and the reversal is not yet real. At the close of the third triad bar, three things happen:

- The previous swing is defined.
- A new pivot marks the end of the previous swing and the birth of the new opposite swing.
- The reversal is complete at that precise instant. Not before. Not after.

This makes the close of the third bar of the descending triad the only natural first entry point after a reversal pivot that confirms a downtrend. Any other entry place would be too early or too late. The close of the third bar of the descending triad is the natural and perfect entry point to sell short. This natural entry point is created by the market itself. It is implied by its own behavior and structure. This is why you must always sell at the close of the third charted bar of a descending triad.

Now that you have your selling point, you need to know the selling short setups – the conditions to satisfy in order to sell short with the least risk and the odds in your favor. You have four main selling short setups. We will review each of them.

The Downside Reversal

The downside reversal occurs when a market makes a top, reverses itself, and then begins a downward movement that can develop into a downward trend. For a downside reversal to occur with a possibility of developing into a downward trend, you need at least a new lower high pivot below the top pivot and a low pivot below the preceding low pivot. This means that, after the top pivot of the previous up movement, the market turns around and creates a lower high and two consecutive lower lows. These are the conditions for a trend reversal. Ideally, the new lower high pivot will not overlap the bar of the top pivot.

As soon as these conditions are satisfied, you sell at the close of the third charted bar of the next descending triad (Figure 6.7 and also see Chart 22 in Appendix II). When this descending triad, your short selling point, is complete and you sell short, a new high pivot has appeared. The newly generated downward movement then has two lower highs and two lower lows, forming a parallelogram structure.

There are four swings in this new downward movement. Your short selling point is after a reaction from the second lower low and the market turns around, producing a second lower high pivot with the completion of the third charted bar of a triad.

Here you see the triads building pivots and swings. The fundamental market structure demonstrates its inner mechanics and its inner logic. What the triads have done here is define a minimum, complex, swing or, in other words, a trend.

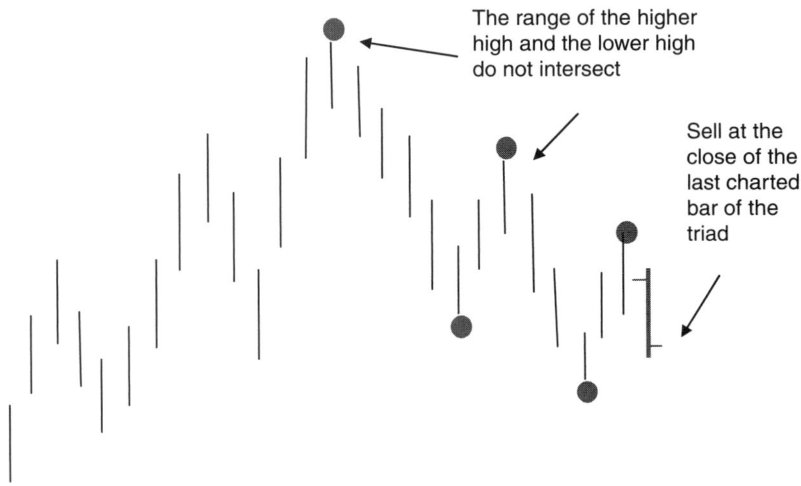

Figure 6.7 The downside reversal setup: selling two lower lows and a lower high.

A simple swing is not a trend. In fact, trends are composed of fluctuations. Each fluctuation is a simple swing. Their combination forms a trend that lasts as long as the market continues, in the case of a downtrend, to make lower consecutive highs and lower consecutive lows.

The minimal trend composed of multiple swings will require a high pivot that is lower than the pivot high of the preceding swing, and a pivot low that is lower than the low preceding pivot of the new downward movement. Your entry point comes after an additional lower high pivot confirms that the downward trend is already underway and validated. You enter when the trend is already underway, as a minimum condition. As mentioned before, these pivots, high and low, are built by the triads that are the market's nanoengineers. Their activity builds the swings and pivots using them to create a diversity of phases and patterns.

Before entering a downward turning point, you wait until the triads have finished building a minitrend. That is your entry point. You do not enter too early on a simple downswing or too late when the swing is already overdeveloped. Your entry point is exactly where the down movement has, at last, become a trend. Although you do not know whether or not your new trend will be short lived, at least you know that you are in a trend and that you have sold at the moment of its birth – not too early or too late.

Of course, this is only a selling setup that enables you to sell a new trend short. We must caution you not to act on all of these setups. Remember first to take into account the market laws, such as the law of action and reaction, the law of alternation, and the law of nonbalance. These laws will define the quality and strength of the selling setup. This is why you must define the type of previous uptrend that will bring about a downtrend – its price length and time frame. All of this has an effect on the new trend to be born.

Therefore, before using this selling setup, you must study the swings and their times and price lengths. Then choose a swing of average time and price length, and test it. Always study the market before acting on it and prove to yourself that a principle or rule really works. This will save you time and money.

Now, we will explain our second selling setup.

The Breakout of an Uptrend Pivot

Here you sell the breakout of a low pivot of the previous uptrend. You sell it after the market has turned around and the new downward movement has broken the previous low pivot of the upward swing. Your selling point here is again a descending triad after a corrective movement following the breakout of the pivot low has created a lower high pivot from the absolute top for that movement.

You sell the close of the third charted bar of the triad that has created the new lower high (Figure 6.8 and also see Chart 23 in Appendix II). Again, you have two lower lows and one lower high. The difference with the former setup is that one low pivot belongs to the old movement and the other low pivot belongs to the new down movement.

The principle at work here to justify your selling is that the breakout of a former pivot, which is a strong support point, means that a new force has entered the market. This new force was able to stop the uptrend and reverse it. The presence of this force

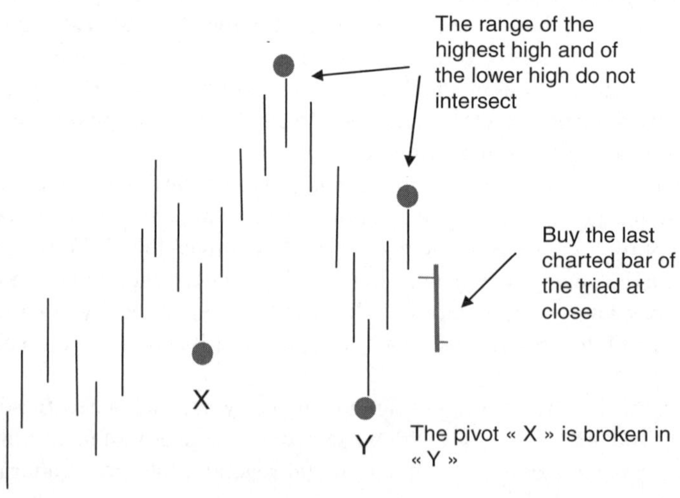

Figure 6.8 The downside reversal setup: selling the breakout of an uptrend low pivot.

is indicated by its ability to break the low pivot of the previous trend. This means that this new force is much stronger than that of the old and dying previous uptrend that it has turned around.

It is possible to give added strength to this setup by combining it with the former setup and waiting for an additional lower low within the same new movement, taking the absolute top of the new down movement as the point of departure. This added condition enables you to avoid the risk of having a corrective complex swing after the breakout. In this case, if you sell the first triad short after the correction, the market could still move up a bit further before it resumes the new trend.

This happens more often than not for the same reason that the low pivot is broken. What has been broken is strong support and, as a consequence, a strong reaction is due, although not strong enough to nullify the previous trend. The high probability of such a correction is deduced from the law of action and reaction. A force great enough to reverse a trend by breaking one of its low pivots and support points is due to test its breakout with an equal force.

This is what brings about the complex correction made of many ascending swings, instead of only one, and is why it is convenient perhaps not to sell the first corrective triad after the breakout of such low pivot, but to wait for the new downtrend to reassert itself by achieving an additional lower low and its corresponding, consecutive, lower high. This lower high then is your entry point at the close of the third charted bar of the triad that gave birth to this lower high pivot.

Again, do not sell any breakout of the low pivot of the former trend outright and without study. Not all pivots are the same and some pivots in uptrends are stronger than others.

Some pivots correspond to the low of a consolidation during an up movement or to a low pivot after a complex, downward, correction made of a multiplicity of swings and with a wide price and time range. This last kind of low pivot is much more significant than the low pivot of a simple swing during an uptrend. This is why the magnitudes of low pivots must be classified and studied.

This study will enable you to choose the best pivots to anticipate a breakout and a sustained change in trend. In this setup, you also have a miniature complex downtrend in the beginning, but with a slight anticipation where an additional bottom is exchanged by greater market strength or force coming into play that broke the pivot to the downside.

Again, studying the market and identifying the best conditions for this setup to work is a must. To do this, take a number of samples of this setup within different time windows – daily, weekly, and monthly – and test them. Begin with the monthly charts and proceed from there to the weekly and daily charts. Experiment with different lengths and durations of uptrends and the breaking of their last significant low pivots. Once you have done this, you can identify a time and price length and its time window, and test a trading scenario based on this setup.

While you study this setup, never stop thinking about the first market laws or principles, such as the principle of action and reaction or the principle of alternation or the principle of inertia, etc. Remember that, although you may think that you are trading a given setup, you are really trading principles and laws.

In this breakout of the pivot setup, the more significant the pivot is, the more meaningful will be its breakout. Action and reaction are proportional. Significant breakouts mean significant movements. Think about it. Prove it to yourself. Always test and experiment.

Now let us define your third selling setup – the simple, double, or triple top.

The Simple, Double, or Triple Top

This is one of your most important selling setups. You will sell short simple, double, or triple tops as soon as a triad appears when the formation ends. As usual, you will sell the third bar of the triad at its close, since this is your general selling setup for all cases. The selling of each kind of top has a different approach. Let us begin with the simple top.

The single, or simple, top is a top that is isolated within a trend. Any top can be considered to be singular, but this is not the case here. For you, a single top is the one that has no company, where no other tops can be found at the same resistance level.

The single top that you will sell is the top that is within a downtrend. A downtrend is made of alternating rising and descending swings that achieve consecutively lower highs at their ending pivots and lower lows at their origin pivots. These lower highs within a trend are the single tops that you will usually trade. In your first setup, the downside reversal, you are selling a single top. This is the same case as for your second setup, the breakout of a pivot. In the case of the second setup, you wait for a correction after the low pivot breakout, and a triad that is the turning point of the correction, by creating a new pivot that constitutes the single top that you are selling.

Single tops enable you to enter a trend at any moment during the ongoing movement. You always sell at the close of the third bar of the triad that builds the top (see Chart 24 in Appendix II). These single tops are created by the presence of a market force. For prices to fall and a trend to exist, you need a force that has not been used to its fullest. The law of nonbalance and the law of inertia are at work here.

The law of nonbalance is pushing the market to seek its new point of equilibrium. This point of equilibrium is an opposing force of opposite direction. As long as such a force does not appear, the trend is bound to continue, and that is the principle of inertia. This nonbalance and inertia are the principles behind the lower single tops. As there is no equilibrium yet, even momentarily, tops cannot be at the same level – only at different and descending levels. Also, as there is no opposing force to create a balance point, the trend must continue and thus its reactions create lower and lower consecutive tops.

These single tops are among the foundations of trend trading according to the fundamental market structure. Your triads, impelled by nonbalance and inertia, create lower and lower pivots, giving you low-risk, short-selling points within a trend.

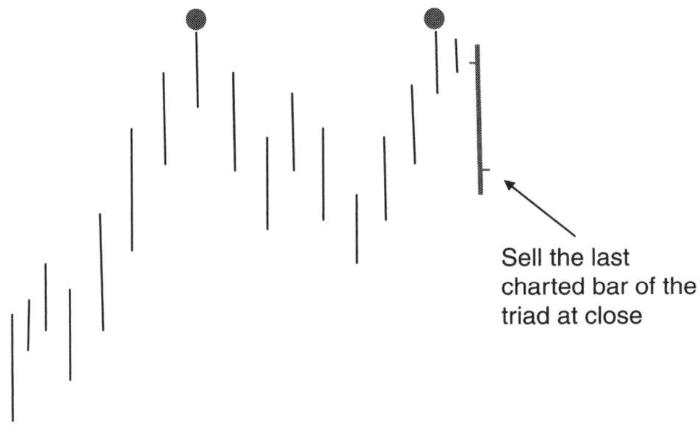

Figure 6.9 Selling tops with triads: double, triple, ...

There is an exception to this kind of single top, one that appears in very volatile markets at an isolated level and not exactly within a trend. This is the case of some markets, such as that for pork bellies, where a single top not within a trend is sometimes seen. In this case, the top is the end of a bull market that ends at a lower level than the previous top. These isolated single tops are not as strong as the downward swing tops within a falling trend.

A double top is a much more reliable top than a single top. Double tops can occur within trends or in isolation. Double tops occur within trends when the trend rests for a while and consolidates before resuming its descent. Double tops within a trend provide a good way to enter an ongoing trend with minimum risk. It is very important to have measured other trends and calculated a target from the double top consolidation area.

Selling the double top short does not happen when the market makes a new top, but when it resumes its course after having made a double top. Here you wait for a triad to be complete in order to have a high pivot created by the triad. You sell short the downward triad that makes the top at the close of its third charted bar or at the open next day (Figure 6.9 and also see Chart 25).

The second way to sell the double top short is to wait for the consolidation to be broken. In that case, you sell short the first triad that is over and does not overlap the consolidation range. You sell at the third triad bar, its end bar, at its close. This second way is safer.

The strongest tops are the triple tops. They are the safest. They are sold short in exactly the same way as the double tops. You sell short the triple top at the close of the third bar that brings it to completion (see Chart 26 in Appendix II).

The second way of selling a triple top short is by selling the first triad that is above and separate from the consolidation range that includes the three tops. You always sell at the close of the third bar of the triad or at the opening of the next bar.

Double and triple tops occur either in isolation or within a trend. They provide a safe way of entering a falling trend or a new trend.

Another safe way of selling single, double, and triple tops, and one of the best, is by combining all previous setups. This gives the maximum possible confirmation that the new trend is on the move (see Charts 27 and 28). In this case, you will sell short the new single, double, or triple top as soon as the market has made a downward reversal setup or a pivot breakout setup, or both. This creates a very strong selling point. The reason for this is that the fundamental market structure, with its triads, creates a cluster structure that defines the new downward trend as fully born and complete.

A double or triple top shows strong selling resistance. The downward reversal setup implies that a new force has been able to create a new trend. The low pivot breakout gives still stronger evidence of the new force.

These three elements cluster together to build a robust structure that uniquely validates the new trend. Now, we will discuss how support that has become resistance, our fourth selling short setup, should be traded.

Support That Becomes Resistance

Selling support that becomes resistance is explained here in the light of triads. There are two main ways of selling support that has become resistance. The first way is selling short old bottoms that become new tops within the same trend. The second way consists in selling short old bottoms that become new tops, but are not within the same trend. Let us examine each.

The first way of selling support that becomes resistance is to wait within a downtrend for a pivot that is lower than the previous low pivot. After this new low pivot, a correction follows that will usually end near the previous low pivot, the resistance point. Within this trend, a new lower, low pivot will occur, making from the previous low pivot the level for a single top. This single top and its defining pivot occur because the market ends its upward correction around the last low, which was the old support.

This old support, now resistance, will stop any corrective upward reaction within a downward trend. It becomes a safe place to sell short and to enter a new ongoing trend. As usual, you sell short at the close of the third bar of the triad that creates the new lower high pivot, which is testing the old support that has now become resistance before the trend resumes its course (Figure 6.10 and also see Chart 29 in Appendix II).

Testing the old support means that the market wants to know if all buying will end at the level of the old support – now new resistance. If this happens, the trend will continue its falling course. You never know in advance what the new trend will do and whether the test of the old support – now new resistance – will succeed. This is why you sell short at the close of the triad or at the open of the next bar.

The reason for this is that, once the triad is in place, the test of the new resistance around the previous low bottom has succeeded, at least in a minimal way. You must

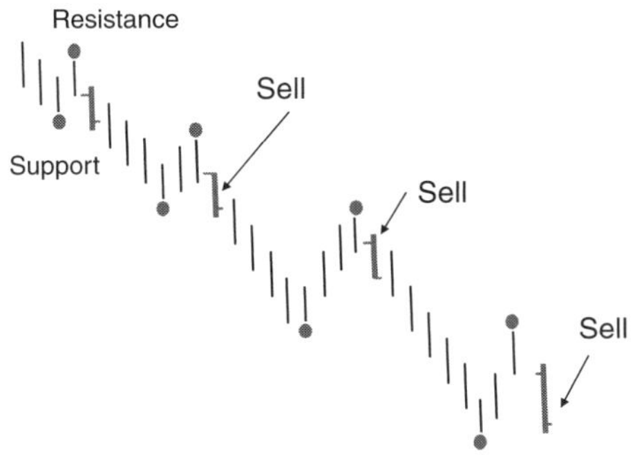

Figure 6.10 Selling old support that has become new resistance within a descending trend.

remember that you do not want to anticipate, but to be in movements that are already on the go. The triad ensures that you will be.

The second way of selling short old support that is now new resistance is to sell short around old bottoms that become the new tops and are not within the same trend. If you examine a chart, you will see how many old bottoms sometimes made years ago become the new tops where the market tends to stop.

The way of selling them short is the same, but with a caveat. They are not the safest way of selling old support that becomes new resistance. If you simply sell short the first triad that appears after the market corrects to such an old bottom, everything could go wrong. The problem here is that there are many levels of old bottoms and not all have the same supporting strength. Therefore, although it is true that the market will always find resistance around an old support bottom, the difficult part is to know around which. In a bear market, for instance, the market could break many former historical bottoms before finding its equilibrium. This is why, when selling short this kind of old support, now resistance, we need to refine our technique.

Again, the previous setups come to our rescue. Triads and the market structure that they build give us an indication of what to do. To trade these old historical bottoms that are months or years apart, and that now have become resistance that will stop a rising market, you will once more combine many setups that integrate themselves naturally. You will wait until the market chooses its old bottom as its new resistance and will ask the market to provide proof that the old bottom is really its new resistance. To do this, you combine some or all of the previous setups.

As soon as the market stops in its rise around an old bottom, whether above or below it, a single, double, or triple top will form. You will wait for one or more of them to form. Then, you will sell them short. If it is a single top, you wait for the downside reversal and the low pivot breakout setups to occur. Then, as usual, you sell the triad that ends the corrective movement, creating a lower high pivot. You sell short at the close of the downward triad or at the next bar. In the case of selling short after a double or a triple top formation around the old bottom that has become new resistance, you follow the setup that previously explained how to trade these kinds of tops.

Here is a word about your selling short setups. All setups combine in a unique mechanism. Each fills and fits perfectly a specific void within the market structure. This is because they are based on a market logic based on pivots, swings, and triads. This enables you to have confirming, rather than conflicting, parameters as trading setups because your setups are market structures in themselves. This is why they fill, fit, and integrate within themselves, which makes your trading more secure and complete. The downward reversal fits perfectly with the previous low pivot breakout, and the tops and old bottoms that become resistance are component parts of a downward reversal movement that, as it goes along, breaks low pivots making them resistance.

Thus, all of these elements, as they integrate and confirm their actions, have an inner logic of their own that give your trades added validity and robustness. In fact, it is not you who are really trading, but the market that is trading for you. Triads and the fundamental market structure teach us how to follow the will of the market, enabling us to go along with its flow. You have studied your selling short patterns where, for all your selling short setups, the unique selling point is at the close of a descending triad or at the next bar after it.

All of these selling patterns are the reverse of the buying patterns that we previously explained.

Now, we will change perspectives and explain a way to swing trade.

7 The Mastery of Fluctuations: How to Develop Your Sixth Sense of the Market

THE ARITHMETIC MEASURING METHOD

A Swing Trade Technique That Relies on Intuition

Here we will present, for illustrative purposes, a swing trading technique based on triads that enables you to trade the market for short-term profits. This method works for all time frames, whether intraday, daily, or weekly. I prefer to use the daily or weekly charts with it.

Swing trading is a science and an art form within trading. It consists of trading the short-term market swings for small profits. Traders of old often relied on their intuition for this kind of trading. Intuition does not mean irrational action. Old traders who succeeded had a highly developed intuition, a subtle market knowledge that came from a long study of market fluctuations and practice. They became so acquainted with market swings that they developed a feeling for the main patterns behind them. An arithmetic intuition and sensibility was the basis of their success. Numbers held the keys to the kingdom for those traders. No charts were needed.[20]

In the era of the spreadsheet and charting software, the task of becoming acquainted with market swings, both numerically and geometrically, becomes easier than for the traders of old. These are the steps that you follow to get an intimate feeling of the market's ebb and flow.

First Define the Market Phase

Using monthly, weekly, and daily charts, identify the market phase that you will trade. It may be a consolidation, a trend, or a turning point. What you are looking for is a trend, a consolidation, or a turning point. Once they have been identified, you will select all possible cases of the same or similar magnitude. You will mark them for further study.

What you are attempting to do is to create a database of trends, consolidations, and turning points for the market of your choice. This must be done for several time frames using monthly, weekly, and daily charts. You will begin with the monthly charts and then move to shorter timeframes.

This top-down analysis will give you a collection in multiple time frames. This will enable you to study them systematically. Your goal is to become familiar with your market of choice and its fluctuations.

This study goes from the present to the past. You will use charts and spreadsheets. The first thing that you will do is measure the price range and the time length of the trends, consolidations, and turning points. With consolidations, you will measure the range from the highest high pivot to the lowest low pivot. Trends will be measured from their lowest low pivot to their highest high pivot for uptrends. For downtrends, you will measure from their highest high pivot to their lowest low pivot. By trend, you mean a movement made of complex swings.

Turning points will be measured in the same way. You measure the price and time range. We suggest a minimum of eight samples for each phase. This can be extended to 25 or more. With both of these measures in their multiple time frames, you proceed to the next step.

Measure all Swings within the Phase

Now, for your collection of trends, consolidations, and turning points, you measure all the swings that they contain for each time frame – monthly, weekly, and daily. These swings that have been measured in time and price are then entered into a spreadsheet. You begin your collection of numbers.

Enter the following data into your spreadsheet for each phase and its specific time frame:

- Date
- Closing price
- Number of charted bars
- Variation in the number of points for the price length of each swing within the phase
- Percentage variation for the number of points of each swing within the phase
- Calendar length: the number of calendar days from the beginning to the end for each swing.

Record the variations in price and percentage of upward swings as positive numbers. Record the variations in price and percentage of downward swings as negative numbers (see Charts 3 and 30 in Appendix II). This immediately gives you a bird's eye view of the value, as a single number, of each of the swings of the corresponding phase in price and time.

In addition, your number sense will be at work and many number patterns will begin to emerge. Some figures will be similar and you will begin to make sense of what at first seems to be a random collection of ciphers. This number sense, which discovers patterns among a set of numbers, works from a different perspective than the visual perspective you have in your charts. The organ of perception of the geometry of the market in charts is the eye and vision is its faculty.

Numbers are perceived differently as arithmetic figures that reveal a hidden harmony and rhythm to you at a different level than the geometrical one. Key numbers, positive and negative, will become meaningful. These numbers will enable you to trade the market fluctuations with a purely numerical approach. The number magic will acquire its full strength. Your tool to identify this number rhythm and its key ciphers is your spreadsheet.

It is possible to mark these numbers in the charts, but what gives full power to the number magic behind this approach to trading are the arithmetic patterns made visible in your spreadsheet. Now, armed with your spreadsheet, it is time to undertake the next step.

Find the Maximal Swing

The first thing to do is to find, for each phase that you have collected and its series of swings, the maximal swing for the series. This maximal swing is the greatest swing of the series in price and in time. The result is that you will have a series of price swings and its maximal swing and a series of time swings and its maximal swing. This maximal swing will give you a number that indicates what a strong reaction is within the phase under study. Every phase has a maximal swing. This swing can be used in a manner of ways.

The maximal swing is useful for stop placement. It gives you an idea of the kind of movement that, without invalidating the phase where it takes place, could take out your stop, even if your trade is correctly placed. This maximal swing could be your choice for stop placement a few points below the maximal reaction. However, it might not be a good choice. The key is its frequency and range. Maybe a swing that is smaller than the maximal swing would be as useful. Only testing can give you the answer, but whatever you do, you must always take into account the maximal swing in stop placement.

The other use for the maximal swing, besides stop placement, is in finding an adequate fluctuation that will enable you to have a profit with low market risk. To wait for a maximal swing correction could be an optimal plan for buying or selling short. The market rarely changes in volatility and the odds are against maximal swings being significantly exceeded, thus making buying or selling points safe.

Here is the next thing to identify once you have the maximal swing.

Find the Minimal Swing

The minimal swing is the opposite of the maximal swing. It is the smallest swing within the series. This minimal swing also has its meaning and its possible uses. The minimal swing tells you about the minimal volatility of the market. Many small swings will not differ much from the minimal swing. When many minimal swings follow one another, you know that an important change in volatility may be near. This could mean a change of phase.

Ideally, minimal swings will not be used for stop placement. If you use them for that purpose, the market could easily take away your stop. The best use of minimal swings is in taking a position, long or short, within a trend.

Often a small reaction and its reversal within an ongoing trend in full strength can give you entry points that are safe. The thing to do is carefully to study the numbers that follow small swings during a trend. The minimal swing signal should only be taken after a reversal has been confirmed and the trend gives a definite sign that it is continuing its course.

Minimal swings and maximal swings are only references here, since most swings will be near the maximal swing or the minimal swing. The really useful swings to trade are those that have enough width to enable a reasonable profit to be made.

This leads to your next type of swing.

Find the Master Swing

The master swing is the most important swing. It is a special type of swing that I also call the meaningful swing. This is because not all swings have the same meaning within a phase. When studying a phase and its set of swings, you must be able to recognize their different meanings and relative importance. By studying your spreadsheet, you will achieve this. Some swings are greater than others.

Some swings are near the maxima, whereas others are near the minima. It is from the swings that are near the maxima that you will choose your master swing. This swing is a meaningful swing that has two conditions.

The first condition is that it should be large enough to be as close as possible to the maximal correction that a market has within a trend or within a consolidation or within a turning point, depending on the phase that you want to trade. A master swing has an amplitude that is greater, and a frequency that is less, than those of the other swings of the phase under observation. The greater in length the master swing is, the more meaningful it becomes. The ideal length is that of the maximal swing. However, this cannot be for a reason that takes us to the second condition necessary for a master swing.

The second condition is that it must repeat itself a number of times to enable you to trade it. If the maximal swing is too large, it may never repeat itself within a swing – or almost never. This makes it impractical to use the maximal swing. You need a swing that is large enough to be near the maximal swing, but not so large that it does not repeat itself a number of times, enabling you to trade it. The greater the number of repetitions, the better. You can visually identify swings within trends that repeat themselves often enough to enable you to trade them for a reasonable profit. To know this, you must count the number of master swings that are meaningful to your trading (see Chart 2 in Appendix II).

Once in possession of your master swing, you have a key number that gives you the vibratory rate of the market that you are trading in accordance with your goals. You now have a practical tool with which to trade swings. Not only can you trade swings with it but you can also take positions – short-term, medium-term, or long-term – in the market. This tool gives you low-risk entry points for any kind of trade that you want to make. The low risk comes from the fact that the master swing is as wide as possible. Therefore, your entry will be at the extreme of the correction for that market, an extreme that is defined by its vibratory rate.

The profit potential arises from the same reason. As it is as large a swing as possible, the master swing has a price length large enough to provide a reasonable profit. It enables you to enter as near the bottom or top as possible. It also gives you an exit point as close to a top or bottom as possible.

This happens because of the law of action and reaction. As the master swing corrects a given amount, the action part, it retraces the corrected amount, the reaction part. What you are really trading is the law of action and reaction for which the master swing is your key vibration number. All your trades will then be grounded on a specific vibration rate, the rate that causes the master swing to exist.

Once in possession of your master swing, you have a number, your master key, which gives you the key vibratory rate of the market that corresponds exactly to your trading objectives and your risk reward ratios.[21] You will now learn how to trade with your master key.

MEASURE MARKET SWINGS BEFORE TRADING

The Entry Point

Once you have identified your master swing and its master key, you have in your possession the location at which to take a position in the market. You now must wait within a trend for a swing to correct at least the amount of your master key number. When that swing appears and arrives at your master key number, you prepare yourself to take a position. When this number is reached, you do not take the position immediately. You wait for a triad to appear and only then do you enter the market.

This entry point at the close of the third bar of the triad enables you to enter the market when it has already reversed into the direction of the main trend and is retracing its previous movement (see Charts 3 and 30 in Appendix II). This enables you to avoid risk and be within the main movement. By waiting for the triad, you prevent, in some measure, the risk that the correction will continue long past your entry point before it reverses. Thus, your stop can be tighter and also your profit potential increases, since you will enter the market as close to the end of the corrective move as possible and as close as possible to the beginning of the new movement that resumes the main trend.

As triads link swings together by building the pivots that link each swing to its contrary one, the swing will appear at the end of the correction. This is the reason for its protective action. The fundamental market structure and its pivots, swings, and triads are at work again. They protect you from entering a correction too soon and enable you to enter at the lowest risk point.

For example, in an upward trend, and once in possession of your master key number, you wait for a swing to correct by an amount equivalent to that value. As soon as this happens and the reversal triad appears, you buy it at its close. In a downward trend, it is the reverse. You wait for a swing to correct an up movement that is equivalent to the master key number, wait for the reversal triad, and then buy it at its close. The correction will often be between 30 and 60 % of the previous upward swing, if trading a downtrend. It will often be between 30 and 60 % of the previous downward swing, if trading an uptrend.

This entry technique can be used to trade swings for small profits. It can also be used to enter positions for the long term. It all depends on your style of trading.

Your next step is the exit.

The Exit Point

Knowing when to exit is even more important than knowing when to enter. Most trades are lost due to exit failures. For example, when the stock market is rising, most stocks are on the bull side. In those conditions, it is sufficient to buy the market to make a profit. The losers here are the ones who overstay the market and do not sell in time. This is why knowing when to exit is so important.

Here we will consider how to exit in short-term swing trades. When it comes to the exit, we have many options. Only testing will give us an acceptable exit.

Basically, the exit can be a target exit or a trailing stop exit. The target exit will do once a risk reward ratio is achieved or if the stop is touched. The trailing stop will trail a stop until the market reverses by an amount that takes the stop away. Each kind of stop has its advantages and disadvantages. The stop should be chosen within your overall strategy and trading plan.

The most important concept for exiting is the risk/reward ratio. Even the trailing stop will depend on it. A series of trades that are unable to achieve a favorable risk/reward ratio can only fail. When choosing an exit strategy, first test your system so that you will achieve a profitable risk/reward ratio. No exit method will ever be successful without it. This is an aspect that we want to emphasize.

Once you have defined a convenient risk–reward, test the market to see if your entry technique and trading method and setup consistently give you that amount of reward for the risk that you are taking. In short-term trading of a few days, it may be better to rely on a risk–reward exit. Your target is your reward relative to your risk.

In long-term or medium-trend trading, it can be convenient to add a trailing stop to the risk/reward ratio.

In the end, the exit that is best for you is the one that gives you profits consistently and easily. This depends on your trading style and personality. It is better to exit a target than not to exit at all or fail to follow your trailing stop. Make it simple to exit. This is more important than the type of exit itself, as long as you keep your favorable risk–reward. Never overrun your risk–reward. This is the secret of successful exits. Also, make your exit as automatic as possible. Once you have a favorable risk–reward, try to reduce the number of steps in your trading execution. This will give added strength to your exit.

Let us talk a little more about minimizing your risk

Minimizing Your Risk

The name of the trading war is minimizing risk. What you are trading is ultimately risk. You are a risk trader. The market is paying you to take a risk. If you take it, you are rewarded. If you do not, you are not.

Traders are professional risk takers. They do not avoid risk. Most people avoid risk in their lives and are fearful. Anything worthwhile entails risk. The thing is not to avoid risk, but to face it courageously. This implies knowing risk and developing a close familiarity with it. This knowledge enables you to become a friend of risk. It is not your enemy, but your ally. The secret of risk is to stack the odds in your favor and minimize it.

Minimizing risk is not avoiding risk, but accepting it intelligently. This is what risk wants of you. The risk will always be there since that is what the market is paying you for. As a trader, you are in the risk business. Because you are in a risky business, you must learn to manage risk. By managing risk, you can use it. The main way to manage it in your trading entries and exits is to be sure that you have a favorable risk/reward and win/loss ratio.

For example, if you win three dollars for each dollar that you lose, you have a risk–reward of one to three. Your reward is three times your risk. This means that you can win only three trades out of ten and come out ahead.[22] If the above is the case, your three winning trades will amount to a total of nine dollars and your seven losing trades will amount to seven dollars. Your profit is two dollars, although you lost seven of ten trades.

This means that you can be a winner, even if the majority of your trades are losers. This example shows you the power of the risk/reward ratio and of controlling risk as you trade. Later, in another chapter, we will delve again into risk control.

Using the master swing and the master key number, waiting for a triad before you enter the market and waiting for the convenient risk/reward ratio are the three ways we use to minimize risk when swing trading. Waiting for a triad before you enter the market, whatever setup you use, helps you to minimize risk. However, we must point out that this does not necessarily apply to exits. These three ways of controlling your risk are the main ones and will define your profits and your success in the markets in the long run. Basically, you need a good setup that gives you a favorable risk reward. That is it.

To this, you can add an additional way of controlling risk while trading – using stops. Let us examine how they help to minimize risk.

How to Use Stops

Using stops should never be your primary way to control risk. We must emphasize this point. Stops will never turn a bad trading system into a good one. All that stops do is avoid extra losses within a winning system and help to prevent the worst case scenario.

This is why stop placement is in some ways an art, as well as a science. It must be placed where it will not be touched, unless the trade goes wrong. What a stop will do is limit losses beyond a certain point. Do not rely on them as your primary risk control. If your system loses without stops, throw it out and begin looking for another one.

It is possible that your stops will not work in a market panic – short or long. If the market overrides your stops, your losses could be devastating. This is why you must never put all of your trust in them, no matter how well placed they may be.

How many times have you entered a trade to see your stop touched and then the market turn around, resuming its trend? The trade would have been a winner had it not been for your stop. This scenario will always occur from time to time, but it should never happen regularly. If it does, your stops are badly placed. To correct this, first refer to your spreadsheet that contains your study of the market's fluctuations. In the spreadsheet, you will find how often a given fluctuation could touch your stop. This will enable you to put your stop at a distance where the market will take it out only exceptionally.[23]

The size of the fluctuation that you allow the market to have before it touches your stop is also a function of your trading system. Sometimes it is convenient to stop even a good trade after a certain number of points are lost. The reason for this is the tradeoff where it is better to have some good trades become losers than to have unnecessary losses. However, no one can know this, except you. It depends on your setups, your entry, your exit, and your risk/reward and win/loss ratio.

Therefore, use your spreadsheet to study the size of those fluctuations that, within a given phase, will not touch your stop, unless the market truly reverses. Then, adjust these data to work within your system.

The Mastery of Oscillations: Other Statistical Measures

Measuring market fluctuations is what will enable you to master them. By using all of the preceding tools, you should be able to gain quite an accurate picture of the markets that you will trade. Nothing can replace your direct contact with the market.

This mastery of market fluctuations never ends. You can add new elements, such as other statistical measures. Adding the average of the price lengths and time lengths of the swings under study is useful You can also add the mode and the median, as well as calculate the standard deviation. You can add a column for each of these measures in your spreadsheet. All of them will give you a clearer view of what the market is doing. These new measures will become useful once you understand their meanings.

These meanings should not become automatic. There is a difference between using a measure blindly as a trading tool, such as buying the crossovers of two moving averages, irrespective of market behavior, and using the tool to get an additional fact that you could be missing. It is important to understand the meaning of each of these measures and how you could use them to get a more accurate view of the market.

For example, if you want to study the repetition of swings, the mode will give you the size of the swing that is repeated most frequently. This can be useful in order to know the impact that certain corrections can have and how important they are. The median will give you the middle value for a series of swings. It is not the average, but a real, existing value. Most important is the standard deviation. It will immediately give the probability for the occurrence of a given swing length in price or time. This can be used as follows to determine the exact probability that something will happen next.

If you want to know how much the market will move in the opposite direction after a given simple or complex swing takes place, all you must do is look at your spreadsheet and find the column where the swing size appears. If the swing is contained within two standard deviations of the arithmetic mean, there is a 95 % probability that such an event will occur again. If the swing exceeds two standard deviations from the mean, its recurrence is a low-probability event.

There is a caveat when using the standard deviation. The standard deviation should not be used to enter trades and it does not mean that we can trade against the main market trend. It is helpful as an additional tool to use eventually with market structure. The market can continue for a very long time before a reversal occurs. This is why the standard deviation is useful to define the area of probability of occurrence of swings of a given size, although it cannot be used as a tool to enter the market anticipating a reversal. More often than not, the result would be catastrophic. Markets are nonlinear. We must always wait for definite confirmation that a reversal has taken place before trading it.

For both sets of events, you can classify the opposite movement that follows and apply again the same measure. If swing a is followed by swing b of a given size and swing c is followed by d, and so on, we measure them. To select a set of swings of the same size, you can use the column where you have posted the standard deviation for each swing of your collection. We measure the contrary swings b, d, e, ... and we obtain their standard deviation. This enables us to know that, for a given swing, there is a 95 % probability that another swing will follow if it is contained within two standard deviations.

All of this can also be done without these statistical measures, but it will not be as precise. You could visually determine which swings have a similar size, inspect their contrary corrective swings, and guess which one has the greatest chance of repeating itself. However, using these measures will give you an accurate answer. With these measures, you can experiment and play in many ways. Only your imagination will limit what you can do with them.

Now we will explain how studying the fluctuations explained above will provide market knowledge of another kind, intuitive knowledge.

BUILDING UP YOUR SIXTH SENSE

Know Your History to Develop Your Intuition

A practical knowledge of market history is the only way to get an accurate and in-depth knowledge of markets.[24] This practical knowledge comes from reading charts and spreadsheets.

The charts enable you to practice pivot recognition, swing recognition, phase recognition, and pattern recognition. You learn how price, time, volatility, rate of change, and volume interrelate. Also, in the charts you will recognize the signs that tell about market force and the laws operating behind market action, such as the law of action and reaction, the law of nonbalance and the law of inertia. Charts will teach you how the different trading setups corresponding to the different setups worked in the past.

Spreadsheets will enable you to classify market movements of all kinds in order to tabulate their prices and time lengths, as well as their statistical measurements. This will give you a numerical sense of past events.

Both of these market senses go together – the geometrical and the arithmetic, the images and the numbers, the charts and the spreadsheets. Both will enable you to perceive markets in a complete way. You need both. In the charts and spreadsheets you will find the past history of markets. This is why you should study them as far back as possible in time. Also, your study should take into account all time frames – yearly, monthly, weekly, and daily. This study of market history by charts is what will build your base of market knowledge. This knowledge should be active. You should record in writing your observations and your thoughts.

You should also commit to memory at least the essential market history. Be aware of the significant past market movements and integrate them in yourself. Know the main bull and bear markets within the different market periods (see Chart 3 in Appendix II). A good exercise is to memorize the chart of the Dow Jones Industrial Index since the beginning of the twentieth century. Memorize the time and price lengths of its main phases through the decades. You can also do this with individual stocks, futures, or any kind of market in which you are interested.

The more you study charts, the more you will study the numbers for each market and the more you measure market past history, the more you will know. By study, I do not mean that you should specialize and trade in all of these markets. What I am saying is that a general knowledge of many markets that have been subject to different conditions will give you an edge This edge will appear even if you specialize in only one market and if you have only one style of trading. Whatever is your way of approaching the market, whether it is as an analyst, investor, or trader, you will benefit from your study.

In summary, become a student of market history in order always to have ongoing market knowledge.

The Market is Unknowable Unless . . .

The study of market history will expand your market knowledge and sharpen your market wits. You will be a better analyst, trader, or investor. However, this knowledge goes far beyond historical data.

This historical data contains a secret clue for us. All market history is in the past. All that the charts and the spreadsheets that you study can do is to convey the past to you. Even when you are day trading with a real time flow, all you will ever see in front of your screen is the past.

You can choose any time frame you want, whether decades, years, months, weeks, days, or even intraday ticks of market history. All that you will be looking up is the past. In summary, the present, the now of the market, does not exist. It does not exist as data. There are no data in the present, at least not any that are known to you. When they become data and materialize, as, for example, a one-minute charted bar on your screen, they already are the past. Therefore, all our market knowledge, even what we think is actual market behavior, is in the past. Not only is market behavior, as seen in our charts, spreadsheets, and real-time screens, in the past but also the way in which this information is organized.

You are using tools from the past to read the past. A chart, a trading setup, a market structure theory, and whatever tool you can think of cannot describe market reality as it is. All it can do is project an image of something that we call the market. Your market image is in itself built with past elements. Even the perception of you as an analyst, investor, or trader is itself in the past. You cannot perceive the present. It will always elude you in the same way that the market does.

In conclusion, the market is unknowable. You will never know market reality by direct perception. For that you must be in the present, but you cannot be. If you were in the present, in the actual market now, you would need no tools to read it. If that was the case, you would have an immediate, transparent knowledge of market reality. The difference between the past and the present in market terms is that the past is past information. It is no longer completely real.

Only the present is what is present – what truly exists. However, you know this as past and only through the past and its tools. All you do is approximate in the past a past market reality. You create useful theories that work. If those actions, such as buying if the market behaves in a given way, make you a profit they become useful.

However, even the best of analyses are not accurate enough and not even the best of setups always succeed.

If all we do is study and act on past information, the only information available, we must be very humble. We must not assume that we know everything about a market. We must never think that markets will behave as we think they will. Although we are only in the past with past information, since all we perceive is already the past, our goal is to be as close to the present as possible, as near as possible to this invisible and ever-eluding market reality now.

To achieve this, we must know that all our tools, market descriptions, and studies, and even ourselves as analysts, investors, or traders, are interpretations that we construct in the past. We must always give market reality, in its invisible present, its own space. We do this by fully acknowledging the past as past and not trusting our impression of the markets or of ourselves.

In contrast are those publicly known wizards who believe that they are infallible and one day go broke, usually by overtrading. The reason is that their perception of themselves in the past was no longer accurate in the invisible present. Then there are those people who think that the market has changed forever and that a severe bear market and a depression are impossible. The answer is that no one knows. I do not. If you do, please send me an email and let me know. Thanks.

Therefore, beware of the past. It is a double-edged sword. This takes us to the mind of the market.

The Mind of the Market

The market seems to have a mind of its own. It has an idea of where and why it wants to go. This mind consists of an indefinite number of thoughts that translate into market action. This market mind is like a huge reservoir where those thoughts spring into existence, develop, and finally transform into other simpler or more complex thoughts. These thoughts are the thinking and acting of every market participant. They build up the market mind. This mind processes instantaneously a huge amount of data and individual thinking about that data.

The processing is done in a multiplicity of different ways to perceive the market and by a multiplicity of market tools to read the market in an attempt to decipher market reality or to act in it to achieve particular results. As an analogy, we can think of the market mind as a huge computer that is running an indefinite number of software programs at the same time, which give different results that integrate into a whole.

As traders or investors, you and I are only thoughts within the market mind. Everything that you think about the market has an influence that will end in a market action, but not necessarily yours. Someone goes to a party, hears someone talk about a stock, and then next day buys it.

All of these combined actions form market reality in the present. This market present is invisible and unknowable. Our past interpretations can only approximate market reality with the hope that they will somewhat coincide, at least in part, with its present reality. We have said that all market knowledge and market tools and actions are in the past, and never in the present. We have also said that it is impossible for us to perceive the now of market reality, its present state. The reason is that we only perceive an action when it is complete. This is synonymous with the past, since a complete action must have been done in order to be complete. If it has been done, it is by definition in the past.

Only unfinished actions – actions in the doing – are in the present. We cannot perceive the present because we cannot perceive what still is not. This is why it does not exist. The present in what concerns the market is the pure potential that it is becoming. To be able to perceive the market would suppose that we are able to perceive the full energy or potential released by the infinitesimal closest past. This we cannot do.

This present state of the market in its potential now cannot be known by us. However, this does not mean that we are forever excluded from this market present. The invisible trader who is in us, not to be confused with our self-image as a trader, always knows the present state of the market and its truth. Most traders are not aware of the invisible trader hidden within them. They confuse their present state with their past reality. Once you become aware of the difference, your invisible trader awakens.

Let us take a look at him.

Your Inner Trader Manifests Itself

The trader, who is never in the past and always in the present, always knows what is going on. He is your inner trader. Here is how to unleash him.

This inner trader emerges when we hear our intuition of the markets. This intuition is a faculty that we must develop. It is the faculty that puts us into immediate contact with present market reality. Intuition is the bridge between visible and perceivable market past reality and the present immediate and invisible market reality. Intuition should not be confused with what it is not. It is not a vague feeling. It is precise and never fails.

Market intuition is a message that your inner trader sends you about the present state of the market. Intuition is never about the past. It is always about how things are. It has nothing to do with your past readings of the market or the tools that you use. Intuition of the market is developed by eliminating the obstacles between market reality and your perception of the market as given by your models, tools, methods, etc. These obstacles are eliminated by using them as stepping stones to go farther. In other words, to be valid, intuition must be educated intuition. Only hard work and study can develop it.[25]

This market present begins to direct invisibly our market study and our performance. While thinking that we are acting in the past and only knowing the past, which is true at the level of our perceptions, the market now is directing our thoughts at a deeper level. The market present instant is invisibly liberated by our practice of constantly studying the market and having a market practice, such as analyzing, trading, or investing. Therefore, the more you study the market and the more you practice, the more freely and effectively your inner trader will direct, without your knowledge and your market action. Your inner trader is above consciousness. He is superconscious and above your perceiving self.

All you must do to make it work for you is to focus on market study and practice, knowing that behind it your inner trader is preparing the bridge to give you, often without you realizing it, the market's present and inner reality. This takes us directly to invention in the markets.

A Trader is an Inventor

The way in which working with your inner trader as an ally occurs is akin to the way in which inventors make discoveries and inventions. This means that you as a trader are, in fact, an inventor. Knowing this is necessary for your market success. Let me explain.

An inventor goes through many steps, but, in the end, the invention is more a kind of revelation that appears when the unconscious has achieved its work. Invention involves the following steps:

1. Accumulation of information
2. Brainstorming for ideas
3. Period of rumination
4. Eureka moment: the new idea surfaces.

The real inventor is the invisible self, the one who is always in the changing present. All the inventor does is put to work his inner inventor deep inside him. Inventions are always about the future, conceived in the present and known in the past.

The first thing that the inventor does is know his subject or field of invention. The same is true for the market student, analyst trader, or investor. Then, based on this knowledge, he looks for new ideas. The market student is also constantly looking for new ideas. He knows that the market does not repeat its past history. He knows that he needs a market edge. Ideas come naturally to the market student.

The inventor then will stop thinking for a time and leave the work to his unconscious mind. This is the ruminating step where all information helps to release true inner knowledge. The same happens with the market student. The market student, after having thought long about what the market might be doing and about his methods of market action, will rest. That resting time will allow his inner trader to integrate and complete this thinking.

Then, his market knowledge will release its true potential that comes from present market reality. This is how the present of market reality gets in touch with us. It is through our inner trader that we learn to trade and the mastery of the markets. He knows!

Now, we will turn to trading with indicators in conjunction with triads and market structure.

8
How to Trade with Indicators while Avoiding False Signals

WHY MATHEMATICAL INDICATORS GIVE SO MANY FALSE SIGNALS

Why Mathematical Indicators Hide Market Reality

Mathematical indicators are created within the context of the normal distribution curve. They are averages. These averages smooth market data and, in doing so, take away market data that is necessary for an understanding of market reality. For instance, a moving average does what its name says. It averages reality and, in doing so, its value at a given point is not a real market price, but an average price that does not exist.

Its market direction is also a smoothing that gives you the direction of the average values, something that does not coincide with the true direction of the market. By smoothing the data, you lose your ability to see the market structure as it really is. Smoothing the data causes you to lose the ability to see the significant data that you need to understand and trade the markets. For example, a moving average may still be telling you that the market is rising when the market long ago reversed and is on a downward course.

The moving average will not tell you about the critical pivots or the significant market swings and their structure. All of these data and their meaning, which is necessary to understand market action, are taken away from you.

This is why you need market structure first. A moving average will never give you market structure. In addition, it gives you false information about prices, market direction, and trading signals. This happens in a moving average crossover. The slower moving average will be crossed by the faster moving average on the upside and you will take this as being a buying signal, whereas if the crossing is in the opposite direction, you will take it as a selling signal.

The signals sometimes do work, but very often do not. Many of these signals, if taken alone, are false. The reason is that, in the act of smoothing market data, the moving average has deformed and falsified it. When this happens, market action will contradict the signal. This is when series of losses occur. This happens when the moving average is not telling the truth.

This is not to say that a moving average is not useful. The smoothing and averaging that it performs is very valuable. However, to be valuable, it must satisfy a condition.

Convergence and Divergence

The condition that an average must satisfy in order to be valid is that market behavior and the moving average behavior must converge. When they converge, the smoothing is able to tell you the dynamic balance of prices while they move. The average will be a kind of middle path that prices will follow in their advance.

In this sense, the moving average will help you to confirm when the market is above or below its relative equilibrium point in its movement. This can be very useful to trade. For example, you can buy below the balance point and sell above it.

When the moving average does not converge with market behavior, you get the opposite – many false signals. This is when moving average signals should be avoided.

This convergence and divergence concept has an added value. It can be used as a trading tool. Do you remember how Charles Dow used the convergence or divergence of two indexes, the industrial index and the transportation index, to get signals on reversals? In this last case, two actual market structures, each telling its own true and objective message, were encountered. The divergence was not a confirmation, but simply a warning that a reversal could happen. Also remember that only a convergence between the two market indexes gave a positive signal to be acted upon. You had real market structures that converged.

In the case of your moving average, things are different. Two realities of different order are encountered. One is a market structure that is real. The other is a mathematical entity that is an abstract of reality. Both their convergence and divergence will ultimately be judged by market structure itself. It is within the primacy of market structure that the divergence acquires its meaning and, eventually, its usefulness. When the market diverges, it is the market that takes the lead, not the moving average. The market is telling you not to obey the moving average any more. It is also telling you that it will soon change its behavior. You must always follow the market first.

How do you know if a moving average is converging or diverging with market behavior? In the next section, you will find the answer.

The Fundamental Market Structure Enables You to Restore the Market's Lost Data

The only way to know whether a moving average is converging or diverging with market behavior is by confronting its behavior with the reality of market structure.

There is no other way out of this dilemma. Only market structure will tell you what the market is doing. By observing market structure, you will know whether the market is in an uptrend achieving higher highs or in a downtrend creating lower lows, or if it is in a horizontal range.

The fundamental market structure and its three elements – pivots, swings, and triads – give you the way in which the market is built at a given moment and the significance of the structure that appears in front of you. The only true meaning is the one that is conveyed by market structure. This is why you must always be aware of market structure. This is why there is nothing else that you need besides knowledge of market structure.

A moving average may or may not tell the truth. Sometimes it does, but more often than not it does not. How can you know? There is only one way – by confronting it with the reality of market structure, the only true market reality. This is why, in order to understand a moving average, you need to look at it within the background of pivots, swings, and triads. They will tell you if the moving average is converging with the market structure direction or not.

Using this knowledge, you can use the moving average for what it was intended, namely to smooth data within a given definite market behavior and, by doing this, giving you a dynamic equilibrium middle path where a movement is in balance. This means that, if the market goes up and the moving average does also, you can use it. If the market goes down and the moving average does also, you can use it. Then, if the market is in a horizontal range and the moving average is also, you can use it.

However, even in this case, there is a warning. Market structure has priority over a moving average when judging market action. For example, market structure can tell you that the market is still in a downtrend, but almost at the point of reversal. At this point, both the market and the moving average converge, but the moving average is not giving you the new information that you need.

The same can be said of the other statistical measures. They always abstract information from market reality without taking into account its structure. This is true of the median, the mode, and the standard deviation.

The information that they all give you is not within the context of market structure. It has been isolated from it. This isolation makes it dangerous to rely blindly on those numbers. You must always confront them with market action according to market structure. This enables you to know not only that they converge but also that, at the moment of observation, they are not about to contradict market action.

This is why you must always rely on market structure first.

Do We Need Indicators?

By what has been explained above and throughout this book, it would seem that you do not need indicators. This is true. All that you need to trade is market structure. Pivots, swings, and triads and the structures that they build are all that you need if you understand their meaning. However, when you restore to indicators their lost data, they become useful because of smoothing and sometimes can provide added insights about the market. Every tool is useful to the trader. He should not reject anything that he can use profitably.

In the act of smoothing, as in the case of a moving average or of isolating a given series of data as in a median or a mode, the context of market structure is lost. Isolated data means nothing. As soon as data are restored within the context of market structure, the indicator acquires its true meaning and function. When this happens, the indicator's true meaning becomes visible to you and you can use it as a trading tool. By restoring the market's lost data indicators, such as stochastics, RSI, MACD, and others, they become useful tools. Then, they are no longer divorced from market reality. They become tools with which to trade the market profitably.

This implies a new approach to indicators. It is not the usual approach of using them as mathematical tools that are limited to giving you signals and then simply taking the trade that they suggest. In fact, the new approach is the oldest. It consists of reading indicators without indicators. This means being able to read the market structure that they are telling you about. This is possible and useful.

Indicators then reveal to you a market pattern with meaning. In order to read it, all you need is market structure. In this way, you can read stochastics without stochastics, or RSI without RSI. Once you know this, you can continue to use indicators as usual, but always against the background of market structure. For example, if you have an uptrend that already has a given time length, according to market structure, you know that a moving average of a given range of value should be going up. Similarly, in the case of a downtrend, it should be going down. There is no need to calculate anything.

In the same way, stochastics average up closes near the end of the range charted bar. You can develop the ability to observe charted bars and see where the closing prices are – near the high or the low of most charted bars. This will give you the stochastic behavior of the market at a glance. This is true of all mathematical indicators. You must never forget that they are only abstractions and averages of real values.

Indicators are based on reality. This is why you must always identify the reality behind the indicator. You will always find an element of market structure – one that was abstracted and averaged to build the indicator. It is that element that you must identify. It has more value than the indicator that it helped to build. It is the source of the indicator. Always go to the source first. They do not need to be optimized any more.

Let us discuss optimization and moving averages briefly.

We Cannot Optimize Market Reality

The reason why some people optimize moving averages is because they think that by so doing they can minimize false signals. This is far from being true or possible. All they are doing is fitting a number, the value of the average, with past information. This past information is no longer valid, since it has already changed when the optimized value of the average is used to trade. Thus, false signals abound again.

However, there is something interesting about optimization. Even if it falsifies the future by fitting a posterior to the past, it does fit the past. This is why you arrive at those staggering profits for some trading systems. What they do is to fit an average or indicator to past market data and events that have already occurred. By doing so, they are trying to make the moving average fit market structure and they succeed, but for the past.

This shows the power of market structure. In fact, when optimizing a moving average, the optimizing is done to fit market structure. Thus optimization is telling us who really rules. The ruler is market structure and the subject is the moving average.

The lesson when optimizing a moving average is twofold. First, the optimization is done against market structure blindly. Second, the market structure against which the optimization is done cannot be optimized. We have two poles. One is the optimized, the moving average, and the second is the optimizer, market structure itself.

To optimize is like a blind person seeking his way by trial and error. Numbers are selected until a satisfactory fit is obtained. All of this is done by trial and error without knowing why. However, when the fit is obtained, there is only one reason. Market structure is validating it.

Why not look directly at market structure, instead of trying blindly by trial and error to get a fit of the past that has no use for the future? Why not go directly to the source of past, present, and future behavior – to market structure itself?

By going directly to market structure, we will need no optimizing. Market structure always tells the truth. No past fitting is necessary. Pivots, swings, and triads and their meaning are all that are needed to study and trade objectively and truthfully. Pivots, swings, and triads build themselves up into the different market structures that we know. They develop into phases of consolidation, trends, and turning points. In turn, these develop different, more specific patterns within themselves. The relative positions and angles of their pivots and swings inform us about market strength, market speed, or market volatility. All this is done in an objective, nonoptimized and truthful way. The market tells us its own message directly. No indicators are needed!

This is why we must never attempt to optimize and fit a moving average. Its usefulness lies in another direction. To discover it, read the next section.

THE POWER OF A SIMPLE MOVING AVERAGE

Welcome Back to the Moving Average

We are back to the moving average. The difference this time is that it will be used to trade in conjunction with market structure as background. By using your moving average against the background of pivots, swings, and triads, a new landscape will appear. The progression of pivots, with some pivots being at the turning point of complex swings, will mark them as significant.

Some pivots, and the swings they complete, will appear more significant than others. They will make the phases of the market visible and they will define the significance of the phases themselves. Not all pivots, swings or phases have the same significance. Significance is given by the time and price factors combined. Some swings and phases are more important than others and so are pivots.

The simple moving average that you will be using immediately will acquire perspective when contrasted with the pivots, swings, phases, and their relative significance. The meaning of the simple moving average will become evident. By evident, we mean that you will know if this simple moving average is converging with market structure and if its message is truly the same as the market's message. You will realize this in a direct visual way.

All you must do to unleash the power of a simple moving average is look at it with new eyes. Look at it and, at the same time, learn its significance from what market structure is telling you.

Now the moving average is no longer the blind tool with no immediate contact with true prices and market reality. The simple moving average now unleashes its power like a snake smoothly moving among pivots, swings, and phases that signal the path that it follows. To use this power practically, the first thing that you need to do is to plot on a chart the fundamental market structure. This is done by defining market swings, simple and complex, by plotting the triads, by marking the pivots they define, and finally by linking those pivots to create swings.

This will cause the market structure to emerge. Once you have finished marking triads, and then its pivots, and then linking those pivots together, the fundamental market structure with its phases and patterns will appear. You will see immediately the simple and complex swings and their pivots and triads. You will see how these swings structure themselves in phases and how the phases form patterns. Also, their relative significance in terms of price, time, and structure will become visible.

Once you have done this, plot a simple moving average that does not need to be optimized. As you have market structure in the background, optimization is not necessary. Choose a moving average that will move smoothly along its pivots, swings, and phases. A 20-day moving average will be fine for daily charts. For longer periods, try a 50-period moving average. Now that you have your simple moving average, you are ready to build a trading system based on it.

We will now examine the methods used to trade a moving average profitably.

Trading a Simple Moving Average: The Three General Conditions

The usual way of trading a simple moving average is to buy as soon as the average is crossed on the upside and to sell as soon as the moving average is crossed on the downside. Many false signals will appear when you do this. These false signals will appear when prices cross the average. Then, they turn around without giving the planned profit and cross back to the downside.

The main reason for this is that the moving average is not in harmony with market behavior. This often happens when the moving average is crossed to the upside and has even a momentary change in its direction to the upside when the market's trend is down. False signals will then proliferate. To avoid this, plot your moving average against the background of market structure. If the market structure is rising, you will only trade on the long side. If the market structure tells you that the market is going down, you will trade on the short side only. If the market is in a range, you will refrain from trading it. Trading ranges with or without moving averages have the added disadvantage of lack of force.

When markets trend, they add to the range within which they vary the force that guides the trend. In horizontal ranges, you have swings between boundaries, but the force that gives its momentum to a trend is lacking. This is why trading ranges always put you at a disadvantage. Force is lacking. However, force within a trend reduces your risk considerably. This is why horizontal ranges should not be traded. For the same reason, moving average false signals abound within them.

This is why, even when trading channels, you should trade within trends and never within horizontal ranges. I do not like saying never as maybe someone can succeed at trading them. However, a force is missing. Why not have all of the odds on our side? Therefore, you will trade your simple moving average within a confirmed trend, up or down. The confirmation will always be given by the fundamental market structure and its setups that you have already studied. When the market structure says that the trend is confirmed and upward, you will only trade the long side. When it says the trend is confirmed and down, you will only trade the short side. Only this will enhance your trading significantly.

To trade the simple moving average, here are the general conditions that apply to all of our moving average trading methods:

1. You want a trend, up or down, confirmed by the fundamental market structure.
2. You want the direction of your simple moving average to be upward if the trend is up or downward if the trend is down.
3. You do not trade horizontal ranges.

These conditions being satisfied, let us explain our first moving average trading strategy.

Trading a Simple Moving Average: The Contrarian Strategy

This method goes against the usual way of trading a moving average. Instead of trading your simple moving average and buying when it crosses to the upside and selling when it crosses to the downside, you will do the opposite This is why I call it the contrarian strategy. You will buy when the average crosses to the downside and you will sell when the simple moving average crosses to the upside.

The conditions to do this are, first, the general conditions that the market is up and the moving average is also rising. Second, when the prices cross the simple moving average to the downside, you must wait for an upside triad to appear and buy it. By waiting for the triad to appear, you are decreasing your downside risk. The downswing could continue after you bought it and then reverse. To diminish the risk of the buying point, you wait for the triad (see Charts 31 and 32 in Appendix II). When the upward triad appears, you buy it at close or you buy the next bar at the open. This is the setup to go long. You must make sure that other elements in the market structure confirm your trade, such as a double bottom or strong support. Otherwise the strategy could be dangerous.

To go short, you sell short when the market structure tells you that the market is in a downward trend, when the moving average is definitely going down, and when prices cross the simple moving average to the upside. Here again market structure must confirm the trade with a resistance point or a double top being made where the trade is initiated. When this happens, you sell short as soon as a downward triad appears. As soon as it appears, you sell it at the close or the bar after it at open (see Chart 28 in Appendix II). Again, waiting for the triad helps selling short, lowering the risk that the market will continue its up move before reversing.

The idea behind this strategy is that, as they say, the trend is your friend. You are buying a correction within a trend because the trend has extra force going for it, which pushes the market upward. If this was not so, you would have a horizontal consolidation within a range. You do not want this. You want all the strength that you can have on your side before trading.

This strategy should be tested and studied. You must study the trend and its inner swings. You must enter into your spreadsheet the size and time length of its corrections. This will give you added confidence in your trades. By knowing your trend and your market, as described by the fundamental market structure, you will know the best swing sizes to apply the strategy to if you are a short-term trader. Also, you will pinpoint more accurately your risk by noting what happens in general when the first reversal triad and your entry point make their appearance.

No trading method should be used blindly without first understanding it and proving it to yourself. Become a market student. Study your trades and your methods.

Trading a Simple Moving Average: The Usual Strategy

This is the classic price crossover. When the simple moving average is crossed to the upside, you buy the crossover as soon as it appears. With your method, you buy the crossover when the following conditions appear. First is the general condition that both the market and the moving average must be rising. Once these conditions have been satisfied, all you need is a buying signal. The buying signal is given when a triad closes above the moving average for the first time. Before that triad, the market is below the moving average. Once the signal is given, you buy at the close of the triad if it closes above the moving average (see Chart 20 in Appendix II). If the triad crosses the simple moving average, but closes below it, you can buy at the open of the next bar, provided it opens above the moving average. You can place your stop at the low pivot of the triad.

In this kind of trade, you expect that once the average is crossed, the trend will continue with renewed vigor. When taking this kind of trade, you must always expect that some trades will fail, even though the trend is still upward. The reason for this is that a trend can take some time before it reaffirms itself. When this happens, a downward reaction can take away your stop. This means that you must re-enter the market as soon as a new signal appears. This new signal must be taken only if the fundamental market structure tells you that the trend is still there.

When entering the market following this signal, the moving average will be somewhat flattened within the trend. During a trend, a moving average is not constantly rising, but flattens from time to time. This is due to the fact that small corrections that do not invalidate the trend, but are resting times during which the market renews its strength, make themselves present. These corrections flatten the simple moving average slightly.

Trading the short side of the market with a simple moving average is similar to trading the long side. To trade short, you wait until the general conditions of the setup are in place. Then, you wait for the short signal to occur.

The general conditions for the short trade setup are that the market structure must show a downtrend in place and that the moving average must be going down. Once these conditions are satisfied, you wait for a short signal. The short signal arrives when the price crosses the simple moving average to the downside. The price must cross with a downward triad. You sell short the close of the downward triad. Your stop can be placed at the high pivot of the triad (see Chart 33 in Appendix II).

This kind of short trade can be followed with a trailing stop until the stop is taken out. It is also possible to follow it with a combination of trailing stop and target. When trading these setups, you must first study the market. This setup is only a general method that must be adapted to your money management, risk control, and trading plan.

Trading a Simple Moving Average: The Crossover Strategy

The next method is the crossover method. Here you use two simple moving averages – a short one and a long one. When the short moving average crosses the longer one, you have your signal.

This method is well known. It was developed by authors like Richard Donchian for the purpose of trading trends. Donchian used a crossover of a 5-day moving average over a 20-day moving average. You can use two setups. The first setup, for short-term or medium-term trading, uses the 5-day and 20-day moving averages. The second setup, for long-term trading, uses a 60-day moving average over a 240-day moving average.

It is better not to tinker with moving averages. Do not try to get a better moving average. The end result will be the same. Instead, rely on what market structure is telling you behind the scenes. Pick two short-term moving averages and two long-term ones and stay with them. We use a ratio of four-to-one for our moving averages. If the short average measures 5, the long average will measure 20. The lengths you choose for the crossover do not matter so much as choosing a pair, staying with it, and using it consistently. The lengths of the moving averages can vary. You can experiment with your own as long as you end up choosing only one pair and staying with it.

Let us discuss the short-term technique first. To trade from the long side, you first need the 20-day moving average to be going up. Second, you need the market structure to tell you that the market is up. The breakout pivot setup or the upward reversal setup, or both, must be in place at the same time. This is because these two setups can be traded independently, but can also be traded together. When both are present at the same time, they reinforce each other and the signal that they give is stronger.

When these conditions are satisfied, you wait for a crossover of the 5-day simple moving average over the 20-day simple moving average. You also want a triad to be present at the crossover. When all these conditions have been met, you buy the triad at its close. Then, you stay in the trade and follow it with a trailing stop. Once your risk/reward ratio has been achieved, you tighten your stop (see Chart 34 in Appendix II).

To trade from the short side, you first need the 20-day moving average going down. Second, you need the market structure telling you that the market is in a downtrend. The breakout pivot setup or the downward reversal setup, or both, must, at a minimum, be complete.

When these conditions are met, you wait for a crossover of the 5-day simple moving average below the 20-day simple moving average. You also want a downward triad to be present at the crossover. When all these conditions have been met, you sell the downward triad at its close. Then, you stay in the trade and follow it with a trailing stop. Once your risk/reward ratio has been achieved, you can tighten your stop (see Chart 35 in Appendix II).

The stop always goes below a triad pivot. For long trades, you use the low pivot of a downward triad. For short trades, use the high pivot of a downward triad.

Moving averages can be useful to trade in the long term. They give easy signals with a minimum of effort. All you do is enter a long-term trade and wait until the market itself exits the trade through your trailing stop.

For long-term trades, use a 60-day or 12-week simple moving average and a 240-day or 48-week moving average. When the 60-day average crosses above or below the 240-day average, you have your entry signal. Long trades are entered when the 60-day average crosses the 240-day average. Only enter if the moving average has been rising for a time. Also, you want market structure in the three main time frames to support your trade (see Chart 36 in Appendix II). The daily, weekly, and monthly trends must be up according to your fundamental market structure.

Once these conditions have been met, you wait for a crossover and a triad. You buy the ascending triad at its close. The stop loss goes at the low pivot of the ascending triad. Follow the trade with a trailing stop.

Short trades are the reverse of long trades. When the market structure and its short setups in the monthly and weekly charts are in a downtrend and the 240-day moving average is going down, you are ready to enter at the crossover. As soon as the 60-day average crosses the 240-day average to the downside, you enter the trade. You sell at the close of a downward triad. You can follow with a trailing stop. The stop loss is placed at the high of the descending triad pivot (see Chart 27 in Appendix II).

TRADING TRIADS WITH INDICATORS

Trading with Indicators

It is not only moving averages that benefit from the fundamental market structure when trading them. Indicators do also. They can be traded using the fundamental market structure as their background. In this way trading indicators enable you to reduce significantly the number of false signals that indicators give. Thus, they become powerful tools in your trader's arsenal. You can use them to build systems.

When trading indicators, you must always remember that the indicator is isolating one element of market structure and averaging it. In this aspect, indicators are not far removed from moving averages. The moving average could be said to be the father of all indicators.

The fact that indicators are ultimately based in market reality tells you that there is a special way to trade them. Every indicator should be referred to its underlying market element. Then, the element should be identified without the indicator.

When using a moving average, you want the market structure to reflect the average. This means that if the moving average is rising, you want the market also to be rising and if the market is in a downtrend, you want the moving average to be going down. In the same way, you want market structure to reflect what the indicator is telling you and want the indicator to behave according to market structure. This means that you should know what an indicator is supposed to do before trading it. This is why, when trading indicators, you should look first to find what the indicator is supposed to do and then look to see if the market structure is validating this. If the market structure is not validating the indicator, you do not do the trade. If, on the contrary, the market structure validates the indicator, you will take the trade as soon as the signal to trade that indicator appears. This is why indicators should never be traded blindly.

Always trade your indicators in conjunction with the market structure. The indicators that you will trade are the best known ones and, in my experience, those that give the best signals.

Besides the moving average, there are the MACD, the stochastic indicator, the RSI, and an indicator of my own called absolute deviation. All of these will be traded in conjunction with the fundamental market structure and its triads.

Now, we will discuss how to trade these indicators. We will explore the core purpose behind the formula of each indicator in the simplest possible terms.

Trading the MACD

MACD stands for moving average convergence/divergence. It was created by Gerald Appel. It is an effective tool that is based on the crossover of two exponential moving averages – one fast and one slow. The slow moving average is subtracted from the fast moving average. The result is averaged, giving a third moving average that is known as the signal line. Its values that correspond to the fast moving average, the slow moving average, and the signal line are 12, 26, and 9, respectively.

The main concept behind the signal line is that the trend is up when the crossover gives a positive number and the trend is down when the crossover gives a negative number. Then the signal line comes into the picture. Without the signal line, you would only have a crossover of two moving averages, one fast and one slow. Positive numbers would indicate that the fast moving average is over the slow moving average and negative numbers would indicate that the fast moving average is below the slow moving average.

However, the inclusion of a 9-period signal line is what gives the MACD its meaning and causes it to differ from a simple crossover of moving averages of different lengths. The signal line itself will be above or below the MACD moving average. When the MACD moving average is below its signal line, you have a positive number since the value of the signal line is the greater of the two. In this case, there are two possibilities. The MACD is either positive or negative. If the MACD is positive and below the signal line, it means that the trend is beginning to move upward but is below the signal line and so the trend is not confirmed. Even if prices seem to be rising, the tendency is still downward. If the MACD is negative and below the signal line, it means that the market has extreme weakness and is continuing its downtrend.

When the MACD is above the signal line, you have two possibilities. You have either a positive number or a negative number. If the number is positive, the market is getting stronger in its uptrend. If the number is negative, the market is getting weaker.

When the MACD crosses its own 9-period moving average, it means that the market is going up first because the 12-period moving average has crossed the 26-period moving average. As a result, you have an upward positive price movement. However, by crossing its own average of 9 periods, it shows that the signal line already had a higher value, meaning that, in the more recent periods, the average shows higher prices. Then, when the MACD itself crosses the signal line, it shows that a more inclusive period of prices is stronger than the signal line and that the market as a whole is strong and rising. The signal line filters the MACD, forcing it to show added strength. In this sense, the MACD with its signal line is an enhanced crossover system. The crossover value itself must be confirmed by crossing a fast average of itself, the 9-period signal line.

There are two main ways to trade the MACD. The first way is to buy when the MACD line crosses its signal line to the upside and sell short when the MACD crosses its signal line to the downside. The other way to trade is by using divergence between the MACD and the market. When prices go lower, while the MACD has turned up, you can expect the market to turn around soon. When prices continue to go up while the MACD turns down, you can expect the uptrend to end soon and a downtrend to begin.

This second approach is more useful as a warning that the market could be preparing a turnaround than as a trading strategy. However, both ways of trading the MACD are inadequate without using the fundamental market structure in conjunction. Here you will learn the first method, trading the MACD's crossing of its signal line. The MACD traded in this way, without triads and the fundamental market structure, gives plenty of false signals.

The first step to trade the MACD is to discover what it is meant to do. The MACD is a moving average crossover where the crossover value is calculated and a fast average of that value is used as signal line. Its function is to confirm two things:

1. That a crossover is in place and the market is continuing in the direction of the crossover.
2. That the value obtained will, at a given moment, cross its own average, with the signal line validating the upturn, if long, or the downturn, if short.

In summary, the MACD ensures that the crossover is a true crossover and that the new trend is valid. This is obtained with the signal line. Once you know this, you know what to look for in the fundamental market structure to validate the MACD. You must look for a confirmation of the trend reversal by the market structure itself. The MACD will give added validity to this.

This confirmation is given by the setups of market structure. If you are going long, you need the market to be in an upward reversal setup or a pivot breaking setup, or both. Then, when the MACD crosses its signal line to the upside, you do so only with a triad. When this crossing of the signal line occurs with a triad, you buy and go long (see Chart 37 in Appendix II). To go short, you do the opposite. Once your signal line is crossed to the downside, you go short only if a downward triad appears. If this happens, you sell it short at its close and only if the market structure has validated the new downtrend (see Chart 38 in Appendix II). The downtrend is validated by either the downward reversal or the low pivot breakout, or both.

In both kinds of trades, the long and the short ones, when using the MACD the ultimate judge of market action is the market structure itself. Trading this indicator, taking into account the market actions, will reduce considerably your false signals. Also, do not forget to analyze each MACD trade in all time frames – daily, weekly, and monthly.

Now, you will learn how to trade with stochastics.

Trading Stochastics

The stochastic oscillator created by George Lane measures the location of closing prices in relation to their range for a given time period. This enables you to identify strong market movements, as well as tops and bottoms. The stochastic measures the closing price minus the low price for a given period and compares the range obtained to the range between the highest high and the lowest low for that period.

This comparison is done by dividing the range obtained from the closing price minus the low by the range obtained by subtracting the highest high from the lowest low for the same period. This price close relative to the range for a given period is called %K, or the fast stochastic. Now, if we average a number of %Ks, we obtain %D, or the slow stochastic. When the fast stochastic crosses the slow stochastic, we have our entry signal. %D is nothing more than the stochastic averaged for a number of periods. It is a simple moving average of the stochastic. The stochastic can be below or above its moving average. It has a definite meaning in each case.

If the stochastic (%K) is below its moving average, it means that the closing prices are near the low of the range. If they are below the 20 % value of the range, the market is oversold and, thus, near a turning point. If the closing range is above 80 %, the market is overbought and the closes tend to be at the upper extreme of the range. This means that a top could be in place or a reversal could be near. In both cases, when oversold or overbought, the stochastic tells us the market's tendency to position its closes.

This gets us to the central concept of stochastics – where the closes are positioned in such a way as to indicate market behavior. When a market is oversold, the number of closes at the low end of the range is greater than the number of closes at the high end of the range. When the opposite happens and the market is overbought, the number of closes at the high end of the range is greater than the number of closes at the low end. This can be verified by simple visual inspection.

You should be able to understand the meaning of the stochastic indicator by simply looking at the market structure. There is no need to plot the indicator to see its basic tendency within the market. The stochastic indicator is useful because it will awaken your awareness of the position of the closes relative to the behavior of the market. By plotting the indicator and comparing it with market behavior in its way of closing, you will become aware of its nuances. As you look at %K and %D, study the sequence of the closing positions. You will then go directly to the market reality that gives life to the indicator.

This observation provides a lesson. The lesson is that isolating the closes relative to the range, even though they give a clue to market behavior, is not enough, in itself, to give a turning point with precision. This is why the stochastic indicator gives so many false signals. The only way to solve this problem is to introduce again the information that the indicator eliminated while isolating a single event. This is why we must reintroduce market structure as the background against which the stochastic oscillator should be judged. This oscillator should always be used in conjunction with the fundamental market structure.

The way to trade the stochastic oscillator is as follows. First, for long entries, the signal is given when the fast %K crosses the slow %D and both lines have recently been below a value of 20. In addition, we want market structure to have confirmed minimally an uptrend through the high pivot breakout setup or the upward reversal setup, or both. Finally, when the signal is given, we also want an upward triad to be present. We buy the triad at its close (see Chart 39 in Appendix II).

For short entries, we wait for the stochastic to be above 80. Then, we wait for %K to cross to the downside %D. Also, we need market structure to have defined, at least minimally, a downtrend with the low pivot breakout setup or the downside reversal setup, or both. In addition, we want a downward triad to be present when our short signal appears. We sell it short at its close (see Chart 40 in Appendix II).

Trading Absolute Deviation

Absolute deviation (AD) is an indicator that I have created. It combines one statistical measure, standard deviation, with market structure. The idea behind it is to combine the best of both worlds – mathematical indicators and market reality – into one. Of course, this is not entirely true since false signals will always be there, although to a lesser degree. Also, my indicator pinpoints one important element of market reality. It is that a market marks a unique price pivot that really exists, when it exhausts itself. It is also an indicator that is easy to understand intuitively.

This new indicator is built in the following way. First, you need a channel with each boundary, the upper and lower, at a distance of two standard deviations from the mean. For this, you take the default form of a Bollinger band with its upper and lower boundaries at two standard deviations. This is the easiest way to create such a measure. You use two standard deviations because they encompass 95 % of the probability of the occurrence of an event. This means that everything outside the boundaries tends to be exceptional.

Next, you wait for a market movement, upward or downward, to go past the upper or lower boundary of the channel and come back and touch the opposite boundary. When this has happened, you mark the pivot high or low. This pivot is the absolute deviation. This means that the portion of the deviation from the mean that exceeds two standard deviations after making that high or low pivot came all the way back to the opposite boundary of the Bollinger band.

This absolute deviation is a deviation without taking into account its value. Wherever the market makes a pivot beyond the band limits, coming back to the opposite side of where the market made the pivot, is an absolute deviation. From this perspective, all absolute deviations have the same value. We must emphasize that the absolute deviation exists as a pivot that belongs to a real market price and market location. It is not an isolated event that is averaged to obtain a statistical measure.

This reality, instead of a mathematical abstraction, is what gives my indicator its validity. Once this absolute deviation pivot has been obtained, you trace a horizontal line across it. This is your signal line for trading. As soon as the market coming from its opposite boundary crosses the horizontal line again, you will buy it or sell it short as soon as a triad appears. You will buy or sell short at the close of the triad (see Charts 41 and 42 in Appendix II).

Here is the other way of trading the indicator. After the absolute deviation is made, wait for the return to the opposite boundary and, after the turnaround, buy or sell a triad at its close. In this case, the exit can be at the mean of the band (see Charts 41 and 43 in Appendix II).

The idea behind absolute deviation is that a movement that goes beyond two standard deviations is a significant movement that exhausts market action. The pivot that is defined is a critical point and a signature. If the market breaks after a full retracement comes back again and breaks that critical point, a new price level will be created that will give momentum to the market until the new balance point is attained. This creates a new trend.

An enormous force is needed to break an absolute deviation pivot. When the pivot is created for the first time, it means very strong resistance or very strong support. This is why it is not every day that an absolute deviation pivot has been broken out.

The absolute deviation can also be used to analyze the market. It is a signature that marks a significant event. Attaining that extreme and highly unlikely pivot point is a test where the market tells you that it is going to break out to a new price level in the near future. This is why the lengths of time between past absolute deviation pivots and their breakouts are important, as well as the calendar dates when they occurred. You can find a use in the future for cycle patterns and key dates that appear. In this sense, absolute deviation is a method to select highly significant pivots that are market signatures. In a way, they are among the most significant and useful pivots that you can find and use to study the market or trade it.

To end this presentation of methods of using indicators, there is a final warning about their link to market reality.

Numbers Are Not Reality: Indicators and the Turing Enigma

You must never forget that all that you obtain about market reality is an image. Prices and their evolution in time are as close as you can get to market reality as a whole. The reason is that prices are a reflection in time of all the fundamental causes behind them. These fundamental causes, as well as the way they are perceived by market operators, define the tug of forces that create prices and price movements. These prices are numbers, but they are real.

More real than the prices is the complex reality behind their numbers. This reality is fundamental and psychological. It goes from the financial statements of a company to the mood of market operators, the general or specific economic condition, and any other factor known or unknown that influences the market. This is why prices and their numbers are the closest that you can get. Even fundamentals, if not supported by prices, can have questionable value.

You must always keep in mind the complexity of the market. This is why indicators do not always work as expected and often give false signals. Indicators are even farther from market reality than prices. They are abstractions that have been created by mathematicians to isolate market behavior that exists only in their minds.

A moving average does not really exist unless you decide to accept it as a mathematical entity. A stochastic indicator isolates closes, compares their ranges, and averages them. Market behavior cannot be reduced to an isolated factor. This reductionist aspect of indicators is the reason for their false signals. By isolating a single element, they exclude the rest of market reality.

Even when using fundamental market structure, pivots, swings, and triads, as well as their phases and patterns that gives structure and meaning to prices and their evolution in time, you receive false signals. The reason is always the same. Prices are numbers. Their structure, which gives existence to market reality, is simply geometry and arithmetic that conceals a deeper reality. This reality is the reason why prices move, creating a fundamental structure. This reality is unknown to us as a whole. We only have glimpses, and lacking the whole, these glimpses are often disqualified by something that we ignore. Thus, fundamental analysis also gives false signals.

The mathematician Alan Turing created a test called the Turing test. The test was devised to answer a question. The question is whether symbols and language enable someone to know if someone else is telling the truth or not. The test consists of a slot in a panel through which you can slide a written question. Behind the panel, someone or something gives you an answer whenever you insert a question into the slot. You have no knowledge of whom or what might be behind the panel. The question that Turing asks is whether you can tell by the answers if the hidden entity behind the panel is human. It could be a computer. The question has not been answered conclusively.

The fact is that you cannot tell if there is a human behind the panel solely by the answers that you receive. The answers are only symbols, and symbols alone do not provide a clue to the true nature of the entity that is concealed behind them.

The same happens with markets. All that we know about them are assumptions, numerical or otherwise. Market structure is a symbol, no matter how apt the synthesis of all the actions and perceptions of market participants may be. The same can be said of financial statements or any other kind of data, numbers, or words. In summary, there will always be an area of ignorance surrounding markets.

The message here is that, if prices and market structure are already symbols of market reality, they are the best that you can get. Indicators, being further removed by isolating an element to signify something, are still less likely to provide a true understanding of market reality. This is why you must never trust indicators alone, but always trade them in conjunction with market structure. In so doing, you will avoid many of the false signals, the reason being that you are a degree closer to the concrete reality of the market.

Nevertheless, even market structure is still a symbol and thus at some distance from market truth in an absolute sense. Therefore, market reality is unknown to you by way of direct perception. This ultimately means that what you know about the market and its fundamental structure is only a reflection of what the market really is and that you will always have false signals. Always. Markets can behave in ways that all our methods and models will never be able to describe and still less be able to anticipate.

This solves the quest for the perfect indicator or perfect descriptive model of market structure. It does not exist and never will. What you can have, and will suffice, are functional tools that work well enough to be profitable. End of story. This means that you should not look for a system that does not give false signals. False signals are unavoidable, due to the fact that we work with symbols that are not market reality. Because they are unavoidable, they are the common element of all trading systems and methods.

In summary, you must learn to trade false signals. This is why trading, in fact, is trading risk. Your job as a trader is to trade risk. Risk comes from false signals. The only way to trade risk is to manage it. To manage it, you must manage your false signals. This can never be done through a trading system. We have therefore found the limits of trading systems. They are false signals. This is the true nature of risk, so far as trading and investing are concerned. This is where money management and risk management come into the picture. No trading system can be successful with it for the reason that no trading system can eliminate risk. This is why some trades are winners and others are losers.

Now, returning to market structure, you will learn how to trade some patterns using triads, pivots, and swings.

9
Trading Patterns with Triads

TRADING TOPS AND BOTTOMS

Among the Strongest Patterns to Trade Are Triple Tops and Head and Shoulders

We still have to learn how to use the fundamental structure in conjunction with some key patterns in order to trade them. We have already explained how to trade tops and bottoms, simple and multiple, within our setups.

Here we will concentrate on the most powerful tops and bottoms pattern, the triple top. By far, this is one of the most powerful patterns to trade. In fact, you could trade only them and make a fortune in the markets. When discussing triple tops, we must make a distinction between true triple tops and false triple tops. For this, we must realize that a triple top is a market consolidation in which prices are testing an upper level where they find resistance.

Many consolidations that seem to be triple tops are broken to the upside of their horizontal range. A triple top is never a triple top until the market turns around and reverses downward. Only when the market has confirmed its reversal does the triple top become one.

Take a chart and identify all of the false triple tops, where what could have developed into a triple top was a range, where a breakout occurred to the upside. They are legion. Never trust what appears to be a triple top.

With this warning, let us discuss how best to trade a triple top.

Trading the Triple Top and the Head and Shoulders

The way to trade the triple top is to wait until it is fully formed and then wait further for a strong downward thrust. The downward thrust can come from the last bar of the downward triad that defines the pivot high of the last top. To have a thrust, you need a triad bar that has a very long range and a down close as near as possible to the bar low. Also, you want the last bar of the triad to close below the first bar of the triad. I call this triad a power triad (see Charts 26 and 28 in Appendix II).

In addition, you want a complete market cycle to have developed. If a complete cycle is ending in the triple top, it is reasonable to suppose that the triple top will begin a new cycle in an indefinite permutation of triple tops and bottoms. To have a complete market cycle, you ask the market to have a triple bottom and an upward trend made by a complex swing with consolidations and gaps. The trend must have a beginning gap, a measuring gap, and an exhaustion gap.

All of these elements add to the probability that what seems to be a triple top is one. Once the four phases of turning phase, trending phase, consolidation phase, and turning phase are in place, you have a full market cycle. This full market cycle is strongest when it goes from triple top to triple top passing through a downtrend with its gaps and consolidations, a triple bottom and an uptrend with its gaps and consolidations, and finally ending in your triple top. When this is the case, you can use either the power triad to initiate a trade or the other setups that define a market turnaround.

There is another key element in trading triple tops – its target.

Triple Top and Head and Shoulders Targets

Targets are a fundamental element in trading any system. In a way, the real secret of trading any system is in establishing targets. Targets are important not only because they give us the potential for a trade. The profit target is not the main reason to define a target. There is a less known and stronger reason. It concerns money management.

Do you remember that we said that traders trade risk and that risk comes from false signals? This meant that the only way to avoid false signals is to have them within a trading system where money management makes the system profitable, despite losses and even with many losses. Thus, losses, in the final analysis, are not what constitute the difference between good and bad systems. The difference between them is that good systems end up winners despite their losses.

However, this is only possible because of money management behind the system. Money management is linked to the fundamental market structure and its pivots, swings, triads, phases, and patterns. This is why a trading method without money management is a sure loser. This is true of the best conceivable method that exists. *No money management* translates to *no winner*.

One of the key elements for success of a system for trading triple tops is the risk/reward ratio. What you should seek is a risk/reward ratio of three. This means that each winning trade wins three times the loss incurred by a losing trade (see Chart 44 in Appendix II). For example, if in trading a triple top, you lose 100 dollars per losing trade and win 300 dollars per wining trade, you have a risk/reward ratio of three-to-one. This means that, with a win/loss ratio of three wins for each seven loses out of ten trades, you are ahead and winning.

The risk/reward is so essential to a winning system that it becomes the first exit priority. If you exited all your trades once their profit ratio had been attained, you would be a winner. This is why all exit methods must be subordinate to your risk/reward ratio. What this means is that your risk/reward ratio is your first, your only, and your true target when trading or investing. Your first priority is to define a risk/reward ratio as your target. This is what will make a winner or a loser of your system.

Forget the false signals and the losses and concentrate on this target ratio. If you are a winner when applying it, you have, in principle, a winning system. This risk/reward target is what truly defines the trader's target when trading a pattern, such as a triple top, although this is not true for the analyst. The real reason behind setting a target when trading a triple top is to ensure that your profit risk/reward target can be achieved.

In summary, the real secret behind target setting in patterns is achieving one of the main goals of money management, a favorable risk/reward ratio. Having said this, here is your first and main rule when trading triple tops: you must only trade triple tops where the pattern target exceeds your risk/reward ratio for that trade. In our method, you want a potential profit that is three times as large as your potential loss (see Chart 44 in Appendix II).

If, when you enter the trade by selling short the triad that makes the pivot high of the triple top, you place your stop at the pivot high, or one or two points above it, the profit target from your entry point to the triple top short target must be at least three times your potential loss. If this is not the case, you should never enter the trade. It is important to emphasize that pattern targets must coincide with risk/reward ratios. The trader sets pattern targets primarily as a money management device (see Chart 44 in Appendix II).

The fundamental market structure makes it easy to identify the target for any pattern. As triads define swing pivots, those pivots are the boundaries of the patterns on which to set a target. In the case of the triple top, the target is set by identifying the highest high triad pivot of the three tops. Next, you identify the lowest low pivot. Then, measure the distance from the high to the low, and project this measure from the low. This gives you the target. The targets that you use are those of classical technical analysis. Pivots and triads make your job of identifying the lengths to measure simpler by giving unmistakable pivots that limit the patterns.

The triple top target, if it allows for your risk/reward target, is your first exit point. From there on, you can stay in the trade by tightening a trailing stop. However, the main exit criterion is always your profit target as a risk/reward ratio.

Let us discuss how to trade triple bottoms.

Trading Triple Bottoms and Inverted Head and Shoulders

The way to trade the triple bottom is to wait until it is fully formed and then wait for a strong upward trust. The upward thrust comes from the last bar of the downward triad that defines the pivot low of the last bottom (see Charts 20, 34, 36, 39 and 45 in Appendix II). In addition, you want a complete market cycle to have developed. If a complete cycle is ending in the bottom, it is reasonable to suppose that the triple bottom will begin a new cycle in an indefinite permutation of triple tops and bottoms.

To have a complete market cycle, you ask the market to have a triple bottom and an upward trend formed of complex swings, consolidations, and gaps. Ideally, the trend will have a beginning gap, a measuring gap, and an exhaustion gap.

Triple Bottom and Inverted Head and Shoulders Targets

In the case of the triple bottom and the inverted head and shoulders, the target is set by identifying the lowest low triad pivot of the three bottoms. Next, you identify the highest high pivot. Then, you measure the distance from the high to the low, and project this measure from the low. This gives you the target.

The targets that you use are those of classical technical analysis. Pivots and triads make your job of identifying the lengths to measure simpler by giving unmistakable pivots that limit the patterns.

The triple top target, if it allows for your risk/reward target, is then your first exit point. From there on, you can stay in the trade by tightening a trailing stop. However, the main exit criterion is always your profit target as a risk/reward ratio. The trailing stop enables you to continue with the trade once the risk/reward pattern has been attained. When the pattern target largely exceeds the risk/reward target, it is logical to continue with the trader expecting further profits.

However, the tightening is important as a way of not having to endure unnecessary risk. Once the favorable risk/reward ratio is obtained, the trade is over. All of the extra profits, however large they may be, do not justify staying in the market after the ratio has been achieved. This is why tightening the trailing stop is advised. The idea is that you cannot allow yourself to add risk to your risk/reward ratio, since this would nullify the logic behind your money management, making your system a losing one.

Now we will explain triangle trading.

TRADING TRIANGLES

Triangle Logic

Triangles have their own market structure logic. They are consolidation phases, usually within a trend. The market swings, as defined by triads and pivots, become smaller in amplitude, thus creating patterns that resemble triangles. The key feature to observe is the progressive reduction in the amplitude of swings. This is what is really going on. This means that you must not seek the perfect triangle pattern. Some patterns develop beautifully and others do not.

The last word is given by market structure – swings of diminishing amplitude within a relatively horizontal range. The meaning of this lessening of amplitude is that the net buying and selling flow is undecided. This uncertain state decreases the buying or the selling, or both. In the first case, we have descending triangles. In the second case, we have ascending triangles, and, in the third, we have symmetrical triangles.

For every buyer, there is always a seller. The number of buyers and sellers are always equal. What makes a price rise or fall is the availability of stock for a given price. This means that, even if there is a buyer for every seller, they will not buy or sell at any price. This is why net buying flow is produced when there is no more supply at a given price. When there is abundant stock to sell, there is abundant money to buy. However, in a rising market in which higher prices are expected, there will be fewer sellers at lower prices than sellers at higher prices – even with an ample supply of stock to sell.

Let us imagine a market in which there are only two traders. One has only stock to sell. The other has only money to buy. The one who has stock has 10 shares to sell. The one who has money to buy has 100 dollars. The seller sells his first share at one dollar. He succeeds since, at that price, his share is immediately purchased. Thus, he decides that perhaps he is selling too cheaply. He then tries to sell a second share from his stock of ten shares at two dollars. Again, he succeeds. His share is sold at double the price. Then, he tries to sell his third share at three dollars. He succeeds again. This means that the net flow is a buying flow, even though the number of buyers and sellers are the same.

Not only are the numbers of buyers and sellers the same, our two traders, but also the number of purchases and sales are the same. The seller sells one share at a time. The buyer buys one share at a time. The net buying flow is up. The difference is not in the number of sellers or buyers or the number of shares sold versus the number of shares purchased. The difference is in the price expected by the seller and the buyer.

Let us continue with the example. The trader seller has sold three shares, each at one dollar higher in price than the price of the previous share. Now, he thinks that he can sell his fourth share from an initial stock of ten shares at four dollars. He offers to sell his fourth share. The buyer refrains from buying and offers only three dollars. The buyer doubts that the market can go higher so easily and thinks that three dollars is a good price for him to pay. The trader, who is the seller, sells another share at that same price. We have a consolidation. Prices stabilize for a while at that three dollar level.

What has been exhausted is not the supply of shares to sell or the supply of money to buy, but the expectation of price. Although he has sufficient money, the buying trader will not go beyond a price of three dollars.

Let us suppose that, in the next trade, the buyer refuses to pay even three dollars. The seller refuses to sell at any price below three dollars. If no one is willing to buy or sell, the volatility is reduced to zero.

From here on, as soon as one of them is ready to buy or sell, a breakout will occur. This is what happens with triangles. This means that their diminishing amplitude is a tug of war to sell or buy shares within a given price range. It is a fight about price, the outcome of which depends on the expectations of the players. When the sellers do not want to sell below a given price and the buyers do not want to buy above a given price, we have a horizontal range. In their tugging, buyers and sellers nullify themselves and the market becomes inactive.

If, within this range, buyers believe that they are perhaps buying too cheaply, they will test higher prices at which to buy and we will have an ascending triangle. If the sellers think they are selling too dearly, they will reduce their prices and you will have a descending triangle. If both buyers and sellers think the same, namely that buyers think that they should buy higher and sellers think that they should sell lower, you will have a symmetrical triangle. If buyers try to buy fewer and fewer shares of stock at each higher price and sellers try to sell fewer and fewer shares of stock at each successively lower price, the amplitude of the swings will diminish.

Then, market volatility diminishes until a point of equilibrium is reached, after which a breakout occurs because something happens that decides the price direction. The inventory of withheld shares of the sellers and the withheld money of the buyers is unleashed explosively. This is what triangle logic is about – a contracting consolidation phase where swings diminish in amplitude due to price indecision. To calculate the target for any kind of triangle, we measure its greatest amplitude from its lowest low pivot to its highest high pivot, as defined by triads. Then, we project this distance from the vertices of the triangle.

Now, we will explain how to trade the different kinds of triangles in conjunction with triads.

Ascending and Descending Triangles

Ascending triangles are contracting consolidations where the lower pivots of the range are ascending and the higher pivots of the range are descending. The meaning of the ascending lower range is that buyers are slowly willing to pay higher prices up to the limit of the upper range. This willingness to pay higher prices means that the sellers are not willing to sell at the same low prices of the lower range.

The pressure is on the buying side and net trading flow has a tendency to rising prices. An upward breakout is therefore probable. As with every consolidation, our consolidation should only be traded at its breakout. You buy the first upward triad after the breakout has occurred. The main concept when trading this kind of triangle is to define a target and trade the triangle only if it includes your risk/reward target within its range.

To calculate the target for the ascending triangle, you measure its greatest amplitude from its lowest low pivot to its highest high pivot, as defined by triads. Then, you project this distance from the vertices of the triangle upward.

The descending triangle is a consolidation that has a descending upper range while the lower range stays level. This means that the flow is to the downside. You sell short the breakout of the descending triad by selling the first descending triad after it.

Remember that you trade this kind of descending triangle, and any other type of triangle as well, only in the direction of the main trend. We go long only in ascending trends and we go short only in descending trends. Also remember that placing a target in harmony with your risk/reward ratio is the main thing to do when trading this pattern. To calculate the target for the descending triangle, you measure its greatest amplitude from its lowest low pivot to its highest high pivot, as defined by triads. Then, you project this distance from the vertices of the triangle downward.

The Symmetrical Triangle

In this triangle, both ranges of the consolidation contract simultaneously. This symmetrical contraction is traded by waiting for a breakout that could take place in any direction. As with the ascending and descending triangles, you establish a target first.

To calculate the target for the symmetrical triangle, you measure its greatest amplitude from its lowest low pivot to its highest high pivot, as defined by triads. Then, you project this distance from the vertices of the triangle in both directions.

You trade in the direction of the breakout. However, accept a note of caution here. Usually symmetrical triangles tend to continue in the direction of the trend. This is due to the fact that they are resting and price-testing locations within the trend. In this sense, you should never trade a symmetrical triangle in the direction contrary to the trend that originated it.

The key idea to trade this triangle is that your risk/reward ratio is included within the triangle's natural target.

The Inverted Triangle

The inverted triangle, also called a megaphone, is a consolidation that progressively increases its amplitude. Swings expand and become larger, with progressively higher tops and lower bottoms. This means that some market participants are ready to pay higher and higher prices, while some others are willing to sell at lower and lower prices. In turn, this means that the market has no clear expectation of its future. Prices do not know in what direction to go. Usually, but not always, this means that the market will turn downward soon. The inverted triangle is traded by selling short the first descending triad after the breakout of its expansive range.

To calculate the target for the inverted triangle, you measure its greatest amplitude from its lowest low pivot to its highest high pivot, as defined by triads. Then, you project this distance from the vertices of the triangle downward.

TRADING GAPS

The Four Kinds of Gap

Gaps are sudden jumps that produce a void between market prices. They signify a sudden change of market sentiment and there is usually a strong reason for it. This is why trading gaps properly can be profitable. There are four kinds of gaps: the gap that occurs within a consolidation range, the gap that occurs next to a consolidation breakout, the gap that occurs at the middle of a trend, and the gap that occurs near the end of a trend.

The only gaps to trade are the three that occur during a trend. These are the breakout gap, the measuring gap and the exhaustion gap. The measuring gap, the one that occurs at approximately the middle of a trend, is called by that name because it measures the trend's length by appearing around its first half. A trend is a market in motion that already has strength in it. A gap then means a sudden jump that gives the trend extra strength.

The way to trade gaps that I will show you is not the usual way. It is Sokyu Honma's method for gap trading. If you want the full explanation, you can read my book, *The Secret Code of Japanese Candlesticks*. We will examine this method.

Trading the Past

You are going to trade in the present a gap of the past. You will not trade gaps that occur during the actual trend that gives us our entry point. For example, if the previous downward trend, after a double or triple top, had three gaps – its breakout gap, its measuring gap, and its exhaustion gap near the bottom of the movement – you will wait for the new uptrend to close the last exhaustion gap.

This means that you trade exhaustion gaps as soon as the market closes them in the opposite direction. This is only after the downtrend has stopped and a double or triple bottom develops and evolves again into an upward trend. You do the same when trading downward trends. You will go short as soon as the exhaustion gap of the previous uptrend is closed by the new downtrend.

You do not need exactly three gaps. You can have more gaps. What is important is that the entry point is the close of the exhaustion gap of the previous move.

The Gap Entry and Target

You buy a trend as soon as it closes the exhaustion gap of its contrary move. As soon as this happens, your entry point is given by the first upward triad in the case of an upward trend or by the first downward triad in the case of a downward trend. As usual, you buy or sell short the triad at its close.

The gap target is the third gap within a trend. This gap is often an exhaustion gap. When trading this kind of pattern, it is important to measure the length of the previous movement, the one where the exhaustion gap occurred. This measurement will give you an approximate value for the trend length so that you can determine whether it satisfies your risk reward target. You must do this since you do not know when the third gap will appear or if it will ever appear.

Exiting a Gap Trade

You do not exit your gap trade until you touch your stop loss or you arrive at your risk/reward target. Once this happens, and if no third gap has arrived, you can tighten your stop to stay in the trend as long as it is profitable. In this case, you can even stay beyond your third gap pattern target since your profit ratio has been obtained long before. However, if the third gap coincides with your risk/reward target, it is better to exit the trade.

Now, we end the trading of patterns using the fundamental market structure. The key to trading patterns is to establish in advance the pattern target, and trade only those pattern targets that include your risk/reward target. Pattern trading, like all trading, is strongly linked to money management. This is why the key pattern trading decision is based on a money management risk/reward ratio. In conclusion, trading patterns is the trading of money management ratios.

The next chapter is about money management.

10 The Only Way to Succeed: Control Your Risk

WHY YOU MUST NEVER OVERTRADE

The Beginner's Blunder

Overtrading becomes a real problem for most beginners, if not for all traders. By overtrading, one loss can become devastating. Also, no amount of money will last and prevent you from losing in the end if you overtrade.[26] That is why you must avoid overtrading.

Even if you know nothing about trading, but do not overtrade, you can survive in the market. You can survive until you learn to trade effectively and trade with controlled risk.

Begin by investing a small amount of your total equity. Do not trade more than 30 %. Also, do not trust your stops. Markets can go through stops and you can lose everything or almost everything.

The Doom Formula

I call overtrading the doom formula. It is the surest path to ruin. Big names in trading history have lost their fortunes by overtrading. Thinking themselves infallible, they risked too much.

The best way to avoid the doom formula is with a robust and simple trading plan. The plan will tell you how much of your assets to allocate to trading, how to diversify and to position size, and how to calculate the more favorable ratios for your trading system or method. (Position sizing is buying or selling only a predetermined portion of your complete position of a particular security on each trade.) Do everything that you can to avoid overtrading. If you are a beginner, risk the minimal possible amount that your trading plan will permit. Also, try to develop a trading plan that can be traded with the smallest possible equity. Usually, this means having a system that takes long-term or medium-term trades with a risk/reward ratio of three.

The doom formula occurs when we fall into another kind of trap, which we will now discuss.

The Fantasy Trap

The fantasy trap is a consequence of false self-images of ourselves as traders. The key here is the difference between trading fantasy and trading imagination.

Imagination is a faculty that enables us to 'see' things before they actually come into existence. It enables us to create things that could exist. Imagination develops reality into its real possibilities before they take place – developing a good trading plan with sound rules. Visualizing how it could trade is an act of imagination.

Imagination is a fundamental faculty of scientific thought. It enables us to create realistic trading systems and to trade them consistently and effectively. Fantasy, on the other hand, creates a false sense of reality. Its basis is wishful thinking. This makes many beginning traders, and even seasoned traders, believe that they can get away with trading bigger positions than they should. Fantasy makes a trader believe that he can find the perfect system that avoids false signals.

Fantasy causes a trader to become greedy and to attempt to maximize his profits. Greed itself is fantasy. This special kind of fantasy is dangerous. It is usually based on desire that has lost touch with reality. This kind of trader hears about systems that make 300 or 1000 %. Even if this were true, once you factor money management into it, the profits drop precipitously to 20 % or even less.

For example, buying an option can make you 300 %. If you use all of your equity to buy an option and you lose, you have lost it all. However, if, as a wise trader, you risk no more than 2 % of your equity per trade, your profit is around 6 % less trading costs.

Greed also manifests itself in a desire to make 40 or 30 or 20 % per year. This is possible. However, it is possible as a result of a sound plan and will not always be achieved. A good trader can make 9 or 12 or 15 % per year on average.

The fantasy trader is thinking about market wizards. One such wizard has made 40 % per year for the last 20 years, while another multiplied his equity 20 times in three months. Forget it. It is not you.

You are a trader who must be profitable. Do not listen to what others tell you about success or their numbers. Often, after a wizard has lost his luster, the true statistics of his record are revealed and his gain is revealed to be much less that what had been publicized.

Simply to trade soundly and profitably is already an achievement. Do not let your fantasy as a trader take over your real personality as a trader. Instead, let the real trader in you come out.

Be Realistic

Being realistic is the best way to become a good trader or investor. This means studying the market and building a sound trading plan with a good system. Profits will take care of themselves if all you ask is to trade consistently.

Once you have traded a plan consistently and profitably for a time, you can refine it and your goals, based on your actual and truthful trading history. Trading is not easy. Learn first.

Be Humble

Humility comes from the Latin word *humus*, earth. Humility is the same as being realistic. All it means is that you must have your feet on the ground, that you must know who you are, and know your strengths and weaknesses.

Humility as a trader does not mean debasing or diminishing yourself. On the contrary, it means being able to be realistic about yourself and letting learning, study, and hard work replace wishful thinking. Create a sound plan with a robust system. That is humility.

LOOKING FOR THE RIGHT RISK/REWARD RATIO

How to Define a Profitable Risk/Reward

To create a robust trading system, you need to define a profitable risk/reward ratio. This is what ultimately defines the profitability of your system. In addition, it defines your win/loss ratio.

Try this simple exercise. Take any of our trading setups with triads. Choose, for instance, an uptrend reversal after a triple bottom where the upward reversal and pivot breakout setups are satisfied. Now test it over 25 trades. Test it with different risk/reward ratios. What do you notice? Your risk/reward ratio will alter your win/loss ratio. In other words, your number of wins will be determined by the reward that you expect for the risk incurred.

This means that what makes a system profitable or not is the risk/reward ratio. Therefore, this is your key ratio. This ratio will determine whether the trading system is valid or not as a profitable system. Let me elaborate.

The first thing that you should do is to test different risk/rewards and graph a distribution curve of them. The win/loss ratio will be a function of the risk/reward ratio. Now, if you have done this and the system is not profitable for any ratio, you must discard it. However, it is the risk/reward ratio that did the selection. Suppose that, instead of not finding any favorable risk/reward for your system, you discover that a three-to-one ratio is profitable.[27] Well, then you have a working system that you can trade.

Signals Do Not Validate a Trading System

This is why trading signals alone do not validate a system. They will not even define its win/loss ratio. This ratio is a variable and is defined as a function of the distribution of the different possible risk/reward ratios that you could use. In the end, this ratio will define the true risk of your system. This is why the fundamental market structure is deeply ingrained with money management and cannot be separated from it. This is why trading targets are so important.

Targets are of two kinds, but one cannot be taken without the other.

The Double Target Approach

You will always find two targets when trading a system. They are inseparable and intertwined in a unique whole. This is why market structure and money management are like two sides of the same coin.

The first target is the market structure target. This target answers questions like how much more in time and price can this trend go according to market structure or what is the target for this double top breakout or this consolidation triangular phase breakout?

This trading target only makes sense within a risk/reward target. This can only be known by testing. If the market structure target includes a risk/reward target, the phase can be traded (see Charts 44 and 46 in Appendix II). It makes no sense to trade market structures if their objectives do not satisfy a profitable risk/reward ratio. Both targets must go hand in hand. They are inseparable and must be traded together.

When adjusting the risk/reward to different levels to fit into market structure, your win/loss ratio will also change. What is important is being profitable with the least possible risk.

11
Money Management Is Easier Than You Think

MONEY MANAGEMENT IS THE SECRET

If There Is a Secret Method, This Is It

The real secret to successful trading is the integration of money management and market structure. They both coincide in the risk/reward ratio, as we have already explained. This secret is what makes trading systems successful.

This is why you must abandon forever the quest for abolition of false signals. As we explained in a former chapter, this cannot be done and should not be attempted. The market is a changing entity. This changing entity, which we call the market, is unknowable through our categories of thinking that are, at best, approximations of something that is going on behind our backs. False signals are a direct consequence of not the market, but of our limits.

When we develop a trading system, we put a frame around the market according to our goals. The market never wins or loses or gives false signals. What we call false signals are unrealized expectations that we impose on the market. For example, a signal makes the market move in one direction and then reverse before it gives us our expected profit. We have defined what that profit should be with, for instance, a pattern target or a risk/reward target or both.

It is never the market. It is always us! This is why a profitable system is a system that gives enough good signals, according to our expectations. We manifest these expectations as targets or risk/reward ratios. Statistics and tests are not tests of the market. Those tests are tests of our expectations applied to the market. Can the market give me such a risk/reward ratio for this trading setup? Can this win/loss ratio combined with this risk/reward ratio be satisfactory for the market sample that I tested? Expectations!

The Truth about Market Behavior

From this viewpoint, you trade your expectations of market behavior – and not market behavior itself. Market reality differs. Market reality appears as an entity that has elasticity. This elasticity enables it to behave, up to a point, as you want it to behave. An analogy could be Silly Putty. You can model it in multiple shapes, make it bounce, contract it, or expand it. When you do that, you impose your thoughts on it. However, it has limits. There are things that you cannot do with it. The same is true for the market. You impose your will on it and the market can coincide with it – to a point.

Silly Putty's flexibility has limits, but the market has no limits. It is your action that is limited relative to it. This is why one of its cycles is going from valid signals to false signals. Of course, false signals depend on your way of framing your expectations.

This is why the fundamental market structure helps to eliminate many false signals since it reframes market behavior in a more concrete way, relative to what you want from the market. However, even here, false signals must exist. This is due to the permanent tradeoff where, if you ask something of the market, you must sacrifice something else. For instance, the higher the risk/reward ratio is, the lower the win/loss ratio is, meaning by this more false signals or, in other words, failed trades.

Becoming Your Own Market Wizard

Other people's expectations are not your own. Forget all those market wizards. Their goals were achievable for them. Emulate those other people in their market knowledge, but do not try to repeat what you hear others say about their success.

Each market wizard is his own market wizard and not someone else. The known market wizards like Warren Buffett, who is a role model for many investors, do not imitate others or seek to be imitated by others. Each has his own unique style that suits his own personality, although they may share similarities.

The same is true for you. You must become your own market wizard. To achieve this, you must trade a system that is profitable to you. Your results will not be those of other people, but only yours. Being ready to achieve results, instead of losing your money, is a worthwhile goal. The only real possibilities of success are those that you will discover by yourself. Research a system that combines being profitable for you and fits your personality and trading style.

THE LOGIC OF MONEY MANAGEMENT

Do Not Trust Your Trading System

You must trust your trading system up to a point. No matter how good your trading system is, it could fail and not work at any moment. Do not trust your trading system to be an infallible money-making device.

If the system fails, you should stop trading it. It should have its own system stop loss built into it. This system stop loss means that you will allow a limited and pre-established equity loss with it. If your equity loss exceeds a certain level because the system has not behaved as it should, you must automatically stop trading the system.

This is where other tools of money management come in, such as asset allocation, position sizing, and diversification.

Never Trust Your Stops

Also, never trust your stops. We have said this before and repeat it here. Imagine that you have bet all of your equity on a single trade and that you place a stop to protect yourself from a devastating loss.

Imagine what would happen if the market does not execute your stop. It happens. I have seen it. Once during a fall, the Dow E-mini future suddenly jumped a very large number of points in seconds. It was such an enormous move that I wondered how many traders had placed short orders without stops.Yes, without stops would only be because they had no time to place stops after their orders were filled. Also, how many trades had their stops not executed or executed at such a distance that their losses were devastating?

Here is another scenario. Imagine a gap. On the following day, the market opens with an immense gap. You have lost all of your equity since your stop was filled after the gap. Never, ever trust your stops. A trading system should work without them.

Even if the worst happens and your stop is not filled, your system should continue to work flawlessly. A system should not depend on stop placement to be profitable. Always test your system without stops. If profitable, keep it.

Stops should be used to avoid unnecessary losses and not to avoid risk. For example, if there is no need for the market to exceed a given dollar amount of loss per trade, even though the loss is within the risk/reward ratio, the stop prevents this waste of money. Suppose that you buy a stock and the risk that you have defined for this specific trade is 10 %. This means that, if the stock falls by 10 %, you sell it at a loss. Now, at the moment when you place the trade, the market structure gives you a location where you can place a secure stop at 5 % from your buying point. What do you do? You place your stop there, risking only 5 % instead of the entire 10 %.

The stop should never be trusted to take you out of a difficult trading impasse. Similarly, you should not trust your ability always to control your trading environment. The unexpected does happen.

Learn to Expect the Unexpected: The Worst Happens

It has happened to me. It can happen to anyone. Imagine that you have a profitable system within a sound trading plan with sound money management. No risk, right? Wrong!

Imagine that you must exit the market on a reversal signal of the fundamental market structure, but you cannot do so because all communication systems are down. Imagine that you must give a stop placement order, but circumstances make that impossible.

Imagine a blackout where nothing works – no electricity, no computers, and no phones – and you have to exit today, but there is nothing that you can do to avoid not exiting. What makes it worse is that you know exactly what you should do, but simply cannot. You say to yourself that it is not your fault. Wrong! It is your fault and only your fault. No excuses accepted. Why? The answer is simple.

When trading depends on a decision that we must make, something can happen that can prevent us from doing so. We can trade a system where our presence is needed, although we know that it is highly unlikely that something could happen. However, unlikely things do happen and we can protect ourselves against not being there at the right time and place.

Make Everything as Automatic as You Can

The way to protect yourself against anything that would hinder your ability to act according to plan is to make everything as automatic as possible. This is valid even when doing discretionary trades. A good system makes no distinction between discretionary and nondiscretionary trades.

If your trading is discretionary, as for instance pattern trading, all else is not. I have explained how pattern targets are used in conjunction with risk/reward ratios. Let us say that you are a discretionary trader. You scan the market for profitable patterns to trade. This means that you have a system. Since you have previously tested the patterns you will trade to verify that it satisfies a risk/reward ratio and a win/loss ratio. Also, you have incorporated the other money management tools, such as asset allocation, position sizing, and diversification.

In summary, you have a system. Truly speaking, you are not a discretionary trader, except for the fact that you select patterns to trade, instead of letting software or an automatic selection system do it for you. Even in the case of having a discretionary system, almost everything is automatic. Only the choice of the pattern to trade and when to trade it is yours.

This is where protecting yourself by making everything as automatic as you can enters the picture. We mean by this that, once you have entered your trade, all that happens afterward is under control, or nearly so. Therefore, both the maximum loss and your exit from the position should be as fully automatic as you can manage it. If this is not feasible, the worst case scenario should be considered and every protective measure against it should be taken in advance.

The first of these measures is your stop loss. Not only will it protect you from unnecessary losses, but it could also protect you from a market crisis. However, do not count on your stop only for protection from a market crisis, because of the reasons that we have given previously. The real protection will come from your main money management tools. We will now examine them.

COMPLEX MATHEMATICS VERSUS INTUITIVE SIMPLICITY: THE TOOLS OF MONEY MANAGEMENT

Numbers Can Be Misleading

Complex mathematics is not always the best tool. Numbers can be misleading, especially when it comes to money management. It is not using advanced mathematics but being profitable that matters. It happens that the old traders' rules of thumb work better than the creations of mathematical geeks. The first demonstration of this is that simple market structure models give you a better description of market behavior than do indicators. The reason for this is that market structure is closer to the whole or totality of the market, whereas indicators isolate only one aspect to manipulate mathematically. The consequence is a distorted perception of the whole and an increase in the number of false signals.

As we have shown, this does not mean excluding market indicators, but using them cautiously within a market structure background. What is true about indicators is also true about asset allocation formulas and diversification formulas. The old tried and true methods are the best. An example of this is the Markowitz approach to diversification, which was far from simple.

Remember what we said about indicators and the Turing enigma. Numbers are not reality. They are only shadows, signs of something behind. Let us get back to Markowitz and his formulas.

A Simple Asset Allocation Method

Harry Markowitz received a Nobel Prize in economics in 1990. What was his Nobel for? It was for an optimal asset allocation model that he had invented. The problem, for which he had an answer, was how to distribute assets so as to minimize risk.

Markowitz created a complex asset allocation formula. For Markowitz, the asset allocation for a given investment depends on the historical market behavior of that investment. Markowitz allocates assets according to the historical relationship existing among the investments to which the assets must be allocated. In short, equity is not distributed equally into all asset classes in his asset allocation formula.

Did Markowitz allocate his own money according to his Nobel Prize winning formula? No, he did not. Why? Because it was not the best formula. What did Markowitz do? He used an old traditional formula. Markowitz divided his money equally among asset classes when investing his own funds. He did not use the asset allocation optimization of his own formula. Instead, he allocated his money equally to each of N asset classes. Simple.

This allocation of equal amounts (its formula is 1/*N*) is an intuitive formula for trades. Investors have probably relied on it for centuries. It is as if a sixth mathematical sense that was acquired through trading and investing history relied on the formula. When a test was undertaken to compare a dozen optimal asset allocation systems, including the Markowitz formula, not one of them could outperform the ageless formula of the traders and investors of old times – the 1/*N* formula.

In conclusion, the lesson is to allocate your assets equally. Allocate 1/*N* to each asset class. Keep it simple. It is better.

I think that this asset allocation formula should be used as a boundary or limit when deciding how much to allocate to trading and how much to allocate to cash or its equivalents. This means that 1/*N* should be the maximum, not the minimum. Never allocate more than 50 % of your assets to trading or investing vehicles. Never allocate less than 50 % of your assets to cash or cash equivalents. This will give you added protection.

For example, if you have two asset classes, never allocate more than 50 % to the trading side. You can allocate 50 % or less. We assume, for our example, that what is not allocated to trading will be held in cash or cash equivalents.

To allocate your assets, the primary practical consideration is how much to allocate to trading or investing and how much to allocate to cash, T-bills, or a money market fund. You should allocate 50 % of your equity to cash, T-bills, etc., and the other half to trading. This should be the maximum. A 10 % loss in your noncash investments, therefore, would be equivalent to a 5 % equity loss.

However, there are other time-tested allocations when trading. Gann allocated 10 % of the total equity to the trading part. Other traders use 30 or 25 %. It is advisable when trading to never allocate more than 30 % to the trading equity, keeping the balance in cash or its equivalents. Trading 30 % of your assets enables you to have a 10 % stop loss per trade while having only around a 3 % risk per trade relative to your whole equity. This is a good figure with which to begin trading.

Allocate 30 % of your equity to trading and, eventually, up to 50 %, but never more. Keep the rest in T-bills or in a money market fund.

A Simple Diversification Method

The 1/*N* formula comes in handy for diversification of investment or trading vehicles, in addition to cash or its equivalents. Invest equally among asset classes. This is the best approach. By allocating equal amounts, you have the optimum. Also, you are free of market history. This allocation does not depend on the specific behavior of each vehicle. Equality is the rule. It not only proves to be the best formula but also simplifies your asset allocation among trading instruments.

Now, how many vehicles, stocks, or commodities should you diversify among? Trading wisdom tells us to diversify among three to twelve stocks or other vehicles. The reason for this is that not all of them will lose at the same time when the signal is valid.[28] A valid signal is often nullified, not because the trade is badly made but because the market for a given vehicle behaves unexpectedly. To compensate for these exceptions, you diversify.

It also may happen that the market reverses unexpectedly and all the trades lose. It can also happen that, by diversifying, losses will average out. Further, a vehicle may move independently, at least momentarily. Thus, you lose less by diversifying. Volatility is smoothed out.

In this way, you automatically optimize your wins without optimizing your signals to artificially fit the market after the fact. Diversification is a powerful tool that minimizes risk and enhances your overall profits. By allocating your equity equally among different asset classes and diversifying your nonasset classes, you make your system automatic. Having only between 30 and 50 % in noncash limits your maximum loss.

By diversifying your vehicles, you further diminish your risk and make your trading as automatic as possible. Even if you are forced to be absent, your equity is at only limited risk. This is a must when trading or investing.

A Simple Position Sizing Method for Entries and Exits

Another way to limit your risk when entering the market, as well as when exiting, is by entering or exiting positions progressively, rather than all at the same time. Traders have known position-sizing numbers.[29] Livermore used five positions. The three first were added after a one-point rise, if long, or a one-point fall, if short. The last two were added at the same time. Sokyu Honma, the Japanese trader and mogul, used two positions.

Both systems are good. Also, positions can be stretched out over time, to make sure that the market follows course. This consistently limits risk. However, entering one half first and the second half some time later is a simple and effective technique.

To exit the market, it is the same. Sokyu Honma advised traders to exit 70 to 80 % of the positions near the end of the trade, leaving the rest for additional profits. Another technique consists of exiting all of your equity near the end and leaving only your profits for further growth. The most commonly used method is exiting half after a given profit has been attained and leaving the other half for further profits.

You should exit after your risk/reward ratio has been achieved with at least half of your positions. I prefer Sokyu Honma's formula – exiting 70 to 80 % of your positions. Once you have done this, you should tighten your stops.

Greed Control is a Must: It is Not as Easy as It May Seem

This may be the most important tool of all. Greed control is a must since greed has a vicious way of making itself almost invisible. The main way by which greed slips in is by overtrading. You invest all of your equity in a single stock and trust your stops, or hope that the market will recover. Imagine having invested in 2007 in Lehman

Brothers, which went broke, or in City Group, which had devastating losses. Also, investing all of your equity in order to maximize profits is a way of not controlling greed. The idea here is to maximize profits. This is the concept that you must fight. Do not look for maximum profits, but for good trading and investing habits.

Say goodbye once and for all to your fantasy trader. Perhaps you do not rely on tips in what concerns trading or investing any more, but still rely on them in what concerns being a successful trader. If you make 9 % per year consistently in trading every year, you are successful. You are in control of your method. This is what you should aim for.

Your fantasy trader will creep in to tell you that someone has made 30 % per year for the last 40 years. Do not listen to the voice that tells you to maximize your profits. Leave profits to your system and the market. Work as well as you can on your trading plan and your system.

Another way that the demon of overtrading uses to insinuate himself is by convincing you that a loss of 50 or 30 % is something that you should be ready to accept easily. This does happen. You look at your tests and see that the trading system, although it had a 50 % loss one year when it was 'paper-traded,' recovered the loss in subsequent years. Factoring in this exceptionally bad year, you discover that your average loss is below 2 % per year and that your system makes, on average, 29 % per year trading stocks. You say to yourself that this is a great system and it really is. However, your fantasy trader sees himself easily handling a 50 % loss.

However, there is a problem. Your fantasy trader is not you. It is once again greed that manifests itself in another disguise. Be warned against greed and against your fantasy trader. Learn to visualize the worst case scenario for each system.

When the loss arrives, it is psychologically devastating to you. The system must stop. In this case, all you had to do was to have good asset allocation. If you had an allocation of half cash and half equity, plus a stop, you would have been fine. You did not because your fantasy trader distorted reality and told you that there was no danger in being fully invested. Now, you know better.

12 How to Find a Trading System or Method That Really Works

WHAT WORKS: ITS KEY ELEMENT

Systems That Work

Many trading methods work. Most work. However, there is a condition. The condition is that the system must be backed by market structure. If this is not the case, the system will not work.

Look inside market structure systems. Within them, you will find swing trading systems, trend trading systems, pattern trading systems, and even, yes, indicator-based trading systems. For instance, the Donchian system is based on market principles and does work.

Robust Systems

A system that works must not only be backed by market structure but also must be robust. By this we mean that it can be traded in any market condition without the need to be optimized. You do not need to fit these systems to the market.

In general, these systems always work – sometimes well, sometimes not so well. During consolidation phases, they will not work. Also, they will give no signals or almost no signals during these periods.

The reason why they are robust is that they have been based on market structure as their background.

Trading Market Structure Systems

This is why I believe that trading market structure systems is the best approach. There are many of those systems, old and new. Systems, such as the ones of Dunnigan among the old masters or of Tom DeMark and John Crane among the recent masters, are top of the line.[30]

Also, trading patterns is an excellent way to trade. Patterns are powerful and robust. Professor Lo of MIT conducted an interesting experiment and, after watching and researching thousands of patterns, he came up with eight key patterns that really worked. There are many other patterns that work if you know how to handle them. However, I mention Professor Lo to emphasize the robustness of the pattern trading systems when they are well built.

It is the direct behavior of the market that is the key decision element in their systems, as well as in my system.

Trading Indicator-Based Systems

Indicator-based systems can also work. Among such systems, I favor moving average systems, especially for medium- and long-term trading. Also, they can be useful adjuncts to tell us that we should begin to watch the market.

I like moving average crossovers and even simple moving average systems. However, it is all right to trade other indicator-based systems.

Where the Real Danger Lies in Selecting a System to Trade

Your greatest danger is not in selecting the wrong system as much as it is constantly changing the system without giving it a chance to work. The key lesson here is to specialize. If you do this, success will come. Of necessity![31]

THE SECRET ABOUT SECRET METHODS

The Best Kept Secrets Are for Everyone to See

Most well-known systems do work. The grail is in front of your eyes. It is our small ego that limits us. Wishful thinking, greed, and ignorance distract our attention from the self-evident truth.

Systems Do Not Work in a Vacuum

Do you want to know what trading systems are not? They are not a series of signals to follow. They are not patterns or moving averages or indicators with their buy and sell signals. All these trading methods are, in fact, entries or exits for given patterns or indicators. They are not trading systems.

For example, assume that you buy a book on technical chart patterns. Next, you read it. Then, you begin trading. This is what you should never do – unless you want to lose it all. Maybe a few trades succeeded. You were lucky. This is worse.

No trading pattern or setup works alone. Without money management, you can be sure that you are going to lose. No trading system or setup works in isolation. For example, you may choose a pattern to trade. Let us look at what can happen. You trade your pattern and enter when you should and exit at the pattern target. If you do this without a convenient risk/reward ratio, you will lose. If you trade this pattern without a favorable win/loss ratio, you will lose.

No pattern or setup wins by itself. Even the win/loss ratio does not depend on the pattern or setup that you are trading. This means that signals and patterns and systems do not mean anything in themselves. They mean nothing.

Trading is another story. Trading has nothing to do with entries and exits and setups only. Trading is a complex structure that must be consistently built.

Having a Blueprint is a Must

To trade, you must create a plan. To create this plan, you must above all integrate a trading setup with trade management tools and money management tools. To do this you must follow a blueprint that will tell you exactly the steps to take. This blueprint should be followed until you have a trading plan with all of its elements. Without such a blueprint, you would be randomly stringing together the elements of your plan. A sense of totality would be missing. To create a trading plan, you need a roadmap that tells you where to begin and where to end.

The elements of this blueprint are, first, your trading setup. You must begin by choosing the right setup. Next, you must add your trade management tools – the ratios that give validity to your setup. Then you add the money management tools. Once you have done this, you have something tradable.

Here is the next step.

Trading the System Prototype

This is the next step of the trading plan. Once you have selected a setup and have integrated trade management and money management in it, you must trade it to see if it works as expected. The main idea here is that you are still not in the trading phase of your system, but in the exploration phase. You must now assign an amount of money that is sufficient to trade the system according to the overall plan.

The amount of money itself is part of the exploration and testing phase. This means that it is money that you can lose. We are not telling you to trade or invest only money that you can afford to lose, as you often read in trading or investing books. No, the concept here is different. The money that you are assigning to the test is written off. It is meant to be lost while testing your system.[32] This money should be the minimum possible for the trades to be executed. Consider it as an expense.

An appropriate analogy would be one concerning an oil drilling company. Once the company thinks that there is a good probability that a particular area has oil underground, it will drill holes that cost millions of dollars in order to discover if there is oil there. Most fail. The money the company invests is meant to be lost in exploration. This goes on and on until the company finds the right spot. With trading it is the same. Once a system, with all of its trade management and money management tools, has been thoroughly tested on paper, it is time for the next phase.

In this phase, money must be risked to see if the trading prototype works as expected in real trading. Also, adjustments are made to the system. Every system needs to be adjusted and debugged. This is why you need exploration money assigned to this final test. Also, in testing, trading psychology tools must be added. Even with the best of systems, losses have an emotional impact that must be dealt with. Preparing for this with the right psychological tools is important.[33]

The first tool is knowledge that your system works in real trading. This is one additional reason to test it in real trading. This is what will contribute most to your confidence in the system that you are trading. The other psychological tool will enable you to remain serene and overcome the emotional impact of the losses your system will incur. This is important, especially when you begin to trade your systems.

Other psychological tools are those that are used to reduce the emotional impact of a loss, assuming that the trading system really works. They range from such activities as walking, yoga, or jogging to taking a coffee break or going out for lunch. The best activity is to re-examine the statistics of the system you use to trade in order to reinforce your confidence in it. Visualize your losses as necessary for the overall success of the system. By knowing that you have a system that works and that you are not overtrading, you will recover from 90 % of the emotional impact of the losing trade. One way to enhance this belief is to write down all your negative feelings and thoughts on the left-hand side of a sheet of paper when you have a losing trade and all the reasons you have to indicate that your system works and that you can trust it on the right-hand side of the sheet of paper.

Real Trading Begins

Only when you have completed all of these steps do you know that you have a system worth trading. You have designed it and then tested it. After testing it, you have refined it and debugged it. Also, you have added any psychological tools that will be needed when future losses are incurred. Your testing has enabled you to know precisely the impact that losses have on you, so that you can choose the best method to remain serene and continue to trade during those periods.[34]

Once all of this is in place, the real adventure begins. It is now that you will begin to consistently trade your system with a profit-making goal. This is where real trading begins. All you did before was to prepare yourself for this moment. In following all of these steps, you have acquired the real secret method for successful trading. If there is a 'trading grail,' this is it.

Now, we will expand on some key trade management and money management ideas.

THE LOGIC OF BOUNDARIES AND MONEY MANAGEMENT

Think 'Ratios' and Not 'Systems'

I do not want to give you all the money management tools here. There are many books on the subject.[35] However, I want to give you ideas that are central to money management.

One of these ideas is that your priority should be thinking about ratios and not of trading systems or setups. Instead of trying to find the perfect setup with no false signals, select a few setups that you find interesting and appear to work. This is only an initial approach. You know that false signals are unavoidable. You also know that the win/loss ratio depends on the risk/reward ratio. Setups, in themselves, do not win or lose. This is why you know better than to lose time by trying to avoid false signals.

So, here you are with a few setups that you would like to test. For example, you would like to test trading support and resistance during a trend or trading triple bottoms or trading the market reversal setup of the pivot breakout setup. Perhaps, you would like to trade an indicator in conjunction with market structure. It does not matter. You take one of your chosen favorite few and here is what you do.

Test Different Ratios for the Same System

You begin to test different money management ratios with it. You test it for different risk/rewards ratios and examine the win/loss ratios that you obtain. Also, in conjunction with those ratios, you calculate your asset allocation. Are you using 10 % of your equity to trade or 30 %? You test for diversification. Are you going to trade one stock, two, three, five, or more?

You must test many risk/reward ratios with their win/loss ratios to apply to your setup and select the most appropriate combination of them. Try to keep your maximum equity loss per trade at 3 %. If it is less, it will be even better. By doing this, you will obtain a curve of your risk/reward ratios and their corresponding win/loss ratios. This will enable you to select the best one, as well as the most appropriate stop loss. You will obtain a perspective of the landscape, so to speak, of your trading setup.

Do not stop here. Remember that you have selected a few possible setups to trade. You must now apply the ratio curve to the other setups. This will enable you finally to select one of them as your trading system.

The Best Ratios Can Be Counterintuitive

When testing your risk/reward ratio and your win/loss ratio, you probably would prefer to trade a system that has many small profits and only a few losses. When you test, the system may seem profitable at first. It is true that, if you reduce your risk/reward ratio, you generally will increase your win/loss ratio. You may think that having many wins will make the system more rewarding psychologically and easier to trade.

There are systems that have inverted risk/reward ratios and win for a long time. An example is a system that has a stop of 0.50 and a profit of 0.25. We find such a kind of system in Dunnigan. This kind of system can be dangerous, since a small series of losses will make the system lose and you will have to stop. If you continue trading it, you will not know when the losses will stop.

This is when counterintuitive ratios are best. Do you think that a series of small wins and very few loses will give you added confidence? Wrong. The opposite is true. Why? Read on.

Think of a system where you win eight times out of ten. In ten trades, your wins amount to $2 and your two losses total $1. This means that you make $0.25 per win and $0.50 per losing trade. You have tested it and it seems to be a winner. When you trade it, everything works out according to your tests. You are now at your trade number 10 and have made $1 per share. With the 1000 shares that you are trading, you now have $1000 in your pocket. However, suddenly the next three trades go wrong. Now, you are down $500 and your wins have evaporated. Of course, if you continue, the system will recover. But when? You do not know.

Now imagine the opposite system. This one makes $3 per winning trade and loses $1 per losing trade. You can lose seven times in a row and still be a winner – and it is not easy to lose seven times in a row.

Which system would you rather trade? Which system gives you more confidence? The one where you can lose seven times in a row and end up a winner or the one where two losing trades not only evaporate your winnings but leave you with a significant loss?

I prefer a system that enables me to lose seven times in a row and still end up a winner. In both types of system, you will have drawdown periods, but I prefer a system with a risk/reward ratio of three.

The Meta System: When Boundaries Underlie Your Trading System

The end result is that, once you have your curve of risk/reward ratios and your win/loss ratios after having it applied to a setup, you will be able to confirm that there are few possible choices. In most systems, the ratios will all be contained within a small range. This means that the ratios tend to cluster around a few key numbers. These key numbers in the end decide the profitability of your system. In general, profitable systems will cluster around a 3/1 risk/reward ratio with a win/loss ratio of 3/7. This means that a winning trade will make around three times what is lost on a losing trade.[36]

These numbers are market structure dependent. They do not work in a void. This is why the fundamental market structure is deeply ingrained in money management ratios. These ratios are powerful clues of what to expect from markets. Thus, if there is an underlying idea behind the successful trading of any kind of setup, pattern, market phase, or method of trading, it is that successful trading is fully dependent on the money management ratios and does not exist without them.

We have already shown how a pattern target means nothing if divorced from its risk/reward ratio. It is this ratio that gives the pattern target its full meaning and not the opposite. This is why money management and its ratios rule the markets. If only this concept remains with you, this book has attained its goal. Ratios validate trading setups and systems. Always think ratios. They are the boundaries underlying all systems.

13
How to Create a Trading Plan

FIND AN IDEA

Trading Ideas Abound

There are many trading ideas. You can specialize and trade a setup, such as a trend upward reversal or a trend downward reversal. You could trade a pattern, such as a symmetrical triangle, or trade a moving average.

All trading ideas should be used in conjunction with the fundamental market structure. You will find many ideas that work. Try a few of them to see which ones you feel more comfortable with and then specialize in one.

The purpose of specializing is twofold. First, it simplifies your work and your trading. Second, it creates a focus on one trading method, thereby making you a real expert. You will learn all the nuances of your trading setup or pattern.

Whether you trade trends or swings, patterns or phases, building expertise in only one setup that will give you an edge. You will know better than anyone how to trade your specific setup. In this way, you are creating a niche. Think of trading setups as selling products. If you find a niche where you are the only one, or where there are very few doing what you do, your competition will be scarce and you will have a definite edge.

Think of the hundreds of trading systems and of the thousands of setups. Trading libraries are full of them. Specialize. Soon you will be ahead of your competition. Most traders try to trade too many things. Do not imitate them. Create your niche.

Keep a Notebook

You should always keep a notebook nearby in which to write your trading ideas. Soon, you will have more than you need. Continue using your notebook. Continue entering your observations, refinements, etc., in it.

Even after you have a working system, continue with your observations. The notebook is not a trading diary. It is an ideas list. Here the trader as inventor is at work. If you hear about an interesting idea, or perhaps awaken in the middle of the night with one, write it down. The notebook is where you will collect your trading ideas. At first, take notes on the setups that you would like to trade. Read about them and take notes of what is useful. Use only one idea per page and date it.

Soon the moment will come to choose a setup to trade.

Choose a System

Once you have a number of setups and trading ideas in your notebook, choose a few of them and list them. Below each, enter a brief description of the setup and how you intend to trade it. The moment has come to build a setup into a trading system. For this, you must take your setup and integrate in it trade management elements and money management elements. Write down the system and its elements. This includes the trading setup or pattern, the money management ratios, such as the risk/reward ratio and the win/loss ratio, etc. Also, enter your asset allocation, your diversification, your stops, and your position sizing.

This is only a first rough draft that will have to be polished many times. To do this, you must proceed to test the elements and adjust them. You do this by looking at your charts and spreadsheets.

DEVELOP AND TEST YOUR IDEAS

First Tests

Begin by testing the setups or patterns to see if their natural targets, according to market structure, give you the risk/reward ratio that your trading system needs. Describe each observation and test in detail. Write down its market structure target, its risk/reward ratio, and its win/loss ratio, plus all the other details. Test many risk/reward ratios and their win/loss ratios. Do this even if you have decided beforehand on a specific risk/reward ratio.

By drawing the distribution curve of your risk/reward ratios and the win/loss ratios, you will get an accurate picture of the market structure in relation to your trading system. This will give you a sense of what the market can or cannot do for you and at what price.

Once you have done this for one setup or method, try a few other ones for comparison and to enable you to choose something that fits your expectations objectively. Do some research and throw out some numbers before deciding on a particular setup. After you have done this, you will have a list of setups that satisfy your risk/reward, win/loss, and other ratios. Adjust these to your equity, your asset allocation, your diversification, your stop losses, etc.

Now, you have a first preliminary draft of a system. Remember that a system is not something that you trade using money management as something you add to it. No, a system includes money management within it. Money management defines the results of the setups and validates them. Money management and market structure are one. They make a whole. Market structure without money management is blind. Money management without market structure is empty.

Work on It and Test It Again

Now that you have your first draft, test it again while adjusting stops, asset allocation, diversification, risk/reward ratios, position sizing for entries and exits, and all other elements that you need. This testing, as often as necessary, is a must. Test until you have gone to your limit and everything works smoothly on paper. Once it all works smoothly on paper, you have a first prototype of your trading system.[37]

Your First Prototype

Once everything is working smoothly on paper, you have a first working prototype of your trading system. All inventors build a prototype first to see if their creations actually work. This is what you have done.

You have built your first prototype. You must now test it in real time. This will provide the definite proof that it works. However, before testing your prototype trading system, you must integrate it into a trading plan.

The trading plan is not the trading system. The trading plan includes all elements of your trading action. The trading plan is a blueprint of all your steps to trade the system. Nothing must be left out. It goes from observing the market for your trading signal to placing your order with your broker, writing it down in your spreadsheet, and making an entry in your journal. The plan is the blueprint, a step-by-step list of your actions to trade your system. Within it also are the psychological tools that will enable you to maintain your emotional stability during losing trades or drawdown periods. All of this goes into your trading plan. Thus, having a final draft on paper of your system, you now draft your trading plan.

In your trading plan, you include your system. Once all is in place, you have a trading plan that is ready to be put into action. Your next step is to follow your plan and trade your system in real time with real money. The first moment of truth has come, but your work on your system and your trading plan is far from over. You still have a lot of work ahead of you. This work will appear as soon as your trading begins.

Testing Your Prototype

Now you must test your prototype. For this, you must allocate an amount of money that will be used for the sole purpose of testing and which can be entirely lost during the test. This test money is part of your R&D expense.

Imagine an oil drilling operation. The company drills many times at a cost sometimes of millions of dollars until oil is found. It is the same with trading ideas. You must allocate an amount of money to test the idea. It is better if this money is ready to be lost. This money should be the minimum possible for the trades to be executed. Consider it as a preliminary expense of a trading operation. If your trading idea works like having found oil in a drilling area, you can make a fortune.

This is why you must never trade before having allocated an amount to fully test the system. Knowing in advance that you are ready to lose that money will give you the confidence to test the system fully, not stopping until the testing period is completed.

This approach gives you immediately the amount of money that you should allocate to testing a prototype – the smallest possible amount of money compatible with the testing of the system. This amount should include the entire amount needed for the system to operate. This means that you will use the trading allocation and have a cash reserve. If your system, for example, trades $10 000 in stocks, which represents a 30 % allocation, you need to have the other 70 % in cash.

Your prototype should be traded exactly as you will trade it, if it works. No element must be missing. This will enable you to have an objective perspective of how the system works in real trading and the impact it will have on you as the trader.

During your first tests, you will find that many adjustments need to be made. One adjustment that will be a result of your tests will be slippage. You will know your real slippage, something that cannot be known by paper trading. Also, you will need to make other minor or major adjustments. Only by trading with real money will all of these appear. You will be able to debug your trading system so that it will perform efficiently.

This applies not only to your trading system but also to your trading plan as a whole. You will adjust your order placement, your signal watching, your journal entries, and any of the elements that are part of your trading plan. You should put everything into writing as you go along, from beginning to end.

Now that you have really traded your plan and your prototype and debugged it, you have, at last, a workable and consistent system and plan that you can trade confidently. Once you have this fully working plan and system, it is time for the next step. Do not bypass this.

PUT EVERYTHING INTO WRITING: CREATE AN OPERATING MANUAL

Your Trading Must Be Easy to Follow

To trade, now that you have a working plan and system, all of the elements that you need must be at hand. You need to have all the tools of the trade and the best that you can afford. You need trading software, a spreadsheet on which to record your trades, and access to your plan. You also need a disciplined approach. We do not mean by this the discipline to follow your trading signals, but the discipline to follow your plan in an orderly way. Scan your charts to identify your setups and signals, record your trades, make an entry in your journal, etc.

You need a flowchart of the actions to follow for each day or week. Also, you should have a weekly calendar with the tasks for the days of the week that are indicated in the plan and a yearly calendar with the monthly tasks. You can also include an evening task of preparing for the following day's action. You can note in a visible location the tasks for the next day, such as chart study and placing the order for the next day.

This makes it visual. It helps you to concentrate on your plan and follow it in a disciplined manner. Also, it will make automatic the discipline of following and executing your system's signals.

Your Plan Must Be Followed Precisely

Making your plan visible will help you to follow it precisely. All your trading will benefit from it. There is nothing worse than trading randomly and trying to decide each day what you should do. By having a visible and precise set of instructions to follow, you are not permitting yourself to work in an undisciplined and disorganized fashion. Being organized is paramount for a trader or investor.

You need to have files where all necessary information is immediately available. You need to have software backup in case your computer fails. You should think of everything that could go wrong and have an alternative plan already in place. Then, if something does go wrong, the execution of your trading plan will not be affected. You will be able to continue trading under almost any circumstance. This will give you added confidence in trading your plan.

Put Everything into a Single Place: Your Operating Manual

Although you should have files, you should not trust them with your trading plan and your trading system. Also, do not trust your memory. It is very easy to get confused by doing so. It also shows poor organization.

Your files, for instance, can have many entries for different aspects of your system and your plan. Maybe you have a file where you have collected charts with setups. In another file, perhaps you keep a study of risk/reward ratios, as well as other statistics, and so on. When you begin to trade, you may forget which ratio you were applying to which setup, or exactly which signal you were following. This can easily happen if your information is not organized.

The same may happen if you trust your memory. You may forget all of the elements of your trading plan and your trading system. This is why you should commit not only everything to writing but also to a single place. This single place is your operating manual. In it should be included your trading plan, your trading system, the system signals, the system statistics, and all of the information you require.

In your operating manual, you will find in a single place all that you need to flawlessly execute your trading plan. Your trading plan is the equivalent of a business plan for the trader. It tells you what you are going to do, how you are going to do it, what the steps to follow are, and what the expected results are.

14
Now Try This Simple Experiment

BUILD YOUR TRADING LABORATORY

Your Trading Laboratory

This chapter is a practical exercise in trading. The main idea to understand is that you should never trade a system before it is fully developed and integrated within a plan. Most beginners lose money by lack of research, testing, and the hard work needed to build something robust that they can trade confidently. Losing money here does not means losing amounts specifically designed to be eventually lost.

These amounts to be lost are experimental amounts that are to be part of the costs of research and development of a sound trading system. The same applies to systems that you buy ready-made. They should be understood, researched, and tested, too.

All of the steps used to create a system from scratch should also be followed when trying to understand, test, and use a ready-made system for trading. This means ultimately that all loss of real equity money will be only your fault.

The first thing that I want you to do here is to create a trading laboratory. In it you will research and collect the information that is required to create and test your systems. It will include all elements, such as a trading library, files, a notebook, software, etc.

Your Library

Traders are readers. You are now reading this book. To trade, you need to acquire knowledge of trading. You should read the masters of old and new who have developed the main trading ideas. You should read books by authors such as Charles Dow, Jesse Livermore, W. D. Gann, William Dunnigan, John Crane, Tom DeMark, and others.

This is a must. You must have your collection of trading and investing books and it should be an ever-expanding collection. There are always persons out there who are creating new and interesting things. Be on the lookout for them.

Your Files

You should also have files in which you collect interesting trading information, articles, and the results of your own tests and developments.

Your Notebook

I have already mentioned the need for a notebook in which to record trading ideas, yours and those of others. This is a key tool of your trading laboratory.

Software and Spreadsheets

You need trading software with which to analyze charts, explore various scenarios, and test formulas and systems. I use Metastock. Also, you need an Excel type of spreadsheet to make studies and record trades.

Once you are equipped with the above, you can begin to research and create your first system.

CREATE YOUR FIRST TRADING SYSTEM

Use This Simple System

Now you are going to create a simple system. The system will be based on trading triple bottom breakouts. The entry signal is a triple bottom followed by the upward reversal setup and the pivot breakout setup.

Once these conditions have been met, you enter on the first upward power triad. You keep the trade until your risk/reward ratio, included within the triple top target, has been attained. Once this has been reached, you sell all, with the exception of 20 % of your profits. Then, you will tighten your stop and let the trade continue. You will exit when the trailing stop is taken out. You place your initial stop loss at the triad bottom pivot.

Use This Risk/Reward Ratio and This Win/Loss Ratio

The risk/reward ratio that you will use is three-to-one. The triple top target must be at least three times the loss if your stop is taken out. To establish this risk/reward ratio, you must study the triple bottoms and their targets for the market that you intend to trade. You should only take trades where this target is possible. Here you must study the past. To begin, collect 10 samples and, if successful, extend this to 25. Stay within a 3/10 win/loss ratio. If your system does not win at least three trades out of ten, discard it. Do this until you have adequate win/loss and risk/reward ratios.

Use This Position Sizing

Buy all of your position at entry.

Use This Asset Allocation

Trade only 10 % of your assets. No more. This means that your total loss is limited to 10 %. This allows you to put a stop per trade of up to 10 %. This also means that trades that need an initial stop of more than 10 % should not be entered. This 10 % stop is equivalent to a stop of 1 % of your full equity.

Perform Your Tests

Now, perform your tests, factoring in your broker commissions. The risk/reward ratio should be net of commissions. A trade that wins should net a ratio of three-to-one after commissions have been deducted.

NOW DO IT!

Prepare Yourself to Trade: Begin Paper Trading

Paper-trade your system with different stocks. If, at this stage, anything needs correction, do it. Always record your observations.

Execute Your First Set of Trades

The moment has come to trade your prototype with real money. Remember, this is money that you are ready to lose as part of your research and development expense. This money should be the minimum possible for the trades to be executed and everything should be done according to plan. Risk no more than 1 % of your full equity per trade.

Now execute your trades. If the drawdown exceeds what is expected, you must rethink the system. At first, do 10 trades. If all goes according to plan, do another 10 trades. Then stop.

Back to the Drawing Board

You have traded your system. You have executed 20 trades. Now revise your system. If it needs minor or major adjustments, make them. Once you have made the adjustments, trade again.

Execute Your Second Set of Trades

Again, do 10 trades and then, if successful, another set of 10. Make the necessary adjustments and, again, trade two sets of 10. When no more adjustments are needed, you can trade your system normally. However, before you do, do the following.

Put Everything Together: Now You Have a Plan

Now that you have a working system, write your final operating plan and your instruction manual to trade the system, including all of the final adjustments. Now you are ready to trade your system normally.

Conclusion

The primary objective of this book is to foster greater concentration on the relevance of market structure. Trading the markets without a market structure description that works is like being blind and without a guide. Market structure is the key to market knowledge. I must emphasize that knowledge of the fundamental market structure has no equivalent when it comes to trading or studying the markets. It is this knowledge that enables you to see what is really going on.

Mathematical indicators acquire their true dimensions only when traded with the fundamental market as their background. Moving averages, stochastics, or whatever other indicators you use, are blind without contrasting them with market structure. Market structure itself has an inner link to money management. Our market perception is intimately linked to what we want from the market.

Market participants trade and invest. Their motivations, perceptions, and actions are behind all market behavior. The fundamental market structure describes such behavior only to a certain extent.

The pivots, swings, and triads are the primary elements of this building set that enables us to describe market behavior. They give place to market phases and patterns caused by value/price perceptions and buying or selling strength. For all participants, making money is the goal. This is the common goal of traders and investors alike, and of analysts in a vicarious way. This is why market structure and money management are one. A market phase or pattern will have a target that may or may not justify a given risk/reward ratio. This is why pattern targets and risk/reward targets go together and form an indivisible whole.

The trading and investing wisdom that tells you that it is better to sell too soon than too late is telling us that a win is not a win and a loss is not a loss until the trade is closed. This means that a trade must have a target that includes its risk/reward ratio. Only exits make profits or losses according to where they take place. They occur at the intersection of market structure and money management.

This is where the fundamental market structure is a unique tool for measuring the market precisely, thanks to its swings defined by its pivots and created by its triads.

By measuring the market, the trader can quantify his expectations and build them into a trading system. This is also true of long-term investors who can use the fundamental market structure to find those market conditions that fit their risk/reward expectations favorably. When market reality and your investing goals identify themselves, you achieve success in the markets.

In the end, markets are what you make of them!

Appendix I
Triad Formulas in Metastock Language

FORMULA 1: DESCENDING TRIAD

```
m1:= H>Ref(H,-1) AND L>Ref(L,-1);
m2:= H>Ref(H,-2) AND L>Ref(L,-2) AND
H>Ref(H,-1) AND L<Ref(L,-1);
m3:= H>Ref(H,-3) AND L>Ref(L,-3) AND
H>Ref(H,-2) AND L<Ref(L,-2) AND
H>Ref(H,-1) AND L<Ref(L,-1);
mark:= m1 OR m2 OR m3;
set:=L<ValueWhen(1,mark,L) AND H<ValueWhen(1,mark,H) AND
HighestSince(1,Ref(mark,-1),H) < ValueWhen(1,mark,H);
sig:= If(mark,1, If(set, 0, PREV));
Cross(sig=0,0.5)
```

FORMULA 2: ASCENDING TRIAD

```
m1:=H<Ref(H,-1) AND L<Ref(L,-1);
m2:=H<Ref(H,-2) AND L<Ref(L,-2) AND
H>Ref(H,-1) AND L<Ref(L,-1);
m3:=H<Ref(H,-3) AND L<Ref(L,-3) AND
H>Ref(H,-2) AND L<Ref(L,-2) AND
H>Ref(H,-1) AND L<Ref(L,-1);
```

```
mark:= m1 OR m2 OR m3;
set:=L >ValueWhen(1,mark,L) AND H>ValueWhen(1,mark,H) AND
lowestSince(1,Ref(mark,-1),L) > ValueWhen(1,mark,L);
sig:= If(mark,1, If(set, 0, PREV));
Cross(sig=0,0.5)
```

Appendix II
Chart Examples and Charts

CHART EXAMPLES

Chart 1. The simple and complex triads. Caterpillar (daily)

This chart shows simple and complex triads. In three of them, we have circled and numbered the defining charted bars of the triad.

Chart 2. Master swing and minor corrections. Exxon Mobil (monthly)

Here in Exxon we show minor corrections within two main ascending trends. If we were to trade a correction, we would have a choice when selecting a master swing. For instance, we could choose the seven-point correction.

If we did, we would wait for any correction to have a length of at least seven points before entering. Additionally, we would make sure that the market gives a definite indication of turning around.

Chart 3. Trading oscillations with the master swing. S&P 500 Stock Index continuous chart (monthly)

Here we use the measure of swings as defined by triads to trade the main waves of the S&P 500 using the master swing. We begin by defining the main pivots since 1982. Each main pivot high and low is defined by a triad. Once these pivots are defined, we create the spreadsheet shown on page 216.

By observing this table, we can identify the length of each main wave. The 1987 crash had a length of three months and the market lost 46.67 % of its value. The 2000–2002 bear market lasted 33 months and lost 51.23 % of its value. The bear market that began in October 2007 lasted 18 months and lost 58 % of its value.

Triad wavemeter

S&P 500 Stock Index CME		Main pivots			
Date	Triad pivot	Number of charted bars	VAR points	VAR %	Calendar length (months)
08 09 82 Mon	101,15				
08 25 87 Tue	339,45	61	238,3	235,59	61
10 20 87 Tue	181	3	−158,45	(46,67)	3
07 20 98 Mon	1199,4	130	1018,4	562,65	130
10 08 98 Thu	929	4	−270,4	(22,54)	4
03 24 00 Fri	1574	18	645	69,42	18
10 10 02 Thu	767,5	33	−806,5	(51,23)	33
10 11 07 Thu	1586	61	818,5	106,64	61
03 06 09 Fri	665,7	18	−920,3	(58,02)	18

You can observe two movements of 61 months length, two movements of 18 months length, one movement of three months and one movement of four months. We find that most of these movements have a ratio of around 2. From around 20 to around 30 to around 60 to around 120 or, more precisely, from 18 to 33 to 61 to 130.

As to the downward moves, they approximate values of −20, −50 and −60 %. Their actual values are −22.54, −46.67, −51.23 and −58.02 %, respectively. The upward moves approximate values of 70, 100, 200 and 600 %.

With this information, we choose the master swing to go long the market. We choose the 46.67 % correction as our master swing. This means that, as soon as the market corrects by an amount of 47 %, give or take one percentage point, we will be on the lookout for an opportunity to buy the market.

To find this opportunity, we will rely on market structure. Such an opportunity presented itself in March 2009. The market had a fall that lost more than our master swing. Pivot 8 is a bottom where the market lost 58 % of its value. The ascending monthly triad indicates that an entry point could be there.

Chart 4. Example of a signature. S&P 500 Stock Index continuous chart (monthly)

In this chart of the S&P 500, we have the swings and the high and low pivots, as defined by the triads. The last downswing before the 2007 historical high is a signature. Its greater length than those of all previous downswings of the same uptrend announced the 2008 reversal.

Chart 5. The three market phases. General Electric (daily)

This chart shows the three main market phases. From 0 to 1 is a double bottom turning point, from 1 to 2 an ascending trend, from 2 to 3 a lateral consolidation, from 3 to 4 a descending trend and, at 4, a single bottom turning point that belongs to a simple triad.

Chart 6. Two higher highs and a higher low upside reversal. 3M (daily)

In the same chart, we have an upward reversal with its two higher highs (pivots 1 and 3) and its higher low (pivot 2). At this point, the market has definitely reversed and there is an ascending trend. This is further confirmed when pivot 4 appears as the low of a new simple ascending triad. The 0 pivot charted bar and the 2 pivot charted bar do not intersect.

This indicates a definite market reversal and that a new ascending trend has begun due to the presence of a new force that was able to neutralize the preceding downtrend and give place to a new uptrend.

Chart 7. The pivot breakout upside reversal. 3M (weekly)

This chart shows the pivot breakout turning point structure. In X we have the last high pivot of a minor top of the descending trend. The arrow shows where the market breaks the X pivot when turning around. Breaking this pivot confirms the turn and the beginning of an ascending trend.

As soon as the pivot X is broken, an ascending trend and its series of ascending swings develop. This means that a new force has come into the market that was not only able to stop the descending trend but also to change its polarity to a new ascending trend.

Chart 8. The two lower lows and a lower high downside reversal. Citigroup (weekly)

Here we show a downside reversal. We have a lower high in 2 and two lower lows in 1 and 3. Charted bar 2 and charted bar 0 do not intersect. Once this market structure is in place, the market will have definitely reversed.

Chart 9. The pivot breakout downside reversal. Hewlett Packard (weekly)

Here we have a pivot breakout downside reversal structure. In Y, the market breaks the last significant pivot low, X, of the previous ascending trend. Once this happens, even though the market consolidates for a while, the descending trend is triggered and the market goes south.

Chart 10. Time factor in an ascending trend. Coca Cola (monthly)

The time factor in the ascending trend changes in the downswing AB from three and two to four. This means that AB has four charted bars between its high pivot A and its lowest pivot B. The two previous downswings had two and three charted bars, respectively.

This change in the time factor is a signature that announces a coming reversal. In fact, the market has a long and final upswing before reversing.

Chart 11. Time factor in a descending trend. Soybean composite CBOT continuous chart (weekly)

The time factor changes in AB from one to three in the descending trend. This is a signature that announces the reversal that took place later.

Chart 12. The energy factor. AAR Corp. (monthly)

Here we have the energy factor in action. After a consolidation range of many years, a breakout occurs at the arrow and an ascending trend that will last for two years begins. The consolidation range accumulated the energy needed for the breakout and the new trend.

Chart 13. The energy factor. AAR Corp. (monthly)

Here we have another figure for the energy factor. The multiyear bear market that went from 1998 to 2002 (pivots 1 to 2) accumulated the energy necessary for the bull market that lasted from 2003 to 2008 (pivots 2 to 3). This is why it is important to take into account the length of a movement, since it could give us powerful information about the strength and duration of the next movement in an opposite direction.

Chart 14. The two higher highs and one higher low upside reversal setup. Dow Jones Industrial Average composite continuous chart (weekly)

Here we have an example of an upside reversal setup. As soon as we have one non-intersecting higher low, pivot 2, and two higher highs, pivots 1 and 3, we will buy at the close of the triad whose pivot creates a second higher low at 4.

Chart 15. The pivot breakout upside reversal setup. Dow Jones Industrial Average composite continuous chart (weekly)

This chart shows the downtrend pivot breakout setup. As soon as X is broken in 5, we will buy at the close of the ascending triad. Notice the three higher highs and the two higher lows that are already in place. They provide additional confirmation of the new, ascending trend.

Chart 16. Buying a single bottom. Dow Jones Industrial Average composite continuous chart (weekly)

Here we buy a simple bottom that reverses a downtrend into a new uptrend. We have two buying points. We can buy as soon as the upside reversal setup is ready (first arrow) or at the pivot breakout setup (second arrow). Observe how in this case the first triad pivot high that breaks a pivot of the former down movement appeared in 5, breaking the pivot X.

Chart 17. Buying a double bottom. Boeing (daily)

We have a double bottom within an ascending trend. We buy the close of the ascending triad whose low pivot defined the double bottom. The market rises and the trend continues.

Chart 18. Buying a double bottom. Gold 100 Troy oz COMEX continuous chart (daily)

We have a double bottom within an ascending trend. We buy the close of the first ascending triad that appeared after the breakout of the double bottom consolidation range high. The market rises and the trend continues.

Chart 19. Buying a triple bottom. Procter & Gamble (weekly)

As soon as a triple bottom is defined by three triad low pivots, we buy the ascending triad of the third bottom at close. The diamonds identify the triad's three charted bars. As soon as we buy, the market rises in an uptrend.

Chart 20. Buying the upside penetration of a simple moving average. Apple (daily)

Here we buy the penetration of a 20-day moving average in the usual way. The difference is that, as soon as the prices penetrate the moving average to the upside, we ask the market structure to confirm the trade before we enter the market.

In this trade, the penetration occurs soon after the first bottom. The moving average is still going down. We must wait for it to reverse direction to the upside in a definite way. This happened only after a third bottom occurred. As soon as the average turned up, we waited for a downtrend pivot breakout setup and an uptrend reversal setup. The downtrend pivot is the high pivot between the first and the second bottom.

The breakout of the pivot, as well as the two higher triad pivots and the higher triad low, occurred only after the third bottom. We buy as soon as an ascending triad creates a second higher low. As usual, we buy at close at the last bar of the triad. The market continues to rise for many months after the buying signal is given.

Chart 21. Buying former resistance that has become support. S&P 500 Stock index CME continuous chart (weekly)

This chart shows how we can buy former resistance that is now support. During this ascending trend, as soon as a top is broken and exceeded and the market comes back to it correcting, we will buy it. The correction can stop at the support level of the previous top or penetrate the top slightly.

Chart 22. The two lower lows and a lower high downside reversal setup. British pound composite continuous chart (daily)

Here we sell short the downside reversal setup. As soon as two lower low pivots and a lower high pivot are in place and a second lower high pivot appears, we are ready to sell.

We sell the descending triad that defines the second lower high pivot at its close. The market continues to fall.

Chart 23. The pivot breakout downside reversal setup. Japanese yen composite continuous chart (daily)

Here we sell an uptrend pivot breakout setup in the Japanese yen. As soon as the uptrend pivot 0 is broken in 1, we wait for the next descending triad and sell it at its closing charted bar.

Chart 24. Selling short a single top. 30 Year US T-bond composite CBOT continuous chart (daily)

As soon as top 1 forms at resistance level 0 in this example, we sell at the close of the next descending triad whose pivot makes a simple top. The market falls immediately.

Chart 25. Selling short a double top. Orange juice continuous chart (daily)

We sell short the double top at the closing charted bar of the complex triad that defines its second high pivot. The market drops immediately.

Chart 26. Selling short a triple top. Intel (weekly)

Here we have a triple top in the Intel weekly chart. We sell it at the closing charted bar of the simple triad whose pivot defines the third top. We always sell at the close or at the open of the next charted bar.

Chart 27. Selling short a 12 week under a 48 week Simple Moving Average Crossover. S&P 500 Stock Index continuous chart (weekly)

In the S&P, we sell short the crossover to the downside of the 12-week moving average below the 48-week moving average. We wait for the moving average to point down, to the breakout of the uptrend pivot and the downtrend reversal setup. We sell the first descending triad that puts into place the second lower high after the two lower lows are in place. The market reacts to the upside, taking out the stop at the high pivot of the descending triad.

The second selling signal comes after a low pivot that is lower than the two previous ones made and both averages point down. The second descending triad after this last low is sold short. The first descending triad is not sold because its last charted bar closes above its opening and above the previous close. The market falls.

Chart 28. Selling short the contrarian upside penetration of a simple moving average. Alliance One International (daily)

In this example, we are selling a contrarian penetration to the upside of a daily 20-day simple moving average. For this, we require the moving average to be clearly pointing down and to have the market structure on our side.

The moving average points down, the uptrend pivot has been broken and a triple top is in place. As soon as the moving average is penetrated to the upside, we sell the descending triad that closes below it, confirming the resumption of the downtrend. The diamonds identify the triad's charted bars. The market goes down for many months.

Chart 29. Selling short support that has become resistance. Crude oil light sweet continuous chart (daily)

Within this downtrend, as soon as a former triad's bottom pivot is penetrated to the downside, becoming resistance, and the market corrects to the upside, coming back and stopping at the previous bottom, we sell the first descending triad that appears. The market must stop at the resistance pivot or slightly exceed it to the upside.

Chart 30 (continues Chart 3). Trading oscillations with the master swing. S&P 500 Stock Index continuous chart (weekly)

The S&P 500, after correcting beyond the master swing, stops at pivot 8 and turns around. We then have a breakout of the last pivot high of the descending trend and, as soon as this pivot is broken, the market corrects a few points and makes an ascending triad.

The weekly triad is bought at the close of its closing bar. The market continues to rise. As I write these words, the S&P is still in an uptrend!

Chart 31. Buying the contrarian downside penetration of a simple moving average. General Electric (daily)

We buy the penetration to the downside of a moving average. Our conditions to do this are satisfied. We have a moving average that is rising and also have market structure on our side. We have bought an ascending triad that is below the moving average because the moving average is rising and the market is in a confirmed uptrend, having made a double bottom after having corrected.

Notice that we have not bought penetrations to the downside of the moving average when the market is in a range, the 'tunnel of death,' even though the average is rising. Notice also that we do not buy the first ascending triad after the consolidation is broken to the downside, since the market could have evolved into a downtrend.

We only buy when the market gives us a definite indication that the trend should continue. Our second buying signal comes when the average is up and the market has corrected to a support pivot. Here we also buy the ascending triad at its close.

Chart 32. Second method of buying the contrarian downside penetration of a simple moving average. Apple (daily)

Here the method to buy the penetration of a simple moving average to the downside is different from the preceding one. As in the previous example, we only buy when the moving average is pointing up, but in this case, we wait for the market to come back with a triad that closes above the moving average. Also, we ask the market structure to confirm our trades.

The market has made double bottoms within an uptrend at our buying points. This gives added strength to our trades.

Chart 33. Selling short the penetration of a simple moving average. ALCOA (daily)

Here we sell short the penetration of a 20-day moving average in the usual way. The moving average is going down and market structure confirms the downward direction of the market. During the downtrend a consolidation was broken to the downside, the moving average always pointing down. We buy the first descending triad at close after the consolidation breakout.

All the conditions for a short sell are satisfied: a moving average going down and a descending trend according to fundamental market structure that additionally included a breakout of a consolidation to the downside.

Chart 34. Buying a simple moving average crossover. Apple (daily)

Here we buy a crossover of the 5-day moving average over the 20-day moving average. We wait for both averages to be pointing up, as well as for definite confirmation of the uptrend from the market structure. We buy at the same place and for the same reasons as we did in the previous chart when buying the penetration of a simple moving average.

Chart 35. Selling short a simple moving average crossover. AM Castle & Co. (daily)

We sell short the crossover of the 5-day simple moving average below the 20-day simple moving average. We make sure that both averages are pointing down within a confirmed downtrend. To sell we wait for a pivot breakout of a double bottom in the previous ascending trend.

Chart 36. Buying a 12-week over a 48-week simple moving average crossover. S&P 500 Stock Index continuous chart (weekly)

This is an example of a long-term trade in the S&P 500. We buy the crossover of a 12-week moving average over a 48-week moving average. We buy the upside reversal after the crossover. This happens as soon as two higher highs and a higher low occur.

As soon as the complex triad that creates the second higher low is in place, we buy it at its close. The market reacts immediately to the upside.

Chart 37. Buying with the MACD. Coffee C continuous chart (daily)

This chart shows us buying with an MACD. After a six-month consolidation, coffee breaks out. The pivot high of the consolidation, 0, is broken in 1. The MACD crossed the zero line around two months ago and both of its averages have been pointing up since the zero line was crossed.

We buy the first ascending triad after the consolidation pivot high 0 was broken in 1. The trend continued its upward move.

Chart 38. Selling short with the MACD. US Dollar Index continuous chart (daily)

Here we sell short the Dollar Index. We wait for the MACD to cross the zero line to the downside and for both of its averages to point down. We also wait for the market structure to define a downward trend with an upward trend pivot breakout and a downside reversal setup. We then sell the first descending triad at its close.

Did we really need the MACD? Probably not! It simply gave us added confidence by confirming what the market structure was telling us.

Chart 39. Buying with the stochastic oscillator. Crude oil light sweet continuous chart (daily)

Trading the stochastic indicator. Here we buy the stochastic oscillator as soon as both of its lines point upward and have crossed the 20 % line. We also need confirmation from the market structure. This comes in the form of a triple bottom.

Instead of buying the first ascending triad whose pivot defines the third bottom, we buy the next ascending triad at its close. The triad that defined the third bottom did not satisfy the condition of having the stochastic oscillator above the 20 % line with both stochastics lined up. As soon as the buying took place, the market went up!

Chart 40. Selling short with the stochastic oscillator. Crude oil light sweet continuous chart (daily)

Using the stochastic oscillator, we sell a double top. Here the descending triad that defines the second top has its third charted bar (in red) when both lines of the oscillator cross to the downside (arrow) and are below the 80 % line. The stochastic oscillator's downward divergence is additional confirmation.

We sell at the close of the descending triad whose pivot defined the second top. The market falls and a six-month downtrend begins.

Chart 41. Selling short with the absolute deviation (first and second methods). General Electric (daily)

The two main ways of trading the absolute deviation are shown in these two short trades. In a descending market, the absolute deviation occurs in the lower Bollinger band, the 0 point. The absolute deviation pivot 0 is only known when the market turns around and touches or penetrates the upper band. As soon as this happens, we sell the first descending triad that occurs in 1. The market initiates a fall.

The second short sale occurs when the market, in its down movement, penetrates the absolute deviation line. This line is a parallel line traced at the absolute deviation pivot. We sell short the first triad to close below this line. The charted bar of the triad where the second sell signal occurs has closed just below the line, so we sell the triad. As soon as this happens, the market continues to fall in what is to be a long downtrend of almost two months.

Chart 42. Buying with the absolute deviation (second method). Exxon Mobil (daily)

This is an example of a long trade that buys the penetration of the absolute deviation line. The absolute deviation occurs at 0 and is known to us in 1, when the market has turned around to the opposite side band. Here we trace our absolute deviation line. We buy the first triad to either penetrate the line or to occur above the line.

We have to buy the first triad that penetrates the line and whose last bar has its close above its opening. The market continues its ascending trend.

Chart 43. Buying with the absolute deviation (first method). General Electric (daily)

Here is an example of absolute deviation trading. Absolute deviation occurs at 0, after the market has penetrated to the upper Bollinger and at two standard deviations from the central moving average. After this initial penetration, the market continues until its exhaustion point at 0. This is the absolute deviation pivot. We know the absolute deviation only at 1, when the market goes in the opposite direction and touches or penetrates the lower band moving average.

As soon as this occurs, we buy the first ascending triad at its close. The market begins a new upswing.

Chart 44. Selling short using the double target approach. Exxon Mobil (daily)

This is an example of a short sale using the money management target and the pattern target. The money management target is included in the pattern target. The pattern target is obtained by taking the multiple top highest pivot and lowest pivot and projecting it downwards. This gives us a pattern target of 60.

We sell the symmetrical triangle at its breakout triad. The stop goes at the high of the last bar of the triad that we sell at its close. This gives us a money management target at 68.84 for a risk/reward ratio of three.

As the money management target is included in the pattern target, the short trade can be taken. The market goes down and first hits the money management target and later the pattern target. If there is a trading Holy Grail, this is it.

Chart 45 (continues Chart 36). Buying a 12-week over a 48-week simple moving average crossover. S&P 500 Stock Index continuous chart (weekly)

This is the continuation of the previous trade in chart 36. Our buying point was at the beginning of a multiyear bull market.

Chart 46. Buying using the double target approach. Exxon Mobil (daily)

This is an example that can be applied to trading all patterns. Our main purpose here is to illustrate the importance of the intersection between the pattern target and the money management target. The money management target must be a subset of the pattern target and be included in it. This is the condition that gives a go signal for the trade.

In this example, the distance from 0 to 1 has been projected from the low of the triangle. This gives us the pattern target at 3. We buy the triad breakout of the triangle at the close of its last charted bar. The stop is placed below the triad low. The diamonds identify the triad's charted bars. The reward is defined as three times the risk and gives us the money management target.

The money management target (first arrow) is included in the pattern target (second arrow). This means that the trade can be taken. As soon as this happens, the market goes up until it attains the predefined target.

CHARTS

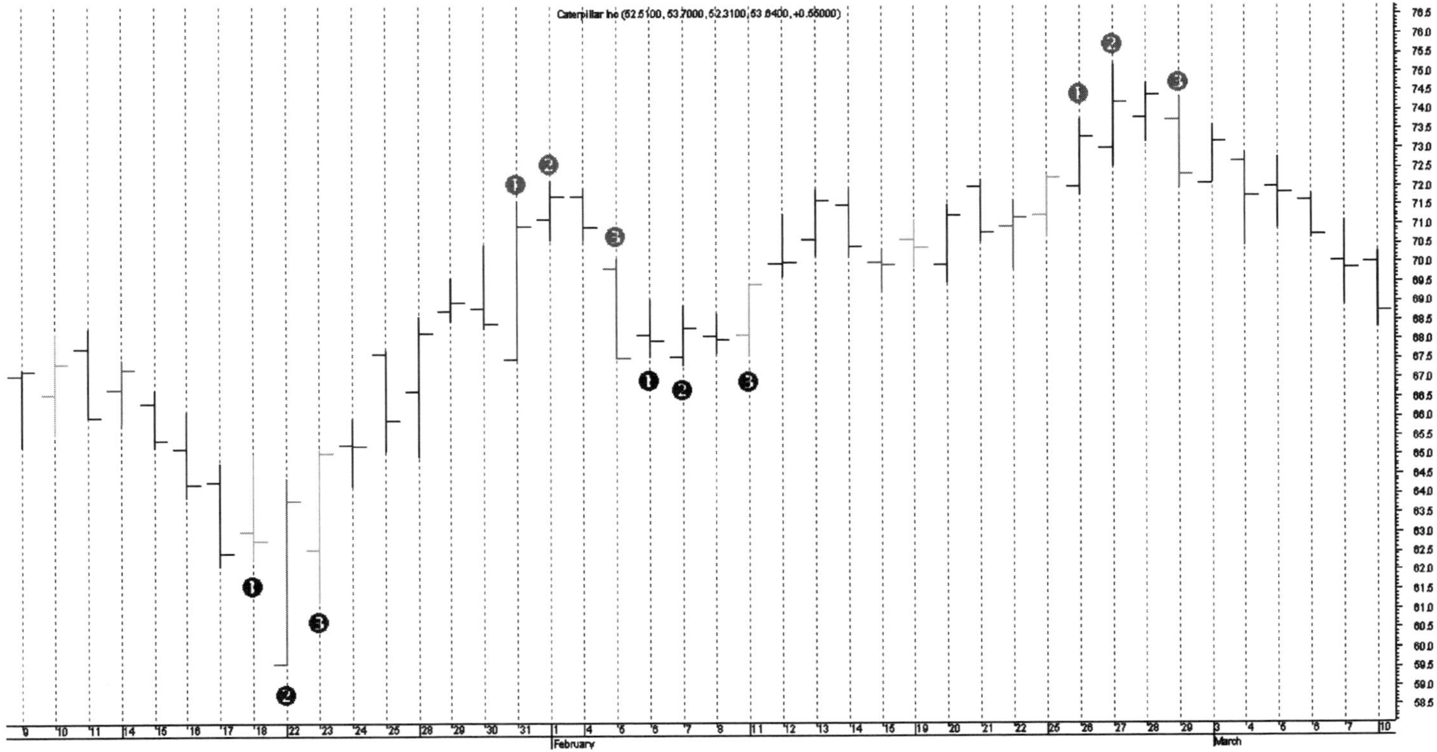

Chart 1 Caterpillar (daily) (Metastock Chart Courtesy of Equis International)

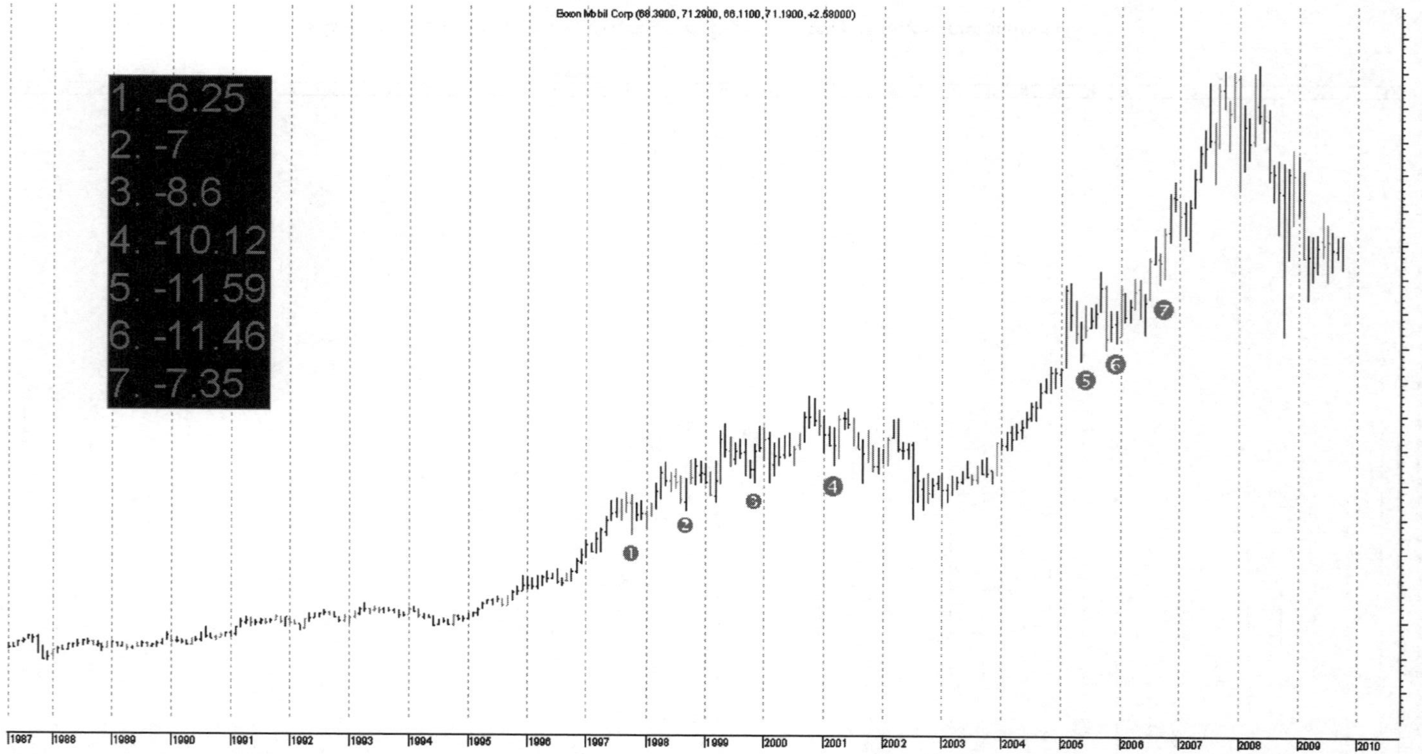

Chart 2 Exxon Mobil (monthly) (Metastock Chart Courtesy of Equis International).

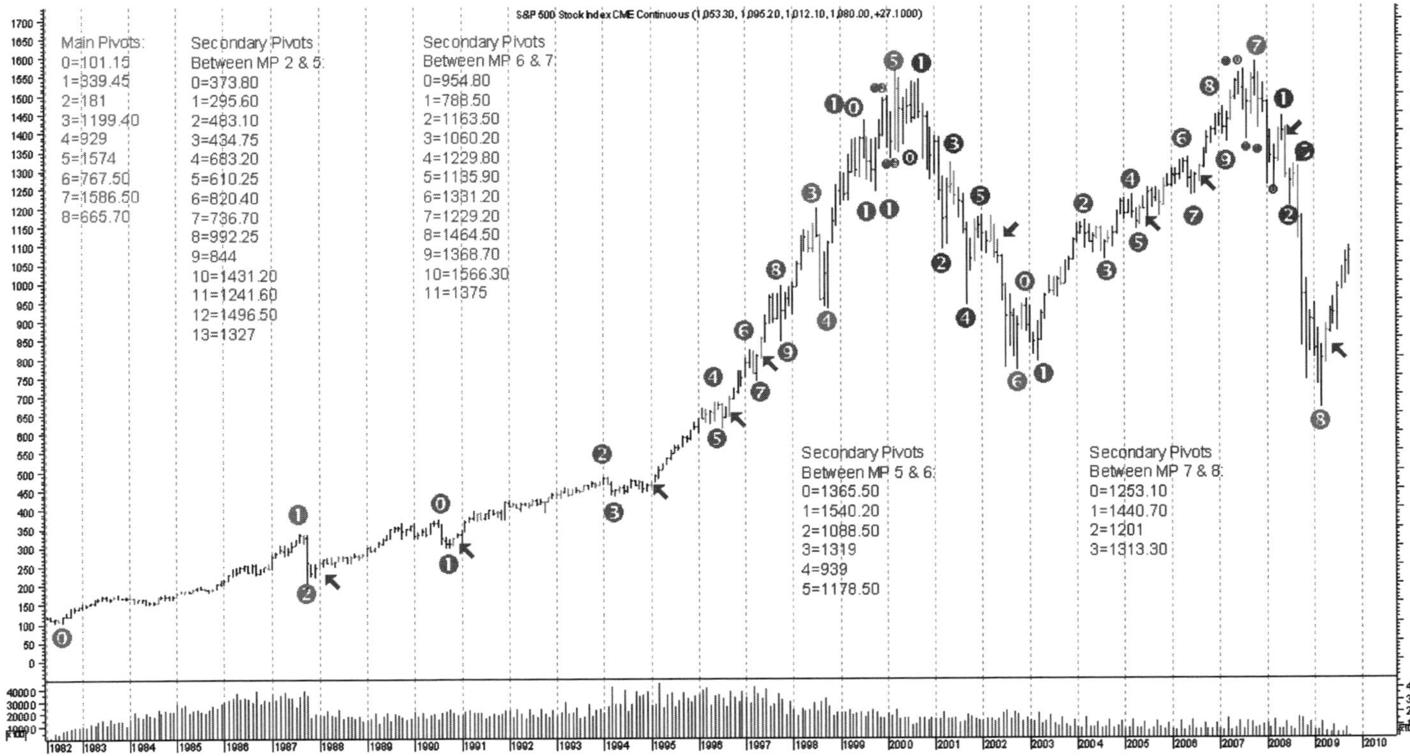

Chart 3 S&P 500 Stock Index continuous chart (monthly) (Metastock Chart Courtesy of Equis International).

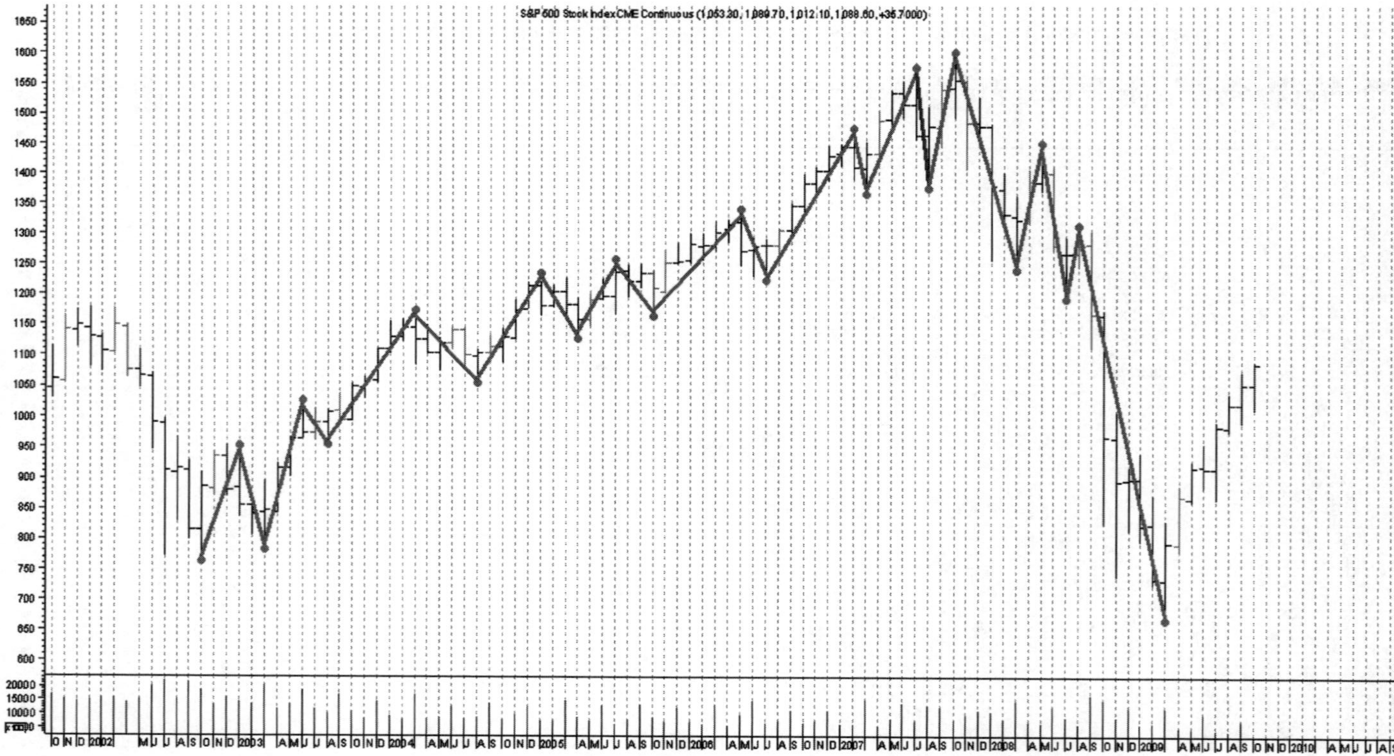

Chart 4 S&P 500 Stock Index continuous chart (monthly) (Metastock Chart Courtesy of Equis International).

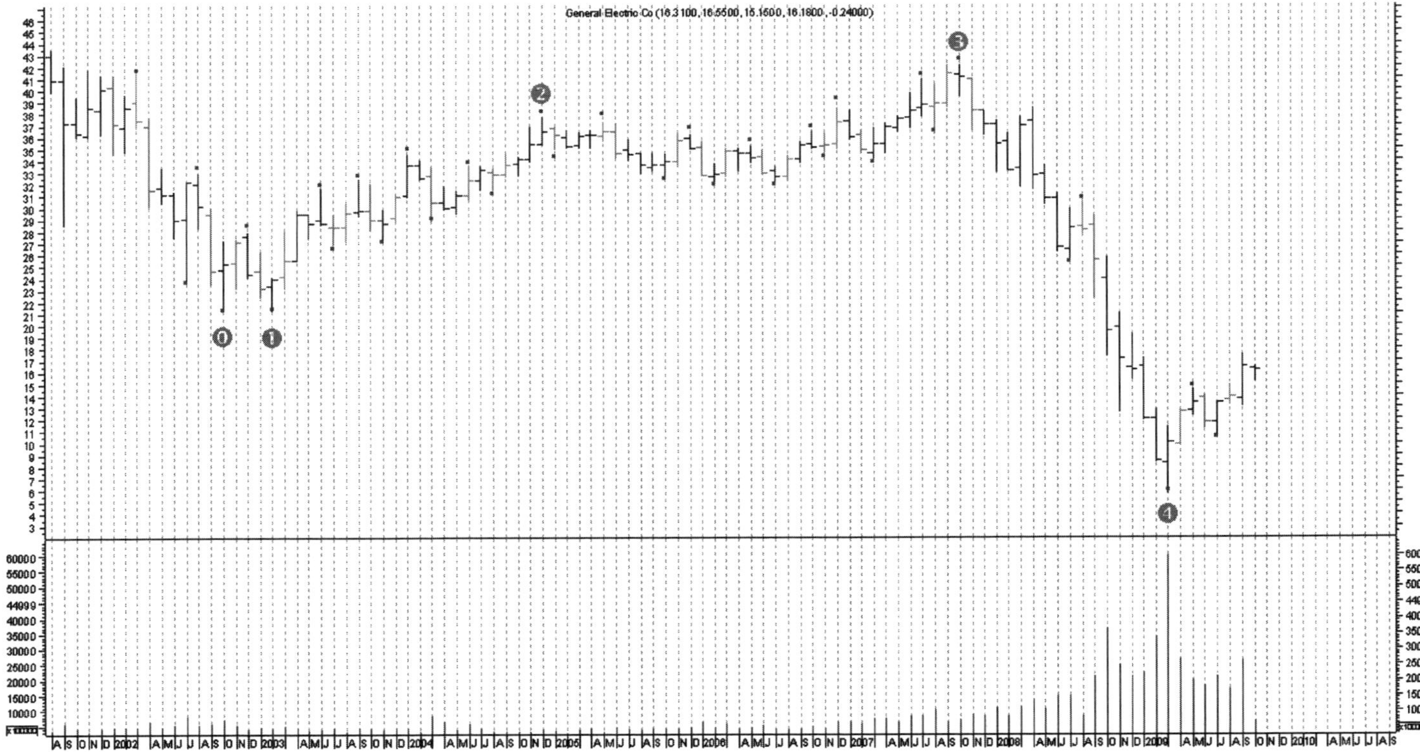

Chart 5 General Electric (daily) (Metastock Chart Courtesy of Equis International).

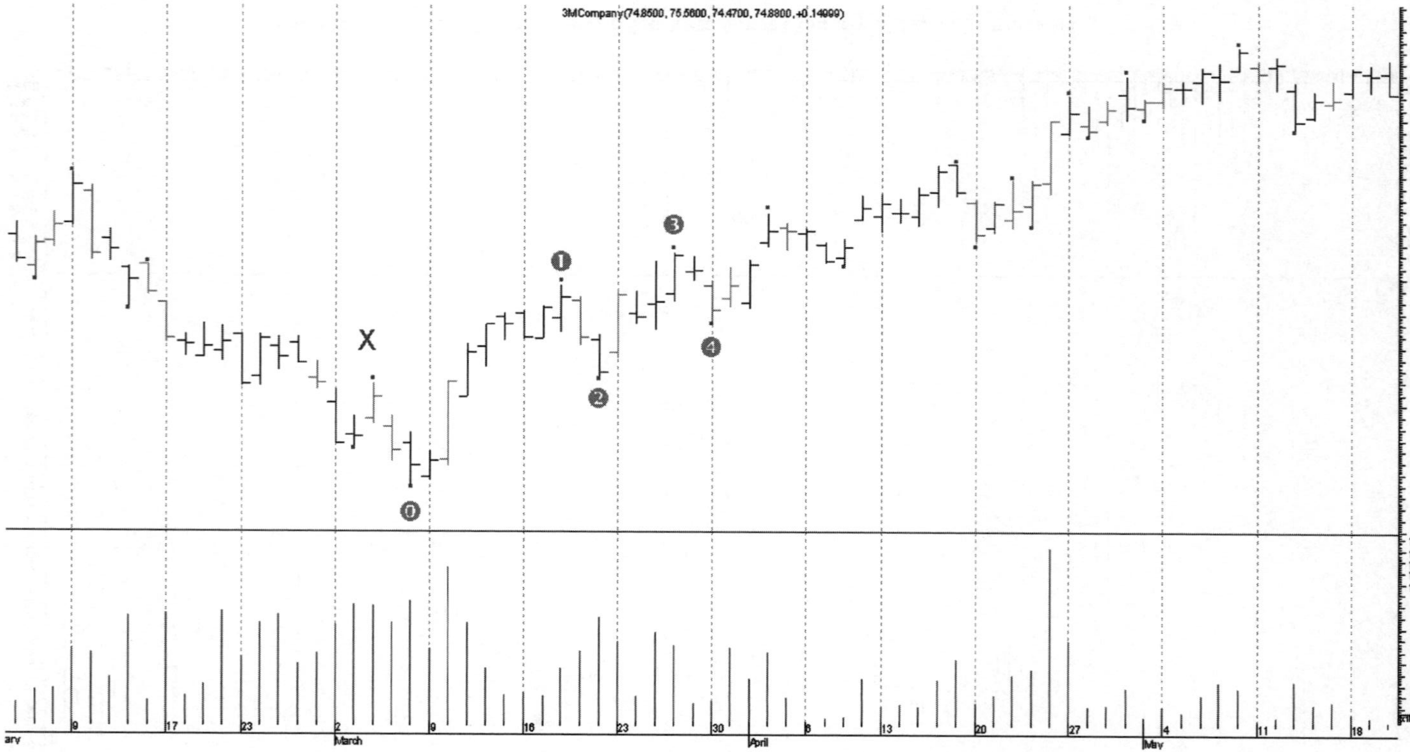

Chart 6 3M (daily) (Metastock Chart Courtesy of Equis International).

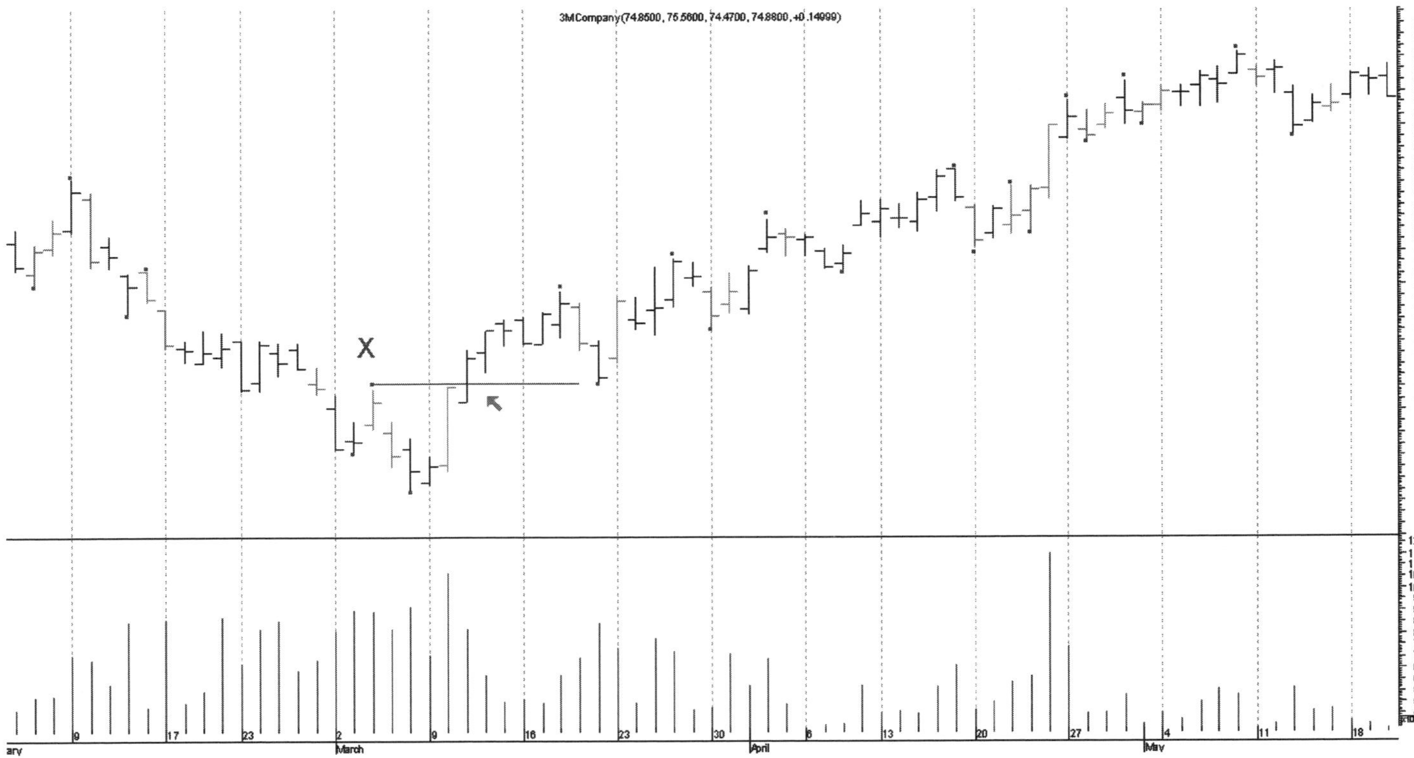

Chart 7 3M (weekly) (Metastock Chart Courtesy of Equis International).

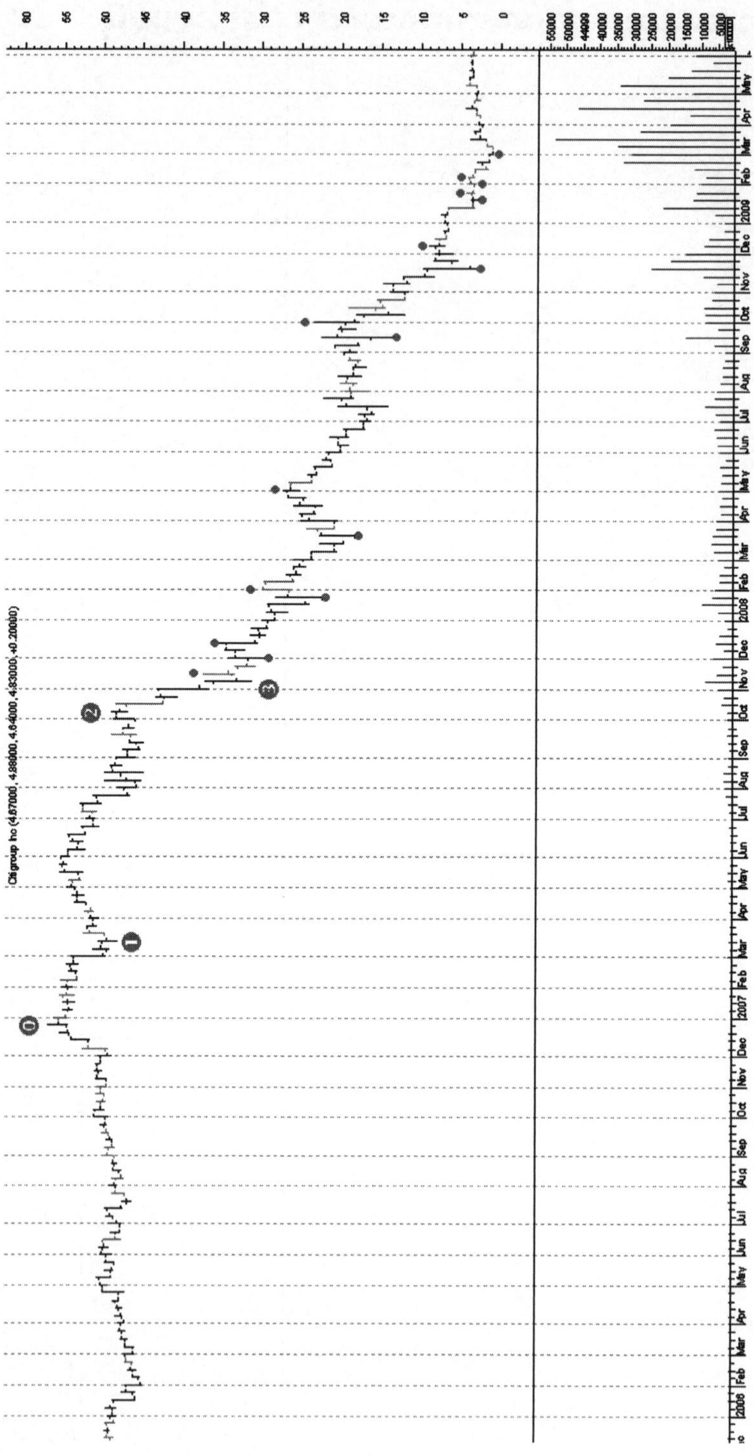

Chart 8 Citigroup (weekly) (Metastock Chart Courtesy of Equis International).

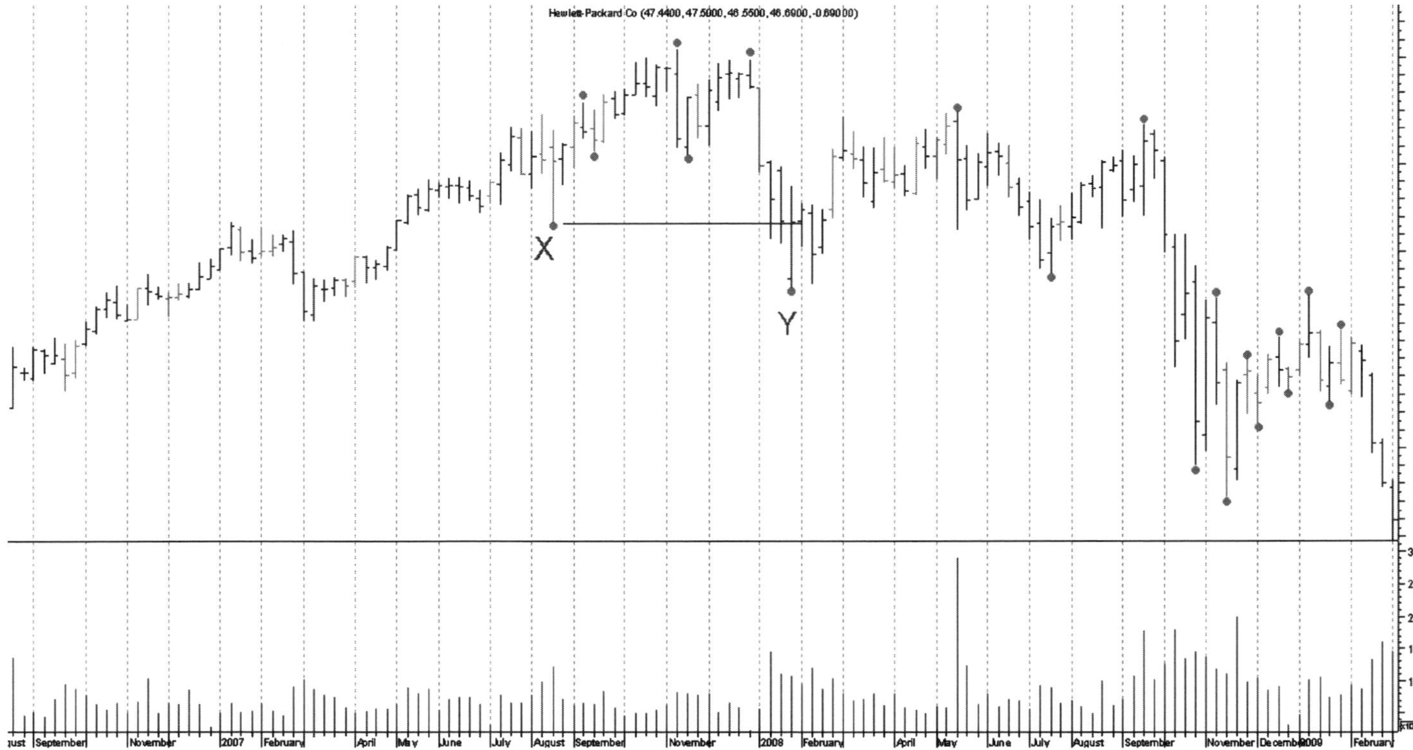

Chart 9 Hewlett Packard (weekly) (Metastock Chart Courtesy of Equis International).

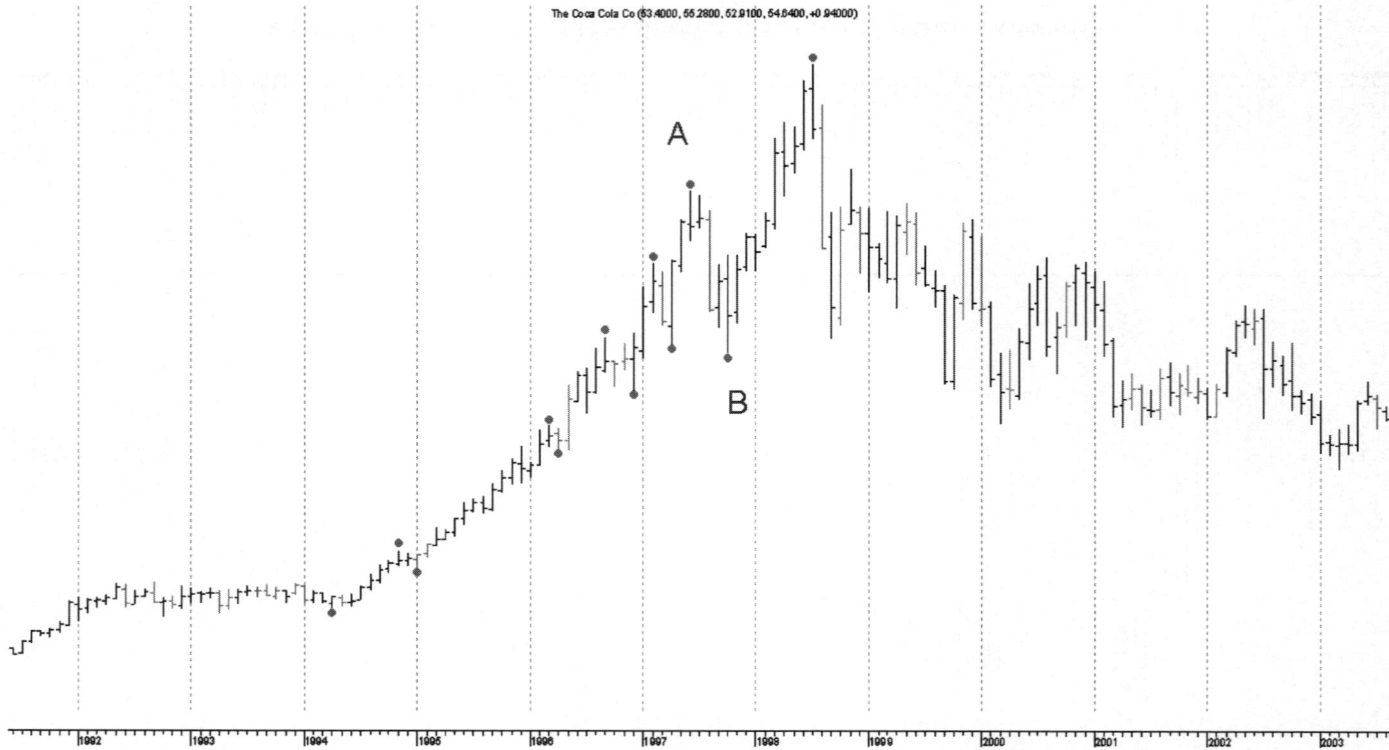

Chart 10 Coca Cola (monthly) (Metastock Chart Courtesy of Equis International).

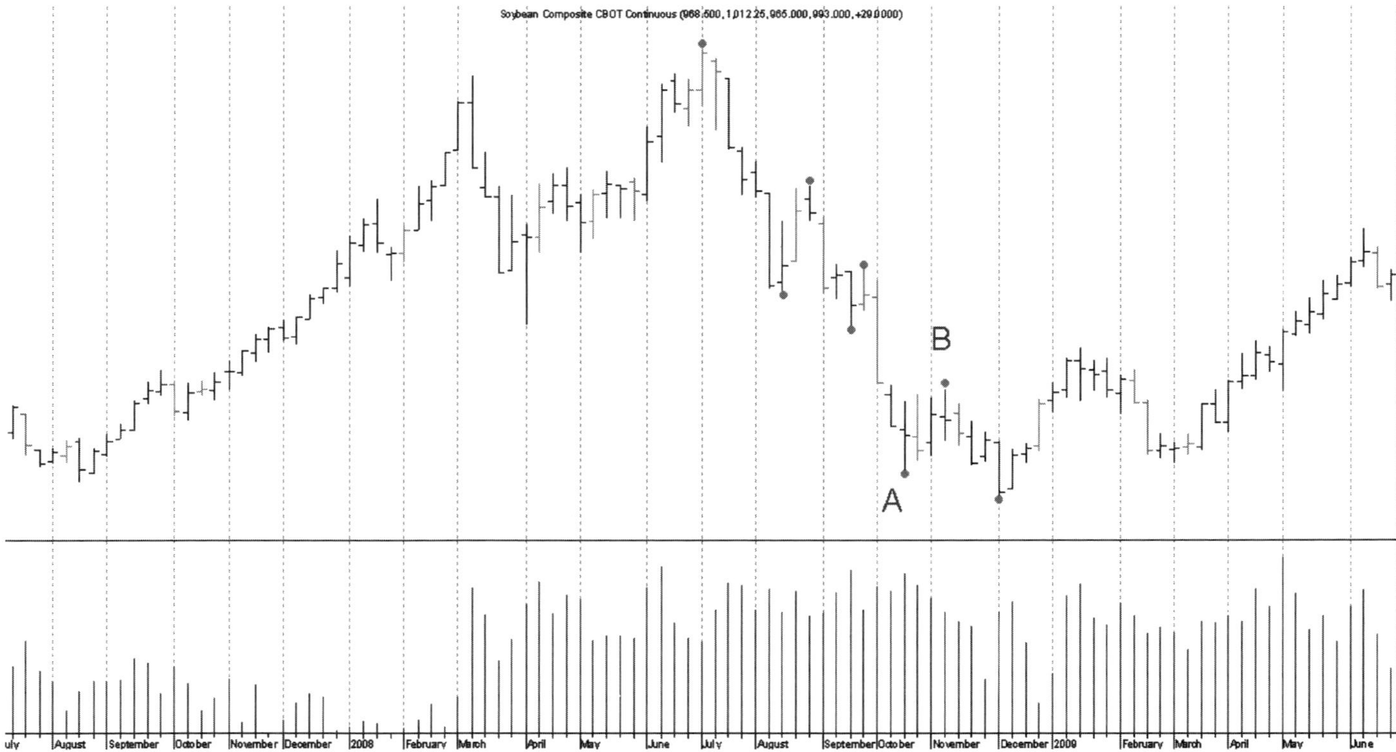

Chart 11 Soybean composite CBOT continuous chart (weekly) (Metastock Chart Courtesy of Equis International).

Chart 12 AAR Corp. (monthly) (Metastock Chart Courtesy of Equis International).

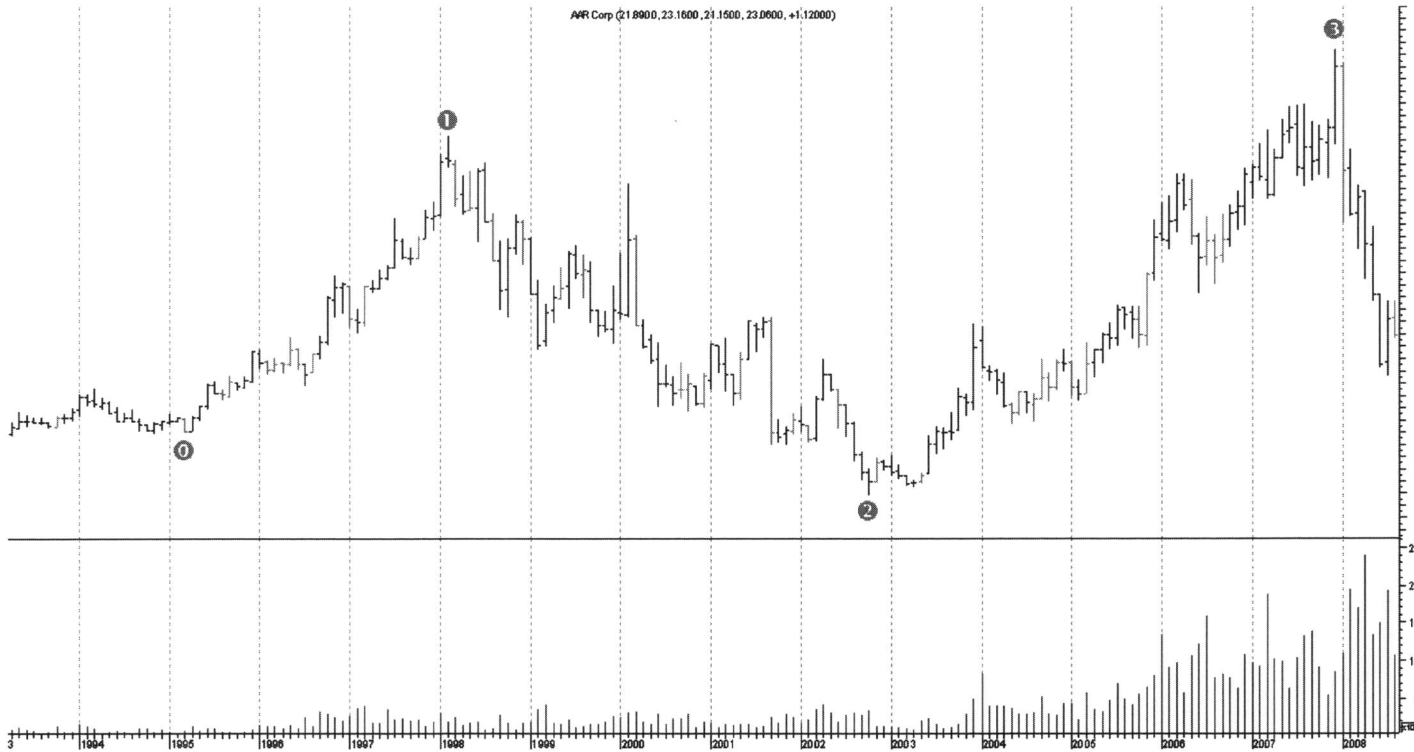

Chart 13 AAR Corp. (monthly) (Metastock Chart Courtesy of Equis International).

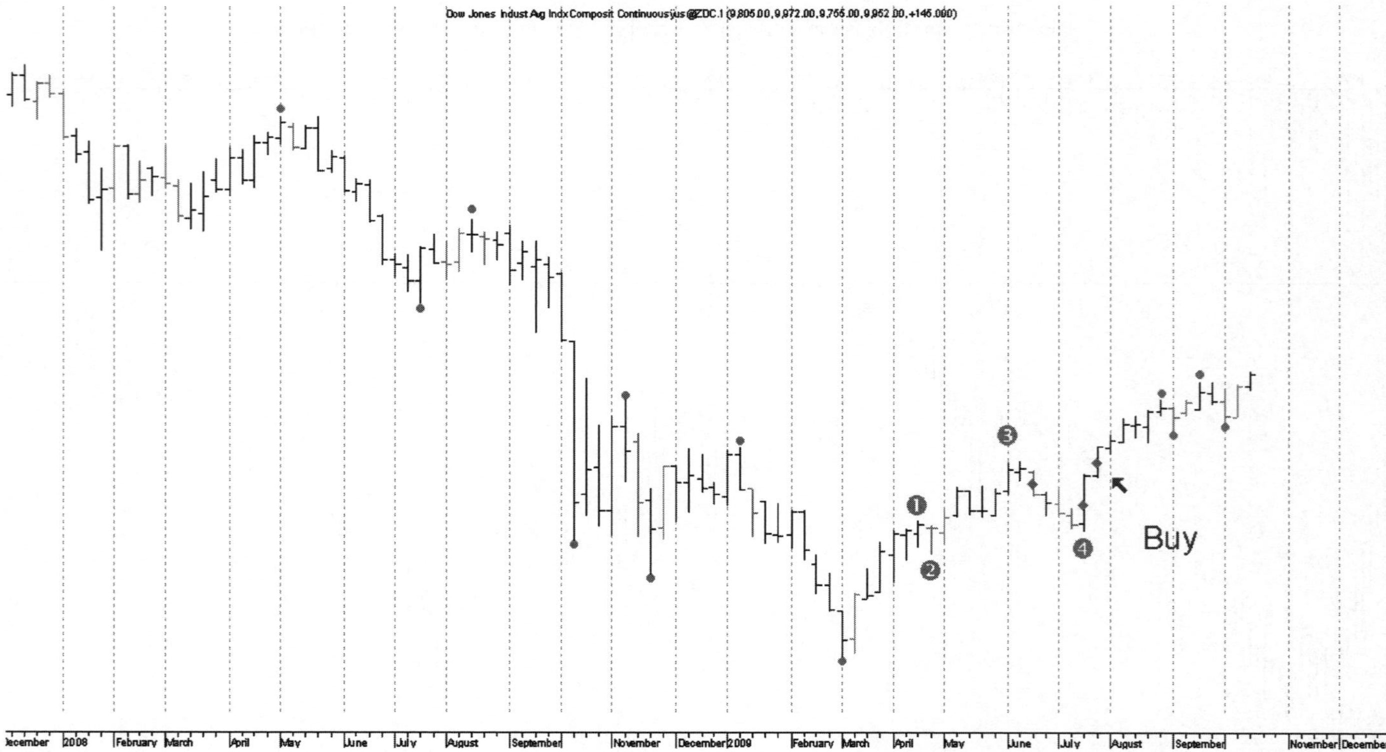

Chart 14 Dow Jones Industrial Average composite continuous chart (weekly) (Metastock Chart Courtesy of Equis International).

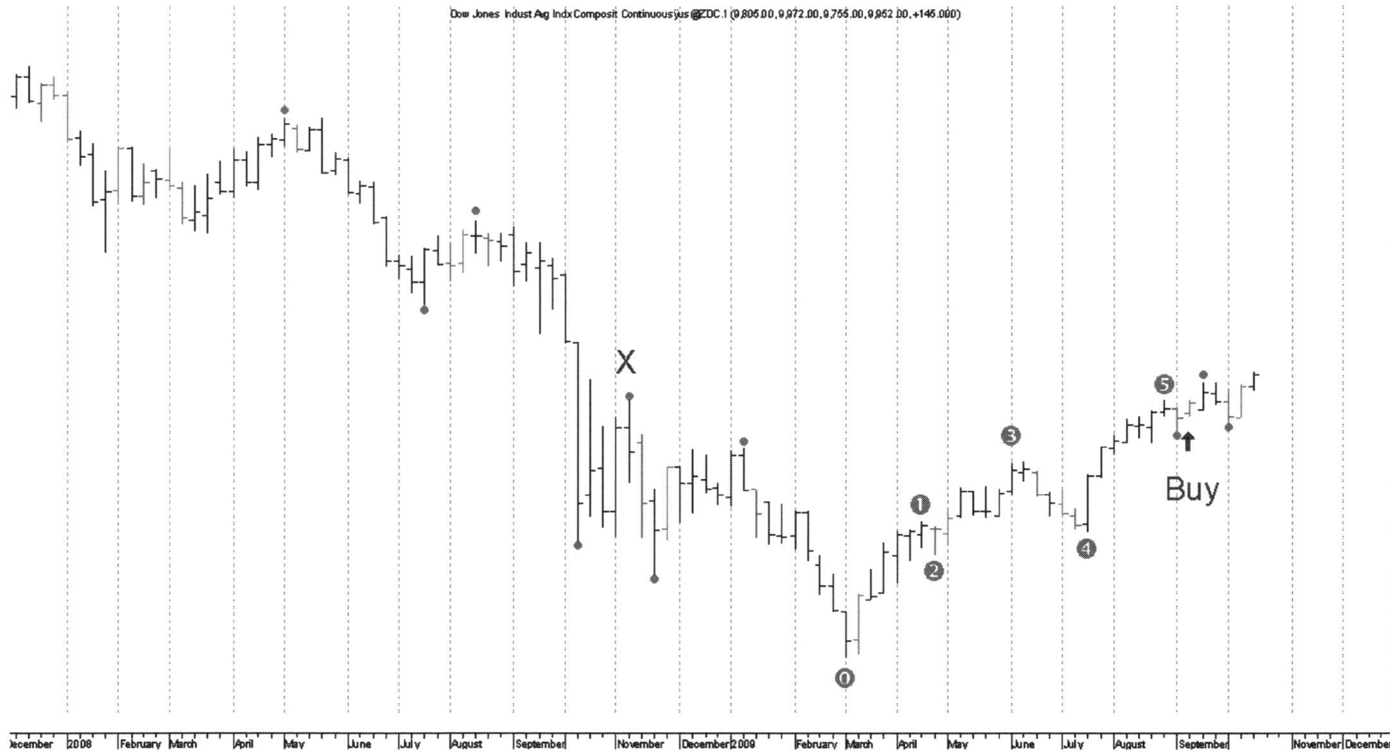

Chart 15 Dow Jones Industrial Average composite continuous chart (weekly) (Metastock Chart Courtesy of Equis International).

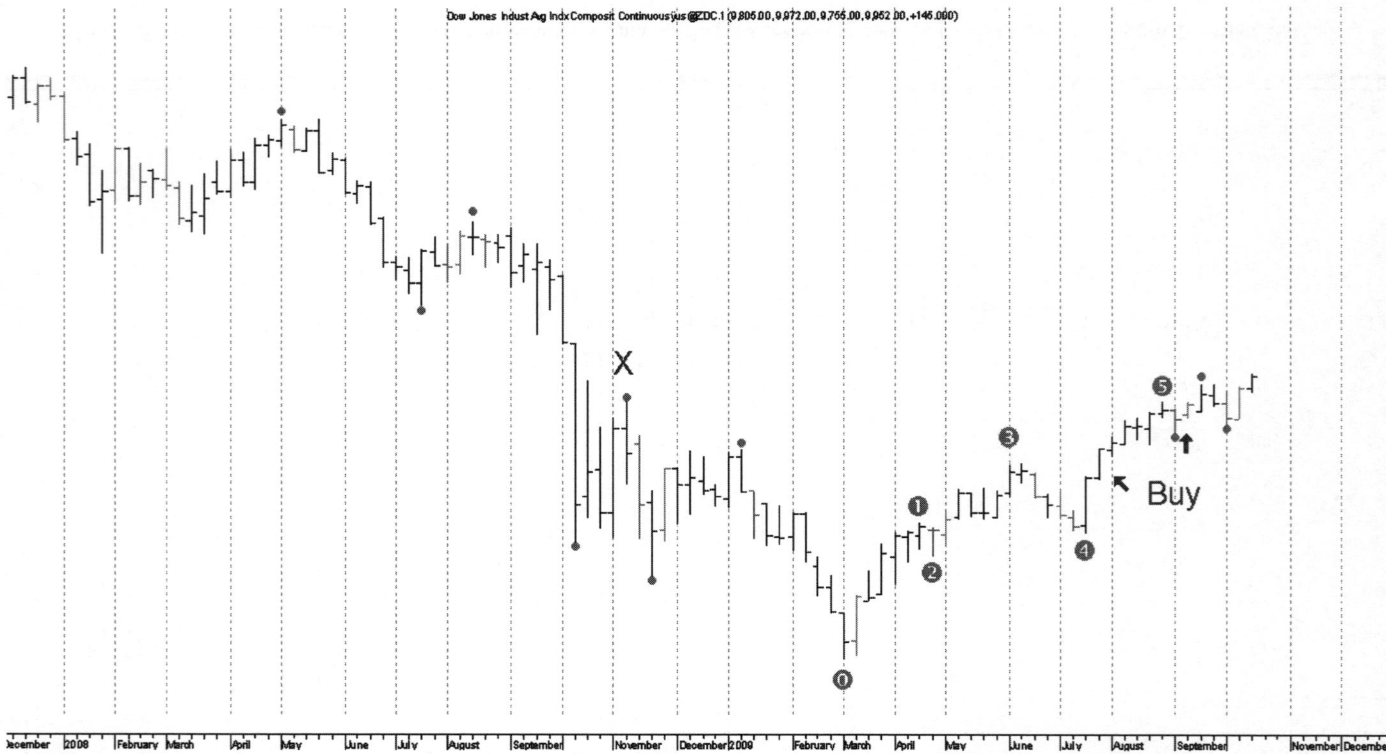

Chart 16 Dow Jones Industrial Average composite continuous chart (weekly) (Metastock Chart Courtesy of Equis International).

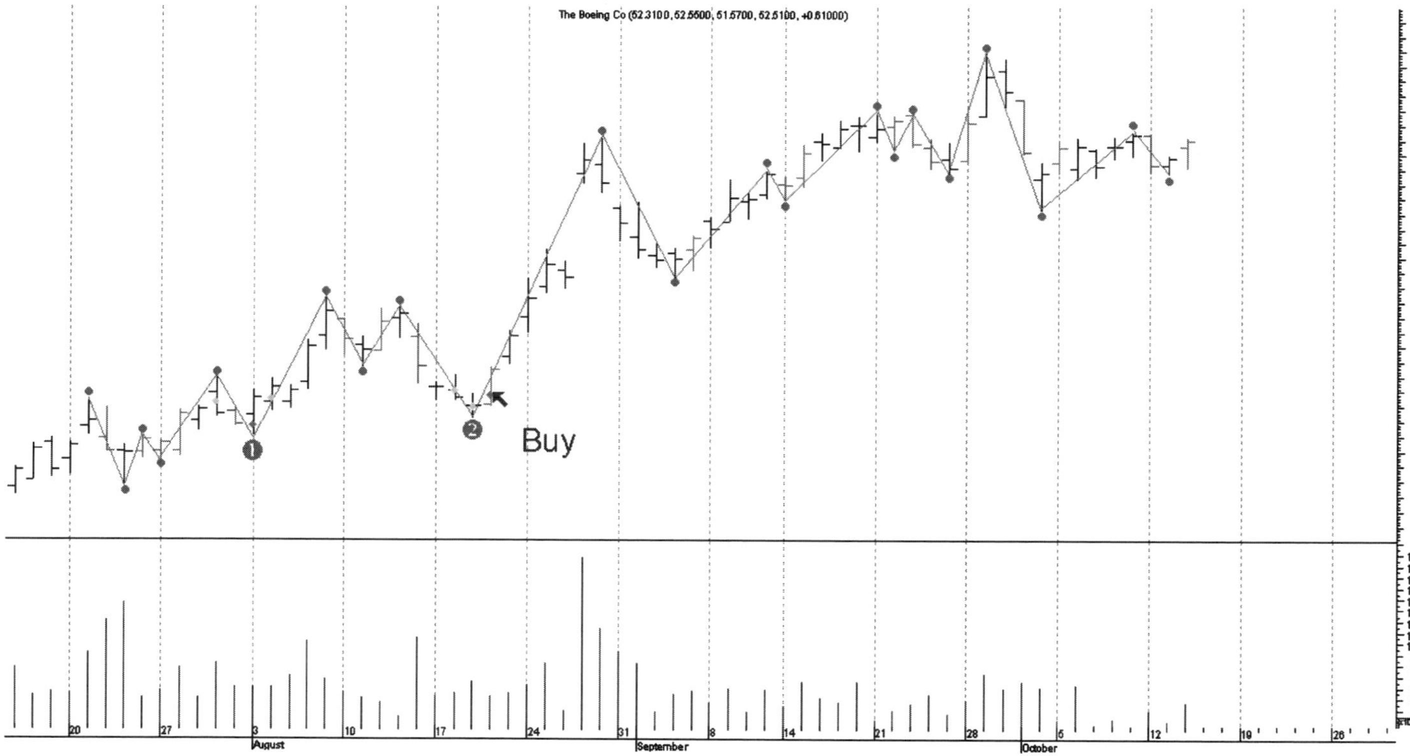

Chart 17 Boeing (daily) (Metastock Chart Courtesy of Equis International).

Chart 18 Gold 100 Troy oz COMEX continuous chart (daily) (Metastock Chart Courtesy of Equis International).

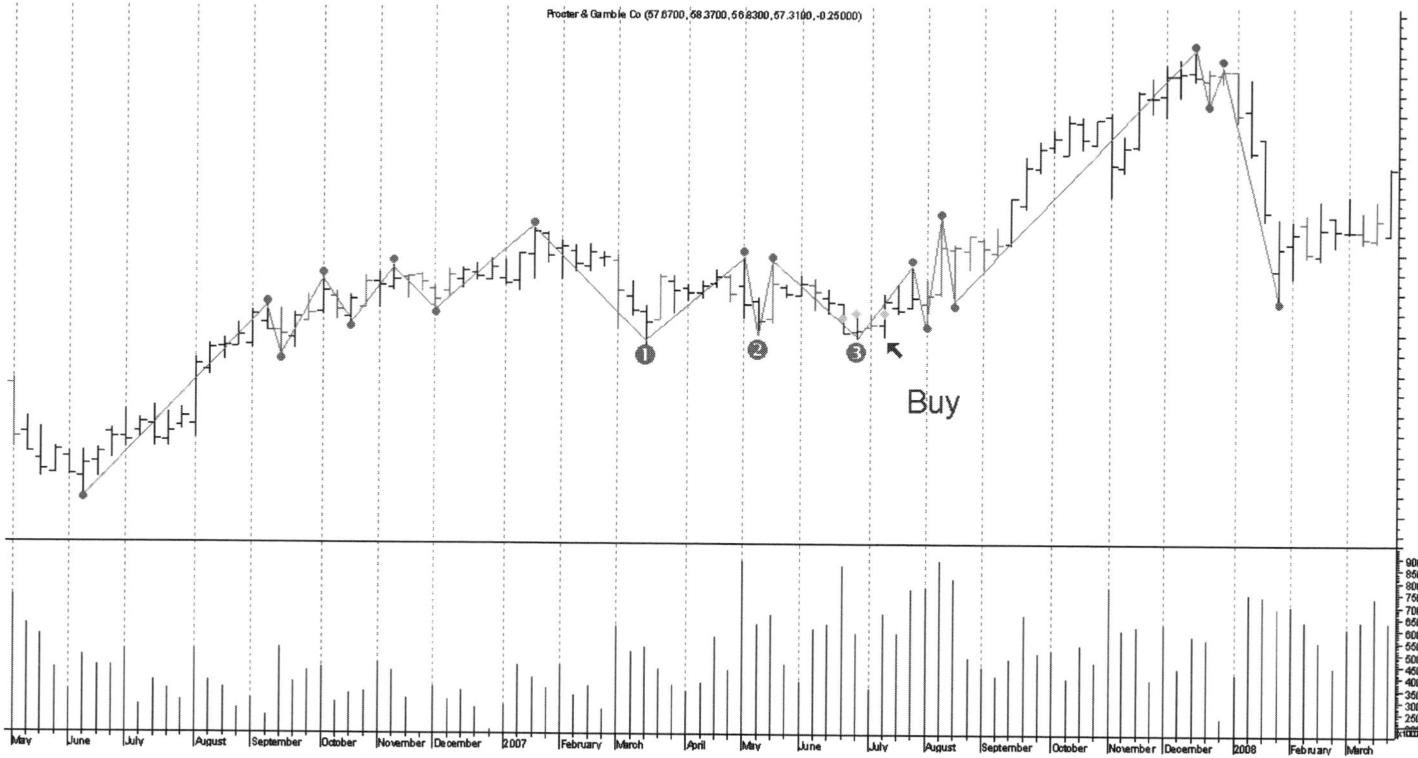

Chart 19 Procter & Gamble (weekly) (Metastock Chart Courtesy of Equis International).

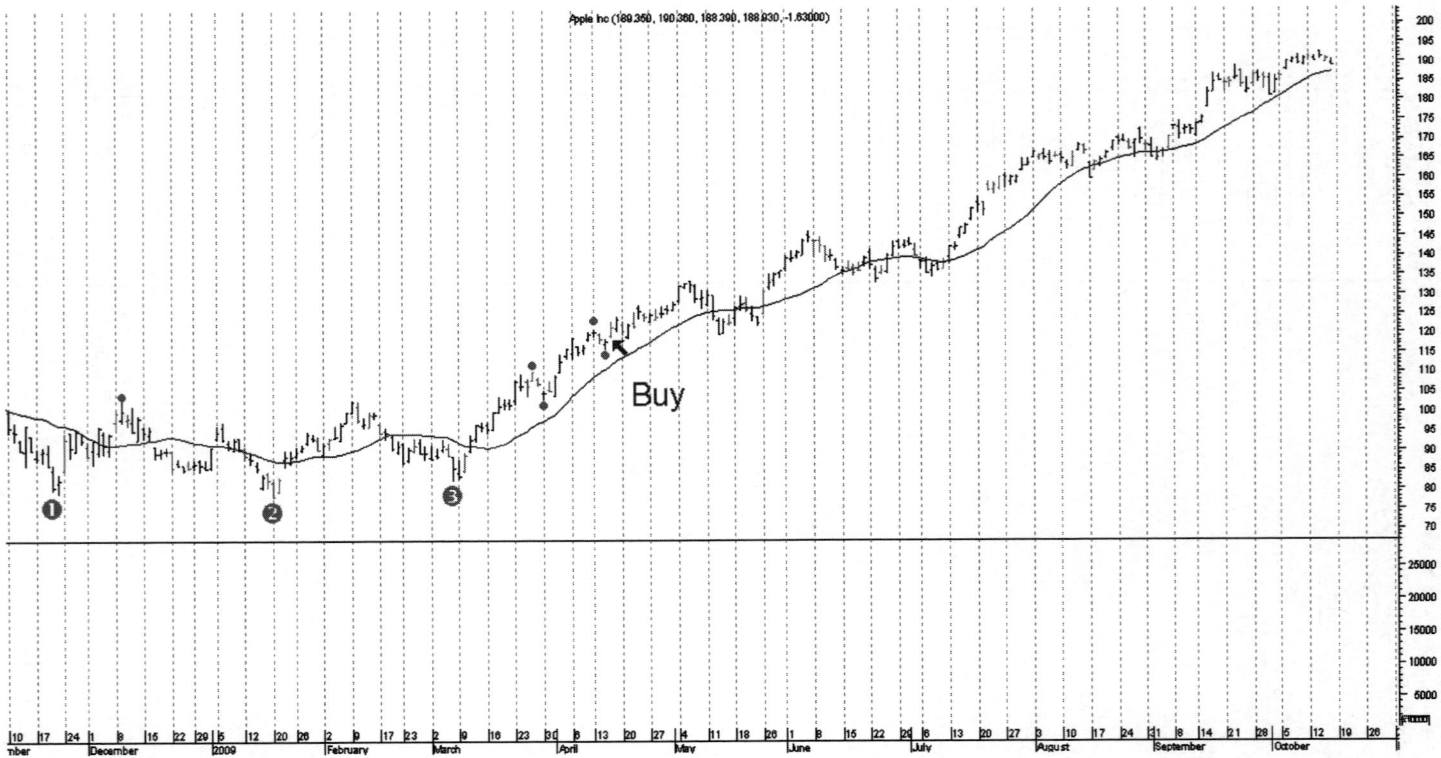

Chart 20 Apple (daily) (Metastock Chart Courtesy of Equis International).

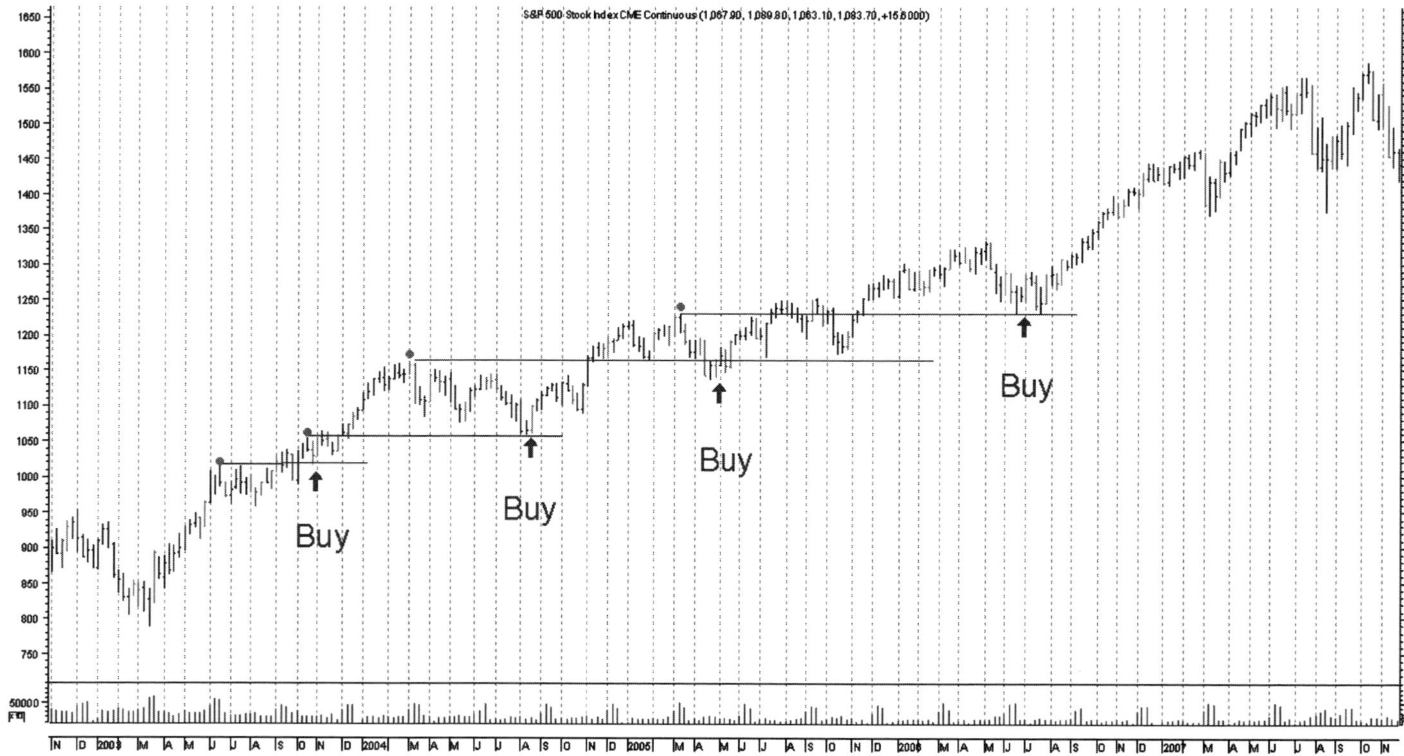

Chart 21 S&P 500 Stock Index CME continuous chart (weekly) (Metastock Chart Courtesy of Equis International).

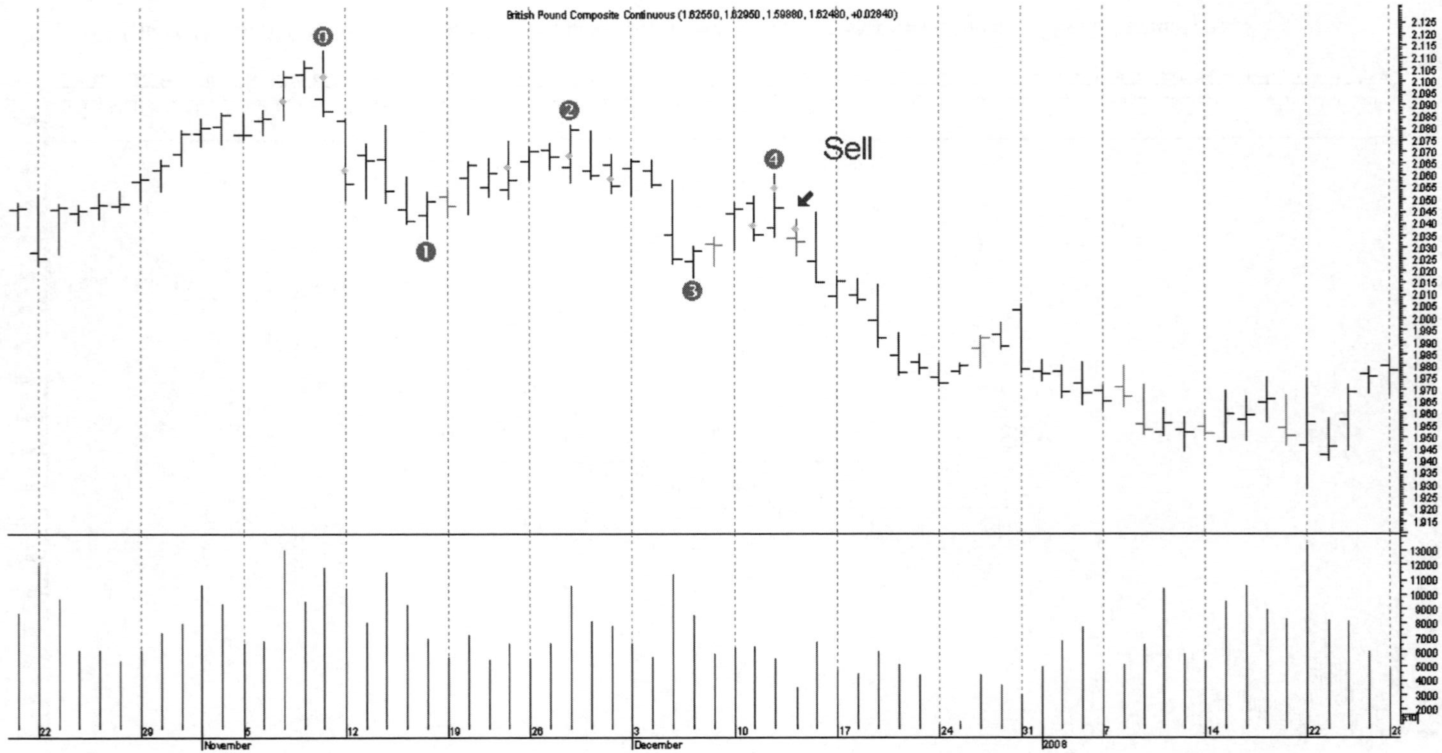

Chart 22 British pound composite continuous chart (daily) (Metastock Chart Courtesy of Equis International).

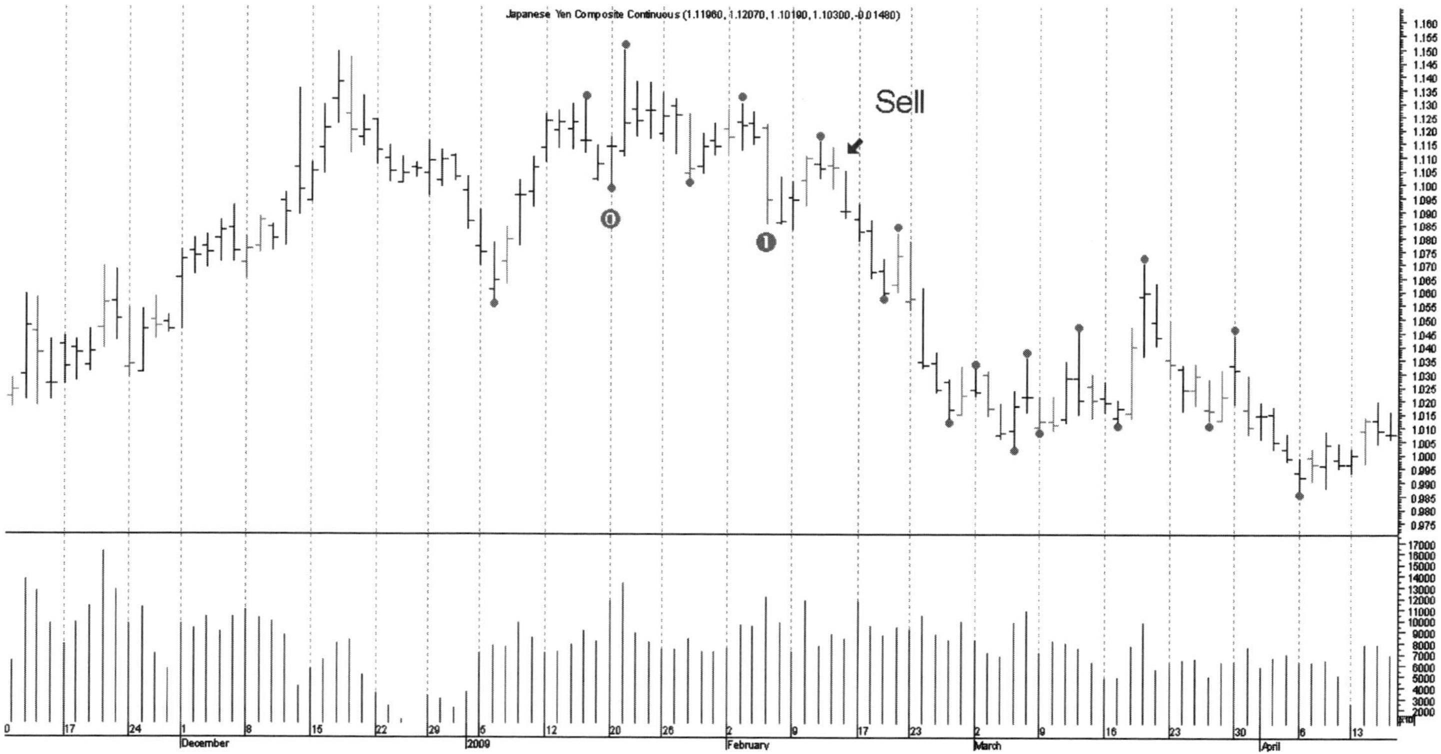

Chart 23 Japanese yen composite continuous chart (daily) (Metastock Chart Courtesy of Equis International).

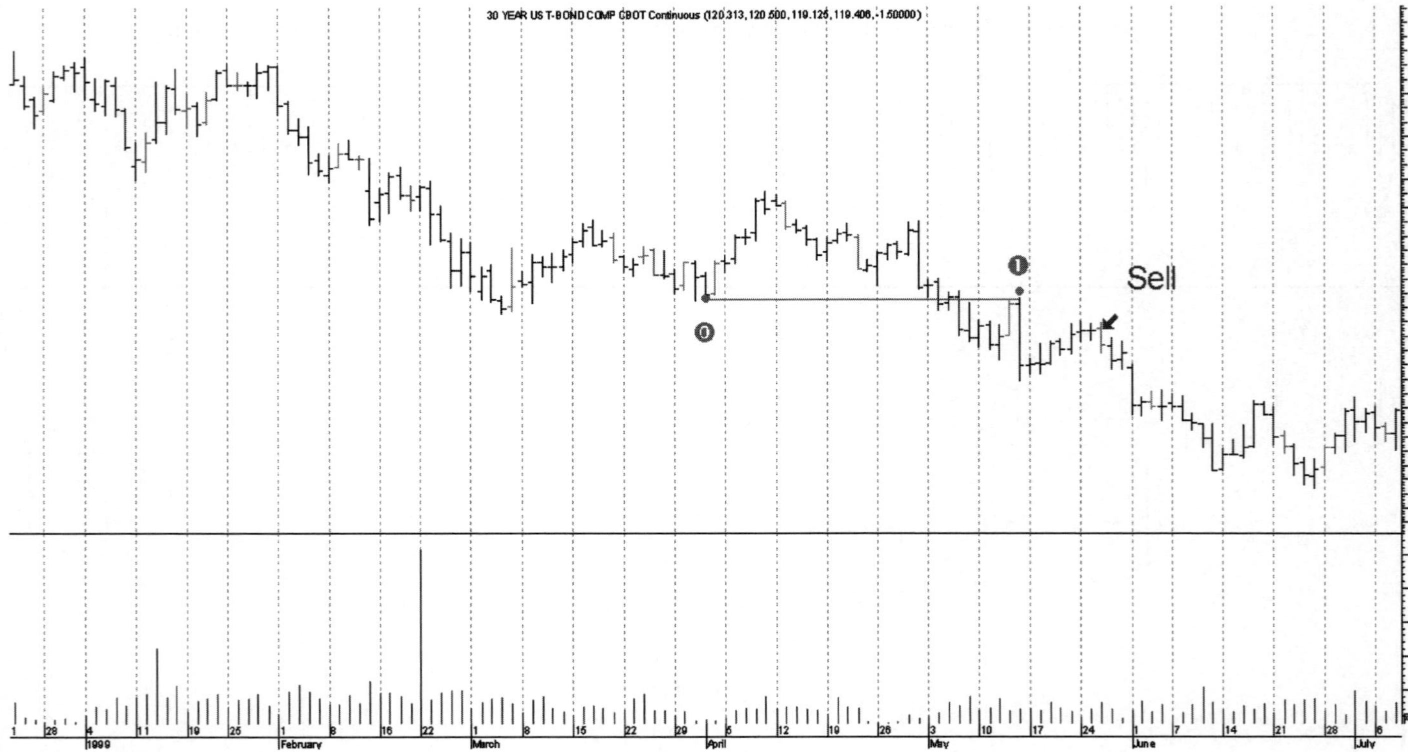

Chart 24 30 Year US T-bond composite CBOT continuous chart (daily) (Metastock Chart Courtesy of Equis International).

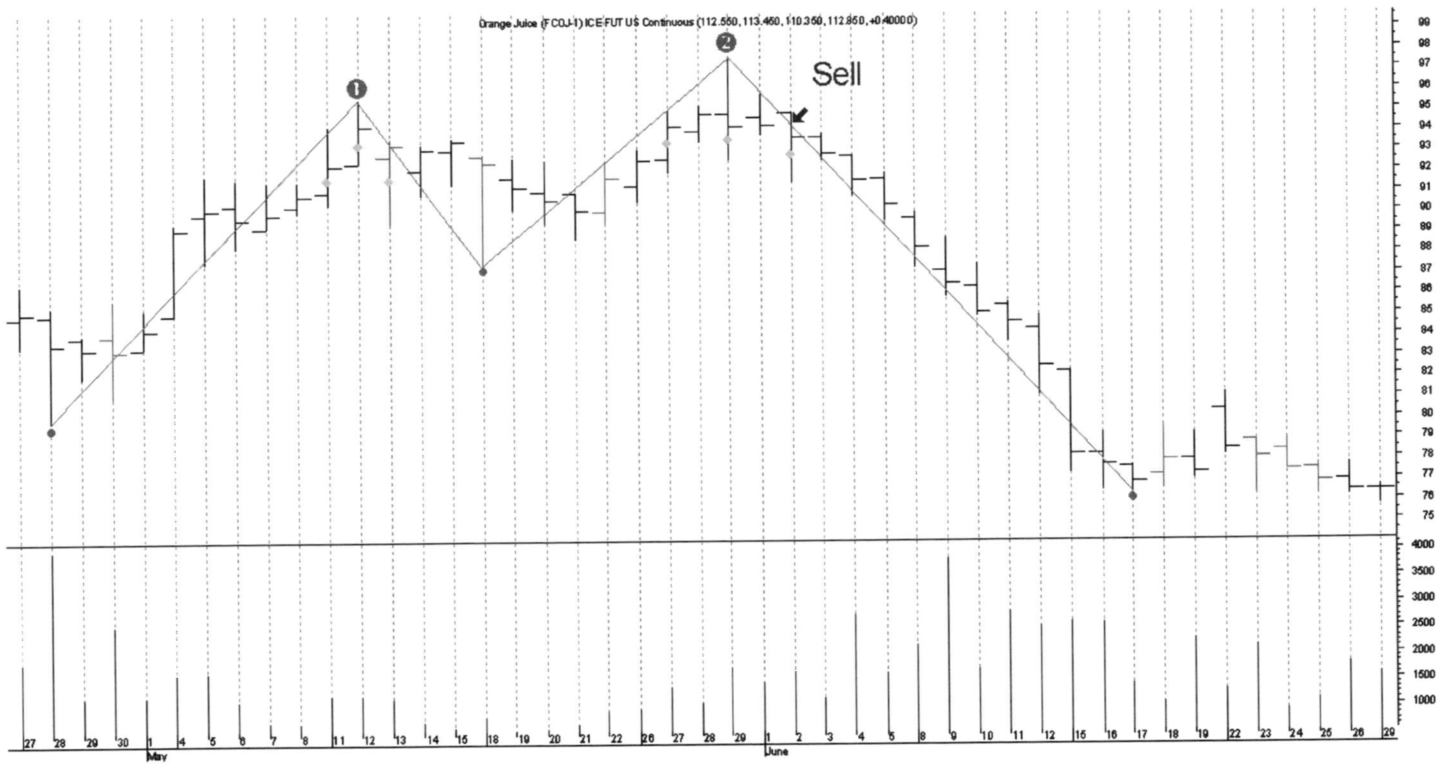

Chart 25 Orange juice continuous chart (daily) (Metastock Chart Courtesy of Equis International).

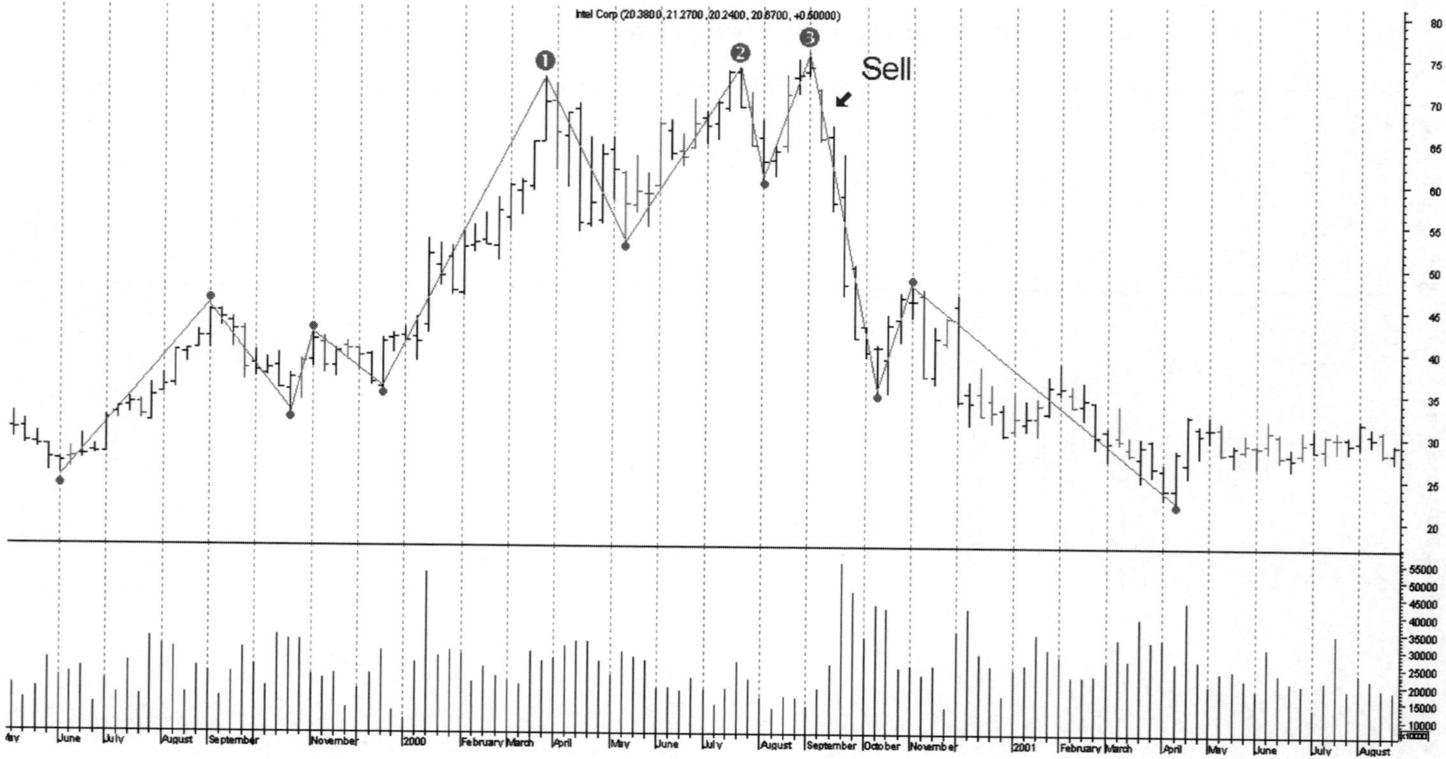

Chart 26 Intel (weekly) (Metastock Chart Courtesy of Equis International).

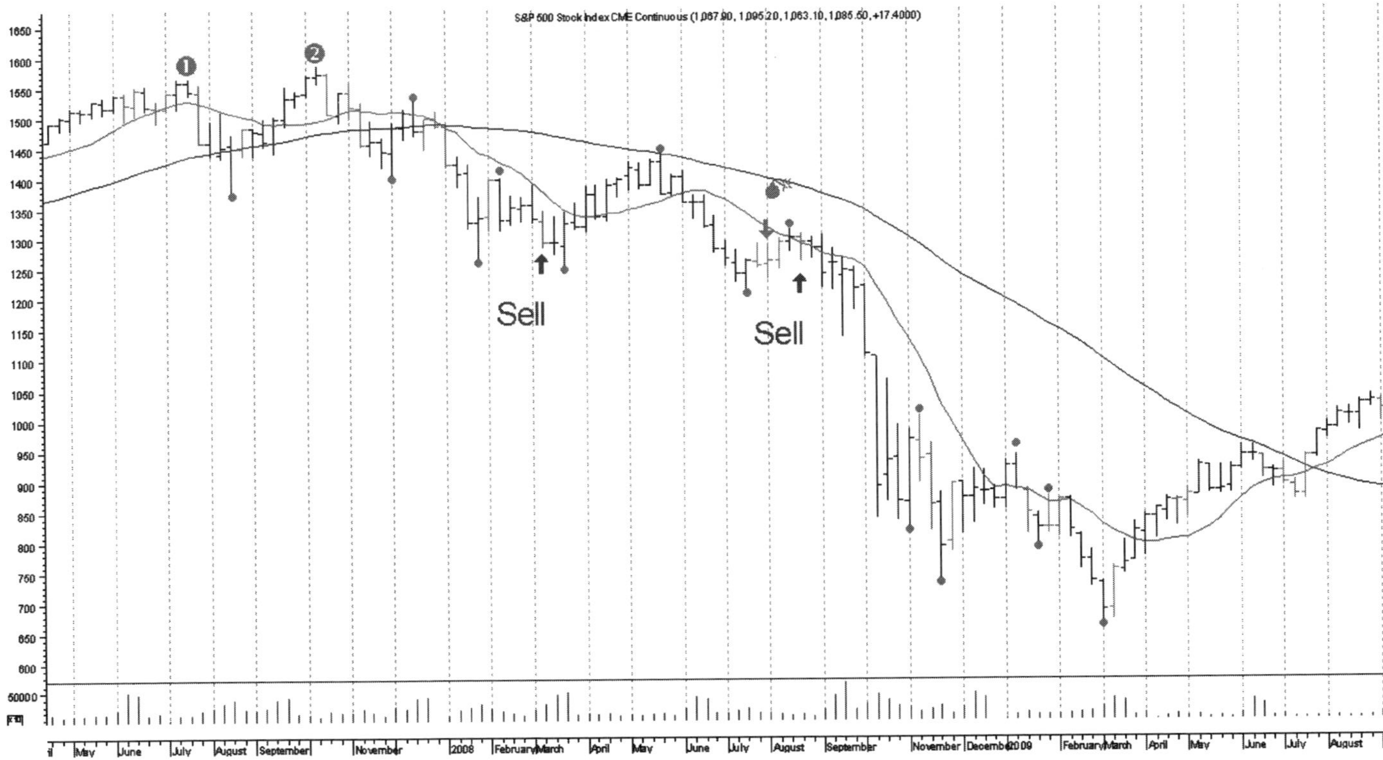

Chart 27 S&P 500 Stock Index continuous chart (weekly) (Metastock Chart Courtesy of Equis International).

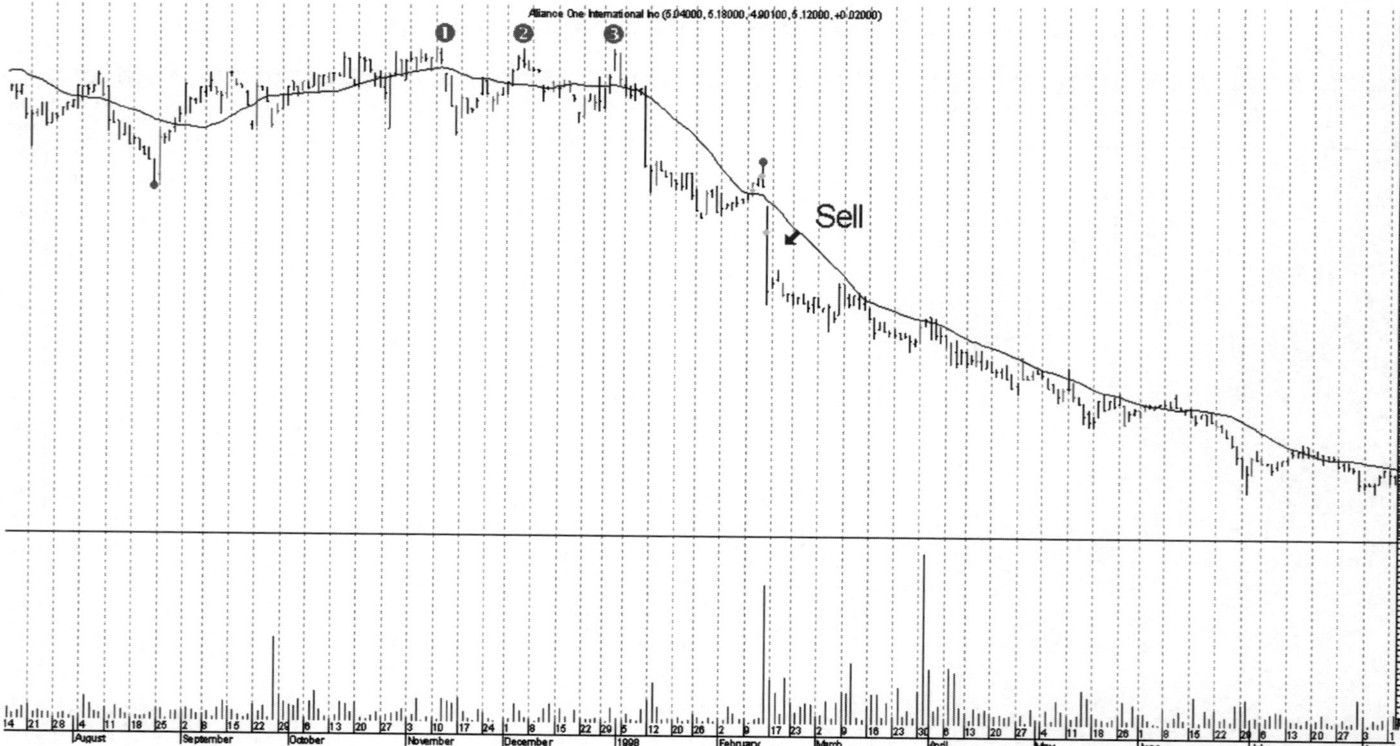

Chart 28 Alliance One International (daily) (Metastock Chart Courtesy of Equis International).

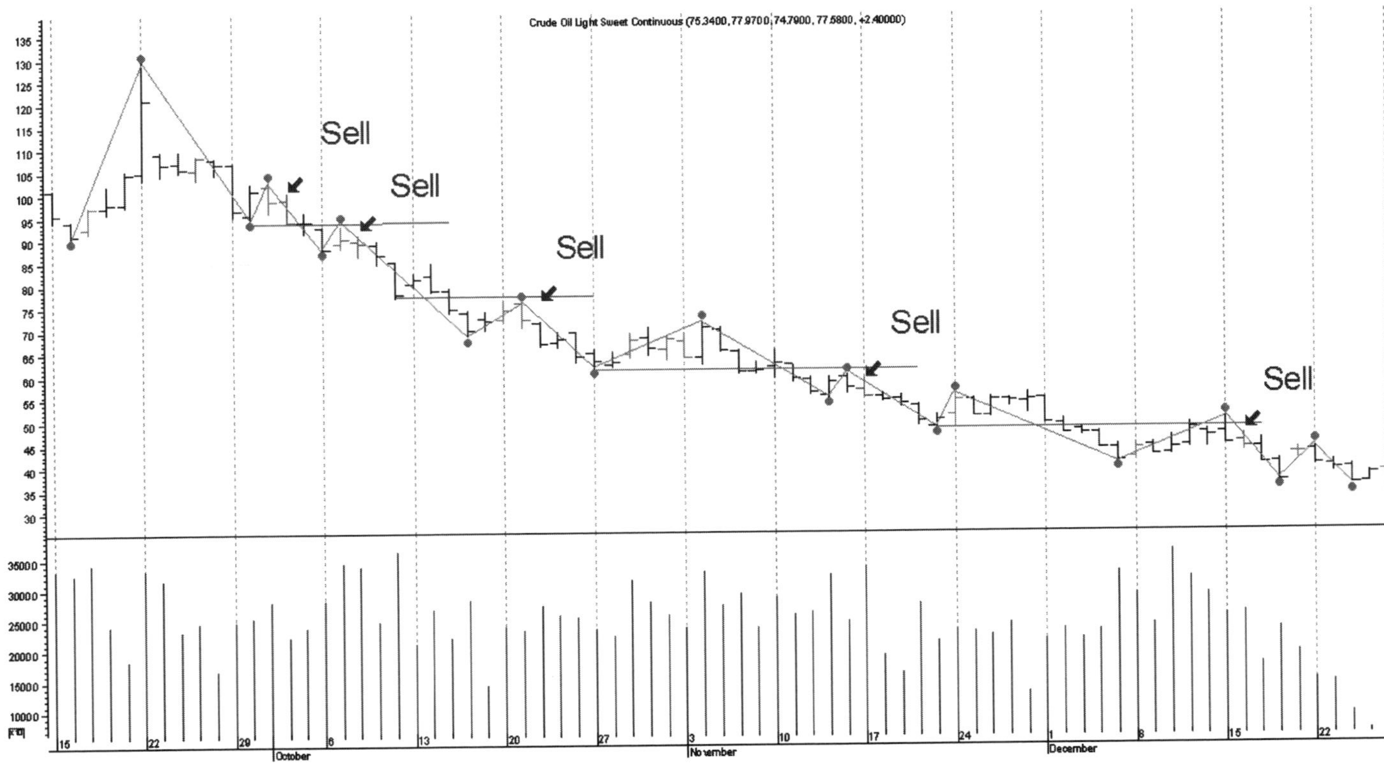

Chart 29 Crude oil light sweet continuous chart (daily) (Metastock Chart Courtesy of Equis International).

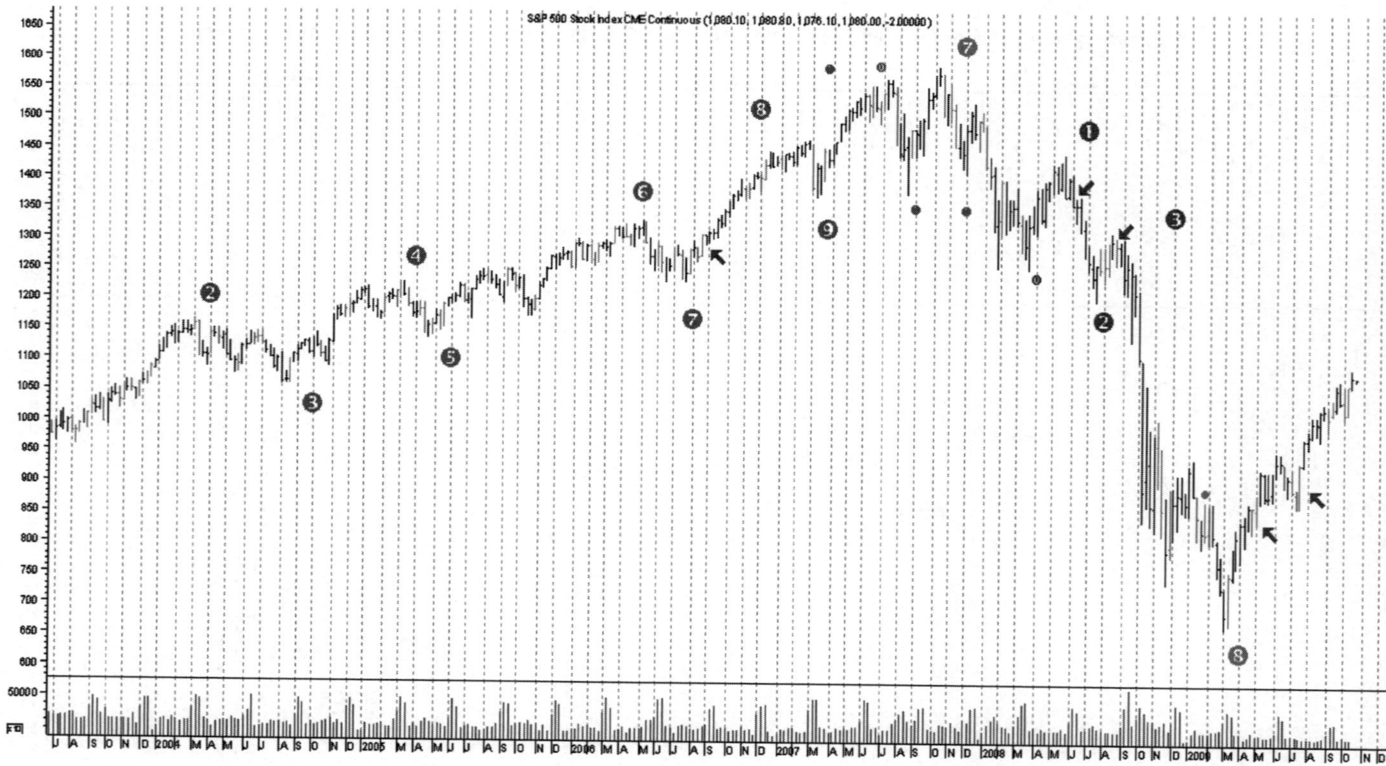

Chart 30 S&P 500 Stock Index continuous chart (weekly) (Metastock Chart Courtesy of Equis International).

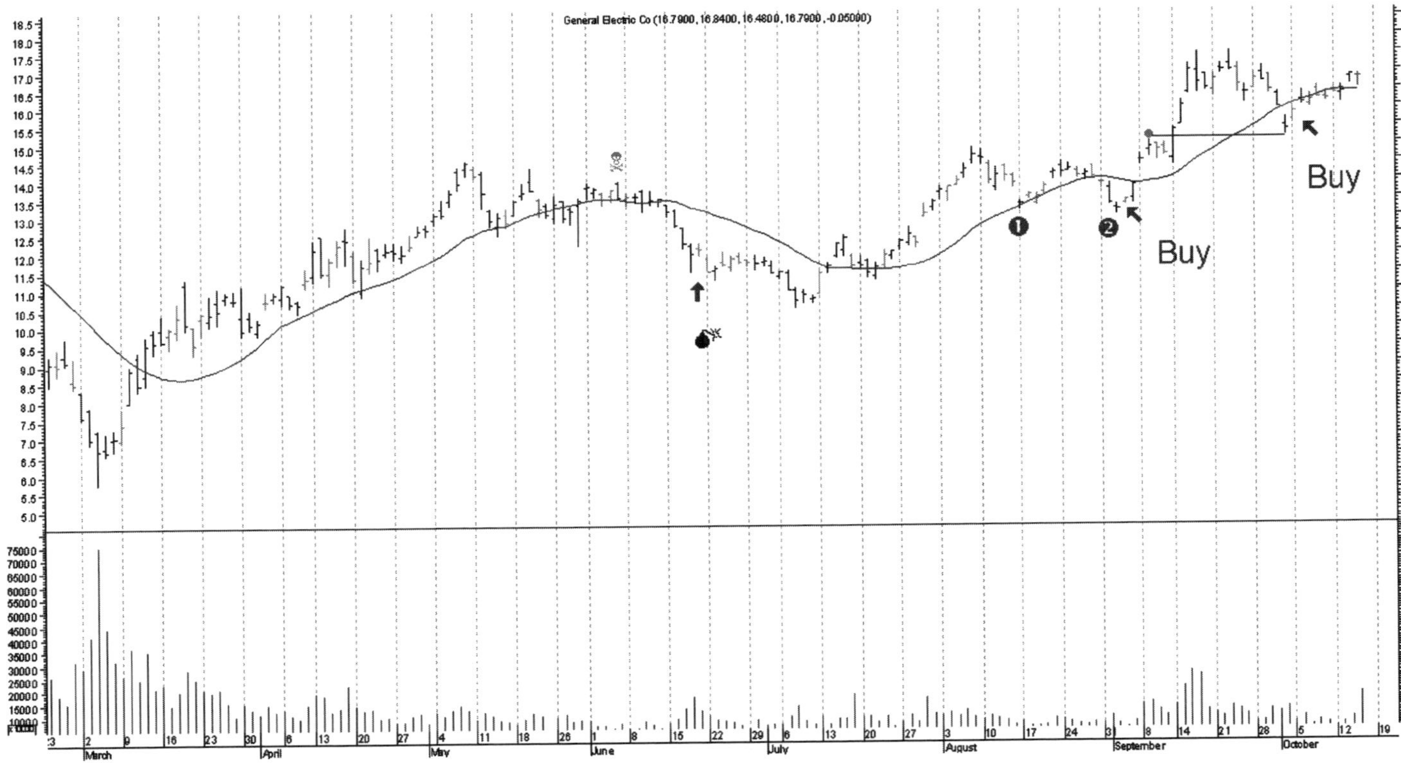

Chart 31 General Electric (daily) (Metastock Chart Courtesy of Equis International).

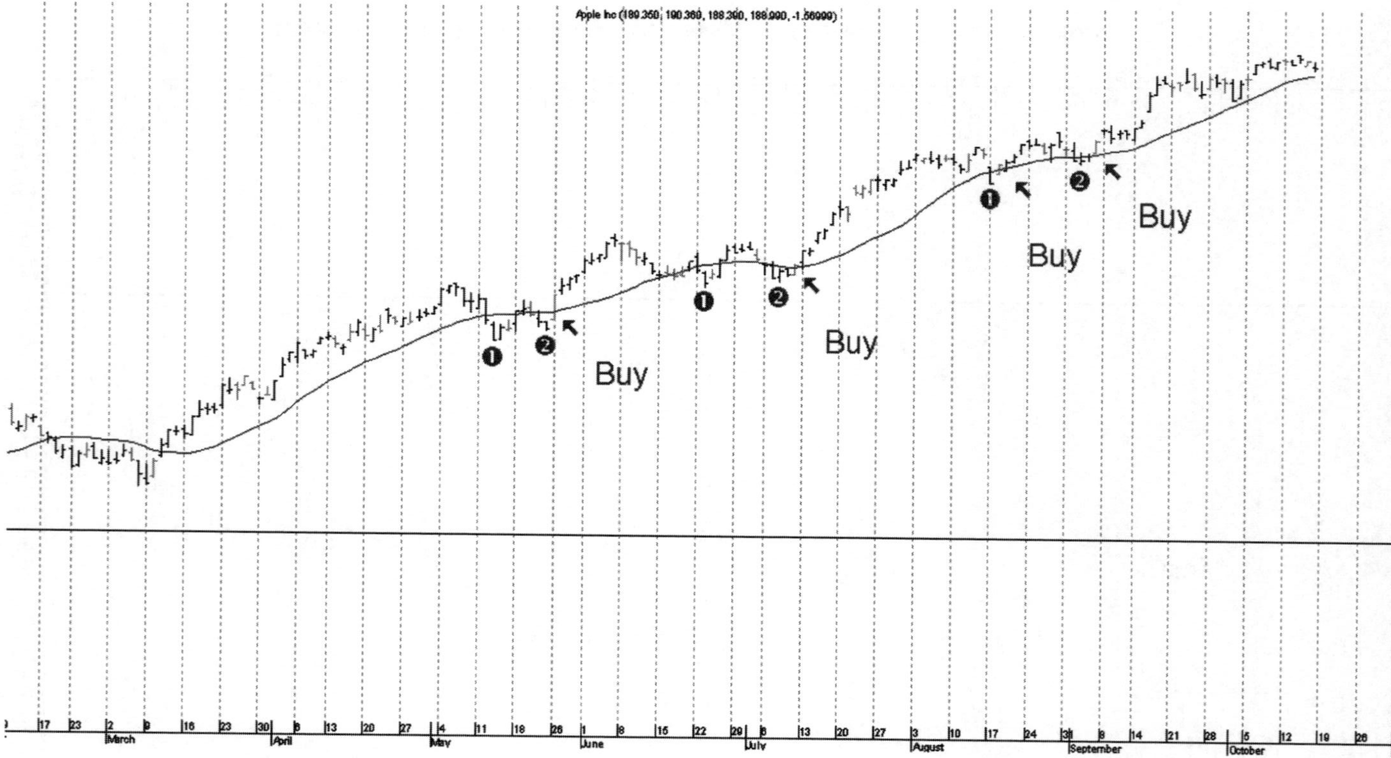

Chart 32 Apple (daily) (Metastock Chart Courtesy of Equis International).

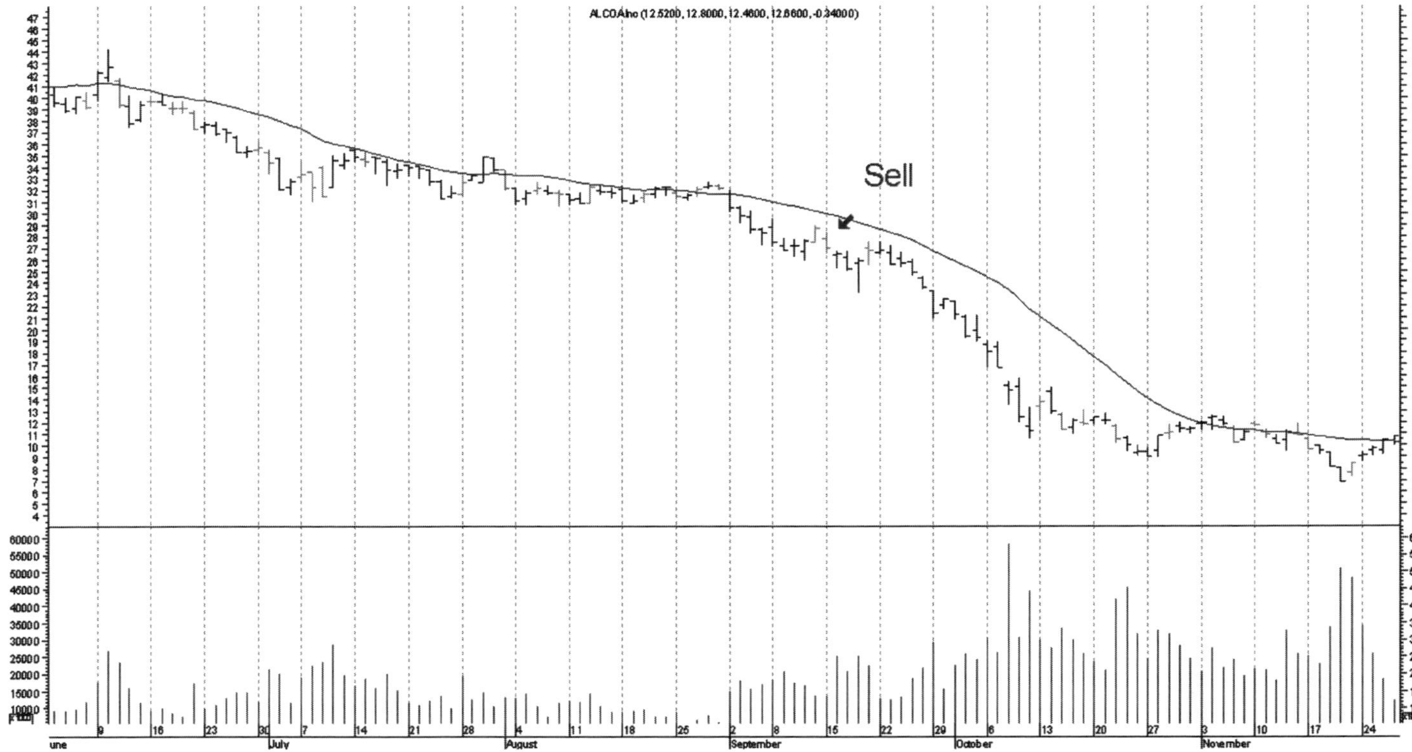

Chart 33 ALCOA (daily) (Metastock Chart Courtesy of Equis International).

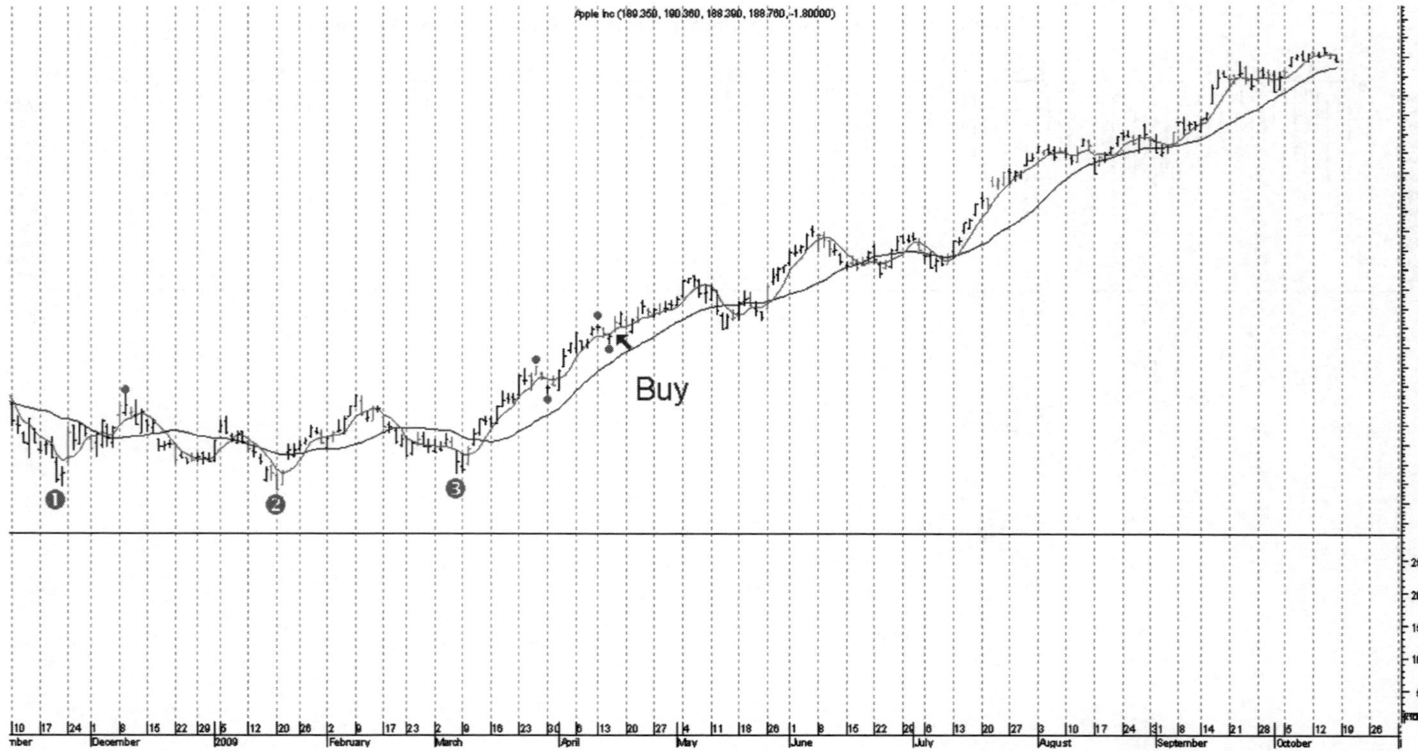

Chart 34 Apple (daily) (Metastock Chart Courtesy of Equis International).

Chart 35 AM Castle & Co. (daily) (Metastock Chart Courtesy of Equis International).

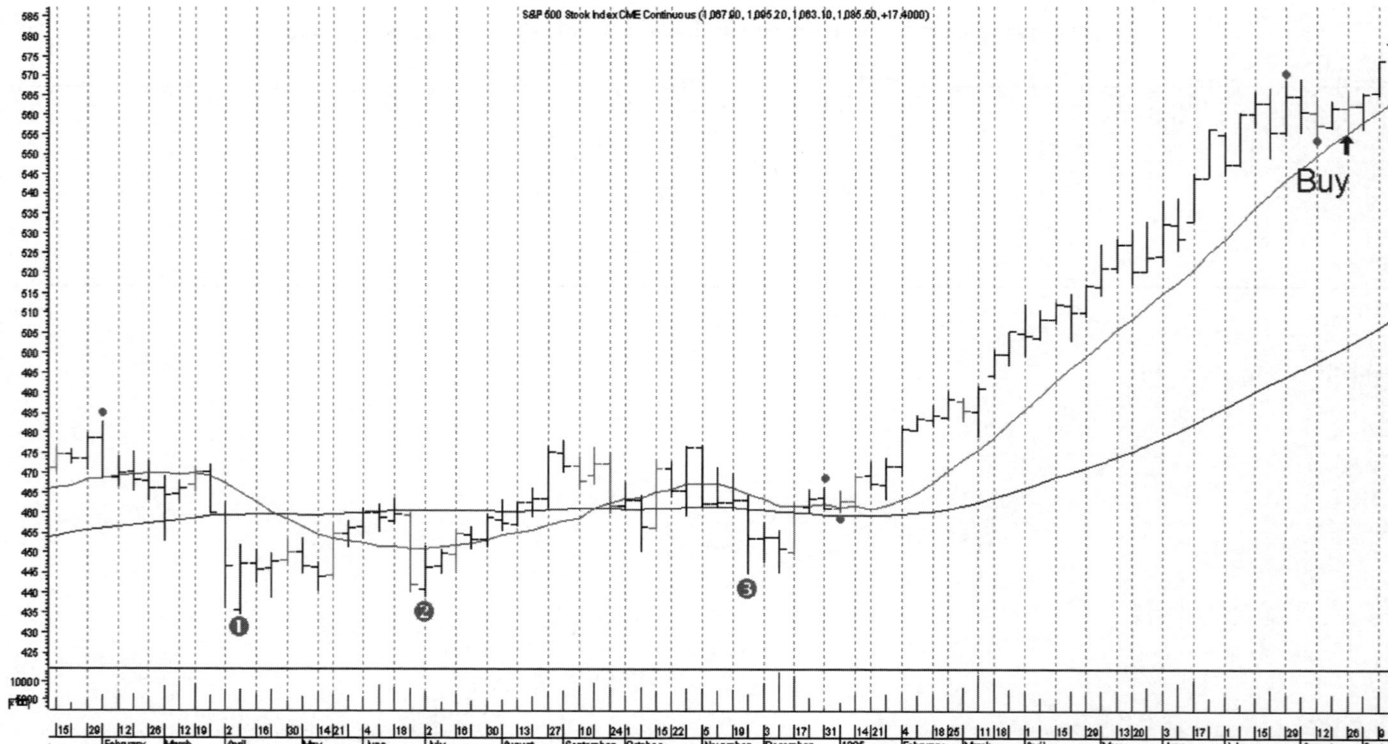

Chart 36 S&P 500 Stock Index continuous chart (weekly) (Metastock Chart Courtesy of Equis International).

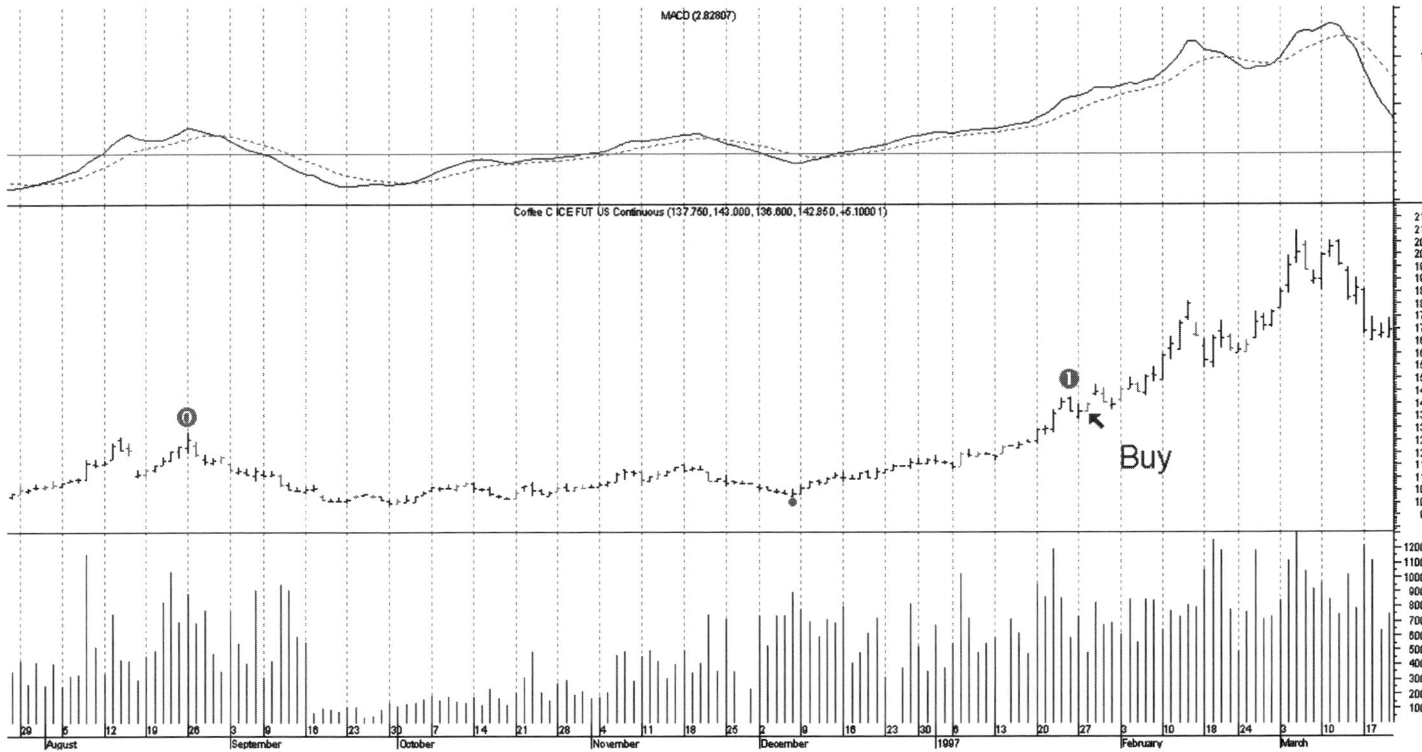

Chart 37 Coffee C continuous chart (daily) (Metastock Chart Courtesy of Equis International).

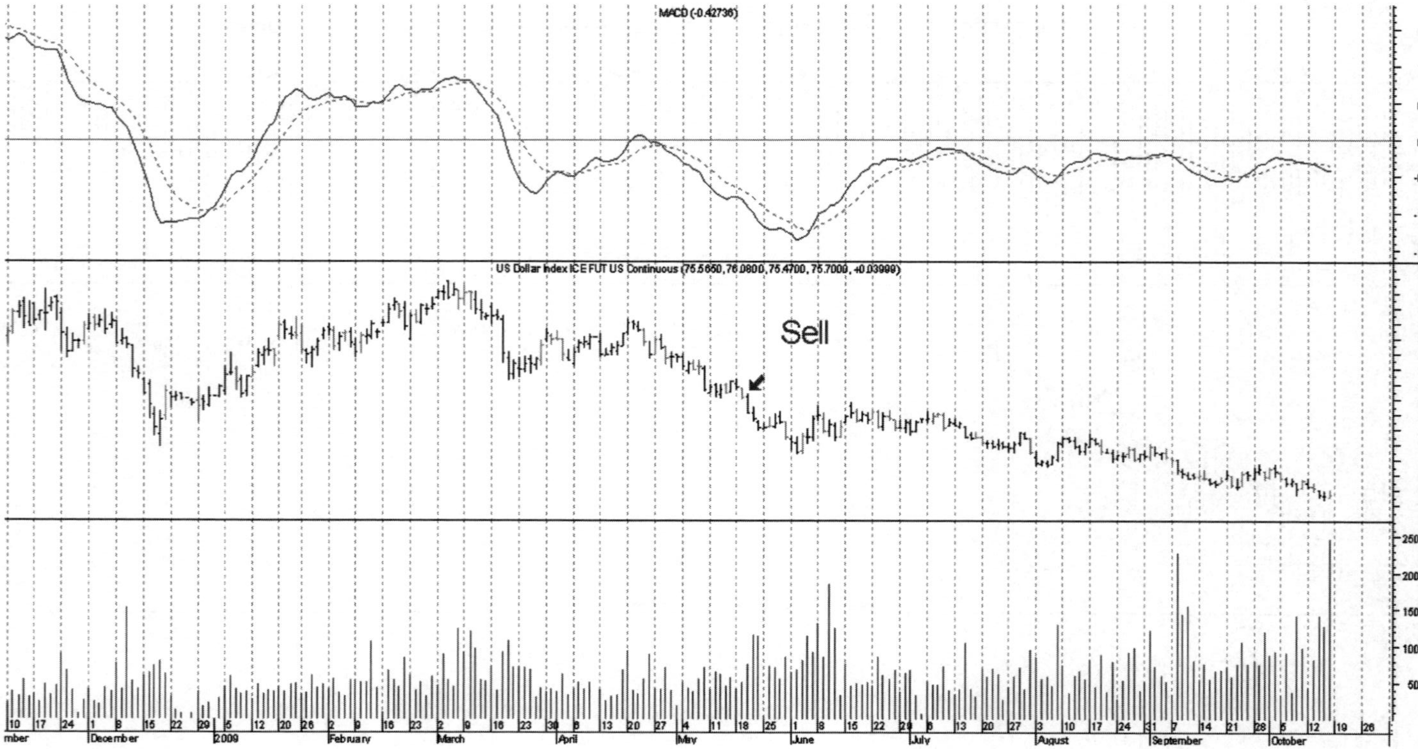

Chart 38 US Dollar Index continuous chart (daily) (Metastock Chart Courtesy of Equis International).

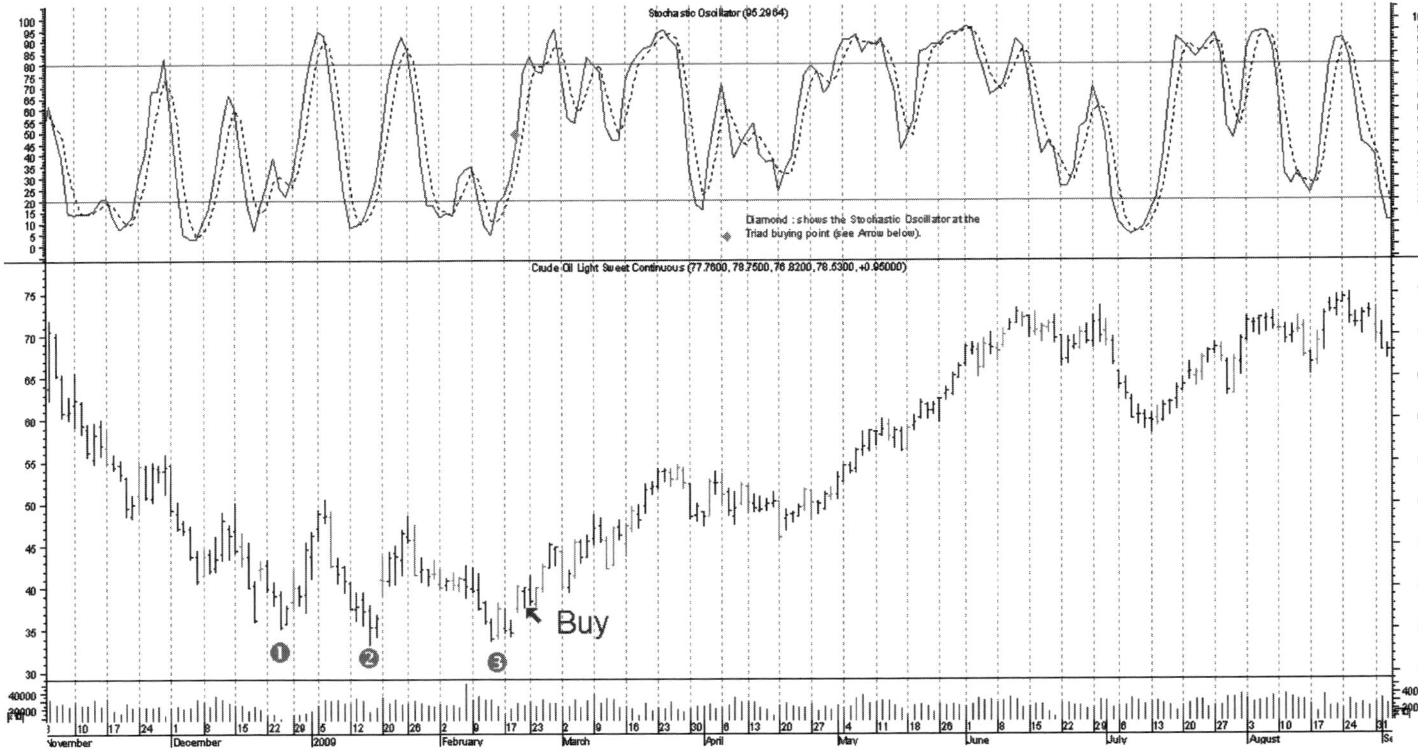

Chart 39 Crude oil light sweet continuous chart (daily) (Metastock Chart Courtesy of Equis International).

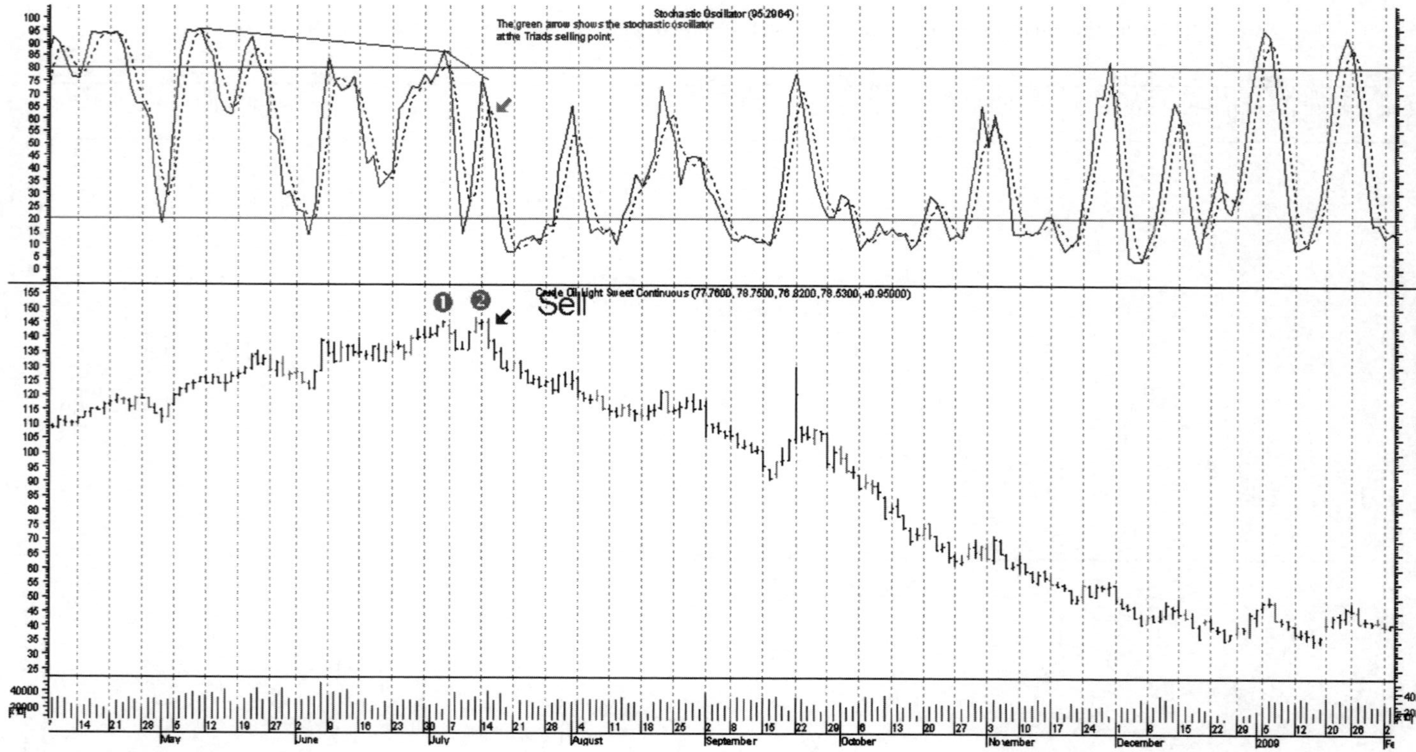

Chart 40 Crude oil light sweet continuous chart (daily) (Metastock Chart Courtesy of Equis International).

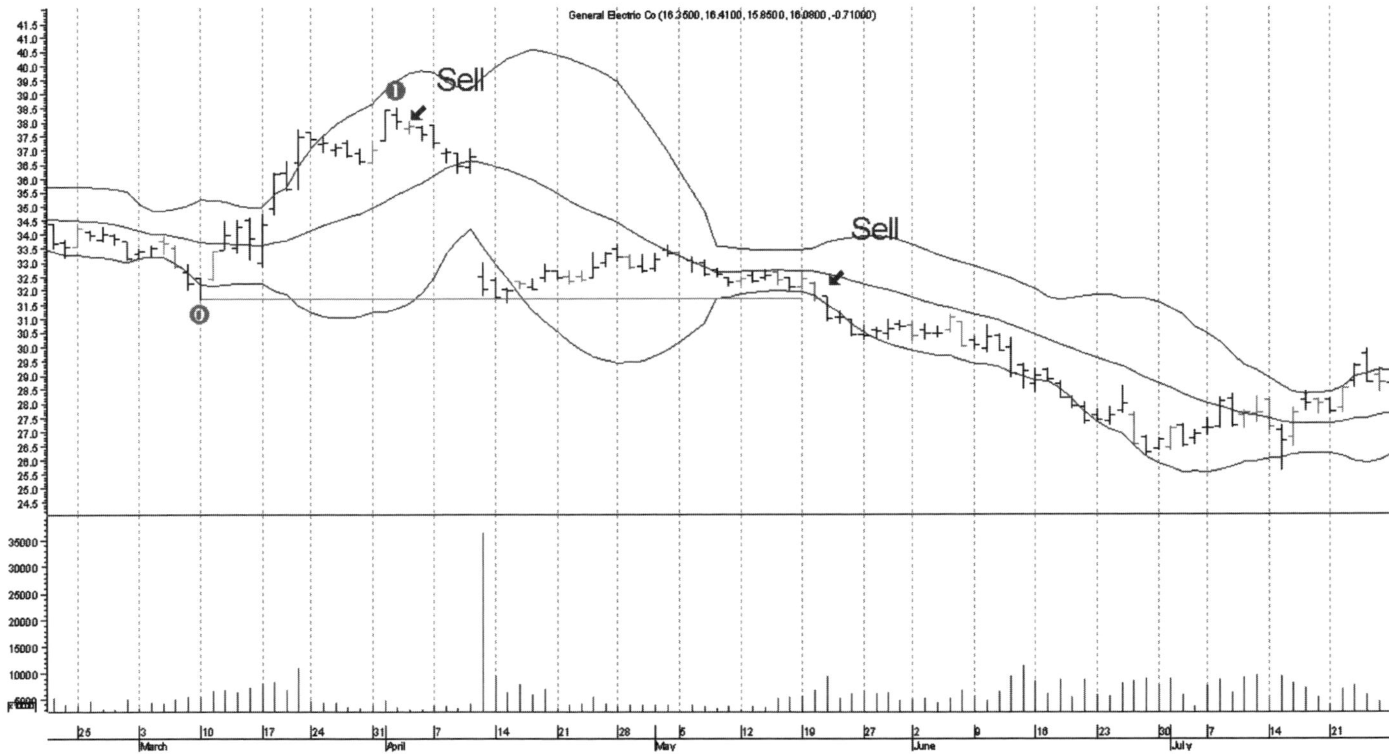

Chart 41 General Electric (daily) (Metastock Chart Courtesy of Equis International).

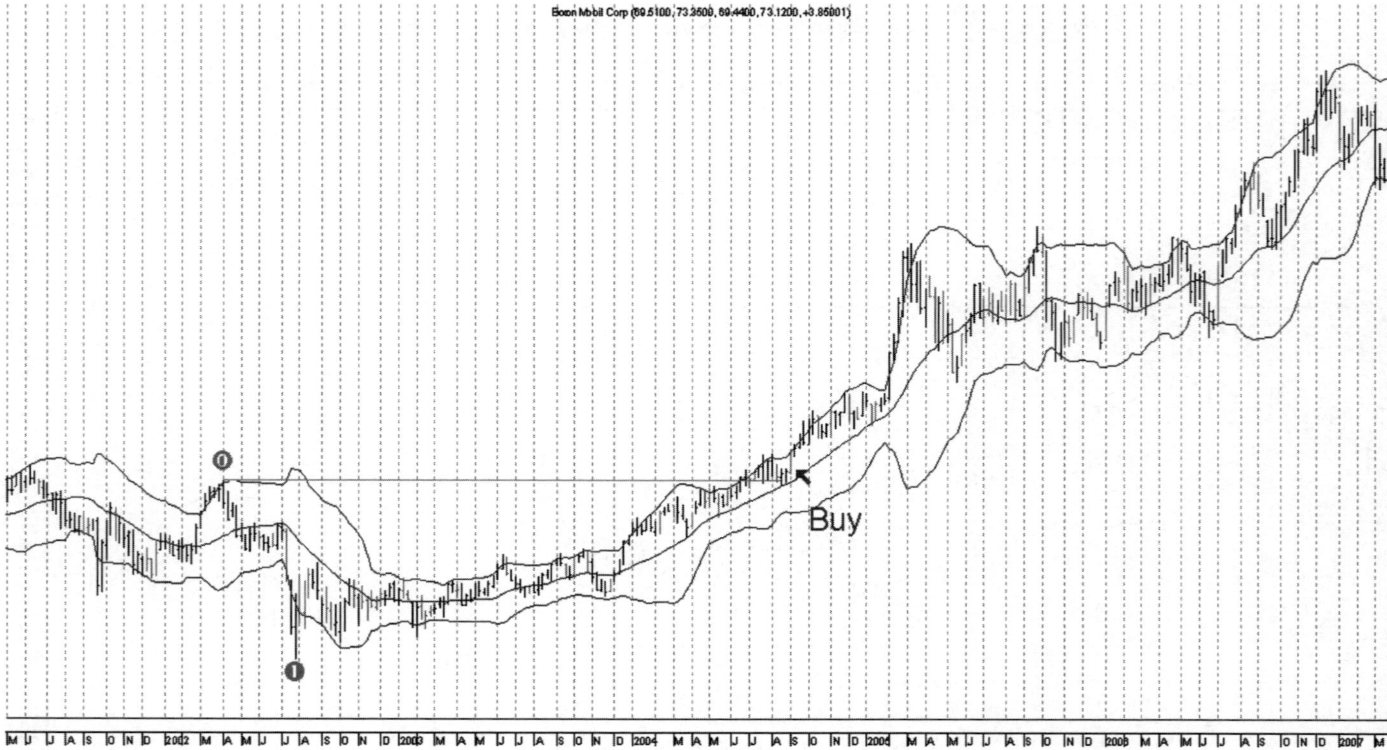

Chart 42 Exxon Mobil (daily) (Metastock Chart Courtesy of Equis International).

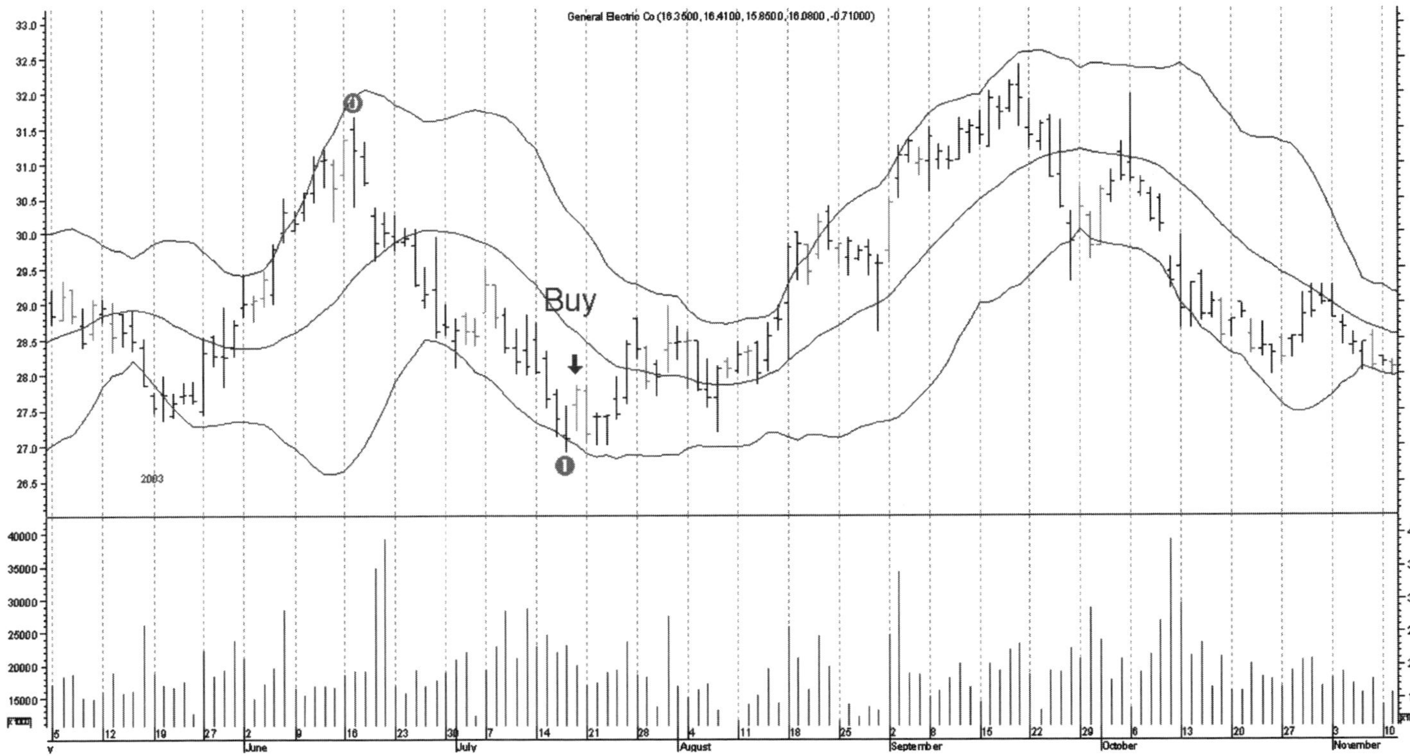

Chart 43 General Electric (daily) (Metastock Chart Courtesy of Equis International).

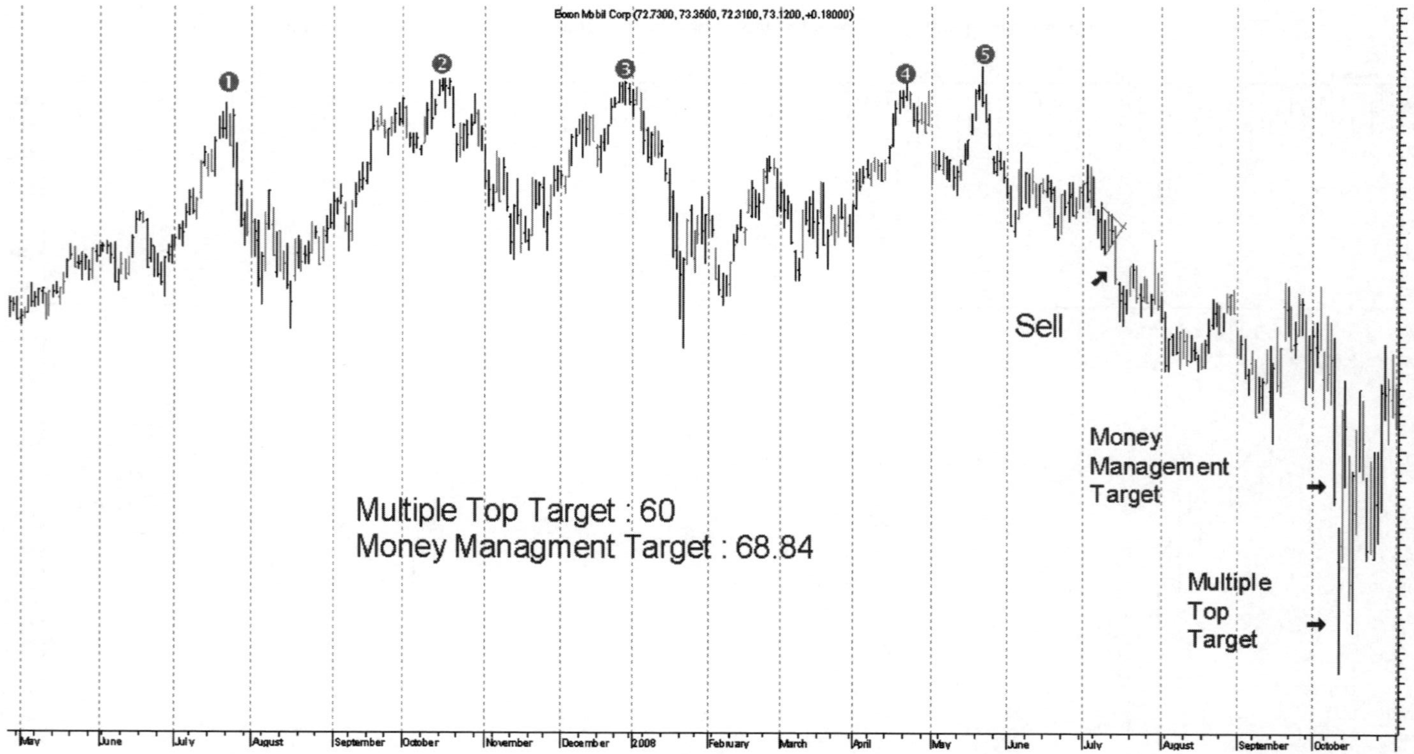

Chart 44 Exxon Mobil (daily) (Metastock Chart Courtesy of Equis International).

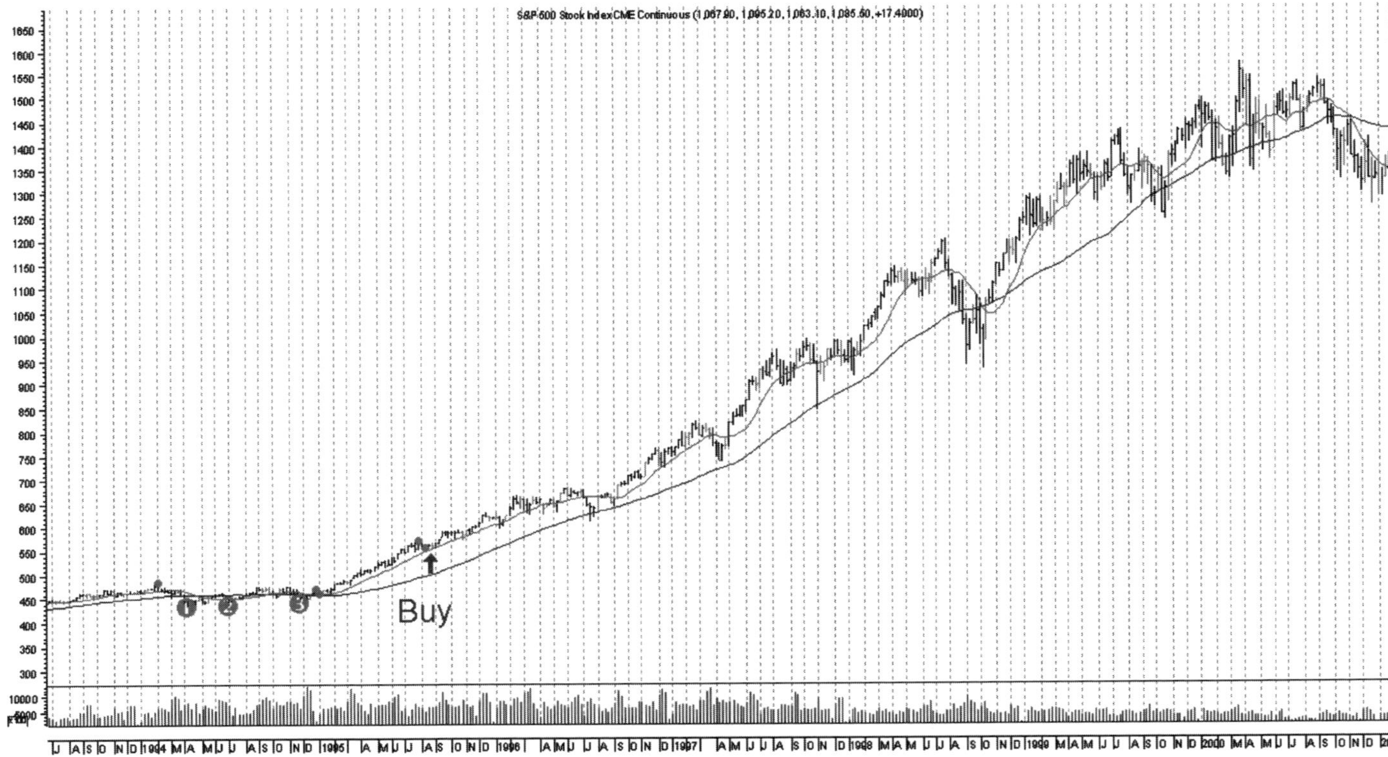

Chart 45 S&P 500 Stock Index continuous chart (weekly) (Metastock Chart Courtesy of Equis International).

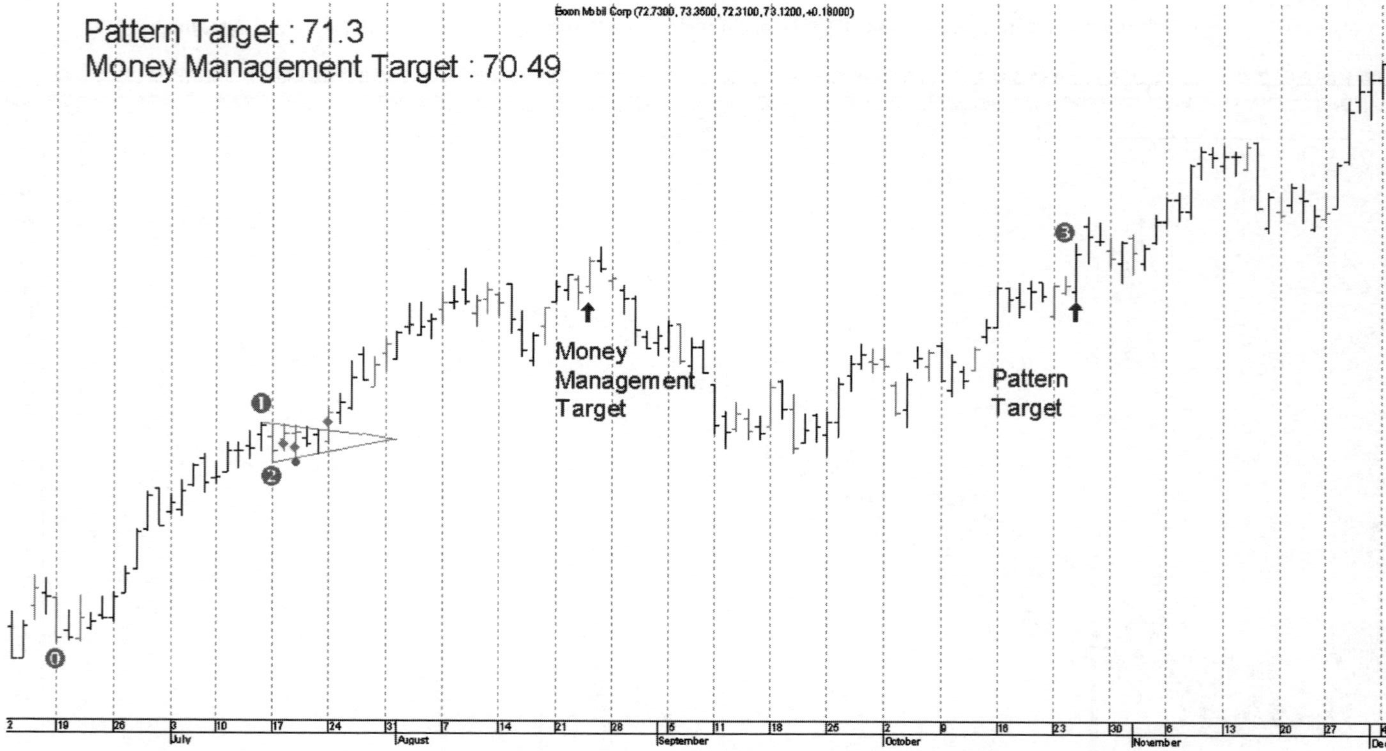

Chart 46 Exxon Mobil (daily) (Metastock Chart Courtesy of Equis International).

Notes

1. George Douglas Taylor, *The Taylor Trading Technique*, Traders Press, 1950. In his book, the author tells how he actually traded market swings for short-term profits. He offers us a glimpse of market structure as the foundation of swings.
2. Wyckoff is aware that each stock has its own personality. He says, 'Stocks have habits and characteristics which are as distinct as those of human beings or animals. By a close study the trader becomes intimately acquainted with these habits,' and then he says that the 'moods' of the stocks should be studied. For Wykoff, stocks can be 'leaders' or 'followers,' 'stubborn,' 'aggressive,' etc. (Rollo Tape (R. D. Wyckoff), *Studies in Tape Reading*, 1910, Fraser Publishing Co., 1987).
3. In his Trading Courses, Gann teaches the Gann swings, such as the 'Three Day Chart Swing.' They are based on counting a selected minimum number of up days with higher highs and higher lows to define ascending swings or a selected minimum number of down days with lower highs and lower lows (see 'Rule for Keeping up 3-Day Chart,' in W. D. Gann, *45 Years in Wall Street*, Lambert Gann Publishing Co., 1976, p. 63).
4. Rhea systematized Dow theory. He gives the designation of 'hypothesis' to the main three postulates of Dow theory. Additionally, he added twelve theorems to the three basic postulates (Robert Rhea, *The Dow Theory*, Fraser Publishing Co., 1993, 12).
5. Both fundamental and technical analyses encompass the market. Fundamental analysis deals with value, whereas technical analysis deals with price. However, for trading, technical analysis beats fundamental analysis. The reason is that technical analysis provides the best timing tool. A stock with strong fundamentals can stay in the same price range for years without significant gains for the investor. The way to avoid this is to use technical analysis. This was the experience of Schwartz, who lost at playing the markets while he worked as a securities analyst. This caused him to react, distancing himself from fundamental analysis and recognizing that technical analysis afforded a much greater probability of

winning. From then on, he became a trader using mainly technical analysis and market timing tools (Martin Schwartz, *Pit Bull, Lessons from a Wall Street Champion Trader*, HarperCollins, 1998, pp.16, 23).

Technical analysis does give false signals, but the same is true of fundamental analysis. Dreman explains the reasons for these failures. What is little known is that the forecast error of fundamental analysis 'as a percent of reported earnings' was in the range of 44 % for the 1991–1996 period (David Dreman, *Contrarian Investment Strategies: The Next Generation*, Simon & Schuster, 1998, pp. 91, 92).

6. Thrust has been used by many master traders, such as Bayer, Livermore, Wyckoff, or Gann, but it is Dunnigan who gives 'thrust' its full importance and scope in trading (William Dunnigan, *New Blueprints for Gains in Stocks and Grains*, FT, Pitman Publishing, 1997, p. 122)
7. The mean swing was calculated by adding the lengths or sizes of a set of swings and dividing the total by the number of swings in the set. The median swing is the value in the middle of a set of swings that have been arranged in ascending or descending order of size. The mode swing is the swing size that occurs most frequently in a given set of swings.

   Sperandeo is a good example of a master trader for whom the study of the fluctuations in price and time of each market, combined with measures of central tendency, has been important. Before buying gold in October 1999, he studied the time/price history of this market since 1981. He measured and tabulated all movements that had durations of three weeks to three months. He found 18 such movements. Measurements of these movements were: minima, 9.4 %; maxima, 68.8 %; and median, 15.2 % (see Victor Sperandeo, *Trader Vic – Methods of a Wall Street Master*, JohnWiley & Sons, Inc., 1994, p. 172).
8. For Gann, the time/price ratio is essential, with time more important than price. He tells us, 'Time is the most important factor of all,' and, 'The time factor will overbalance both Space and Volume' (W. D. Gann, *How to Make Profits in Commodities*, Traders Press, 1976, p. 56).
9. The White House, following the advice of Paul Volcker who was Chairman of the Fed at the time, announced on 15 April 1980, a package of credit controls to curb the double-digit inflation. This unprecedented measure caused the economy to plunge and President Carter to lose the election. This was a Signature announcing the Reagan era and the end, at least for a time, of Keynesianism as the main foundation of economic policy in the US.
10. According to the nineteenth century French economist Bastiat, we only see the first effect, but the chain of effects that follows is unseen. Therefore, the unknown factors, invisible to us, are the most important ones. If we apply this principle to our twenty-first century traders and investors, what they actually know is minimal compared to the unknown factors behind the market scene (Fréderic Bastiat, *What Is Seen and What Is Not Seen*, 1850).

11. See note 10 on Fréderic Bastiat and the invisible chain of effects. Once more, when trying to understand the mind of the market participants, we are confronted by the invisible realm of the markets.
12. Triads are helpful in trading any kind of pattern. One of the best books on patterns is the classic by Richard W. Schabaker, *Technical Analysis and Stock Market Profits*, FT, Pitman Publishing, 1997. In it is an in-depth study of patterns. Schabaker's book is the source that Edwards and Magee used for their book on TA. An excellent up-to-date manual is Thomas N. Bulkowski, *Encyclopedia of Chart Patterns*, John Wiley & Sons, Inc., 2005.
13. See note 8.
14. Ted Warren, *How to Make the Stock Market Make Money for You*, Buccaneer Books, 1994.
15. Boucher explains why vehicle selection is best. Vehicle selection beats market timing by 10 to 1 and profits come mainly from vehicle selection (see Mark Boucher, 'Stock Selection 20,' in *The Science of Trading*, IRA, 1996, and also Mark Boucher, *The Hedge Fund Edge*, John Wiley & Sons, Inc., 1999).
16. Jesse Livermore constantly insists on the need to study general conditions (see Edwin Lefèvre, *Reminiscences of a Stock Operator*, John Wiley & Sons, Inc., 1994, p. 69). For Gann, the first rule is to determine the trend of the general market (see W. D. Gann, *45 Years in Wall Street*, Lambert Gann Publishing Co., 1976).
17. Contrary to the current belief, Keynes, in fact, lost heavily in the markets. He was almost wiped out in the 1929 crash. This was due to his flawed economic thinking. He was not able to predict either the crash or the Great Depression at a time when the Austrian economists already knew that the New Era Boom was about to end. For a complete explanation see Mark Skousen, *The Making of Modern Economics: The Lives and Ideas of the Great Thinkers*, ME Sharpe, 2001. Mark Boucher uses Austrian School economics plus market timing to trade the markets. Austrian economics enabled him to anticipate moves in his trading portfolios. His Midas fund had many years of above average returns. See the chapter on Austrian Alchemy in his course, *The Science of Trading*, IRA, 1996.
18. Gann's Rule 2 for trading stocks is: 'Buy at Single, Double and Triple Bottoms' (W. D. Gann, *45 Years in Wall Street*, Lambert Gann Publishing Co., 1976, p. 7).
19. When explaining rule 2 for trading stocks, Gann explains why the Triple Bottoms or Triple Tops are the strongest. About the Triple Top or Bottom, he says, 'This is often the safest place to buy or sell because the market moves away from a Triple Top or a Triple Bottom much faster' (W. D. Gann, *45 Years in Wall Street*, Lambert Gann Publishing Co., 1976, p. 8).
20. About tape reading, R. D. Wyckoff says, 'It is not trading on chart indications or by other mechanical methods,' and he defines tape reading as, 'The science of determining from the tape the immediate trend of prices.' He gives us *Swing*

Trading Secret Tape Readers Used: Determine 'The Immediate Trend.' Trading market fluctuations must be done only when the market provides a clear indication that a trend is on (see Rollo Tape (R. D. Wyckoff), *Studies in Tape Reading*, 1910, Fraser Publishing Co., 1987, pp. 9, 10).

21. In Gann, we find rules for buying market fluctuations based on their numbers. Some of his rules for buying stocks are: 'Rule 3. Buy and Sell on Percentages.' He mentions buying or selling on the following percentage numbers: 3 to 5 %, 10 to 12 %, 20 to 25 %, 33 to 37 %, 45 to 50 %, 62 to 67 %, 72 to 78 %, and 85 to 87 %. Then he adds, 'The most important resistance levels are 50% and 100 % and the proportional parts of 100%.' 'Rule 6: Buy or Sell on 5 to 7 Point Moves.' In Rule 6, he tells us to watch for reactions of 5 to 7 points, 9 to 10 points, 10 to 12 points and 18 to 21 'points up or down from any important Top or Bottom' (W. D. Gann, *45 Years in Wall Street*, Lambert Gann Publishing Co., 1976, pp. 8, 9).
22. Many successful traders use a 3:1 risk/reward ratio. One of them is Sperandeo (see Victor Sperandeo, *Trader Vic – Methods of a Wall Street Master*, John Wiley & Sons, Inc., 1994, p. 25).
23. The stops that Gann used came from observing the history of market fluctuations and learning to place the stop where the market could not touch it if the trade was correct. He said, 'As a rule, when you buy or sell grain and it goes against you, 3 to 5 cents, you are wrong and you may as well get out.' He added, 'See how far advancing markets have run and how small their rallies have been' (W. D. Gann, *How to Make Profits in Commodities*, Traders Press, 1976).
24. Gann was an advocate of studying market history as the biggest help for a trader. He said, 'Nothing will help you more than going over the past history of commodities, studying its actions under different periods . . .' (W. D. Gann, *How to Make Profits in Commodities*, Traders Press, 1976, p. 1).
25. Gann emphasizes the need for 'long years of study and research.' He places 'knowledge' and 'hard work' above all else as the key to success in trading. He says, 'There is only one key (. . .) and that key is KNOWLEDGE.' He also says, 'Without knowledge, money is worthless' (see W. D. Gann, *How to Make Profits in Commodities*, Traders Press, 1976, p. 3).
26. For Jesse Livermore, as well as for W. D. Gann, overtrading is a trader's worst mistake. Overtrading must be avoided at any cost. The second rule of Gann's well-known 'Twenty Four Never Failing Rules' says, 'Never overtrade.' Wyckoff tells us that lack of capital in Wall Street is caused by 'overtrading' and he brings forward the epigram, 'Overtrading is financial suicide.' This is a common belief among all successful traders (see W. D. Gann, *How to Make Profits in Commodities*, Traders Press, 1976, p. 16, and Rollo Tape (R. D. Wyckoff), *Studies in Tape Reading*, 1910, Fraser Publishing Co., 1987, p. 23).
27. See note 22.

28. Livermore used to trade between 8 and 12 stocks. These stocks were from four sector groups. This means that he used to follow two to three stocks per group (Jesse Livermore, *How to Trade in Stocks*, Traders Press, 1991, p. 35, and Edwin Lefèvre, *Reminiscences of a Stock Operator*, John Wiley & Sons, Inc., 1994, p.182). Steward also advised during the 1950s to have between 8 and 12 stocks (Cliff Steward, *Magic of Making Money in the Stock Market*, Sacred Science Library, 2003, p. 30). Gann, in his rules, suggests trading four or five stocks (W. D. Gann, *45 Years in Wall Street*, Lambert Gann Publishing Co., 1976, p. 16).
29. Jesse Livermore added, after the initial position, each new lot after a one-point rise (Edwin Lefèvre, *Reminiscences of a Stock Operator*, John Wiley & Sons, Inc., 1994, p. 84). Steward, in 1951, advised traders to add after a rise of 3 to 5 points in stocks under $25 or 5 to 7 points in stocks over $25 (Cliff Steward, *Magic of Making Money in the Stock Market,* Sacred Science Library, 2003, p. 10).
30. William Dunnigan, John Crane, Tom DeMark, W. D. Gann, and Jesse Livermore are authors and traders who base their perspectives on market structure and not on indicators. This is the reason why their market understanding and trading setups really do work and are excellent trading tools. These authors should be studied in depth by all market students.
31. Rashke advises new traders to first specialize in mastering one pattern only (see Laurence A. Connors and Linda Bradford Raschke, *Street Smarts*, M. Gordon Publishing Group, 1995, p. 2).
32. The difference between the Apollo projects and the Shuttle projects is illustrative of deficient testing – the result of not asking the questions, the answers to which would protect against worst-case scenarios. Jim Longuski, an Aerospace engineer, who worked for the Jet Propulsion Laboratory, tells us how the Apollo engineers asked 'what if' questions about all of the worst case scenarios and that the answers were taken into account in the planning of Apollo missions. This was not the case, he tells us, with the Shuttle missions, where many important 'what if' questions were left 'unanswered or poorly answered.' This illustrates the difference between good planning and bad planning and the consequences in reality. The same thing can be said of trading, for which we must plan in advance for any adverse event that could occur before even thinking of 'launching' our prototype in real trading. For the NASA example, see Jim Longuski, *Think Like a Rocket Scientist*, Copernicus Books, 2007, pp. 51–53.
33. Among the best trading psychology books today are: Mark Douglas, *The Disciplined Trader*, NYIF, 1990, Ari Kiev, *Trading to Win*: *The Psychology of Mastering the Markets*, John Wiley & Sons, Inc., 1998, and Van K. Tharp, *Trade Your Way to Financial Freedom*, McGraw-Hill, 2006.
34. When you have a losing trade, a way to recover from the emotional impact is to review the trading statistics and also put down on paper all of your feelings

and thoughts, negative and positive. This can be combined with a period of silent meditation to detach yourself from your emotions and negative thoughts.

35. Some good money management and asset allocation books are: Ralph Vince, *The New Money Management*, John Wiley & Sons, Inc., 1995, Nauzer J. Balsara, *Money Management Strategies for Futures Traders*, John Wiley & Sons, Inc., 1992, and Fred Gehm, *Quantitative Trading and Money Management*, Irwing, 1995.
36. See note 22.
37. See note 32.

Bibliography

Nauzer J. Balsara, *Money Management Strategies for Future Traders*, John Wiley & Sons, Inc., 1992.
Mark Boucher, *The Science of Trading*, IRA, 1996.
Laurence A. Connors and Linda Bradford Rashke, *Street Smarts*, M. Gordon Publishing Group, 1995.
John Crane, *A Trader's Handbook, The Reversal Day Phenomenon*, Tradenet Publishing Co., 1998.
John Crane, *Unlocking Wealth, The Secret to Market Timing*, Tradenet Publishing Co., 2007.
Tom DeMark, *The New Science of Technical Analysis*, John Wiley & Sons, Inc., 1994.
Tom DeMark, *New Market Timing Techniques, Innovative Studies in Market Rhythm and Price Exhaustion*, John Wiley & Sons, Inc., 1997.
George Douglass Taylor, *The Taylor Trading Technique*, Traders Press, 1950.
Mark Douglas, *The Disciplined Trader*, NYIF, 1990.
William Dunnigan, *New Blueprints for Gains in Stocks and Grains*, FT, Pitman Publishing, 1997.
W. D. Gann, *How to Make Profits in Commodities*, Traders Press, 1976.
W. D. Gann, *45 Years in Wall Street*, Lambert Gann Publishing Co., 1976.
Fred Gehm, *Quantitative Trading and Money Management*, Irwing, 1995.
Ari Kiev, *Trading to Win: The Psychology of Mastering the Markets*, John Wiley & Sons, Inc., 1998.
Edwin Lefèvre, *Reminiscences of a Stock Operator*, John Wiley & Sons, Inc., 1994.
Jesse L. Livermore, *How to Trade in Stocks*, Traders Press, 1991.
Jim Longuski, *Think Like a Rocket Scientist*, Copernicus Books, 2007.
Robert Rhea, *The Dow Theory*, Fraser Publishing Co., 1993.
Rollo Tape (R. D. Wyckoff), *Studies in Tape Reading*, 1910, Fraser Publishing Co., 1987.
Richard W. Schabaker, *Technical Analysis and Stock Market Profits*, FT, Pitman Publishing, 1997.
Martin Schwartz, *Pit Bull, Lessons from a Wall Street Champion Trader*, HarperCollins, 1998.
Mark Skousen, *The Making of Modern Economics: The Lives and Ideas of the Great Thinkers*, M. E. Sharpe, 2001.
Victor Sperandeo, *Trader Vic – Methods of a Wall Street Master*, John Wiley & Sons, Inc., 1994.

Cliff Steward, *Magic of Making Money in the Stock Market*, Sacred Science Library, 2003.
Van K. Tharp, *Trade Your Way to Financial Freedom*, McGraw-Hill, 2006.
Felipe Tudela, *The Secret Code of Japanese Candlesticks*, John Wiley & Sons, Ltd, 2008.
Ralph Vince, *The New Money Management*, John Wiley & Sons, Inc., 1995.

Index